SIXTH EDITION

Methods in Behavioral Research

SIXTH EDITION

Methods in Behavioral Research

Paul C. Cozby
California State University, Fullerton

Mayfield Publishing Company
Mountain View, California
London • *Toronto*

Library of Congress Cataloging-in-Publication Data

Cozby, Paul C.
   Methods in behavioral research / Paul C. Cozby. — 6th ed.
     p.   cm.
   Includes bibliographical references (p.   ) and index.
   ISBN 1-55934-659-0
   1. Psychology—Research—Methodology. 2. Social sciences—
Research—Methodology. I. Title.
BF76.5.C67 1996   96-12005
150'.72—dc20   CIP

Manufactured in the United States of America

10   9   8   7   6   5

Mayfield Publishing Company
1280 Villa Street
Mountain View, California 94041

Sponsoring editor, Franklin C. Graham; production, Robin Lockwood and
Associates; manuscript editor, Tom Briggs; art director, Jeanne M. Schreiber;
cover illustration, Paul Schulenburg; cover designer, Jean Mailander; manu-
facturing manager, Randy Hurst. The text was set in 10/12 Zapf International Light by TBH Typecast, Inc. and printed on 50# Butte des Mortes
by The Banta Company.

 This book is printed on acid-free, recycled paper.

Contents

CHAPTER 4
Studying Behavior   52

CHAPTER 5
Descriptive Methods   77

CHAPTER 6
Experimental Design: Purposes and Pitfalls   105

CHAPTER 7

Conducting Experiments   125

CHAPTER 8

Complex Experimental Designs   146

CHAPTER 9

Quasi-Experimental and Single-Subject Research Designs   162

CHAPTER 10

Understanding Research Results: Description and Correlation 174

CHAPTER 11

Understanding Research Results: Statistical Inference 195

CHAPTER 12

Generalizing Results 217

APPENDIX A

Writing Research Reports   231

APPENDIX B

Statistical Tests   277

APPENDIX C

Statistical Tables   299

Preface

Teaching and learning about research methods is both challenging and a great deal of fun. This new edition of *Methods in Behavioral Research* has benefited from the input of many instructors and students who have used previous editions. Clear communication of concepts to students is my highest priority. I have tried to present material clearly, use interesting examples, and mention the same concepts at numerous points throughout the text. An outline precedes each chapter; study terms and review and activity questions appear at the end of each chapter. Important terms are boldfaced in the text; and the Glossary defines these terms. The Instructor's Manual contains many student activities and homework assignments, as well as exam questions.

ORGANIZATION

The organization generally follows the sequence of planning and conducting a research investigation. However, the chapters are relatively independent to provide instructors maximum flexibility in assigning the order of chapters. Chapter 1 gives an overview of the scientific approach to knowledge and distinguishes between basic and applied research. Chapter 2 discusses sources of ideas for research and exploration of library resources. Chapter 3 focuses on issues of research ethics, a concept that is stressed here and throughout the text. Chapter 4 examines psychological variables, reliability and validity of measures, relationships among variables, and the distinction between correlational and experimental methods. Chapter 5 contains a description of both quantitative and qualitative approaches to describing behavior, including naturalistic observation, case studies, archival research, and surveys. Chapters 6 and 7 present the basics of designing and conducting experiments. Complex experimental designs and the special issues raised by the use of quasi-experimental and single-subject designs are described in Chapters 8 and 9. Chapters 10 and 11 focus on the use of statistics to understand the results of research. Finally, Chapter 12 discusses generalization issues and emphasizes the importance of replications. Appendices on writing research reports, analyzing data, and constructing Latin Squares are included as well.

CHANGES IN THIS EDITION

This edition incorporates a number of changes suggested by instructors and students who have used the previous editions. The coverage of ethical research is now earlier, in Chapter 3. Coverage of some topics has been rearranged to make assignment of topics easier for instructors. For example, quasi-experimental and single-subject designs are now combined in Chapter 9. Descriptive statistics and correlation are discussed together in Chapter 10, and inferential statistics are covered separately in Chapter 11.

I am always interested in comments and suggestions from students and instructors who are using the text. My postal address is Department of Psychology, California State University, Fullerton, CA 92834; my e-mail address is *cozby@fullerton.edu*.

ACKNOWLEDGMENTS

Many individuals helped to produce this and the previous editions of this book. A special note of thanks is due to Claire Palmerino, Jeanne King, Gregory Robinson, Heidi Weller, David Perkins, and Dan Kee for their help in developing the book and the Instructor's Manual. Frank Graham at Mayfield Publishing Company has been an invaluable resource. Thanks go to Tom Briggs for editing the manuscript and Robin Lockwood for production management. Most importantly, I thank the many students and instructors who have sent suggestions, and I particularly thank the following individuals who provided detailed reviews of this edition: Kellina M. Craig, University of Illinois; Leslie E. Fisher, Cleveland State University; Monica Harris, University of Kentucky; Howard S. Hock, Florida Atlantic University; Linda Petty, Hampton University; and Harold Sigall, University of Maryland.

SIXTH EDITION

Methods in Behavioral Research

CHAPTER

1

Scientific Understanding of Behavior

What are the causes of aggression and violence? How do we remember things, what causes us to forget, and how can memories be improved? What are the effects of stressful environments on health and social interactions? How do early childhood experiences affect later development? Curiosity about questions such as these is probably the most important reason that many students decide to take courses in the behavioral sciences. Scientific research provides us with a means of addressing such questions and providing answers. In this book, we will examine the methods of scientific research in the behavioral sciences. In this introductory chapter, we will focus on ways in which a knowledge of research methods can be useful in understanding the world around us. Further, we will review the characteristics of a scientific approach to the study of behavior and the general types of research questions that concern behavioral scientists.

USES OF RESEARCH METHODS

A knowledge of research methods is increasingly needed by informed citizens in our society. Daily newspapers, general-interest magazines, and other media are continually reporting research results: "Type A Personalities More Likely to Suffer from Heart Attacks" or "Smoking Linked to Poor Grades." Articles and books make claims about the beneficial or harmful effects of particular diets or vitamins on one's sex life, personality, or health. Survey results are frequently reported that draw conclusions about how we feel about a variety of topics. How do you evaluate such reports? Do you simply accept the findings because they are supposed to be scientific? A background in research methods will help you to read these reports critically, evaluate the methods employed, and decide if the conclusions are reasonable.

Many occupations require the use of research findings. For example, mental health professionals must make decisions about treatment methods, assignment of patients to different types of facilities, medications, and testing procedures. Such decisions are made on the basis of research; to make good decisions, the mental health professional must be able to read the research conducted by others and judge its adequacy and relevance for the particular setting in which he or she works. Similarly, people who work in business environments frequently rely on research to make decisions about marketing strategies, ways of improving employee productivity and morale, and methods of selecting and training new employees. Educators must keep up with research on topics such as the effectiveness of different teaching strategies or programs to deal with special student problems. Knowledge of research methods and the ability to evaluate research reports are useful in many fields.

It is also important to recognize that scientific research has become increasingly important in public policy decisions. Legislators and political leaders at all levels of government frequently take political positions and propose legislation based on research findings. Research may also influence judicial decisions. A prime example of this is the *Social Science Brief* that was pre-pared by psychologists and accepted as evidence in the landmark 1954 case of *Brown v. Board of Education*, in which the U.S. Supreme Court banned school segregation in the United States. One of the studies cited in the brief was con-ducted by Clark and Clark (1947). The study found that when allowed to choose between light-skinned and dark-skinned dolls, both black and white children preferred to play with the light-skinned dolls (see Stephan, 1983, for a further discussion of the implications of this study). More recently, legisla-tion and public opinion regarding the availability of pornographic materials have been informed by behavioral research investigations of this topic (see, for example, Koop, 1987; Linz, Donnerstein, & Penrod, 1987), and psycholog-ical research on sex stereotyping greatly influenced the outcome of a Supreme Court decision on sex discrimination by employers (Fiske, Bersoff, Borgida, Deaux, & Heilman, 1991). Research is also important when developing and assessing the effectiveness of pilot programs designed to achieve certain goals —for example, to increase retention of students in school or to influence peo-ple to engage in behaviors that reduce their risk of contracting AIDS. If suc-cessful, such programs may be implemented on a large scale. The fact that so many policy decisions and political positions are based on research makes knowledge of research methods particularly important for all of us as informed citizens who must ultimately evaluate the policies at the voting booth.

THE SCIENTIFIC APPROACH

We opened this chapter with several questions about human behavior and suggested that scientific research is a valuable means of answering them. How does the scientific approach differ from other ways of learning about behavior? People have always observed the world around them and sought explanations for what they see and experience. However, instead of using a scientific approach, many people rely on intuition and authority as ways of knowing.

The limitations of intuition and authority

Intuition Most of us know of a married couple who, after years of trying to conceive, adopts a child. Then, within a very short period of time, the couple finds that the woman is pregnant. This observation leads to a common belief that adoption increases the likelihood of pregnancy among couples who are having difficulties conceiving a child. Such a conclusion seems intuitively rea-sonable, and people usually have an explanation for this effect—for example, the adoption reduces a major source of marital stress, and the stress reduc-tion in turn increases the chances of conception (see Gilovich, 1991).

When you rely on intuition, you accept unquestioningly what your own personal judgment tells you about the world. The intuitive approach takes

3

many forms. Often, it involves finding an explanation for our own behaviors or the behaviors of others. For example, you might develop an explanation for why you keep having conflicts with a co-worker, such as "that other person wants my job" or "having to share a telephone puts us in a conflict situation." Other times, intuition is used to explain intriguing events that you observe, as in the case of concluding that adoption increases the chances of conception among couples having difficulty conceiving a child.

A problem with intuition is that numerous cognitive and motivational biases affect our perceptions, and so we may draw erroneous conclusions about cause and effect (cf. Fiske & Taylor, 1984; Gilovich, 1991; Nisbett & Ross, 1980; Nisbett & Wilson, 1977). Gilovich points out that there is in fact no relationship between adoption and subsequent pregnancy according to scientific research investigations. So why do we hold this belief? Most likely it is because of a cognitive bias called *illusory correlation* that occurs when we focus on two events that stand out and occur together. When an adoption is closely followed by a pregnancy, our attention is drawn to the situation, and we are biased to conclude that there must be a causal connection. Such illusory correlations are also likely to occur when we are highly motivated to believe in the causal relationship. While this is a natural thing for us to do, it is not scientific. A scientific approach requires much more proof before drawing conclusions.

Authority   The philosopher Aristotle was concerned with the factors associated with persuasion or attitude change. In his *Rhetoric*, Aristotle describes the relationship between persuasion and credibility: "Persuasion is achieved by the speaker's personal character when the speech is so spoken as to make us think him credible. We believe good men more fully and readily than others." Thus, Aristotle would argue that we are more likely to be persuaded by a speaker who seems prestigious, trustworthy, and respectable than by one who lacks such qualities.

Many of us might accept Aristotle's arguments simply because he is considered a prestigious "authority" and his writings remain important. Similarly, many people are all too ready to accept anything they learn from the news media, books, government officials, or religious figures. They believe that the statements of such authorities must be true. The problem, of course, is that the statements may not be true. The scientific approach rejects the notion that one can accept on faith the statements of any authority; again, more proof is needed before we can draw scientific conclusions.

Skepticism, science, and the empirical approach

The scientific approach to knowledge recognizes that both intuition and authority are sources of ideas about behavior. However, scientists do not unquestioningly accept anyone's intuitions—including their own. Scientists recognize that their ideas are just as likely to be wrong as are anyone else's. Also, scientists do not accept on faith the pronouncements of anyone, regard-

4

less of that person's prestige or authority. Thus, scientists are very skeptical about what they see and hear. They insist that scientific methods be used to evaluate assertions about the nature of behavior.

The essence of the scientific method is the insistence that all propositions be subjected to an empirical test. This means that the propositions are tested using scientific methods of observation and experimentation. This empirical approach to knowledge has two basic components. First, an idea must be studied under conditions in which it may be either supported or refuted: The empirical test allows the proposition to be shown to be false. Second, the research is done in a way that can be observed, evaluated, and replicated by others.

Thus, the scientific method, in contrast to intuition or authority, does not rely on accepting assertions generated by someone else or on one's own personal perceptions of the world. The scientific method embodies a number of rules for testing ideas through research—ways that observations are made and experiments are designed and conducted. These will be explored throughout the book.

Integrating intuition, skepticism, and authority

The advantage of the scientific approach over other ways of knowing about the world is that it provides an objective set of rules for gathering, evaluating, and reporting information, such that our ideas can be refuted or replicated by others. This does not mean that intuition and authority are not important, however. As noted previously, scientists often rely on intuition and assertions of authorities for ideas for research. Moreover, there is nothing wrong with accepting the assertions of authority as long as we don't accept them as scientific evidence. Often, scientific evidence isn't obtainable—as, for example, when religions ask us to accept certain beliefs on faith. Some beliefs cannot be tested and thus are beyond the realm of science. In contrast, scientific ideas must be testable—there must be some way of verifying or refuting them.

There is also nothing wrong with having opinions or beliefs as long as they are presented simply as opinions or beliefs. However, we should always ask whether the opinion can be tested scientifically or whether scientific evidence exists that relates to the opinion. For example, opinions on whether exposure to television violence increases aggression are only opinions until scientific evidence on the issue is gathered.

As you learn more about scientific methods, you will become increasingly skeptical of the assertions of scientists. You should be aware that scientists often become authorities when they express their ideas. When someone claims to be a scientist, should we be more willing to accept what he or she has to say? The answer depends on whether the scientist has scientific data that support his or her assertions. If there is no such evidence, the scientist is no different from any other authority; if scientific evidence is presented, you will want to evaluate the methods used to gather it. Also, there are many "pseudoscientists," who use scientific terms to substantiate their claims (e.g.,

**Figure 1-1
Ebbinghaus
forgetting curve**

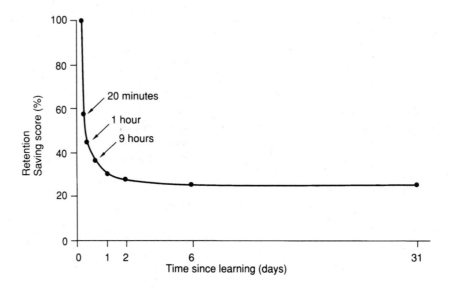

astrologers or new age channelers). A general rule is to be highly skeptical whenever someone who is labeled as a scientist makes assertions that are supported by only vague or improbable evidence.

GOALS OF SCIENCE

Scientific research has four general goals: (1) to describe behavior, (2) to predict behavior, (3) to determine the causes of behavior, and (4) to understand or explain behavior.

Description of behavior

The scientist begins with careful observation, because the first goal of science is to describe events. In a classic experiment conducted in the late 19th century, experimental psychologist Hermann Ebbinghaus carefully observed his own rate of forgetting material after it had been learned. He studied the amount of retention of material (actually, nonsense syllables like *TAV*) at periods ranging from 20 minutes to 31 days after the original learning. His results produced the "forgetting curve" shown in Figure 1-1 (see Schwartz, 1986). Many questions that interest researchers concern describing the ways in which events are systematically related to one another. Does greater speaker credibility lead to greater attitude change? In what ways do intellectual abilities change throughout the life cycle? Does noise affect performance on cognitive tasks?

Prediction of behavior

Another goal of science is to predict behavior. Once it has been observed with some regularity that two events are systematically related to one another (e.g., greater credibility is associated with greater attitude change), it becomes possible to make predictions. One implication of this is that we can anticipate events. If we know that one candidate in an election is considered more credible than the other, we may be able to predict the outcome of the election. Further, the ability to predict often helps us make better decisions. For example, many college students take a measure of occupational interests such as the Strong-Campbell Interest Inventory at the college counseling center because awareness of their scores can help them make better decisions about possible career goals and choice of a major.

Determining the causes of behavior

A third goal of science is to determine the causes of behavior. Although we might accurately predict the occurrence of a behavior, we might not have correctly identified its cause. For example, college grades are not caused by aptitude test scores. The aptitude test is an indicator of other factors that are the actual causes; research may be undertaken to study these factors. Similarly, research has shown that a child's aggressive behavior may be predicted by knowing how much violence the child views on television. Unfortunately, unless we know that exposure to this violence is a *cause* of behavior, we cannot assert that aggressive behavior can be reduced by limiting scenes of violence on television. Thus, to know how to *change* behavior, we need to know the *causes* of behavior.

Explanation of behavior

A final goal of science is to explain the events that have been described. The scientist seeks to understand *why* the behavior occurs. Thus, for example, it is important to ask why the forgetting curve in Figure 1-1 has the shape it does. Clearly, forgetting increases over time, but time is not sufficient to explain the psychological processes that might be responsible for the forgetting. To explain the finding, you might ask whether there is a decay in the memory trace or whether other events increasingly interfere with the ability to remember what was learned. Or consider the relationship between television violence and aggression; even if we know that TV violence is a cause of aggressiveness, we need to explain this relationship. Is it due to imitation or "modeling" of the violence seen on TV? Is it the result of psychological desensitization to violence and its effects? Or does watching TV violence lead to a belief that aggression is a normal response to frustration and conflict? Further research is necessary to shed light on possible explanations of what has been

7

observed. Usually, additional research like this is carried out by testing theories that are developed to explain particular behaviors.

Description, prediction, determination of cause, and explanation are all closely intertwined. Determining cause and explaining behavior are particularly closely related because it is difficult ever to know the true cause or all the causes of any behavior. An explanation that appears satisfactory may turn out to be inadequate when other causes are identified in subsequent research. For example, when early research showed that speaker credibility is related to attitude change, the researchers explained the finding by stating that people are more willing to believe what is said by a person with high credibility than by one with low credibility. However, this explanation has given way to a more complex theory of attitude change that takes into account many other factors that are related to persuasion (Petty & Cacioppo, 1986). In short, there is a certain amount of ambiguity in the enterprise of scientific inquiry. New research findings almost always pose new questions that must be addressed by further research; explanations of behavior often must be discarded or revised as new evidence is gathered. Such ambiguity is part of the excitement and fun of science.

BASIC AND APPLIED RESEARCH

Basic research

Basic research tries to answer fundamental questions about the nature of behavior. Studies are often designed to address theoretical issues concerning phenomena such as cognition, emotion, motivation, learning, psychobiology, personality development, and social behavior. Here are citations of a few journal articles that pertain to some basic research questions:

> Eich, E. (1995). Mood as a mediator of place dependent memory. *Journal of Experimental Psychology: General, 124,* 293–308.
>
> Dewhurst, S. A., & Conway, M. A. (1994). Pictures, images, and recollective experience. *Journal of Experimental Psychology: Learning, Memory, and Cognition, 20,* 1088–1098.
>
> Siegal, E., & Rachlin, H. (1995). Soft commitment: Self-control achieved by response persistence. *Journal of the Experimental Analysis of Behavior, 64,* 117–128.
>
> Huddy, L., & Virtanen, S. (1995). Subgroup differentiation and subgroup bias among Latinos as a function of familiarity and positive distinctiveness. *Journal of Personality and Social Psychology, 68,* 97–108.

Applied research

The research articles listed previously were concerned with basic processes of behavior and cognition rather than any immediate practical implications. In contrast, applied research is conducted to address issues in which there are practical problems and potential solutions. To illustrate, here are a few journal article titles:

Weiner, R. L., Pritchard, C. C., & Weston, M. (1995). Comprehensibility of approved jury instructions in capital murder cases. *Journal of Applied Psychology, 80,* 455–467.

Scheipis, M. M., & Reid, D. H. (1995). Effects of a voice output communication aid on interactions between support personnel and an individual with multiple disabilities. *Journal of Applied Behavior Analysis, 28,* 73–77.

Faupel, C. E., & Styles, S. P. (1993). Disaster education, household preparedness, and stress responses following Hurricane Hugo. *Environment and Behavior, 25,* 228–249.

Boldero, J. (1995). The prediction of household recycling of newspapers: The role of attitudes, intentions, and situational factors. *Journal of Applied Social Psychology, 25,* 440–462.

A major area of applied research is called *program evaluation.* Program evaluation research evaluates the social reforms and innovations that occur in government, education, the criminal justice system, industry, health care, and mental health institutions. In an influential paper on "reforms as experiments," Campbell (1969) noted that social programs are really experiments designed to achieve certain outcomes. He argued persuasively that social scientists should evaluate each program to determine whether it is having its intended effect. If it is not, alternative programs should be tried. This is an important point that people in all organizations too often fail to remember when new ideas are implemented; the scientific approach dictates that new programs should be evaluated. Here are some sample journal articles:

Dukes, R. L., Ullman, J. B., & Stein, J. A. (1995). An evaluation of D.A.R.E. (Drug Abuse Resistance Education), using a Solomon four-group design with latent variables. *Evaluation Review, 19,* 409–435.

Land, K. C., McCall, P. L., & Williams, J. R. (1991). Something that works in juvenile justice: An evaluation of the North Carolina court counselors' intensive protective supervision randomized experimental project. *Evaluation Review, 14,* 574–606.

Much applied research is conducted in settings such as large business firms, marketing research companies, government agencies, and public polling organizations and is not published, but rather is used within the company or by clients of the company. Whether or not such results are published, however, they are used to help people make better decisions concerning problems that require immediate action.

Comparing basic and applied research

Both basic and applied research are important, and neither can be considered superior to the other. In fact, progress in science is dependent on a synergy between basic and applied research. Much applied research is guided by the theories and findings of basic research investigations. For example, applied research on expert testimony in jury trials is guided by basic research in perception and cognition. In turn, the findings obtained in applied settings often require modification of existing theories and spur more basic research. Thus, the study of actual eyewitness testimony leads to richer and more accurate knowledge of basic perceptual and cognitive processes.

In recent years, many in our society, including legislators who control the budgets of research-granting agencies of the government, have demanded that research be directly relevant to specific social issues. The problem with this attitude toward research is that we can never predict the ultimate applications of basic research. Psychologist B. F. Skinner, for example, conducted basic research in the 1930s on operant conditioning, which carefully described the effects of reinforcement on such behaviors as bar pressing by rats. This research led, years later, to many practical applications in therapy, education, and industrial psychology. Research with no apparent practical value ultimately can be very useful. The fact that no one can predict the eventual impact of basic research leads to the conclusion that support of basic research is necessary both to advance science and benefit society.

Behavioral research is important in many fields and has significant applications to public policy. This chapter has introduced you to the major goals and general types of research. All researchers use scientific methods whether they are interested in basic, applied, or program evaluation questions. The themes and concepts in this chapter will be expanded in the remainder of the book. They will be the basis on which you evaluate the research of others and plan your own research projects as well.

This chapter emphasized that scientists are skeptical about what is true in the world and insist that propositions be tested empirically. In the next two chapters, we will focus on two other characteristics of scientists. First, scientists have an intense curiosity about the world and find inspiration for ideas in many places. Second, scientists have strong ethical principles; they are committed to treating those who participate in research investigations with respect and dignity.

STUDY TERMS

Applied research	Empirical test	Intuition
Authority	Goals of science	Skepticism
Basic research		

REVIEW QUESTIONS

1. Why is it important for anyone in our society to have a knowledge of research methods?

2. Why is scientific skepticism useful in furthering our knowledge of behavior? How does the scientific approach differ from other ways of gaining knowledge about behavior?

3. Distinguish among description, prediction, determination of cause, and explanation as goals of scientific research.

4. Distinguish between basic and applied research.

ACTIVITY QUESTIONS

1. Read several editorials in your daily newspaper and identify the sources used to support the assertions and conclusions. Did the writers use intuition, appeals to authority, scientific evidence, or a combination of these? Give specific examples.

2. You are interested in studying psychological depression. What would you try to accomplish if your goal was to describe depression, predict depression, understand the causes of depression, and explain depression?

3. Imagine a debate on the following assertion: Behavioral scientists should only conduct research that has immediate practical applications. Develop arguments that support ("pro") and oppose ("con") the assertion.

4. Imagine a debate on the following assertion: Knowledge of research methods is unnecessary for students who intend to pursue careers in clinical and counseling psychology because their professional lives will be spent helping people. Develop arguments that support ("pro") and oppose ("con") the assertion.

CHAPTER 2

Where to Start

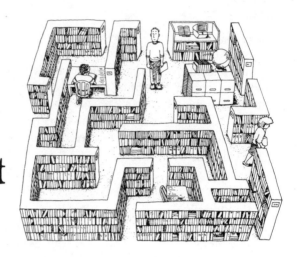

The motivation to conduct scientific research derives from a natural curiosity about the world. Most people have their first experience with research when their curiosity leads them to ask, "I wonder what would happen if . . . ," followed by an attempt to answer the question. What are the sources of inspiration for such questions? And how do you find out about other people's ideas and past research? In this chapter, we will explore some sources of scientific ideas. We will also consider the nature of research reports published in professional journals.

HYPOTHESES AND PREDICTIONS

Most research studies are attempts to test a **hypothesis** formulated by the researcher. A hypothesis is really a type of idea or question; it makes a statement about something that may be true. A hypothesis therefore is only a tentative idea or question that is waiting for evidence to support or refute it. Sometimes, hypotheses are very general and informal questions. For example, Geller, Russ, and Altomari (1986) had general questions about beer drinking among college students: How much beer is consumed in an average sitting in a college bar? How long do the students stay? Do males and females differ in their drinking? With such questions in mind, the researchers developed a procedure for collecting data to answer the questions. Research problems formulated in this way are informal hypotheses or simply questions about behavior.

Hypotheses are often stated in more specific and formal terms. Usually, such formal hypotheses state that two or more variables are related to one another. Thus, researchers might formulate hypotheses such as "crowding results in lowered performance on mental tasks" or "attending to more features of something to be learned will result in greater memory." Such hypotheses are formulated on the basis of past research findings and theoretical considerations. The researcher will then design a study to test the hypothesis. In the crowding example, the researcher might place research participants in either a crowded room or an uncrowded room to work on a series of tasks and then observe their performance.

At this point, the researcher would make a specific **prediction** concerning the outcome of this experiment. Here the prediction might be that "participants in the uncrowded condition will perform better on the tasks than will participants in the crowded condition." If this prediction is confirmed by the results of the study, the hypothesis is supported. If the prediction is not confirmed, the researcher will either reject the hypothesis (and believe that crowding does not lead to poor performance) or conduct further research using different methods to study the hypothesis. It is important to note that when the results of a study confirm a prediction, the hypothesis is only *supported*, not *proven*. Researchers study the same hypothesis using a variety of methods, and each time a hypothesis is supported by a research study, our confidence that the hypothesis is correct increases.

13

You should note the use of the term *participants* to refer to the individuals who participated in a research project. An equivalent term is *subjects*. Until recently, "subjects" was used most frequently, and so you will see both terms when you read about research. The American Psychological Association *Publication Manual* (APA, 1994) recommends "participants."

SOURCES OF IDEAS

It is not easy to say where good ideas come from. Many people are capable of coming up with worthwhile ideas, but verbalizing the process by which they are generated is difficult. Cartoonists know this—they show a brilliant idea as a light bulb flashing on over the person's head. But where does the electricity come from? Let's consider five sources of ideas: common sense, observation of the world around us, theories, past research, and practical problems.

Common sense

One source of ideas that can be tested is the body of knowledge called common sense—the things we all believe to be true. Do "opposites attract" or do "birds of a feather flock together"? If you "spare the rod," do you "spoil the child"? Is a "picture worth a thousand words"? Asking questions such as these can lead to research programs studying attraction, the effects of punishment, and the role of visual images in learning and memory.

Testing a commonsense idea can be valuable because such notions don't always turn out to be correct, or research may show that the real world is much more complicated than our commonsense ideas would have it. For example, pictures can aid memory under certain circumstances, but sometimes pictures detract from learning (see Levin, 1983). Actually conducting research to test commonsense ideas often forces us to go beyond a commonsense theory of behavior.

Observation of the world around us

Observations of personal and social events can provide many ideas for research. The curiosity sparked by your observations and experiences can lead you to ask questions about all sorts of phenomena. In fact, this type of curiosity is what drives many students to engage in their first research project.

Have you ever had the experience of storing something away in a "special place" where you were sure you could find it later (and perhaps where no one else would possibly look for it), only to later discover that you couldn't recall where you had stored it? Such an experience could lead to systematic research on whether it is a good idea to put things in special places. In fact, Winograd and Soloway (1986) conducted a series of experiments on this very topic. Their research demonstrated that people are likely to forget where something is placed when two conditions are present: (1) The location where the object is placed is judged to be highly memorable *and* (2) the location is considered a very unlikely place for the object. Thus, while it may seem to be a good idea at the time, storing something in an unusual place is generally not a good idea.

Events you read or hear about can also lead to research ideas. In 1961, Eliot Aronson read a Gallup Poll showing that President Kennedy's popularity actually increased following a failed attempt to invade Cuba at the Bay of Pigs. The invasion attempt was widely viewed as a tremendous blunder by the United States, so Aronson wondered why Kennedy's popularity would increase rather than drop. Aronson hypothesized that the rise in popularity resulted from the fact that Kennedy was almost "too perfect," with his good looks, charm, athletic ability, sense of humor, and intelligence. Perhaps the blunder of the invasion made him more "human" in the eyes of the public, thus causing the increase in popularity. This was an intriguing idea, but it had not been proven; there was no necessary connection between the blunder and the rise in popularity because many other events were occurring simultaneously that could have caused Kennedy's increased popularity.

To rule out the possible contribution of these other events, Aronson conducted an experiment to test the hypothesis that a blunder committed by a perfect person will result in increased liking for that person (see Aronson, 1984). In the experiment, participants listened to tape recordings of candidates for the "College Quiz Bowl." Some participants heard a person who was nearly perfect, with high scores on the quiz answers and an impressive series of accomplishments in his background; other participants listened to an average person. Some of the participants listening to each candidate then heard that person commit a blunder: He spilled coffee all over himself. Thus, four conditions were created: a perfect person who did or did not commit the blunder and an average person who did or did not commit the blunder. Subjects then indicated how much they liked the person they listened to. The results showed that participants most liked the perfect person who had spilled coffee and least liked the average person who had done so. Thus, the research supported Aronson's idea that a blunder by a perfect person can increase liking for that person.

A more recent example demonstrates the diversity of ideas that can be generated by curiosity about things that happen around you. During the past few years, there has been a great deal of controversy about the effects of rock music on teenagers—specifically, a fear that rock music leads to sexual promiscuity, drug use, and violence. Some groups, such as the Parents' Music Resource Center (PMRC), would like to censor song lyrics and have persuaded record companies to place warning labels on records. There have even been congressional hearings on this topic. Some researchers noted this controversy and decided to conduct research to examine the issue. In one study, Prinsky and Rosenbaum (1987) asked teenagers to name their favorite songs and explain what the songs were about. Most of the participants could explain the songs in only vague terms, such as "the beat is good" or "it's about love." The researchers concluded that teenagers do not pay a great deal of attention to the lyrics of songs.

15

The world around us is a rich source of material for scientific investigation. When psychologist Robert Levine was teaching in Brazil several years ago, he noticed that Brazilian students were much more casual about both getting to class on time and leaving afterwards than were their counterparts in the United States. That observation led him to begin studying the pace of life in a variety of countries, as well as in numerous U.S. cities (Levine, 1990). Investigations such as these illustrate a point made in Chapter 1: Personal opinions and personal experiences provide insights about behavior, but scientific thinking requires us to test ideas through research.

Theories

Much research in the behavioral sciences tests theories of behavior. **Theories** serve two important functions in increasing our understanding of behavior. First, theories *organize and explain* a variety of specific facts or descriptions of behavior. Such facts and descriptions are not very meaningful by themselves, and so theories are needed to impose a framework on them. This framework makes the world more comprehensible by providing a few abstract concepts around which we can organize and explain a variety of behaviors. As an example, consider how Charles Darwin's theory of evolution organized and explained a variety of facts concerning the characteristics of animal species. Similarly, in psychology, one theory of memory asserts that there are separate systems of short-term memory and long-term memory. This theory accounts for a number of specific observations about learning and memory, including such phenomena as the different types of memory deficits that result from a blow to the head versus damage to the hippocampus area of the brain and the rate at which a person forgets material he or she has just read.

Second, theories *generate new knowledge* by focusing our thinking so that we notice new aspects of behavior: Theories guide our observations of the world. The theory generates hypotheses about behavior, and the researcher conducts studies to see if these are correct. If the studies confirm the hypotheses, the theory is supported. A theory is never proven, though; research can only provide support for a theory. However, research also can reveal weaknesses in a theory and force researchers to modify the theory or develop a new, more comprehensive one.

The necessity of modifying theories is illustrated by the theory of short-term versus long-term memory mentioned previously. The original conception of the long-term memory system described long-term memory as a storehouse of permanent, fixed memories. However, research by cognitive psychologists, including Loftus (1979), has shown that memories are easily reconstructed and reinterpreted. In one study, participants watched a film of an automobile accident and later were asked to tell what they saw in the film. Loftus found that participants' memories were influenced by the way they were questioned. For example, participants who were asked whether they saw "the" broken headlight were more likely to answer yes than were participants who were asked whether they saw "a" broken headlight. Results such as these have required a more complex theory of how long-term memory operates.

Past research

A fourth source of ideas is past research. Becoming familiar with a body of research on a topic is perhaps the best way to generate ideas for new research. Because the results of research are published, researchers can use the body of past literature on a topic to continually refine and expand our knowledge. Virtually every study raises questions that can be addressed in subsequent research. The research may lead to an attempt to apply the findings in a different setting, to study the topic with a different age group, or to use a different methodology to replicate the results. The Geller et al. (1986) study on beer drinking reported that students who buy pitchers drink more beer than those who purchase bottles, that males drink more than females, that students in groups drink more than those who are alone, and that females stay longer in the bar than males. Knowledge of this study and its results might lead, for example, to research on ways to reduce excess drinking by college students.

In addition, as you become familiar with the research literature on a topic, you may see inconsistencies in research results that need to be investigated, or you may want to study alternative explanations for the results. Also, what you know about one research area often can be successfully applied to another research area.

Let's look at a concrete example of a study that was designed to address methodological flaws in previous research. The study was concerned with a method of helping children who are diagnosed with autism. Childhood autism is characterized by a number of symptoms, including severe impairments in language and communication ability. Recently, parents and care providers have been encouraged by a technique called "facilitated communication" that apparently allows an autistic child to communicate with others by pressing keys on a keyboard showing letters and other symbols. A facilitator holds the child's hand to facilitate the child's ability to determine which key to press. With this technique, many autistic children begin communicating their thoughts and feelings and answer questions posed to them. Most people who see facilitated communication in action regard the technique as a miraculous breakthrough.

The conclusion that facilitated communication is effective is based on a comparison of the autistic child's ability to communicate with and without the facilitator. The difference is impressive to most observers. Recall, however, that scientists are by nature skeptical. They examine all evidence carefully and ask whether claims are justified. In the case of facilitated communication, Montee, Miltenberger, and Wittrock (1995) noted that the facilitator may be unintentionally guiding the child's fingers to type meaningful sentences. In other words, the facilitator, and not the autistic individual, is controlling the communication. Montee et al. conducted a study to test this idea. In one condition, both the facilitator and the autistic child were shown a picture, and the child was asked to indicate what was shown in the picture by typing a response with the facilitator. This was done on a number of trials. In another condition, only the child saw the pictures. In a third condition, the child and facilitator were shown different pictures (but the facilitator was unaware of this fact). Consistent with the hypothesis that the facilitator is controlling the child's responses, the pictures were correctly identified only in the condition in which both saw the same pictures. Moreover, when the client and facilitator viewed different pictures, the child never made the correct response, and usually the picture the facilitator had seen was the one identified.

Practical problems

Research is also stimulated by practical problems that can have immediate applications. Groups of city planners and citizens might survey bicycle riders to determine the most desirable route for a city bike path, for example. On a larger scale, researchers have guided public policy by conducting research on the effects of exposure to pornographic materials, as well as other social and health issues. Much of the applied research described in Chapter 1 addresses issues such as these.

LIBRARY RESEARCH

Before an investigator can conduct any research project, he or she must have a thorough knowledge of previous research findings. Even if the basic idea has been formulated, a review of past studies will help the researcher clarify the idea and design the study. Thus, it is important to know how to search the literature on a topic and how to read research reports in professional journals. In this section, we will discuss only the fundamentals of conducting library research; for further information, you may refer to the excellent guides to library research in psychology and to preparing papers that review research by Reed and Baxter (1992) and Rosnow and Rosnow (1995), respectively.

The nature of journals

If you've wandered through the periodicals section of your library, you've noticed the enormous number of professional journals. In these journals, researchers publish the results of their investigations. After a research project has been completed, the study is written as a report, which then may be submitted to the editor of an appropriate journal. The editor solicits reviews from other scientists in the same field and then decides whether the report is to be accepted for publication. Because each journal has a limited amount of space and receives many more papers than it has room to publish, most papers are rejected. Those that are accepted are published about a year later.

Most psychology journals specialize in one or two areas of human or animal behavior. Even so, the number of journals in many areas is so large that it is almost impossible for anyone to read them all. Table 2-1 lists some of the major journals in several areas of psychology. Clearly, it would be difficult to read all of them, even in a single research area in psychology such as learning and memory. Further, if you were seeking research on a single specific topic, it would be impractical to look at every issue of every journal in which relevant research might be published. Fortunately, you don't have to.

Psychological Abstracts

Psychological Abstracts, or "*Psych Abstracts*," contains "nonevaluative summaries of the world's literature in psychology and related disciplines." *Psych Abstracts* is published monthly by the American Psychological Association; each of its volumes contains thousands of abstracts (summaries) of recently published articles. To find articles on a specific topic in which you are interested, you would consult the index at the end of each volume. The summaries of the articles are brief descriptions of the research findings. On the basis of the abstract, you can determine the relevance of a particular article for your purposes.

To use *Psychological Abstracts*, you must first locate the index that accompanies each volume. The index is organized by subject category. Some categories, such as "cognitive development" or "mental retardation," are quite large; others, such as "clothing fashions" or "startle reflex," are narrower and contain relatively few references. The more general the category, the greater the number of references. As a general rule, you can search most efficiently when you have narrowed the category as much as possible—that is, when it is as specific as you can get it.

Suppose you are interested in finding out about research on test anxiety. You locate the index for a volume of *Psych Abstracts*; for this example, I chose Volume 79 (1992). There you find a category labeled "anxiety," as well as one on "test anxiety." If you want to know more about the categories used in the abstracts, you can consult the separate thesaurus of terms. In each category, the publications are listed under serials (articles in periodicals), chapters, and books. For test anxiety, there are 19 articles, 5 chapters, and no books. Here are four of the serial listings:

> extraversion & neuroticism & social contacts & support, test anxiety, college students, 5415
>
> feasibility & reliability & validity of daily diary, assessment of anxiety disorders, 3rd–6th graders with vs without test anxiety, 12970
>
> microcomputer program for assessment & relaxation & desensitization treatment of test anxiety, female graduate students, 13768
>
> perceived control over test content, stress symptoms prior to test & perceived control over & actual test performance, college students, 37046

Typically, only some of the articles will be of interest. You can locate those that do appear relevant in the appropriate volume of abstracts (in this case,

19

Table 2-1
Some major
journals in
psychology

General

---

*American Psychologist** (general articles on a variety of topics)
*Contemporary Psychology** (book reviews)
*Psychological Bulletin** (literature reviews)
*Psychological Review** (theoretical articles)
Psychological Science
*Psychological Methods**
Current Directions in Psychological Science

Experimental areas of psychology

---

*Journal of Experimental Psychology: General**
*Journal of Experimental Psychology: Applied**
*Journal of Experimental Psychology: Learning, Memory, and Cognition**
*Journal of Experimental Psychology: Human Perception and Performance**
*Journal of Experimental Psychology: Animal Behavior Processes**
*Journal of Comparative Psychology**
*Behavioral Neuroscience**
Bulletin of the Psychonomic Society
Learning and Motivation
Memory and Cognition
Cognitive Psychology
Cognition
Cognitive Science
Discourse Processes
Journal of the Experimental Analysis of Behavior
Animal Learning and Behavior
*Neuropsychology**

Clinical and counseling psychology

---

*Journal of Abnormal Psychology**
*Journal of Consulting and Clinical Psychology**
*Journal of Counseling Psychology**
Behaviour Research and Therapy
Journal of Clinical Psychology
Behavior Therapy
Journal of Abnormal Child Psychology
Journal of Social and Clinical Psychology

Developmental psychology

---

*Developmental Psychology**
*Psychology and Aging**
Child Development
Journal of Experimental Child Psychology
Journal of Applied Developmental Psychology
Developmental Review
Infant Behavior and Development
Experimental Aging Research

Table 2-1
(continued)

Personality and social psychology

*Journal of Personality and Social Psychology**
Personality and Social Psychology Bulletin
Journal of Experimental Social Psychology
Journal of Research in Personality
Journal of Social Issues
Social Psychology Quarterly
Journal of Applied Social Psychology
Basic and Applied Social Psychology
Journal of Social and Personal Relationships

Applied areas of psychology

*Journal of Applied Psychology**
*Journal of Educational Psychology**
Journal of Applied Behavior Analysis
*Health Psychology**
*Psychological Assessment**
Journal of Human Stress
Educational and Psychological Measurement
American Educational Research Journal
Evaluation Review
Evaluation and Program Planning
Evaluation and Change
Environment and Behavior
Journal of Environmental Psychology
Journal of Consumer Research
Journal of Marketing Research

Family studies and sexual behavior

*Journal of Family Psychology**
Journal of Marriage and the Family
Journal of Marital and Family Therapy
Journal of Sex Research
Journal of Sexual Behavior
Journal of Homosexuality

Ethnic, gender, and cross-cultural issues

Hispanic Journal of Behavioral Sciences
Journal of Black Psychology
Sex Roles
Psychology of Women Quarterly
Journal of Cross-Cultural Psychology

Some Canadian and British journals

Canadian Journal of Psychology
Canadian Journal of Behavioral Science
British Journal of Psychology
British Journal of Social and Clinical Psychology

* Published by the
American Psychological
Association.

Volume 79). The abstracts are listed in numerical order. If you looked up article 5415, you would find the following information:

> **5415. Belger, Niall & Eckenrode, John.** (New York U) **Social relationships, personality, and anxiety during a major stressful event**. *Journal of Personality & Social Psychology*, 1991 (Sep), Vol 61(3), 440–449.
>
> —Although it is commonly believed that social relationships buffer the effects of stress on mental health, these apparent buffering effects may be spurious reflections of personality or prior mental health. This possibility was investigated in a prospective study of a medical school entrance examination. Five weeks before the examination, Ss ($N=56$; mean age=30.3 yrs) rated their personality (extraversion and neuroticism) and social relationships (number of social contacts and perceived support). They then rated their anxiety for 35 days surrounding the examination. Controlling for personality and prior anxiety, social contacts buffered against increases in anxiety, whereas perceived support did not. Further analyses revealed that discretionary social contacts were beneficial whereas obligatory contacts were not.
>
> —*Journal abstract.*

After copying the information about this article, you could look up any other abstracts that seem relevant. To continue the search, you would then go to other volumes. (Note the reference to "Ss" in the abstract. This is an abbreviation of the word "subjects" and is used in *Psychological Abstracts* to save space; the abbreviation is not used in the actual research article.)

After you complete the abstract search, your final step is to find the most useful original articles in the journals. If your library has the journal, you can read it in the library or make a photocopy. If the journal is not in your library, simply ask a librarian for help in obtaining a copy through an interlibrary loan service.

The reference section of your library has abstracts of literature in many disciplines. For example, sociology journal articles are abstracted in *Sociological Abstracts*, while research on topics related to education can be found in the ERIC *Resources in Education* abstracting system. A reference librarian can help you use these and other abstract sources.

Computer-assisted searches

A manual search through the volumes of *Psychological Abstracts* can be very time-consuming. Thus, a computer-assisted search is often a much more efficient way to find articles relevant to your topic of interest. The contents of *Psychological Abstracts*, as well as other bibliographic information sources, have been stored in computer databases. The *Psych Abstracts* database called *PsycLIT* is stored on a CD-ROM used with a microcomputer; Box 2-1 offers a brief guide to using *PsycLIT*. Your library may provide access to other computer databases using either microcomputers or a connection to information retrieval services such as Lexis/Nexis and FirstSearch. The Internet is also

Box 2-1
Using PsycLIT

In a search using *PsycLIT*, the first step is to specify the database to be used. On my library's computer, I can choose either *PsycLIT Journal Articles 1/90 to current PsycLIT Journal Articles prior to 1/90*, or *PsycLIT Chapters & Books 1/87 to current*. During my session at the computer, I can use function keys to give me more information about searching. For example, F1 is a help key, F3 gives information about the database, and F9 provides me with the thesaurus of psychological terms.

Suppose I decide to search through the most current journal articles. The computer program gives me a FIND: prompt; I now have to tell the computer the topics I want it to search for in the database. The easiest way to do this is to type in specific terms to search on. For example, I can ask for a search on test anxiety:

FIND: test anxiety

When I enter these two words, the computer finds all the abstracts that contain the word "test" and all the abstracts that contain the word "anxiety." It then lists only those abstracts that contain both words—in this case, 284 abstracts. Next, I press the F4 key to show the actual abstracts. Here is one that was found:

TI: Psychopathology and cognition in adolescents experiencing severe test anxiety.
AU: King, -Neville-J.; Mietz, -Angelique; Tinney, -Leesa; Ollendick, -Thomas-H.
IN: Monash U Faculty of Education, School of Graduate Studies, Clayton, Vict, Australia
JN: Journal-of-Clinical-Child-Psychology; 1995 Mar Vol 24(1) 49–54
IS: 0047228X
LA: English
PY: 1995
AB: Screened 600 Australian adolescents in Grades 9 and 10 for test anxiety (TA) using the Test Anxiety Scale for Children. 22 Ss (mean age 15 yrs) with high TA and 25 Ss (mean age 15 yrs) with low TA completed the Diagnostic and Statistical Manual of Mental Disorders-III-Revised (DSM-III-R), a measure of mathematical and language skills, a cognitive assessment, and self-report measures of fearfulness, anxiety, depression, and hopelessness. High and low TA Ss differed significantly on the presence of DSM-III-R diagnoses; 61% of high TA Ss were diagnosed with an anxiety or a phobic disorder. High TA Ss had significantly higher levels of psychopathology on the self-report measures than the low TA Ss did. High TA Ss reported higher levels of depression and hopeless-

Box 2-1
(continued)

ness than the low TA Ss did. Moreover, dysfunctional thinking was reported by the high TA Ss in an evaluative situation. (PsycLIT Database Copyright 1995 American Psychological Assn, all rights reserved)

KP: psychopathology & dysfunctional thinking; severe test anxiety; 9th–10th graders; Australia

DE: TEST-ANXIETY; PSYCHOPATHOLOGY-; THINKING-; HIGH-SCHOOL-STUDENTS; ADOLESCENCE-

CC: 3560; 35

PO: Human

AG: Adolescent

UD: 9508

AN: 82-31092

JC: 1377

The output is actually a series of data "fields" that have abbreviations such as TI (title), AU (authors), JN (journal name), PY (publication year), AB (abstract), KP (key phrase), and DE (descriptors). I can review the search results on the computer monitor. If the computer is connected to a printer, I can print one or more of the abstracts by pressing the F6 key. I can also specify the fields that I want printed. I can even download the results to a diskette that I can use later in a word processing program. To download information, press F10.

The search I just described found the terms in any of the fields. Suppose I want to narrow the search so that I will only get articles in which the phrase "text anxiety" is actually in the key phrase field. The way to do this is to specify the field of interest:

FIND: test anxiety in KP

This search results in 158 matches. Of course, I could limit the search to other fields as well.

Suppose that I want to further narrow my search to articles in which the research participants were college students. Note in the abstract shown above that the DE (descriptors) field includes HIGH-SCHOOL-STUDENTS. Consider the following search request:

FIND: test anxiety in KP and college-students in DE

The "and" is a logical operator that narrows the search to only those abstracts that match both conditions specified. This search results in 32 abstracts. I could also use the "or" as a logical operator to include abstracts that meet either condition specified.

The procedures for searching other library databases will be quite similar. The reference librarians in your library can provide you with guidance and information on the specific requirements of your school's computer system.

becoming increasingly useful as a means of locating information via computer.

Social Science Citation Index

Another resource in searching for articles is the *Social Science Citation Index* (SSCI), which uses the "key article" method. Here you need to first identify a "key article" on your topic, usually one published sometime in the past that is particularly relevant to your interests (this article is often identified through your search of *Psychological Abstracts*). The SSCI then allows you to search for subsequent articles that cited the key article. This will give you a bibliography of articles relevant to your topic. As you become familiar with this list, one or more of the articles might become new "key articles," and you can conduct further searches. Eventually, you become thoroughly familiar with the research on your topic. As with *Psych Abstracts*, the SSCI may also be available to you on a computer, and a computer search of the SSCI database is much more efficient than a manual search.

Literature reviews

Articles that summarize the research in a particular area are also useful. The *Psychological Bulletin* publishes reviews of the literature in various topic areas in psychology. The *Annual Review of Psychology* each year publishes articles that summarize recent developments in various areas of psychology. A number of other disciplines have similar annual reviews.

ANATOMY OF A RESEARCH ARTICLE

Now that you have selected a research article, what can you expect to find in it? Research journal articles usually have five sections: (1) an *abstract*, such as the ones found in *Psychological Abstracts*, (2) an *introduction* that explains the problem under investigation and the specific hypotheses being tested, (3) a *method* section that describes in detail the exact procedures used in the study, (4) a *results* section in which the findings are presented, and (5) a *discussion* section in which the researcher may speculate on the broader implications of the results, propose alternative explanations for the results, discuss reasons that a particular hypothesis may not have been supported by the data, and/or make suggestions for further research on the problem.

Abstract

The abstract is a summary of the research report and typically runs no more than 150 words in length. It includes information about the hypothesis, the procedure, and the broad pattern of results. Generally, little information is abstracted from the discussion section of the paper.

Introduction

In the introduction, the researcher outlines the problem that has been investigated. Past research and theories relevant to the problem are described in detail. The specific expectations of the researcher are noted, often as formal hypotheses. In other words, the investigator introduces the research in a logical format that shows how past research and theory are connected to the current research problem and the expected results.

Method

The method section is divided into subsections, with the number of subsections determined by the author and dependent on the complexity of the research design. Sometimes, the first subsection presents an overview of the design in order to prepare the reader for the material that follows. The next subsection describes the characteristics of the participants. Were they male or female, or were both sexes used? What was the average age? How many participants were there? If the study used human participants, some mention of how participants were recruited for the study would be needed. The next subsection details the procedure used in the study. In describing any stimulus materials presented to the participants, the way the behavior of the participants was recorded, and so on, it is crucial that no potentially important detail be omitted. Such detail allows the reader to know exactly how the study was conducted, and it provides other researchers with the information necessary to replicate the study. Other subsections may be necessary to describe in detail some piece of equipment or testing materials that were used.

Results

In the results section, the researcher presents the findings, usually in three ways. First, there is a description in narrative form—for example, "The location of items was most likely to be forgotten when the location was both highly memorable and an unusual place for the item to be stored." Second, the results are described in statistical language. And third, the material is often depicted in tables and graphs.

The statistical terminology of the results section may appear formidable. However, lack of knowledge about the calculations isn't really a deterrent to understanding the article or the logic behind the statistics. Statistics are only a tool the researcher uses in evaluating the outcomes of the study.

Discussion

In the discussion section, the researcher reviews the research from various perspectives. Do the results support the hypothesis? If they do, the author should give all possible explanations for the results and discuss why one explanation is superior to another. If the hypothesis has not been supported, the author should suggest potential reasons for this. What might have been wrong with the methodology, the hypothesis, or both? The researcher may also discuss how the results compare with past research results on the topic. This section may also include suggestions for possible practical applications of the research and for future research on the topic.

You should read as many research articles as possible to become familiar with the way information is presented in reports. As you do so, you will develop ways of efficiently processing the information in the articles. It is usually best to read the abstract first, then skim the article to decide whether you can use the information provided. If you can, go back and read the article closely. Note the hypotheses and theories presented in the introduction, write down anything that seems unclear or problematic in the method, and read the results in view of the material in the introduction. Be critical when you read the article; students often generate the best criticism. Most importantly, as you read more research on a topic, you will become more familiar with the variables being studied, the methods used to study the variables, the important theoretical issues being considered, and the problems that need to be addressed by future research. In short, you will find yourself generating your own research ideas and planning your own studies.

STUDY TERMS

Abstract	Method section	Results section
Discussion section	Prediction	*Social Science Citation*
Hypothesis	*Psychological Abstracts*	*Index* (SSCI)
Introduction section	*PsycLIT*	Theory
Literature review		

REVIEW QUESTIONS

1. What is a hypothesis? What is the distinction between a hypothesis and a prediction?
2. What are the two functions of a theory?
3. Describe the difference in the way that past research is found when you use *Psychological Abstracts* versus the "key article" method of the *Social Science Citation Index*.
4. What information does the researcher communicate in each of the sections of a research article?

ACTIVITY QUESTIONS

1. Think of at least five "commonsense" sayings about behavior (e.g., "Spare the rod, spoil the child"; "Like father, like son"; "Absence makes the heart grow fonder"). For each, develop a hypothesis that is suggested by the saying and a prediction that follows from the hypothesis. (Based on Gardner, 1988.)

2. Choose one of the hypotheses formulated in item 1 and develop a strategy for finding research on the topic. Use *Psychological Abstracts* or *PsycLIT* to locate abstracts of studies that investigated the topic.

3. Theories serve two purposes: (1) to organize and explain observable events and (2) to generate new knowledge by guiding our way of looking at these events. Identify a consistent behavior pattern in yourself or somebody close to you (e.g., you consistently get into an argument with your sister on Friday nights). Generate two possible theories (explanations) for this occurrence (e.g., because you work long hours on Friday, you're usually stressed and exhausted when you get home; because your sister has a chemistry quiz every Friday afternoon and she's not doing well in the course, she is very irritable on Fridays). How would you gather evidence to determine which explanation might be correct? How might each explanation lead to different approaches to changing the behavior pattern, either to decrease or increase its occurrence?

4. The sample research paper by Robert A. Baron in Appendix A is an investigation of the effect of cologne and perfume on evaluations of job applicants. Use this as the key article to do a search using the *Social Science Citation Index*.

3

Ethical Research

Ethical concerns are paramount when planning, conducting, and evaluating research. In this chapter, we will explore in detail the nature of ethical problems that arise in research, and we will examine some guidelines for dealing with these problems.

MILGRAM'S OBEDIENCE EXPERIMENT

Stanley Milgram conducted a series of experiments (1963, 1964, 1965) to study the phenomenon of obedience to an authority figure. He placed an ad in the local newspaper in New Haven, Connecticut, offering to pay $4.50 to men to participate in a "scientific study of memory and learning" being conducted at Yale University. The participants reported to Milgram's laboratory at Yale, where they met a scientist dressed in a lab coat and another participant in the study—a middle-aged man named "Mr. Wallace." Mr. Wallace was actually a confederate of the experimenter, but the participants didn't know this. The scientist explained that the study would examine the effects of punishment on learning. One person would be a "teacher" who would administer the punishment, and the other would be the "learner." Mr. Wallace and the volunteer participant then drew slips of paper to determine who would be the teacher and who would be the learner. The drawing was rigged, however—Mr. Wallace was always the learner and the volunteer was always the teacher.

The scientist attached electrodes to Mr. Wallace and placed the teacher in front of an impressive-looking shock machine. The shock machine had a series of levers that, the individual was told, when pressed would deliver shocks to Mr. Wallace. The first lever was labeled 15 volts, the second 30 volts, the third 45 volts, and so on up to 450 volts. The levers were also labeled "Slight Shock," "Moderate Shock," and so on up to "Danger: Severe Shock," followed by red X's above 400 volts.

Mr. Wallace was instructed to learn a series of word pairs. Then he was given a test to see if he could identify which words went together. Every time Mr. Wallace made a mistake, the teacher was to deliver a shock as punishment. The first mistake was supposed to be answered by a 15-volt shock, the second by a 30-volt shock, and so on. Each time a mistake was made, the learner received a greater shock. The learner, Mr. Wallace, never actually received any shocks, but the participants in the study didn't know that. In the experiment, Mr. Wallace made mistake after mistake. When the teacher "shocked" him with about 120 volts, Mr. Wallace began screaming in pain and eventually yelled that he wanted out. What if the teacher wanted to quit? This happened—the real participants became visibly upset by the pain that Mr. Wallace seemed to be experiencing. The scientist told the teacher that he could quit but urged him to continue, using a series of verbal prods that stressed the importance of continuing the experiment.

The study purportedly was an experiment on memory and learning, but Milgram really was interested in learning whether participants would continue to obey the experimenter by administering ever higher levels of shocks to the learner. What happened? Approximately 65 percent of the participants continued to deliver shocks all the way to 450 volts. Milgram's study received a great deal of publicity, and the results challenged many of our beliefs about our ability to resist authority. Milgram's study is important, and the results have implications for understanding obedience in real-life situations, such as Nazi Germany and the Jonestown mass suicide (see Miller, 1986). But what about the ethics of the Milgram study? What aspects of the experimental procedure might we find objectionable?

MAJOR ETHICAL ISSUES IN RESEARCH

Stress and psychological harm

The first problem concerns the stress that the research participants experienced while delivering intense shocks to an obviously unwilling learner. A film that Milgram made shows participants protesting, sweating, and even laughing nervously while delivering the shocks. You might ask whether subjecting people to such a stressful experiment is justified, and you might wonder whether the experience had any long-range consequences for the volunteers. For example, did participants who obeyed the experimenter feel continuing remorse or begin to see themselves as cruel, inhumane people? A defense of Milgram's study follows, but first let's consider some potentially stressful research procedures.

Procedures that could conceivably cause some physical harm to participants are rare but nonetheless possible. Many medical procedures would fall in this category—for example, administering some sort of drug, such as alcohol or caffeine, or depriving people of sleep for an extended period of time. The risks in such procedures require that great care be taken to make them ethically acceptable.

More common than physical stress is psychological stress. For example, participants might be told that they will receive some extreme-intensity electric shocks. They never actually receive the shock—it is the fear or anxiety during the waiting period that is the variable of interest. Research by Schachter (1959) employing a procedure like this showed that the anxiety produced a desire to affiliate with others during the waiting period.

In another procedure that produces psychological stress, participants are given unfavorable feedback about their personalities or abilities. Researchers interested in self-esteem have typically given a subject a bogus test of personality or ability. The test is followed by an evaluation that lowers or raises self-esteem by indicating that the participant has an unfavorable personality trait or a low ability score.

As you can see, some research procedures involve physical or psychological stress. Whether such research should be conducted is a difficult issue, one we'll grapple with a little later.

31

Deception

The Milgram experiment also illustrates the use of deception. Participants in the Milgram experiment agreed to take part in a study of memory and learning, but they actually took part in a study on obedience. Who could imagine that a memory and learning experiment (that title does sound tame, after all) would involve delivering high-intensity, painful electric shocks to another person? Participants in the Milgram experiment didn't know what they were letting themselves in for. The procedure lacked what is called **informed consent:** The research participants were not given an accurate account of the purpose of the study and the risks involved before they consented to take part in the experiment.

The problem of deception is not limited to laboratory research. Procedures in which observers conceal their purposes, presence, or identity are also deceptive. For example, Humphreys (1970) studied the behavior of male homosexuals who frequent public restrooms (called "tearooms"). Humphreys did not participate in any homosexual activities, but he served as a lookout who would warn the others of possible intruders. In addition to observing the activities in the tearoom, Humphreys wrote down license plate numbers of tearoom visitors. Later, he obtained the addresses of the men, disguised himself, and visited their homes to interview them. Humphreys' procedure is certainly one way of finding out about homosexuality, but it employs considerable deception.

Herbert Kelman (1967) noted several problems with the use of deception. First, deception is unethical. Kelman wrote:

> In our other interhuman relationships, most of us would never think of doing the kinds of things that we do to our subjects—exposing others to lies and tricks, deliberately misleading them about the purposes of the interaction or withholding pertinent information, making promises or giving assurances that we intend to disregard. We would view such behavior as a violation of the respect to which all fellow humans are entitled and of the whole basis of our relationship with them. Yet we seem to forget that the experimenter-subject relationship . . . is a real interhuman relationship, in which we have responsibility toward the subject as another human being whose dignity we must preserve.[1]

A second problem noted by Kelman is that deception may fail to achieve its intended goals. The primary justification for deceiving participants is that knowledge of the purpose of an experiment would contaminate the results. If the subject is unaware of the real purpose, he or she will behave more naturally. Kelman believed, however, that participants are aware of psychologists' tricks and that they come to experimental situations expecting to be lied to.

---

1. From Kelman, H. C. (1967). Human use of human subjects: The problem of deception in social psychological experiments. *Psychological Bulletin*, *67*, 1–11. Copyright © 1967 by the American Psychological Association. Reprinted by permission.

Thus, they take nothing the researcher says at face value. This may be an extreme statement of the problem, but it is a possibility worth considering.

Another problem with deception has been noted by Rubin (1970) and by Ring (1967). These authors look beyond the possible harmful effects of deception to the motivation of some researchers who use deception. Rubin refers to many of these researchers at work in the 1960s as "jokers wild in the lab," and Ring talks about a "fun and games" approach to research. The official justification for deception is that it helps ensure that the participants behave naturally and spontaneously, so that researchers get a better picture of real behavior. This justification is based on scientific grounds and so has some merit. Observers such as Rubin and Ring note, however, that some researchers are motivated by the desire to devise clever and elaborate experimental manipulations mainly to win attention. Ring (1967) states that "there is a distinctly exhibitionist flavor to much current experimentation, while the experimenters often seem to equate notoriety with achievement."

Rubin (1970) describes the following procedure: The research participant sits behind a large machine and is shown how to operate it by pushing the proper buttons. He is then told, "All my research money is tied up in this contraption and I'll never get my master's degree if it doesn't function properly." However, there is an explosion, and smoke begins to billow out of the machine. The experimenter now says, "I'll never get my master's now . . . (choke) . . . What did you do to the machine? . . . (sob) . . . Well, I guess that ends the experiment . . . (long pause and then, solemnly) . . . The machine is broken."[2] The real purpose of the experiment is to see if this experience will increase the likelihood that the participant will sign a petition being circulated by the experimenter (it does). The description of this little drama staged by the experimenter makes for amusing reading, but how amused were the participants? In this example, was the researcher employing a deception procedure primarily to draw attention to the research rather than for its scientific necessity? If so, it arguably is an unethical procedure.

Informed consent

Ideally, all research should provide research participants with full informed consent. As noted previously, informed consent means that research participants are informed about the purposes of the study, the risks involved with the procedures, and their rights to refuse or terminate participation in the study. In other words, participants are provided with all information that might influence their decision to participate prior to making that decision.

Also as previously stated, the use of deception deprives participants of full informed consent. If the participants in Milgram's experiment had participated only after giving informed consent, they would first have been told that

---

2. From Rubin, Z. (1970, December). Jokers wild in the lab. *Psychology Today*, pp. 18ff. Copyright © 1970 by Ziff-Davis Publishing Company. All rights reserved.

obedience was being studied and that they would be required to inflict painful shocks on another person. They would also have been told that they could withdraw from the experiment at any time. You can immediately see why full informed consent is not a completely satisfactory solution to the deception problem. First, knowledge that the research is designed to study obedience is bound to alter the behavior of the participants. Few of us like to think of ourselves as obedient, and we would probably go out of our way to prove that we are not. Research indicates that providing informed consent may in fact bias participants' responses, at least in some research areas. For example, research on stressors such as noise or crowding has shown that a feeling of "control" over a stressor reduces its negative impact. If you know that you can terminate a loud, obnoxious noise, the noise produces less stress than when the noise is uncontrollable. Studies by Gardner (1978) and Dill, Gilden, Hill, and Hanslka (1982) have demonstrated that informed consent procedures do increase perceptions of control in stress experiments and therefore can affect the conclusions drawn from the research.

A second problem with informed consent is that it may bias the sample. In Milgram's experiment, if participants had had prior knowledge that they would be asked to give severe shocks to the other person, some might have declined to be in the experiment. Therefore, we might limit our ability to generalize the results only to those "types" who agreed to participate. If this were true, anyone could say that the obedient behavior seen in the Milgram experiment occurred simply because the people who agreed to participate were sadists in the first place!

This discussion has assumed that full informed consent is the only alternative to a situation in which there is no informed consent. Full informed consent is absolutely necessary when there are major risks associated with participation. However, there are frequently good reasons to withhold information such as the hypothesis of the study or the condition an individual is participating in (see Sieber, 1992). Researchers commonly provide a general description of the topic of the study and assure participants that they can withdraw from the study without penalty at any time. Most people who volunteer for experiments do not expect full disclosure about the study prior to participation. They do, however, expect a thorough debriefing after they have completed the study.

Debriefing

The traditional solution to the problem of deception is to thoroughly debrief participants after the experiment. Debriefing has become a standard part of experimental procedure, even when there is no stress and virtually no possibility of harm to participants. Researchers believe that participation should be an educational experience, so they communicate their ideas about human behavior to the participants. Is debriefing sufficient to remove any negative effects when stress and elaborate deception are involved? Let's turn again to Milgram's research.

Milgram went to great lengths to provide a thorough debriefing session. Participants who were obedient were told that their behavior was normal in that they had acted no differently from most other participants. They were made aware of the strong situational pressure that was exerted on them, and efforts were made to reduce any tension they felt. Participants were assured that no shock was actually delivered, and there was a friendly reconciliation with the confederate, Mr. Wallace. Milgram also mailed a report of his research findings to his participants and at the same time asked about their reactions to the experiment. The responses showed that 84% were glad that they had participated, and 74% said they had benefitted from the experience. Only 1% said they were sorry they had participated. When participants were interviewed by a psychiatrist a year later, no ill effects of participation could be detected. We can only conclude that debriefing did have its intended effect. Other researchers who have conducted further work on the ethics of Milgram's study reached the same conclusion (Ring, Wallston, & Corey, 1970).

Other research on debriefing has also concluded that debriefing is effective as a way of dealing with deception in experiments (Smith, 1983; Smith & Richardson, 1983). However, deception remains a controversial issue (see Rubin, 1985; Smith & Richardson, 1985). You may be wondering, then, whether there are alternatives to deception.

Alternatives to deception

After criticizing the use of deception in research, Kelman (1967) called for the development of alternative procedures. One procedure Kelman suggests is role-playing; other options include simulation studies (a variation on role-playing) and "honest" experiments.

Role-playing   In one **role-playing** procedure, the experimenter describes a situation to participants and then asks them how they would respond to the situation. Sometimes, participants are asked to say how they themselves would behave in the situation; other times, they are asked to predict how real participants in such a situation would behave. It isn't clear whether these two instructions produce any differences in results.

Role-playing is not generally considered to be a satisfactory alternative to deception (Freedman, 1969; Miller, 1972). One problem is that simply reading a description of a situation does not involve the participants very deeply— they are not part of a real situation. Also, because the experimenter gives the participants a complete description of the situation, the experimenter's hypothesis may become transparent to the participants. When people can figure out the hypothesis, they may try to behave in a way that is consistent with the hypothesis. Features of the experiment that may inform participants about the hypothesis are called "demand characteristics." The problem of demand characteristics is described in detail in Chapter 7.

The most serious defect of role-playing is that, no matter what results are obtained, critics can always claim that the results would have been different if the participants had been in a real situation. This criticism is based on the assumption that people aren't always able to accurately predict their own behavior or the behavior of others. This would be particularly true when undesirable behavior—such as conformity, obedience, or aggression—is involved. For example, if Milgram had used a role-playing procedure, how many people do you think would have predicted that they would be completely obedient? In fact, Milgram asked a group of psychiatrists to predict the results of his study and found that even these experts could not accurately anticipate what would happen. A similar problem would arise if people were asked to predict whether they would help someone in need. Most of us would probably overestimate our altruistic tendencies.

Simulation studies   A different type of role-playing involves simulation of a real-world situation. A simulation study that impressed Kelman (1967) is the Inter-Nation Simulation, in which participants role-play being leaders of nations and the researchers observe processes of negotiation, problem solving, and so on. Such simulations can create high levels of involvement, as anyone who has played an all-night game of Monopoly or become thoroughly engrossed in a computer game will appreciate.

Even with simulations, there may be ethical problems. A dramatic example is the Stanford Prison Experiment conducted by Zimbardo (1973). Zimbardo set up a simulated prison in the basement of the psychology building at Stanford University. He then recruited college students who were paid $15 per day to play the role of either prisoner or guard for a period of two weeks. Guards were outfitted in uniforms and given sunglasses and clubs. Prisoners were assigned numbers and wore nylon stocking caps to simulate prison haircuts and reduce feelings of individuality. The participants became deeply involved in their roles, so much so that Zimbardo had to stop the simulation after six days because of the cruel behavior of the "guards" and the stressful reactions of the "prisoners." This was only a simulation—participants knew that they were not really prisoners or guards. Yet they became so involved in their roles that the experiment produced levels of stress that were higher than almost any other experiment one can imagine. Fortunately, the Zimbardo experiment is an unusual case—most simulation studies do not raise the ethical issues seen in this particular study.

Honest experiments   Rubin (1973) described what he called "honest" experimental strategies. None of these involve role-playing. The first strategy is one in which the participants are made completely aware of the purposes of the research. In a study by Byrne, Ervin, and Lamberth (1970), the researchers told college students that they were interested in the effectiveness of computer dating. They used a computer program to match male and female students who held either similar or dissimilar attitudes. Each couple had a brief date on campus, and then the researchers measured how much the members of each couple liked one another. The students who were similar were more attracted to each other than were students who were dissimilar. The study involved neither deception nor misrepresentation of the purposes of the research.

A second honest strategy is used in situations in which programs explicitly seek to change people's behavior. Examples cited by Rubin include educational programs, health appeals, charity drives, political campaigns, and solicitations for volunteers. In such situations, people are aware that someone is trying to change their behavior. For instance, people may voluntarily expose themselves to an appeal to quit smoking. Researchers can then investigate the effectiveness of such an appeal while manipulating variables such as the amount of fear aroused (Leventhal, 1970).

Rubin also stated that many field experiments involve honest procedures. In contrast to laboratory experiments such as the Milgram study in which behavior is studied in a laboratory setting, field experiments introduce the experimental manipulation in a natural context. Rubin cites a study in which an experimenter stared at drivers of cars while they were waiting for a red light to change (Ellsworth, Carlsmith, & Henson, 1972). The drivers crossed the intersection faster than did drivers in a control condition in which no staring experimenter was present. This particular experiment does not seem particularly unethical. We have all experienced being stared at. The researchers merely applied experimental methods in order to systematically study this situation. Much research in field settings is indeed honest. Researchers are observing the behavior of people in public places and everyday situations. However, just because an experiment is conducted in the field does not mean that no ethical issues are involved. For example, what are the ethical (and legal) implications of taking up the time of auto salespersons while posing as a customer in order to study different types of price offers or of exposing subway passengers to a person who collapses between stations (cf. Silverman, 1975)?

The final honest strategy discussed by Rubin involves situations in which a naturally occurring event presents an opportunity for research: "Nature, fate, government, and other unalterable forces often impose their will on people in random or nonsystematic ways." For example, researchers were able to study the effects of crowding when a shortage of student housing forced Rutgers University to assign entering students randomly to crowded and uncrowded dormitory rooms (Aiello, Baum, & Gormley, 1981). Baum, Gachtel, and Schaeffer (1983) studied the stressful effects associated with nuclear power plant disasters by comparing people who lived near the Three Mile Island nuclear plant with others who lived near an undamaged nuclear plant or a conventional coal-fired power plant. Such natural experiments occur frequently enough that they are worthwhile sources of data.

Is deception still a problem?

Psychologists obviously have thought a great deal about the problems of deception since the Milgram experiment in the 1960s. A reasonable question to ask is whether deception is still a problem in research. The answer to the question isn't easy. Deception has never been a major problem in many areas of experimental psychology, such as human perception, learning, memory, and motor performance. Even in these areas, however, the experimenter rarely tells participants everything that will happen in the experiment. Further, researchers may use a cover story to make the experiment seem plausible and involving (e.g., telling participants that they are reading actual newspaper stories for a study on readability when the true purpose is to examine memory errors or organizational schemes). As noted previously, such deception is often necessary and expected by the research participants.

Traditionally, deception has been most problematic in social psychology and research on motivation and emotion. In these areas, researchers have used complex event manipulations designed to produce various emotions and other psychological states or to simulate events such as an emergency in which someone needs help. Thus, machines break down to produce guilt, false feedback is given on a personality test, or a bookcase appears to fall on a person in the next room. Gross and Fleming (1982) reviewed 691 social psychological studies published in the 1960s and 1970s. While most research in the 1970s still used deception, the deception primarily involved false cover stories. There were far fewer questionable deceptions in which blatant lies were told or participants were exposed to physically or psychologically stressful events.

Has this trend continued? Sieber, Iannuzzo, and Rodriguez (1995) examined the studies published in the *Journal of Personality and Social Psychology* in 1969, 1978, 1986, and 1992. The number of studies that used some form of deception decreased from 66% in 1969 to 47% in 1978 and to 32% in 1986 but increased again to 47% in 1992. The large drop in 1986 may be due to an increase that year in the number of studies on such topics as personality that require no deception to carry out. Also, informed consent was more likely to be explicitly described in 1992 than in previous years, and debriefing was more likely to be mentioned in the years after 1969. However, false cover stories are still frequently used.

Thus, the answer to our original question is that there seem to be fewer problematic instances of deception in psychological research. There are three primary reasons for this change. First, more researchers have become interested in cognitive variables rather than emotions and so use methods that are similar to those used by researchers in memory and cognitive psychology. Second, the general level of awareness of ethical issues as described in this chapter has led researchers to conduct studies in other ways. Third, ethics committees at universities and colleges now review proposed research more carefully (ethics review boards are described later in this chapter).

OTHER ETHICAL ISSUES IN RESEARCH

Stress and deception are the two major sources of ethical concern in research. Several other ethical issues must be considered as well, however.

Privacy and confidentiality

Researchers must take care to protect the privacy of individuals. When studying topics such as sexual behavior, divorce, family violence, or drug abuse, researchers may sometimes need to ask people sensitive questions about their private lives. It is extremely important that responses to such questions be both anonymous and confidential. The researcher may need to carefully plan ways of coding questionnaires and explaining the procedures to participants so that there is no question concerning the anonymity of responses. Similar safeguards must be taken when individuals are studied on multiple occasions over time; in such cases, there must be some way to identify the individuals but to separate the information about their identity from the actual data collected in the study. Researchers are very conscientious in maintaining the privacy of the participants in research with surveys and questionnaires.

A more problematic privacy issue concerns concealed observation of behavior. In some studies, researchers make observations of behavior in public places. Observing people in shopping malls or in their cars does not seem to present any major ethical problems. But what if a researcher wishes to observe behavior in more private settings or in ways that may violate individuals' privacy or sense of personal space (see Wilson & Donnerstein, 1976). For example, would it be ethical to rummage through people's trash or watch people in public bathrooms? In one study, Middlemist, Knowles, and Matter (1977) measured the time to onset of urination and the duration of urination of males in restrooms at a college. The purpose of the research was to study the effect of personal space on a measure of physiological arousal (urination times). The students were observed while alone or with a confederate of the experimenter, who stood at the next stall or a more distant stall in the restroom. The presence and closeness of the confederate did have the effect of delaying urination and shortening the duration of urination. In many ways, this is an interesting study; also, the situation is one that males experience on a regular basis. However, one can question whether the invasion of privacy was justified (Koocher, 1977). The researchers can, in turn, argue that through pilot studies and discussions with potential participants they determined that ethical problems with the study were minimal (Middlemist et al., 1977). Middlemist et al. employed a method for determining whether a procedure is ethically acceptable that was first proposed by Berscheid, Baron, Dermer, and Libman (1973). Role-playing is used to gather evidence about participants' perceptions of a potential experiment. If the role-playing participants indicate that they would participate in the experiment, at least one objection to deception has been addressed.

Special populations of research participants

Another ethical issue concerns the degree of voluntary participation. Most of us believe that college students are able to make free choices about whether to participate in a study or whether to walk away from research they consider unethical. But what about special populations such as children, psychiatric patients, or prisoners? Clearly, researchers must take special precautions when dealing with groups such as these; obtaining appropriate informed consent becomes especially important. When minors are asked to participate, for example, a written consent form signed by a parent or guardian is generally required. The Division of Developmental Psychology of the American Psychological Association and the Society for Research on Child Development have established their own guidelines for ethical research with children.

Experimenters' obligations

Researchers make several implicit "contracts" with participants during the course of a study. For example, if participants agree to be present for a study at a specific time, the researcher should be there. The issue of punctuality is never mentioned by researchers, yet research participants note it when asked about the obligations of the researcher (Epstein, Suedfeld, & Silverstein, 1973). If researchers promise to send a summary of the results to participants, they should do so. If participants are to receive course credit for participation, the researcher must immediately let the instructor know that the person took part in the study. These are "little details," but they are very important in maintaining trust between participants and researchers.

FORMULATION OF ETHICAL PRINCIPLES

Psychologists recognize the ethical issues we have discussed, and the American Psychological Association (APA) has provided leadership in formulating ethical principles and standards. The Ethical Principles of Psychologists and Code of Conduct—also called the Ethics Code (APA, 1992)—and Ethical Principles in the Conduct of Research With Human Participants (APA, 1982) are the primary sources. The preamble to the Ethics Code states:

> Psychologists work to develop a valid and reliable body of scientific knowledge based on research. They may apply that knowledge to human behavior in a variety of contexts. . . . Their goal is to broaden knowledge of behavior and, where appropriate, to apply it pragmatically to improve the condition of both the individual and society. Psychologists respect the central importance of freedom of inquiry and expression in research, teaching, and publication. They also strive to help the public in developing informed judgments and choices concerning human behavior. . . . It is the individual responsibility of each psychologist to aspire to the highest possible standards of conduct. Psychologists respect and protect human and civil rights, and do not knowingly participate in or condone unfair discriminatory practices.

Six general principles relate to psychologists' competence, integrity, professional and scientific responsibility, respect for people's rights and dignity, concern for others' welfare, and social responsibility. Eight ethical standards address specific issues concerning the conduct of psychologists in teaching, research, therapy, and other professional roles. We will be most concerned with Ethical Standard 6: Teaching, Training Supervision, Research, and Publishing.

RESEARCH WITH HUMAN PARTICIPANTS

The sections of Ethical Standard 6 that most directly deal with research with human participants are:

6.06 Planning Research

(a) Psychologists design, conduct, and report research in accordance with recognized standards of scientific competence and ethical research.

(b) Psychologists plan their research so as to minimize the possibility that results will be misleading.

(c) In planning research, psychologists consider its ethical acceptability under the Ethics Code. If an ethical issue is unclear, psychologists seek to resolve the issue through consultation with institutional review boards, animal care and use committees, peer consultations, or other proper mechanisms.

(d) Psychologists take reasonable steps to implement appropriate protections for the rights and welfare of human participants, other persons affected by the research, and the welfare of animal subjects.

6.07 Responsibility

(a) Psychologists conduct research competently and with due concern for the dignity and welfare of the participants.

(b) Psychologists are responsible for the ethical conduct of research conducted by them or by others under their supervision or control.

(c) Researchers and assistants are permitted to perform only those tasks for which they are appropriately trained and prepared.

(d) As part of the process of development and implementation of research projects, psychologists consult those with expertise concerning any special population under investigation or most likely to be affected.

6.08 Compliance With Law and Standards

Psychologists plan and conduct research in a manner consistent with federal and state law and regulations, as well as professional standards governing the conduct of research, and particularly those standards governing research with human participants and animal subjects.

6.09 Institutional Approval

Psychologists obtain from host institutions or organizations appropriate approval prior to conducting research, and they provide accurate information about their research proposals. They conduct the research in accordance with the approved research protocol.

6.10 Research Responsibilities

Prior to conducting research (except research involving only anonymous surveys, naturalistic observations, or similar research), psychologists enter into an agreement with participants that clarifies the nature of the research and the responsibilities of each party.

41

6.11 Informed Consent to Research

(a) Psychologists use language that is reasonably understandable to research participants in obtaining their appropriate informed consent (except as provided in Standard 6.12, Dispensing With Informed Consent). Such informed consent is appropriately documented.

(b) Using language that is reasonably understandable to participants, psychologists inform participants of the nature of the research; they inform participants that they are free to participate or to decline to participate or to withdraw from the research; they explain the foreseeable consequences of declining or withdrawing; they inform participants of significant factors that may be expected to influence their willingness to participate (such as risks, discomfort, adverse effects, or limitations on confidentiality, except as provided in Standard 6.15, Deception in Research); and they explain other aspects about which the prospective participants inquire.

(c) When psychologists conduct research with individuals such as students or subordinates, psychologists take special care to protect the prospective participants from adverse consequences of declining or withdrawing from participation.

(d) When research participation is a course requirement or opportunity for extra credit, the prospective participant is given the choice of equitable alternative activities.

(e) For persons who are legally incapable of giving informed consent, psychologists nevertheless (1) provide an appropriate explanation, (2) obtain the participant's assent, and (3) obtain appropriate permission from a legally authorized person, if such substitute consent is permitted by law.

6.12 Dispensing With Informed Consent

Before determining that planned research (such as research involving only anonymous questionnaires, naturalistic observations, or certain kinds of archival research) does not require the informed consent of research participants, psychologists consider applicable regulations and institutional review board requirements, and they consult with colleagues as appropriate.

6.13 Informed Consent in Research Filming or Recording

Psychologists obtain informed consent from research participants prior to filming or recording them in any form, unless the research involves simply naturalistic observations in public places and it is not anticipated that the recording will be used in a manner that could cause personal identification or harm.

6.14 Offering Inducements for Research Participants

(a) In offering professional services as an inducement to obtain research participants, psychologists make clear the nature of the services, as well as the risks, obligations, and limitations. (See also Standard 1.18, Barter [With Patients or Clients].)

(b) Psychologists do not offer excessive or inappropriate financial or other inducements to obtain research participants, particularly when it might tend to coerce participation.

6.15 Deception in Research

(a) Psychologists do not conduct a study involving deception unless they have determined that the use of deceptive techniques is justified by the study's prospective scientific, educational, or applied value and that equally effective alternative procedures that do not use deception are not feasible.

(b) Psychologists never deceive research participants about significant aspects that would affect their willingness to participate, such as physical risks, discomfort, or unpleasant emotional experiences.

(c) Any other deception that is an integral feature of the design and conduct of an experiment must be explained to participants as early as is feasible, preferably at the conclusion of their participation, but no later than at the conclusion of the research. (See also Standard 6.18, Providing Participants With Information About the Study.)

6.16 Sharing and Utilizing Data

Psychologists inform research participants of their anticipated sharing or further use of personally identifiable research data and of the possibility of unanticipated future uses.

6.17 Minimizing Invasiveness

In conducting research, psychologists interfere with the participants or milieu from which data are collected only in a manner that is warranted by an appropriate research design and that is consistent with psychologists' roles as scientific investigators.

6.18 Providing Participants With Information About the Study

(a) Psychologists provide a prompt opportunity for participants to obtain appropriate information about the nature, results, and conclusions of the research, and psychologists attempt to correct any misconceptions that participants may have.

(b) If scientific or humane values justify delaying or withholding this information, psychologists take reasonable measures to reduce the risk of harm.

6.19 Honoring Commitments

Psychologists take reasonable measures to honor all commitments they have made to research participants.

These standards stress the importance of informed consent as a fundamental part of ethical practice. However, fully informed consent may not always be possible, and deception may sometimes be necessary. In such cases, the researcher's responsibilities to the participant are increased. Obviously, decisions as to what should be considered ethical or unethical are not simple; there are no ironclad rules. Each piece of research has to be evaluated in terms of whether there are any ethical problems with the procedure, whether alternative, more ethical procedures are available, and whether the importance of the study is such that the ethical problems are justified.

You probably noted that the Ethics Code gives special consideration to research "involving only anonymous questionnaires, naturalistic observations, or certain kinds of archival research." Such research has been placed in a special category by the U.S. Department of Health and Human Services (HHS) regulations for the protection of human research participants (Department of Health and Human Services, 1981). Under these regulations, every institution that receives funds from the HHS must have an Institutional Review Board (IRB) that decides whether proposed research may be conducted (note that institutional review boards are referred to in the Ethics Code). The IRB is composed of both scientists and nonscientists, members of the community, and legal specialists. The 1981 HHS regulations categorized research according to the amount of risk imposed on the subject in order to facilitate the ethical review of research. The rationale was that older regulations required the same type of review for a relatively harmless project and one that might involve physical or psychological harm (cf. Gergen, 1973).

Research in which there is "no risk" is exempt from review. Thus, research that involves only anonymous questionnaires, surveys, and educational tests is exempt, as is naturalistic observation in public places when there is no threat to subject anonymity. Archival research in which the data being studied are publicly available or the participants cannot be identified is exempt as well.

A second type of research activity is called "minimal risk." Minimal risk means that the risks of harm to participants are no greater than risks encountered in daily life or in routine physical or psychological tests. When minimal-risk research is being conducted, elaborate safeguards are less of a concern, and approval by the IRB is routine. Some of the research activities considered minimal risk are (1) recording routine physiological data from adult participants (e.g., weighing, tests of sensory acuity, electrocardiography, electroencephalography, diagnostic echography, and voice recordings; note that this would not include recordings that might involve invasion of privacy or invasive recordings such as x-rays); (2) moderate exercise by healthy volunteers; and (3) research on individual or group behavior or characteristics of individuals, such as studies of perception, cognition, game theory, or test development in which the researcher does not manipulate participants' behavior and the research will not involve stress to participants.

Any research procedure that places the subject at greater than minimal risk is subject to thorough review by the IRB. Complete informed consent and other safeguards may be required before approval is granted.

We can conclude that with the ethical principles of the American Psychological Association, the HHS regulations, and the review of research by the IRB the rights and safety of human participants are well protected. We might note at this point that researchers and review board members tend to be very cautious in terms of what is considered ethical. In fact, several studies have shown that students who have participated in research studies are more lenient in their judgments of the ethics of experiments than are researchers or IRB members (Epstein et al., 1973; Smith, 1983; Sullivan & Deiker, 1973). Moreover, individuals who have taken part in research that used deception report that they did not mind the deception and evaluated the experience positively (Christensen, 1988).

ETHICS AND ANIMAL RESEARCH

Although this chapter has been concerned with the ethics of research with humans, you are no doubt well aware that psychologists sometimes conduct research with animals. About 7% of the articles in *Psychological Abstracts* in 1979 studied animals (Gallup & Suarez, 1985). Animals are used for a variety of reasons. The researcher can carefully control the environmental conditions of the animals, study the same animals over a long period, and monitor their behavior 24 hours a day if necessary. Animals are also used to test the effects of drugs and to study physiological and genetic mechanisms underlying behavior. Most commonly, psychologists work with rats and mice, and to a lesser extent, birds; according to one survey of animal research in psychology, over 95% of the animals in research were rats, mice, and birds (see Gallup & Suarez, 1985).

In recent years, groups opposed to animal research in medicine, psychology, biology, and other sciences have become more vocal and militant. For example, animal rights groups have staged protests at conventions of the American Psychological Association, and animal research laboratories in numerous cities have had animals stolen by members of these groups. The groups are also lobbying for legislation to prohibit all animal research.

Scientists argue that animal research benefits humans and point to many discoveries that would not have been possible without animal research (Miller, 1985). Also, animal rights groups often have exaggerated the amount of research that involves any pain or suffering (Coile & Miller, 1984). Most importantly, scientists point to the fact that strict laws and ethical guidelines govern both research with animals and teaching procedures in which animals are used. Such regulations deal with the need for proper housing, feeding, cleanliness, and health care. They specify that the research must avoid any cruelty in the form of unnecessary pain to the animal. In addition, institutions in which animal research is carried out must have an Institutional Animal Care and Use Committee (IACUC) composed of at least one scientist, one veterinarian, and one community member. The IACUC is charged with reviewing animal research procedures and ensuring that all regulations are adhered to (see Holden, 1987). This section of the Ethics Code is of particular importance here:

6.20 Care and Use of Animals in Research

(a) Psychologists who conduct research involving animals treat them humanely.

(b) Psychologists acquire, care for, use, and disposal of all animals are in compliance with current federal, state, and local laws and regulations, and with professional standards.

(c) Psychologists trained in research methods and experienced in the care of laboratory animals closely supervise all procedures involving animals and are responsible for ensuring appropriate consideration of their comfort, health, and humane treatment.

(d) Psychologists ensure that all individuals using animals under their supervision have received explicit instruction in research methods and in the care, maintenance, and handling of the species being used, to the extent appropriate to their role.

(e) Responsibilities and activities of individuals assisting in a research project are consistent with their respective competencies.

(f) Psychologists make reasonable efforts to minimize the discomfort, illness, and pain of animals.

(g) A procedure subjecting animals to pain, stress, or privation is used only when an alternative procedure is unavailable and the goal is justified by its prospective scientific, educational, or applied value.

(h) Surgical procedures are performed under appropriate anesthesia; techniques to avoid infection and minimize pain are followed during and after surgery.

(i) When it is appropriate that the animal's life be terminated, it is done rapidly, with an effort to minimize pain, and in accordance with accepted procedures.

A more complete set of detailed guidelines for researchers who study animals has also been developed (American Psychological Association, 1986). Clearly, psychologists are concerned about the welfare of animals used in research. Nonetheless, this likely will continue to be a controversial issue.

SUMMING UP:
MAKING A DECISION ABOUT A RESEARCH PROJECT

You are now familiar with the ethical issues that confront researchers who study human and animal behavior. If you do your own research or evaluate the research of others, how do you ultimately decide that the research is or is not ethically acceptable? You will consider the many factors described in this chapter: who the research participants are and how they were recruited, what types of procedures are being used, whether there are risks of psychological harm or loss of confidentiality, how debriefing will be carried out, and so on. According to research on decision making, you are likely to take all of this information into account and use it in a cost-benefit analysis. That is, either implicitly or explicitly, you calculate the costs and the benefits that are likely to result and then make your decision. The costs include all of the potential risks to the participants. In addition, the cost of not conducting the study if in fact the proposed procedure is the only way to collect potentially valuable data can be considered (cf. Christensen, 1988).

The first benefits to consider are direct benefits to the participants, such as an educational benefit, acquisition of a new skill, or treatment for a psychological or medical problem. Other benefits include the scientific contribution of the investigation, the potential beneficial applications of the research findings, and the educational benefit for student researchers. If you ultimately decide that the costs outweigh the benefits, you must conclude that the study cannot be conducted in its current form; in some cases, changes can be made to make it acceptable. If the benefits outweigh the costs, you will likely decide that the research should be carried out. Obviously, your calculation might differ from another person's calculation. That is precisely why having ethics review boards is such a good idea. An appropriate review of research proposals makes it highly unlikely that unethical research will be approved.

FRAUD

One final ethical problem should be mentioned: fraud. When a research finding is published, it is imperative that we have confidence that the research was actually conducted, that the procedures were accurately described, and that the results reported were actually obtained. Two standards in the Ethics Code relate to this topic:

6.21 Reporting of Results
(a) Psychologists do not fabricate data or falsify results in their publications.
(b) If psychologists discover significant errors in their published data, they take reasonable steps to correct such errors in a corrections, retraction, erratum, or other appropriate publication means.

6.22 Plagiarism
Psychologists do not present substantial portions or elements of another's work or data as their own, even if the other work is cited occasionally.

We must be able to believe the reported results of research; otherwise, the entire foundation of the scientific method as a means of knowledge is threatened. In fact, although fraud may occur in many fields, it probably is most serious in relation to two areas: science and journalism. This is because science and journalism are both fields in which written reports are assumed to be accurate descriptions of actual events. There are no independent accounting agencies to check on the activities of scientists and journalists.

Instances of fraud in the field of psychology are considered to be very serious (cf. Hostetler, 1987; Riordan & Marlin, 1987), but fortunately, they have been rare. Perhaps the most famous case is that of Sir Cyril Burt, who reported that the IQ scores of identical twins reared apart were highly similar. The data were used to support the argument that genetic influences on IQ are extremely important. However, Kamin (1974) noted some irregularities in Burt's data. A number of correlations for different sets of twins were exactly the same to the third decimal place, virtually a mathematical impossibility. This observation led to the discovery that some of Burt's presumed co-workers had not in fact worked with him or had simply been fabricated. Ironically, though, Burt's "data" were close to what has been reported by other investigators who have studied the IQ scores of twins.

Burt's fraudulent data were not easy to detect. It took the careful eye of a skilled scientist to notice the unusual pattern of results and to suspect a problem with the data. Fraud may also be detected by a colleague who has worked with the researcher. In a more recent case of fraud in psychology, Stephen Breuning was guilty of faking data showing that stimulants could be used to reduce hyperactive and aggressive behavior in severely retarded children (Byrne, 1988). In this case, another researcher who had worked closely with Breuning had suspicions about the data; he then informed the federal agency that had funded the research.

The most common reason for suspecting fraud is when an important or unusual finding cannot be replicated. Fraud is not a major problem in science because researchers know that others will read their reports and conduct further studies, including replications. They know that their reputations and careers will be seriously damaged if other scientists conclude that the results are fraudulent.

Why, then, do researchers sometimes commit fraud? For one thing, scientists occasionally find themselves under extreme pressures to produce impressive results. However, this is not a sufficient explanation because many researchers maintain high ethical standards under such pressures. Another reason is that researchers who feel a need to produce fraudulent data have an exaggerated fear of failure, as well as a great need for success and the admiration that comes with it. If you wish to explore further the dynamics of fraud and the controversies that still surround the Burt case, you might begin with Hearnshaw's (1979) book on Sir Cyril Burt and with Green's (1992) analysis.

We should make one final point: Allegations of fraud should not be made lightly. If you disagree with someone's results on philosophical, political, religious, or other grounds, it does not mean that they are fraudulent. Even if you cannot replicate the results, the reason may lie in aspects of the methodology of the study. Scientific rigor demands that we carefully consider all hypotheses. However, the fact that fraud could be a possible explanation of results stresses the importance of careful record keeping and documentation of the procedures and results.

These points are illustrated by a case in which fraud was suspected but not substantiated (see Marlatt, 1983). In the early 1970s, two psychologists (Sobell & Sobell, 1973) reported a study of the effectiveness of a "controlled drinking" treatment for alcoholics. Controlled drinking is a procedure designed to produce moderate social drinking, in contrast to the more traditional treatment that attempts to produce abstinence. The Sobells' finding is controversial, especially among anti-alcohol groups.

Ten years later, another group of researchers (Pendery, Maltzman, & West, 1982) reported on the patients in the Sobells' controlled-drinking condition. These authors reported that the participants in the study were in fact not helped, and they went on to describe the serious drinking problems of the persons whom they interviewed. Two of the authors made statements to the press that their findings cast "grave doubt on the scientific integrity of the original research" and "beyond any reasonable doubt, it's fraud" (Marlatt, 1983). As a result of the Pendery et al. study, a "blue-ribbon panel" of researchers and legal experts investigated the Sobells' original work. Fortunately, the Sobells had kept extensive records of their research activities, including audiotapes of interviews of the patients in a follow-up study. The panel concluded that there was "no reasonable cause to doubt the scientific or personal integrity" of the Sobells. In this case, careful record keeping by the researchers and a reasoned scientific examination of the original research prevented substantiation of a serious allegation of fraud.

We should note in conclusion that ethical guidelines and regulations are constantly evolving. The new APA Ethics Code addresses many areas not previously covered, and federal, state, and local regulations may be revised periodically. Researchers need to always be aware of the most current policies and procedures. In the following chapters, we will be discussing many specific procedures for studying behavior. As you read about these procedures and apply them to research you may be interested in, remember that ethical considerations are always paramount.

STUDY TERMS

Confidentiality	Honest experiments	Risk
Cost-benefit analysis	IACUC	Role-playing
Debriefing	Informed consent	Simulation studies
Deception	IRB	Special populations
Ethics Code	Plagiarism	
Fraud	Responsibility	

REVIEW QUESTIONS

1. Discuss the major ethical issues in behavioral research: physical and psychological harm, deception, debriefing, and informed consent. How can researchers weigh the need to conduct research against the need for ethical procedures?

2. Why is informed consent an ethical principle? What are the problems with full informed consent?

3. What alternatives to deception are described in the text?

4. Summarize the principles concerning research with human participants in the APA Ethics Code.

5. What is the difference between "no-risk" and "minimal-risk" research activities?

6. What is an Institutional Review Board?

7. Summarize the ethical procedures for research with animals.

8. What constitutes fraud, what are some reasons for its occurrence, and why doesn't it occur more frequently?

ACTIVITY QUESTIONS

1. Consider the following experiment, similar to one that was conducted by Smith, Lingle, and Brock (1978). Participants interacted for an hour with another person who was actually a confederate. After this interaction, both persons agreed to return one week later for another session with each other. When the real participants returned, they were informed that the person they had met the week before had died. The researchers then measured reactions to the death of the person.

   a. Discuss the ethical issues raised by the experiment.
   b. Would the experiment violate the guidelines articulated in APA Ethical Standard 6 dealing with research with human participants? In what ways?
   c. What alternative methods for studying this problem (reactions to death) might you suggest?
   d. Would your reactions to this study be different if the participants had played with an infant and then later been told that the infant had died?

2. In a procedure described in this chapter, participants are given false feedback about an unfavorable personality trait or a low ability level. What are the ethical issues raised by this procedure? Compare your reactions to that procedure with an analogous one in which people are given false feedback that they possess a very favorable personality trait or a very high ability level.

3. A social psychologist conducts a field experiment at a local bar that is popular with college students. Interested in observing flirting techniques, the investigator instructs male and female confederates to smile and make eye contact with others at the pub for varying amounts of time (e.g., 2 seconds, 5 seconds, etc.) and varying numbers of times (e.g., once, twice, etc.). The investigator observes the responses of those receiving the gaze. What ethical considerations, if any, do you perceive in this field experiment? Is there any deception involved?

4. Should people who are observed in field experiments (such as the one described in question 3) be debriefed? Write a paragraph supporting the "pro" position and another paragraph supporting the "con" position.

5. Dr. George conducted a study to examine various aspects of the sexual behaviors of college students. The students filled out a questionnaire in a classroom on campus; about 50 students were tested at a time. The questionnaire asked about prior experience with various sexual practices. If a student had experience, a number of other detailed questions were asked. However, if the student did not have any prior experience, he or she skipped the detailed questions and simply went on to answer another general question about a sexual experience. What ethical issues arise when conducting research such as this? Do you detect any specific problems that might arise because of the "skip" procedure used in this study?

Studying Behavior

In this chapter, we will explore some of the basic issues and concepts that are necessary for understanding the scientific study of behavior. We will begin by looking at the nature of variables, including their measurement and the types of relationships among them. We will then examine general methods for studying these relationships.

VARIABLES

A **variable** is a general class or category of objects, events, or situations. Examples of variables a psychologist might study include cognitive task performance, word length, spatial density, intelligence, gender, reaction time, rate of forgetting, aggression, speaker credibility, attitude change, anger, stress, age, and self-esteem. Each of these variables represents a general category; within the category, specific instances will vary. These specific instances are called the *levels* or *values* of the variable. A variable must have two or more levels or values. For some variables, the values will have true numeric, or quantitative, properties. Suppose that task performance is a score on a cognitive test on which the values can range from a low of 0% correct to a high of 100% correct; these values have numeric properties. The values of other variables are not numeric, but instead simply identify different categories. An example is gender; the values for gender are male and female. These are different categories, but they do not differ quantitatively.

Variables can be classified into three general categories. *Situational* variables describe characteristics of a situation or environment: the length of words that you read in a book, the spatial density of a classroom, the credibility of a person who is trying to persuade you. *Response* variables are the responses or behaviors of individuals, such as reaction time, performance on a cognitive task, and aggression. *Subject* or *individual difference* variables are the characteristics of individuals, including gender, intelligence, and personality traits such as extraversion.

OPERATIONAL DEFINITIONS OF VARIABLES

In actual research, the researcher has to decide on a method by which to study the variables of interest. It is important to know that a variable is an abstract concept that must be translated into concrete forms of observation or manipulation. Thus, a variable such as "aggression," "cognitive task performance," "amount of reward," "self-esteem," or even "word length" must be defined in terms of the specific method used to measure or manipulate it. Scientists refer to the **operational definition** of a variable—a definition of the variable in terms of the operations or techniques the researcher uses to measure or manipulate it.

53

Variables must be operationally defined so they can be studied empirically. Thus, a variable such as "speaker credibility" might be conceptualized as having two levels and operationally defined as a speaker described to listeners as a "Nobel Prize recipient" or as a "substitute teacher in the Central High School District." The variable of "cognitive task performance" might be defined as the number of errors detected on a proofreading task during a 10-minute period.

There also may be several levels of abstraction when studying a variable. A variable such as "word length" is concrete and easily operationalized in terms of numbers of letters or syllables, but the exact words for the study must still be selected. The concept of "stress" is very general and more abstract. When researchers study stress, they might focus on any number of stressors—noise, crowding, major health problems, job burnout, and so on. A researcher interested in stress would probably choose one stressor to study and then develop operational definitions of that specific stressor. He or she would then carry out research investigations pertaining both to the specific stressor and to the more general concept of stress. The key point is that researchers must always translate variables into specific operations in order to manipulate or measure them.

The task of operationally defining a variable forces scientists to discuss abstract concepts in concrete terms. The process can result in the realization that the variable is too vague to study. This does not necessarily indicate that the concept is meaningless, but rather that systematic research is not possible until the concept can be operationally defined. Once an operational definition is found, progress in understanding a psychological phenomenon is often dependent on the development of increasingly sophisticated technology. For example, the concept of "brain activity" is not new. The study of how brain activity is related to behavior was facilitated first by the development of electrophysiological recording techniques and more recently by brain-imaging technologies.

Operational definitions also help us communicate our ideas to others. If someone wishes to tell me about aggression, I need to know exactly what is meant by this term because there are many ways of operationally defining it. For example, aggression could be defined as (1) the number and duration of shocks delivered to another person, (2) the number of times a child punches an inflated toy clown, (3) the number of times a child fights with other children during recess, (4) homicide statistics gathered from police records, or (5) a score on a personality measure of aggressiveness. Communication with another person will be easier if we agree on exactly what we mean when we use the term *aggression* in the context of our research.

There is rarely a single, infallible method for operationally defining a variable. A variety of methods may be available, each of which has advantages and disadvantages. Researchers must decide which one to use given the particular problem under study, the goals of the research, and other considerations such as ethics and costs. To illustrate how complex it can be to develop an operational definition of a variable, consider the choices faced by a researcher interested in studying crowding. The researcher could study the effects of crowding on college students in a carefully controlled laboratory experiment. However, the focus of the researcher's interest may be the long-term effects of crowding; if so, it might be a good idea to observe the effects of crowding on laboratory animals such as rats. The researcher could examine the long-term effects of crowding on aggression, eating, sexual behavior, and maternal behavior. But what if the researcher wants to investigate cognitive or social variables such as intellectual performance or family interaction? Here, the researcher might decide to study people who live in crowded housing and compare them to people who live in less crowded circumstances. Because no one method is perfect, complete understanding of any variable clearly involves studying the variable using a variety of operational definitions. Several methods will be discussed throughout this book.

MEASUREMENT OF VARIABLES

Recall from Chapter 1 that describing behavior is one of the primary goals of scientific research. To do this, researchers must measure variables. Sometimes, the aim of the research is primarily to describe one or more variables. A social psychologist, for example, might want to develop a taxonomy of ways that people relate to love partners; a cognitive psychologist might seek to describe the ways that people approach a problem-solving situation. Other research focuses on relationships among variables. Do males and females differ in their love relationships? Which problem-solving strategies are most effective in different situations? Measuring variables is a fundamental part of every research investigation. The researcher begins with an abstract, conceptual variable and then must operationally define it. In this section, three aspects of measurement are discussed: reliability, validity, and the problem of reactivity.

Reliability of measures

A reliable measure is one that is both consistent and, because it gives a stable measure of a variable, precise. **Reliability,** then, refers to the consistency or stability of a measure of behavior.

Your everyday definition of reliability is quite close to the scientific definition. For example, you might say that you have a "reliable" watch: Your reliable watch always gives you the precise time, and you rarely find that it is running slow or fast. Similarly, a reliable measure of a psychological variable such as intelligence will yield the same result each time you administer the test to the same person. A measure of intelligence would be unreliable if it measured the same person as average one week, low the next, and bright the next. Put simply, a reliable measure does not fluctuate from one reading to the next. If the measure does fluctuate, there is error in the measurement device.

Figure 4-1
Comparing data of
a reliable and
unreliable measure

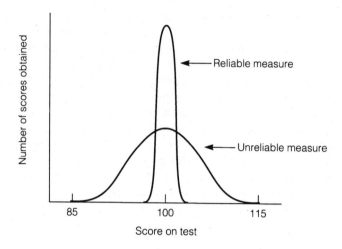

Any measure can be thought of as comprising two components: (1) a **true score,** which is the actual score on the variable, and (2) **measurement error.** An unreliable measure of intelligence contains measurement error and so does not provide an accurate indication of an individual's true intelligence. In contrast, a reliable measure of intelligence—one that contains little measurement error—will yield an identical (or nearly identical) intelligence score each time the same individual is measured.

To illustrate the concept of reliability further, imagine that you know someone whose "true" intelligence score is 100. Suppose that you administer an unreliable intelligence test to this person each week for a year. After the year, you calculate the person's average score on the test based on the 52 scores you obtained. Now suppose that you test another friend who also has a true intelligence score of 100; however, this time you administer a highly reliable test. Again, you calculate the average score. What might your data look like? Typical data are shown in Figure 4-1. In each case, the average score is 100. However, scores on the unreliable test range from 85 to 115, whereas scores on the reliable test range from 97 to 103. The *error* in the unreliable test is revealed in the greater variability shown by the person who took the unreliable test.

When conducting research, you can only measure each person once; you can't give the measure 50 or 100 times to discover a true score. Thus, it is very important that you use a reliable measure. Your single administration of the measure should closely reflect the person's true score.

The importance of reliability is obvious. An unreliable measure of length would be useless in building a table; an unreliable measure of a variable such as intelligence is equally useless in studying that variable. Researchers cannot use unreliable measures to systematically study variables or the relationships among variables. Trying to study behavior using unreliable measures is a waste of time because the results will be unstable and unable to be replicated.

Reliability is most likely to be achieved when researchers use careful measurement procedures. In some research areas, this might involve carefully training observers to record behavior; in other areas, it might mean paying close attention to the way questions are phrased or placing recording electrodes on the body to measure physiological reactions.

There are several ways of assessing reliability. We cannot directly observe the true score and error components of an actual score on the measure. However, we can assess the stability of measures using correlation coefficients. Correlation coefficients are discussed in detail in Chapter 10; for now, you should know that a correlation coefficient is a number that tells us how strongly two variables are related to each other. The size of the coefficient ranges from 0.00, indicating no relationship, to 1.00, the strongest possible relationship. The closer a coefficient is to 1.00, the stronger the relationship. When scores on two variables are very similar, the correlation coefficient describing the strength of the relationship will be high. To assess reliability of a measure, we will need to obtain at least two scores on the measure from many individuals. Let's examine specific methods of assessing reliability.

Test-retest and alternate forms reliability

Test-retest reliability and **alternate forms reliability** measure the same individuals at two points in time. For example, the reliability of a test of intelligence could be assessed by giving the measure to a group of individuals on one day and again a week later. We would then have two scores for each person, and a correlation coefficient could be calculated to determine the relationship between the test score and the retest score. Recall that high reliability is indicated by a high correlation coefficient. It is difficult to say how high the correlation should be before we accept the measure as reliable, but for most measures, the correlation should probably be at least +.80.

Given that test-retest reliability involves administering the same test twice, the correlation might be artificially high because the individuals remember how they responded the first time. Alternate forms reliability is sometimes used to avoid this problem. Alternate forms reliability involves administering two different forms of the same test to the same individuals at two points in time.

Intelligence is a variable that can be expected to stay relatively constant over time; thus, we expect the test-retest reliability for intelligence to be very high. Test-retest and alternate forms reliability should be used for variables that remain stable over time, such as intelligence and achievement. However, some variables may be expected to change from one test period to the next. For example, a mood scale designed to measure a person's current mood state is a measure that might easily change from one test period to another. Thus, methods to assess reliability without two testings also may be used.

57

Split-half, odd-even, and item-total reliability

It is possible to assess reliability by measuring individuals at only one point in time. We can do this because most psychological measures are made up of a number of different items. For example, an intelligence test might have 100 items; a person's test score would be based on the total of his or her scores on all items. Thus, methods to assess reliability at only one point in time are referred to as *internal consistency measures* of reliability. **Split-half reliability** is the correlation between the individual's total score on the first half of the test and his or her total score on the second half of the test. **Odd-even reliability** involves finding the correlation between the total score on the odd-numbered items and the total score on the even-numbered items. Finally, with **item-total reliability,** a correlation between the score on each item of a measure and the total score is calculated. If there are 10 items in the measure, 10 correlation coefficients are obtained; reliability is simply the average of the correlations. In all cases, if the test is reliable, the correlation coefficients will be high.

Construct validity

If something is valid, it is "true" in the sense that it is supported by available evidence. In research, **validity** generally refers to the extent to which a variable has been adequately measured or manipulated. Several types of validity are described in the book. The type of validity most relevant to the current discussion is construct validity.

Construct validity may be defined as the extent to which the operational definition of a variable actually reflects the true theoretical meaning of the variable. Remember that a variable is an abstract concept that can be operationally defined in many ways. Memory, intelligence, attitude, motivation, and self-esteem are all abstract concepts that have theoretical definitions. Operational definitions are necessary to study the variables in empirical research. Construct validity is the extent to which an operational definition does, in fact, reflect the underlying variable.

In terms of the measurement of behavior, construct validity is a question of whether the measure that is employed actually measures what it is intended to measure. A measure of scholastic aptitude (such as the Scholastic Aptitude Test, or SAT) is supposed to measure the ability to succeed in school. The validity of such a test is determined by whether it does, in fact, measure this ability. A measure of self-esteem is an operational definition of the self-esteem variable; the validity of this measure is determined by whether it does measure the theoretical self-esteem construct.

The first test of whether a measure has validity is to examine its **face validity,** which tells whether the measure appears (on the face of it) to measure what it is supposed to measure. Face validity is not very sophisticated; it involves only a judgment of whether, given the theoretical definition of the variable, the measure appears to actually measure the variable. That is, do the procedures used to measure the variable appear to be an accurate operational definition of the theoretical variable? Thus, a measure of a variable such as self-esteem will usually appear to measure self-esteem. The measure might include an item such as "I feel comfortable attending a social function with strangers" but not an item such as "I learned to ride a bicycle at an early age"; the first item appears to be more closely related to self-esteem than does the second one. Most researchers prefer to use measures that have face validity.

Face validity is not entirely satisfactory, however. Some measures of variables do not have obvious face validity. For example, is it obvious that rapid eye movement during sleep is a measure of dream occurrence? Also, psychological variables are usually discussed in terms of their theoretical meaning. Self-esteem is measured and studied because researchers have developed theories of self-esteem that relate this construct to other variables. People with high self-esteem are hypothesized to differ from people with low self-esteem in a variety of ways—for example, to behave differently in different situations. Further, certain variables are hypothesized to result in low or high self-esteem.

When a measure does relate to other variables in meaningful ways, our confidence that the measure has construct validity increases. There is a formal term for this: **Convergent validity** means that the measure is related in predicted ways to other variables. Such validity emerges from research studies in which investigators use the measure to study behavior. For example, the construct validity of rapid eye movement as a measure of dream occurrence is demonstrated when studies find that people who are awakened during rapid eye movement are more likely to report dreaming than are people who are awakened when their eyes are not moving. Similarly, a measure of self-esteem should be related to variables that are theoretically predicted to be related to self-esteem. Also, the measure should *not* be related to variables with which it should not be related; this is formally referred to as **discriminant validity.**

The construct validity of a measure is rarely established in a single study, but rather is built up over time as numerous studies investigate the theory of the particular construct being measured. Further, measures of variables usually have a limited life span. As research findings accumulate, researchers discover problems with the measure and develop new measures to correct the problems. This process leads to better measures and fuller understanding of the underlying variable being studied.

The Sensation Seeking Scale (Zuckerman, 1979) is an excellent illustration of construct validity issues. Zuckerman's research was stimulated by a psychological theory of optimal levels of physiological arousal. The theory states that people have a need to maintain an optimal level of arousal. When arousal is too low, people will be motivated to do things to increase arousal; when arousal is too high, an attempt to reduce arousal should be observable. The theory helps to explain many behaviors, such as the hallucinations and other disturbances that people experience when they are placed in sensory deprivation environments. Zuckerman decided to study this theory by focusing on individual differences; he asked why some people consistently seem to seek out novel or arousing sensations (e.g., parachuting, listening to loud music, driving in car races) while other people avoid arousing sensations.

The Sensation Seeking Scale was developed to study such individual differences in personality. The scale itself includes items intended to measure thrill seeking, susceptibility to boredom, and other aspects of sensation seeking. The reliability of the scale was assessed, of course. After determining that the scale was reliable, construct validity research could begin. Over a period of many years, research by Zuckerman and others has shown that people who score high on the scale do in fact behave differently from people who score low. High sensation seekers engage in more dangerous activities, drive faster, and prefer less intellectual activities, for example. The measure is also related in expected ways to other personality traits: High sensation seekers are more extraverted. Work on the Sensation Seeking Scale has ultimately led to research on the biological basis for sensation seeking, such as what brain mechanisms are responsible for arousal needs and whether the trait has a genetic basis. Zuckerman's research illustrates a systematic program of research on the validity of a measure of a psychological construct. In other areas of research, the construct validity of measures may be studied less systematically. In all research, though, measures must be useful in studying the variables being investigated.

The problem of reactivity

A potential problem when measuring behavior is **reactivity.** A measure is said to be reactive if awareness of being measured changes the individuals' behavior. A reactive measure tells what the person is like when he or she is aware of being observed, but it doesn't tell how the person would behave under natural circumstances. Simply having various devices such as electrodes and blood pressure cuffs attached to your body may change the physiological responses being recorded. Knowing that a researcher is observing you or recording your behavior on tape might change the way you behave. Measures of behavior vary in terms of their potential reactivity. There are also ways to minimize reactivity, such as allowing time for individuals to become used to the presence of the observer or the recording equipment.

A book by Webb, Campbell, Schwartz, Sechrest, and Grove (1981) has drawn attention to a number of measures that are called *nonreactive* or *unobtrusive.* Many such measures involve clever ways of indirectly recording a variable. For example, an unobtrusive measure of preferences for paintings in an art museum is the frequency with which tiles around each painting must be replaced—the most popular paintings are the ones with the most tile wear. Levine's (1990) study on the pace of life in cities, mentioned in Chapter 2, used indirect measures such as the accuracy of bank clocks and the speed of processing standard requests at post offices to measure pace of life. Some of the measures described by Webb et al. (1981) are simply humorous. For instance, in 1872, Sir Francis Galton studied the efficacy of prayer in producing long life. Galton wondered whether British royalty, who were frequently the recipients of prayers by the populace, lived longer than other people. He checked death records and found that members of royal families actually led shorter lives than other people, such as men of literature and science. The book by Webb and his colleagues is a rich source of such nonreactive measures. More importantly, it draws attention to the problem of reactivity and sensitizes researchers to the need to reduce reactivity whenever possible. We will return to this issue at several points in this book.

RELATIONSHIPS BETWEEN VARIABLES

Recall from Chapter 1 that researchers are often interested in studying the relationship between two variables. The relationship between two variables is the general way in which changes in the values of one variable are associated with changes in the values of the other variable. That is, do the levels of the two variables vary systematically together? As age increases, does the amount of cooperative play increase as well? Does viewing television violence result in greater aggressiveness? Is speaker credibility related to attitude change?

Recall that some variables have true numeric values while the levels of other variables are simply different categories. This distinction will be expanded on in Chapter 10 because it has implications for determining appropriate statistical analyses of data. For the purposes of describing relationships among variables, we will begin by discussing relationships in which both variables have true numeric properties.

When both variables have values along a numeric scale, many different "shapes" can describe their relationship. We begin by focusing on the four most common relationships: the positive linear relationship, the negative linear relationship, the curvilinear relationship, and, of course, the situation in which there is no relationship between the variables. These relationships are best illustrated by line graphs that show the way changes in one variable are accompanied by changes in a second variable. The four graphs in Figure 4-2 show these four types of relationships.

Positive linear relationship

In a **positive linear relationship,** increases in the values of one variable are accompanied by increases in the values of the second variable. We have previously described a positive relationship between communicator credibility and persuasion: Higher levels of credibility are associated with more attitude change. Consider another communicator variable, rate of speech. Are "fast talkers" more persuasive? In a study conducted by Smith and Shaffer (1991), students listened to a speech delivered at a slow (144 words per minute), intermediate (162 wpm), or fast (214 wpm) speech rate. The speaker advocated a position favoring legislation to raise the legal drinking age; the students disagreed with this position. Graph A in Figure 4-2 shows the positive linear relationship between speech rate and attitude change that was found

61

Figure 4-2
Four types of
relationships
between variables

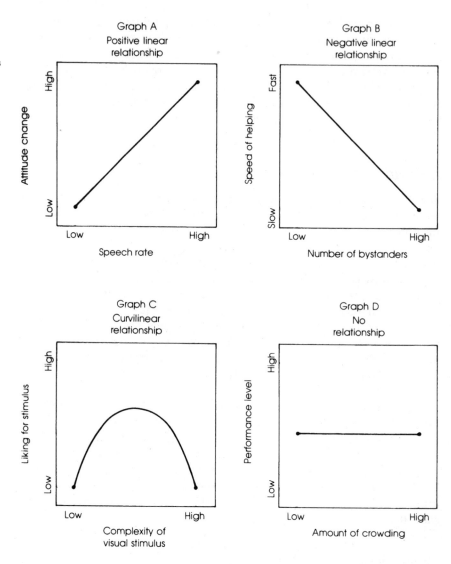

в this study. In a graph like this, there is a horizontal and a vertical axis. Values of the first variable are placed on the horizontal axis, labeled from low to high. Values of the second variable are placed on the vertical axis. Graph A shows that higher speech rates are associated with greater amounts of attitude change.

Negative linear relationship

Variables can also be negatively related. In a **negative linear relationship,** increases in the values of one variable are accompanied by *decreases* in the values of the other variable. Darley and Latané (1968) were intrigued with a widely publicized incident in which a woman named Kitty Genovese was repeatedly stabbed outside her apartment building in New York City while 38 of her neighbors failed to respond to her cries for help. Subsequent research on the effect of bystanders on helping behavior revealed a negative relationship between the number of bystanders present at an emergency and the speed with which the victim receives help. Each person in the experiment was alone in a cubicle in the laboratory and overheard what he or she thought was another person having an epileptic seizure (actually each heard a tape recording). Some individuals believed that they were the only ones to hear the emergency; others thought that there was one other bystander; still others believed that there were four other bystanders present. Graph B in Figure 4-2 illustrates the negative relationship between number of bystanders and speed of helping. As the number of bystanders *increased*, the speed of helping *decreased*. The two variables are systematically related, just as in a positive relationship; only the direction of the relationship is reversed.

Curvilinear relationship

In a **curvilinear relationship,** increases in the values of one variable are accompanied by both increases and decreases in the values of the other variable. In other words, the direction of the relationship changes at least once. This type of relationship is sometimes referred to as a *nonmonotonic function*. Graph C in Figure 4-2 shows a curvilinear relationship between complexity of visual stimuli and ratings of preferences for the stimuli. This particular relationship is called an inverted-U relationship. Increases in visual complexity are accompanied by increases in liking for the stimulus, but only up to a point. The relationship then becomes negative, as further increases in complexity are accompanied by *decreases* in liking for the stimulus (Vitz, 1966).

No relationship

When there is no relationship between the two variables, the graph is simply a flat line. Graph D in Figure 4-2 illustrates the relationship between crowding and task performance found in a study by Freedman, Klevansky, and Ehrlich (1971). Unrelated variables vary independently of one another. Increases in crowding are not associated with any particular changes in performance; thus, a flat line describes the lack of relationship between the two variables.

These graphs illustrate several kinds of shapes; almost any shape can describe the relationship between two variables. Other relationships are described by more complicated shapes than those in Figure 4-2. For example, the positive and negative linear relationships just described are examples of a more general category of relationships described as monotonic because the relationship between the variables is always positive or always negative (it does not change directions as in the curvilinear, or nonmonotonic, relationship in Graph C). An example of a positive monotonic function that is not strictly linear is shown in Figure 4-3. We will return to this topic in Chapter 8.

Remember that these are general patterns. Even if, in general, a positive linear relationship exists, that does not necessarily mean that everyone who

Figure 4-3
Positive monotonic
function

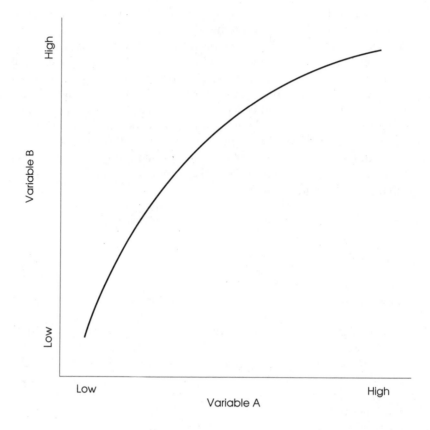

scores high on one variable will also score high on the second variable. Individual deviations from the general pattern are possible. In addition to knowing the general type of relationship between two variables, it is also necessary to know the strength of the relationship. That is, we need to know the size of the correlation between the variables. Sometimes, two variables are strongly related to each other and there is very little deviation from the general pattern. Other times, the two variables are not highly correlated. As noted previously, a correlation coefficient is an index of the strength of the relationship between variables; we will return to this issue in Chapter 10.

CORRELATIONAL VERSUS EXPERIMENTAL METHODS

There are two general approaches to the study of relationships among variables: the correlational method and the experimental method. The **correlational method** is nonmanipulative; the researcher observes or measures the variables of interest (the terms "observation" and "measurement" will be used interchangeably throughout the text). That is, behavior is observed as it occurs naturally. This may be done by asking people to describe their behavior, by directly observing behavior, or even by examining various public records such as census data. The second approach to the study of relationships between variables is called the experimental method. In contrast to the correlational method, the **experimental method** involves manipulation of variables. The researcher directly manipulates one or more variables by establishing the conditions for studying behavior; the behavior is then observed under the different conditions. For example, Loftus (1979) used the experimental method when participants who viewed a film of an auto accident later were asked whether they saw "a" broken headlight or "the" broken headlight. The method of questioning was manipulated, and the participants' answers were then measured.

The correlational method

Suppose a researcher is interested in the relationship between exercise and anxiety. How could this topic be studied? Using the correlational method, the researcher would devise operational definitions to measure both the amount of exercise that people engage in and their level of anxiety. There could be a variety of ways of operationally defining either of these variables; for example, the researcher might simply ask people to provide self-reports of their exercise patterns and current anxiety level. The important point to remember here is that both variables are measured when using the correlational method. Now suppose that the researcher collects data on exercise and anxiety from a number of people and finds that exercise is negatively related to anxiety. That is, the more people exercise, the lower their level of anxiety.

The correlational method seems to be a reasonable approach to studying relationships between variables such as exercise and anxiety. However, two problems arise when interpreting results obtained using the correlational method: (1) direction of cause and effect and (2) the third-variable problem —that is, extraneous variables that may affect the results.

Direction of cause and effect   The first problem is that of direction of cause and effect. With the correlational method, it is difficult to determine which variable causes the other. In other words, it can't really be said that exercise causes a reduction in anxiety. Although there are plausible reasons for this particular pattern of cause and effect, there are also reasons that the opposite pattern might occur. Perhaps anxiety level causes exercise, or perhaps the experience of high anxiety interferes with the ability to exercise. This is an important difference. If exercise reduces anxiety, then undertaking an exercise program would be a reasonable way to lower one's anxiety. However, if anxiety causes people to stop exercising, simply forcing someone to exercise would not be likely to reduce the person's anxiety level.

The problem of direction of cause and effect is not the most serious drawback to the correlational method, however. Scientists have pointed out, for example, that astronomers can make accurate predictions even though they cannot manipulate variables in an experiment. In addition, the direction of cause and effect is often not crucial because, for some pairs of variables, the causal pattern may operate in both directions. For instance, there seem to be two causal patterns in the relationship between the variables of similarity and liking: (1) Similarity causes people to like each other, and (2) liking causes people to become more similar. In general, the third-variable problem is a much more serious fault of the correlational method.

The third-variable problem   When the correlational method is used, there is the danger that no direct causal relationship exists between the two variables. Exercise may not influence anxiety, and anxiety may have no causal effect on exercise. Instead, there may be a relationship between the two variables because some other variable causes both exercise *and* anxiety. This is known as the third-variable problem. Any number of other *third variables* may be responsible for an observed relationship between two variables. In the exercise and anxiety example, one such third variable could be income level. Perhaps high income allows people more free time to exercise (and the ability to afford a health club membership!) and also lowers anxiety. If income is the determining variable, there is no direct cause-and-effect relationship between exercise and anxiety; the relationship was caused by the third variable, income level.

As you can see, direction of cause and effect and potential third variables represent serious limitations of the correlational method. Often, they are not considered in media reports of research results. For instance, a newspaper may report the results of a correlational study that found a positive relationship between amount of coffee consumed and likelihood of a heart attack. Obviously, there is not necessarily a cause-and-effect relationship between the two variables. Numerous third variables (e.g., occupation, personality, or genetic predisposition) could cause both a person's coffee-drinking behavior and the likelihood of heart attack. In sum, the results of such studies are ambiguous and should be viewed with skepticism.

The experimental method

The experimental method reduces such ambiguity in the interpretation of results. With the experimental method, one variable is manipulated and the other is then measured. If a researcher used the experimental method to study whether exercise reduces anxiety, exercise would be manipulated—perhaps by having one group of people exercise each day for a week and another group refrain from exercise. Anxiety would then be measured. Suppose it was found that people in the exercise group are lower in anxiety than the people in the no-exercise group. The researcher could now say something about the direction of cause and effect: In the experiment, exercise came first in the sequence of events. Thus, anxiety level could not influence the amount of exercise that the people engaged in.

Another characteristic of the experimental method is that it attempts to eliminate the influence of all extraneous "third" variables. This is called control of extraneous variables. Such control is usually achieved by making sure that every feature of the environment except the manipulated variable is held constant. Any variable that cannot be held constant is controlled by making sure that the effects of the variable are random. Through randomization, the influence of any extraneous variables is equal in the experimental conditions. Both procedures are used to ensure that any differences between the groups are due to the manipulated variable.

Experimental control   With experimental control, all extraneous variables are kept constant. If a variable is held constant, it cannot be responsible for the results of the experiment. In the experiment on the effect of exercise, the researcher would want to make sure that the only difference between the exercise and no-exercise groups is the exercise. Because people in the exercise group are removed from their daily routine to engage in exercise, the people in the no-exercise group should be removed from their daily routine as well. Otherwise, the lower anxiety in the exercise condition could have resulted from the "rest" from the daily routine rather than the exercise.

Experimental control is accomplished by treating people in all groups in the experiment identically; the only difference between groups is the manipulated variable. In the Loftus experiment on memory, both groups will witness the same accident, the same experimenter will ask the questions in both groups, the lighting and all other conditions will be the same, and so on. When there is a difference between the groups in reporting memory, one can be sure that the difference is the result of the method of questioning rather than of some other variable that was not held constant.

Randomization   Sometimes, it is difficult to keep a variable constant. The most obvious such variable is any characteristic of the participants. If, in a study using the experimental method, one group of subjects is in the exercise condition and a different group of subjects is in the no-exercise condition, the subjects in the two conditions might differ on some extraneous variable, such as income. This difference could cause an apparent relationship between exercise and anxiety. How can the researcher eliminate the influence of such extraneous variables in an experiment?

The experimental method eliminates the influence of such variables by **randomization.** Randomization ensures that the extraneous variable is just as likely to affect one experimental group as it is to affect the other group. To eliminate the influence of individual characteristics, the researcher assigns subjects to the two groups in a random fashion. In actual practice, this means that assignment to groups is determined using a list of random numbers. To understand this, think of the people in the experiment as forming a line. As each person comes to the front of the line, a random number is assigned, much like random numbers are drawn for a lottery. If the number is even, the individual is assigned to one group (e.g., exercise); if the number is odd, the individual is assigned to the other group (e.g., no exercise). By using a random assignment procedure, the researcher can guarantee that the individual characteristic composition of the two groups will be virtually identical. In this "lottery," for instance, people with low, medium, and high incomes will be distributed equally in the two groups. In fact, randomization ensures that the individual characteristic composition of the two groups will be virtually identical in every way. This ability to randomly assign people to groups is an important difference between the experimental and correlational methods.

To make the concept of random assignment more concrete, you might try an exercise such as the one I did with a box full of old baseball cards. The box contained cards of 50 American League players and 50 National League players. The cards were thoroughly mixed up; I then proceeded to select 32 of the cards and assign them to "groups" using the list of random numbers in Table C-1 in Appendix C. As I selected each card, I used the following decision rule: If the random number is even, the player is assigned to "group 1," and if the number is odd, the player is assigned to "group 2." I then checked to see whether my two groups differed in terms of league representation. Group 1 had 9 American League players and 7 National League players, while group 2 had an equal number of players from the two leagues. The two groups were virtually identical!

Any other variable that cannot be held constant is also controlled by randomization. For instance, many experiments are conducted over a period of several days or weeks, with participants arriving for the experiment at various times during each day. In such cases, the researcher use a random order for scheduling the sequence of the various experimental conditions. This procedure prevents a situation in which one condition is scheduled during the first days of the experiment while the other is studied during later days. Similarly, participants in one group will not be studied only during the morning and the others only in the afternoon.

Direct control and randomization eliminate the influence of any extraneous variables. Thus, the experimental method allows a relatively unambiguous interpretation of the results. Any difference between groups on the observed variable can be attributed only to the influence of the manipulated variable.

INDEPENDENT AND DEPENDENT VARIABLES

When researchers study the relationship between variables, the variables are usually conceptualized as having a cause-and-effect connection. That is, one variable is considered to be the "cause," and the other variable the "effect." Thus, speaker credibility is viewed as a cause of attitude change, while exercise is viewed as having an effect on anxiety. Researchers using both experimental and correlational methods view the variables in this fashion, even though, as we have seen, there is less ambiguity about the direction of cause and effect when the experimental method is used. Researchers use the terms

independent variable and **dependent variable** when referring to the variables being studied. The variable that is considered to be the "cause" is the independent variable, and the variable that is the "effect" is the dependent variable.

In an experiment, the manipulated variable is the independent variable, and the second variable that is measured is the dependent variable. One way to remember the distinction is to relate the terms to what happens to an individual in an experiment. The researcher devises a situation to which people are exposed, such as watching a violent versus a nonviolent program. This situation is the manipulated variable; it is called the independent variable because the person has nothing to do with its occurrence. In the next step of the experiment, the researcher measures the person's response to the manipulated variable. The person is responding to what happened to him or her; the researcher assumes that what the individual does or says is caused by, or dependent on, the effect of the independent (manipulated) variable. The independent variable, then, is the variable manipulated by the experimenter, and the dependent variable is the measured behavior of the subject that is assumed to be caused by the independent variable.

When the relationship between an independent and a dependent variable is plotted in a graph, the independent variable is always placed on the horizontal axis and the dependent variable is always placed on the vertical axis. If you look back to Figure 4-2, you will see that this graphing method was used to present the four relationships. In Graph B, for example, the independent variable "number of bystanders" is placed on the horizontal axis; the dependent variable "speed of helping" is placed on the vertical axis.

Note that some research focuses primarily on the independent variable, with the researcher studying the effect of a single independent variable on numerous behaviors. Other researchers may focus on a specific dependent variable and study how various situations affect that one behavior. Construct validity research, discussed previously in this chapter, illustrates research that concentrates on a single behavior, such as sensation seeking. To make this distinction more concrete, consider a study of the effect of jury size on the outcome of a trial. One researcher studying this issue might be interested in the effect of group size on a variety of behaviors, including jury decisions and risk taking among business managers. Another researcher interested solely in jury decisions might study the effects of jury size or the judge's instructions on the behaviors of jurors. Both emphases lead to important research.

CAUSALITY

Thus far, causality has been discussed only on an intuitive level. When the experimental method is used, causality is inferred on the basis of the fact that, because everything else is held constant, a change in one variable produces a change in another variable. When psychologists speak of "cause," they mean that evidence exists that one variable does affect another. Such evidence is most easily established using the procedures of the experimental method.

In reality, however, questions of true cause and effect are more difficult than they appear, provoking controversy among both scientists and philosophers. Many argue that a cause-and-effect relationship is proven only if the cause is both necessary *and* sufficient for the effect to occur.

To illustrate, consider the question "What causes a car to start?" Many people might answer that it is turning the ignition key. Admittedly, for two cars in perfect working order, turning the ignition key in only one of the cars means only one of the cars will start. But has causation been proven? The answer is no if we require a cause to be both necessary and sufficient for the effect to occur.

To be necessary, the cause must be present for the event to occur. To prove that turning the ignition key is the cause of the car starting, it must be shown that turning the ignition key must occur for the car to start. To be sufficient, the cause will *always* produce the effect. To prove that turning the key is the cause, it must always result in the car starting.

Is turning the key necessary and sufficient for the car to start? In most cases, turning the key is necessary. However, it is possible to start the car by "hot wiring" the ignition to bypass the ignition key. Thus, turning the ignition key is not necessary; rather, turning on an electrical ignition circuit is necessary. Is turning the key sufficient to start the car? Turning the key is not sufficient because it does not always result in the car starting. The car may not start when the key is turned for any number of reasons, including lack of fuel or a dead battery.

The "necessary and sufficient" requirement for establishing cause is rare in psychology. Whenever psychologists assert that there is a necessary and sufficient cause of a behavior, research soon reveals that this just isn't so. For example, psychologists once asserted that "frustration causes aggression"; whenever frustration occurs, aggression will result, and whenever aggression occurs, frustration must be the preceding cause. This assertion was shown to be inaccurate. Frustration may lead to aggression, but other responses (such as passive withdrawal or increased effort to overcome the frustration) are possible as well. Also, aggression may result from frustration, but other events may produce aggression as well, including pain, insult, or direct attack.

A typical type of cause-and-effect relationship in psychology is one in which the cause is sufficient but not necessary for the effect to occur. For example, through classical conditioning procedures, the pairing of a painful stimulus with a neutral stimulus will produce a fear of the originally neutral stimulus. However, fears may be acquired in other ways.

Another type of cause and effect is observed when a variable is necessary but not sufficient. The variable by itself cannot produce the effect; other conditions must also be present for the effect to occur. For example, it is necessary to be over 18 years of age to vote, but age is not a sufficient cause. Other conditions, such as motivation to vote, must be present.

Behavioral scientists are not unduly concerned with the issues of ultimate cause and effect. Rather, they are more interested in carefully describing behavior, studying how variables affect one another, and understanding the reasons why. The general consensus is that there are few interesting "necessary and sufficient" causes of behavior. Instead, research on numerous variables eventually leads to an understanding of a whole "causal network," in which a number of variables are involved in complex patterns of cause and effect. This book will not focus on these difficult questions, but instead will examine the methods used to study behavior.

CHOOSING A METHOD

In this chapter, we have discussed the importance of describing behavior through careful measurement and of studying relationships among variables using the correlational and experimental methods. The advantages of the experimental method have been stressed. However, there *are* disadvantages to experiments and many good reasons for using methods other than experiments. These reasons include the possible artificiality of a laboratory experiment, ethical considerations, the need to study subject variables, and the goals of description and prediction of behavior. When researchers choose a methodology to study a problem, they must weigh the advantages and disadvantages of their options in the context of the overall goals of the research.

Artificiality of experiments

In a laboratory experiment, the independent variable is manipulated within the carefully controlled confines of a laboratory. This procedure permits relatively unambiguous inferences concerning cause and effect and reduces the possibility that extraneous variables could influence the results. It is an extremely valuable way to study many problems. However, the high degree of control and the laboratory setting may sometimes create an artificial atmosphere that limits either the questions that can be addressed or the generality of the results. For this reason, researchers may decide to use correlational methods. Another alternative is to try to conduct an experiment in a field setting. In a **field experiment,** the independent variable is manipulated in a natural setting. As in any experiment, the researcher attempts to control extraneous variables via either randomization or experimental control.

As an example of a field experiment, consider Langer and Rodin's (1976) study on the effects of giving elderly nursing home residents greater control over decisions that affect their lives. One group of residents was given a great deal of responsibility for making choices concerning the operation of the nursing home; a second group was made to feel that the staff would be responsible for their care and needs. The experimenters measured dependent variables such as activity level and happiness of the residents. The results showed that the members of the group given increased responsibility were more active and happy. In a follow-up study, group members even showed greater improvements in physical health (Rodin & Langer, 1977).

The advantage of the field experiment is that the independent variable is investigated in a natural context. The disadvantage is that the researcher loses the ability to directly control many aspects of the situation. The laboratory

71

experiment permits researchers to more easily keep extraneous variables constant, thereby eliminating their influence on the outcome of the experiment. Of course, it is precisely this control that leads to the artificiality of the laboratory investigation.

Ethical considerations

Sometimes, the experimental method is not a feasible alternative because experimentation would be either unethical or impractical. Child-rearing practices would be impractical to manipulate with the experimental method, for example. Further, even if it were possible to randomly assign parents to two child-rearing conditions, such as using withdrawal of love versus physical types of punishment, the manipulation would be unethical. Instead of manipulating variables such as child-rearing techniques, researchers usually study them as they occur in natural settings. Many important research areas present similar problems—for example, studies of the effects of alcoholism, divorce and its consequences, or the impact of maternal employment on children. Such problems need to be studied, and generally the only techniques possible are nonexperimental.

Subject variables

Subject variables are characteristics of individuals, such as age, gender, personality, or marital status. These variables are by definition nonexperimental. When subject variables are studied, the variables are measured. For example, to study a personality characteristic such as extraversion, you might have subjects complete a personality test that is designed to measure this variable. Such variables may be studied in experiments along with manipulated independent variables (see Chapter 8).

Description of behavior

A major goal of science is to provide an accurate description of events. Thus, the goal of much research is to describe behavior; the issues that experiments address are really not relevant to the primary goals of the research. A classic example of descriptive research in psychology comes from the work of Jean Piaget, who carefully observed the behavior of his own children as they matured and described in detail the changes in their ways of thinking about and responding to their environment (Piaget, 1952). Piaget's descriptions and his interpretations of his observations resulted in an important theory of cognitive development that greatly increased our understanding of this topic. Piaget's theory is still being tested and refined by researchers using a variety of methods (see Flavell, 1985).

Successful predictions of future behavior

In many real-life situations, a major concern is to make a successful prediction about a person's future behavior—for example, success in school, ability to learn a new job, or probable interest in various major fields in college. In such circumstances, there may be no need to be concerned about issues of cause and effect. It is possible to design measures that increase the accuracy of predicting future behavior. School counselors can give tests to decide whether students should be in "enriched" classroom programs; employers can test job applicants to help determine whether they should be hired; and college students can take tests that help them decide on a major. These types of measures can lead to better decisions for many people.

When researchers develop measures designed to predict future behavior, they must conduct research to demonstrate that the measure does, in fact, relate to the behavior in question. You may recognize this as another aspect of the construct validity of a measure. For example, if a clerical aptitude test is designed as a measure of the ability to succeed in a clerical training program, does it in fact measure this ability?

The construct validity of such measures is called **criterion validity.** Research is conducted to examine whether the test, which is called a **predictor variable,** is related to the future behavior, called the **criterion variable.** The criterion validity of a test of clerical aptitude is demonstrated when research shows that people who score high on the test do better in clerical training than people who score low on the test (i.e., there is a positive relationship between the test score and future behavior). When research establishes that the test has criterion validity, the measure can be used to advise people on whether they will be successful in a clerical training program or to select applicants for a program.

SUMMING UP AND LOOKING AHEAD: THREE VALIDITIES

Research can be described and evaluated in terms of three types of validity: construct validity, internal validity, and external validity. Each gives us a different perspective on any particular research investigation.

As discussed previously, construct validity is the extent to which the operational definition of a variable actually reflects the true theoretical meaning of the variable. Most attention to construct validity is directed toward measures of psychological variables, and so the focus in this chapter has been on the validity of measures: face validity, convergent and discriminant validity, and criterion validity. However, construct validity is also important when researchers manipulate variables in experimental research. Here, the issue is how well the independent variable manipulation actually reflects the underlying theoretical variable. For example, a manipulation of anxiety in an experiment should truly affect anxiety levels in the participants to have construct validity. This issue is raised again in Chapter 7.

Internal validity refers to the ability to draw conclusions about causal relationships from our data. A study has high internal validity when strong inferences can be made that one variable caused the other. We have seen that, in general, strong causal inferences can be made more easily when the exper-

73

imental method is used. In subsequent chapters, we will examine ways that experiments can be designed to increase their internal validity.

Finally, the **external validity** of a study is the extent to which the results can be generalized to other populations and settings. In this chapter, concerns over the artificiality of laboratory experiments were addressed. The issue of external validity is a complex one that will be discussed more fully in Chapter 12.

At this point, you may be wondering how researchers select a methodology to study a problem. A variety of methods are available, each with advantages and disadvantages. Researchers select the method that best enables them to address the questions that they wish to answer. No method is inherently superior to another. Rather, the choice of method is made after considering the problem under investigation, any cost and time constraints, and issues associated with the three types of validity. In the remainder of this book, many specific methods will be discussed, all of which are useful under different circumstances. In fact, all are necessary to understand the wide variety of behaviors that are of interest to behavioral scientists. Complete understanding of any problem or issue requires research using a variety of methodological approaches.

STUDY TERMS

Alternate forms reliability	Face validity	Randomization
Construct validity	Field experiment	Reactivity
Convergent validity	Independent variable	Response variable
Correlational method	Internal validity	Situational variable
Criterion validity	Item-total reliability	Split-half reliability
Criterion variable	Measurement error	Subject variable
Curvilinear relationship	Necessary cause	Sufficient cause
Dependent variable	Negative linear relationship	Test-retest reliability
Discriminant validity	Odd-even reliability	Third-variable problem
Experimental control	Operational definition	True score
Experimental method	Positive linear relationship	Variable
External validity	Predictor variable	

REVIEW QUESTIONS

1. What is a variable? List at least five different variables, and then specify the levels of each variable.

2. Define "operational definition" of a variable. Give at least two operational definitions of the variables you thought of in item 1.

3. What is meant by the reliability of a measure? Distinguish between true score and measurement error.

4. Discuss the concept of validity. Distinguish among the types of validity described in this chapter.

5. What is a reactive measure?

6. Distinguish among positive linear, negative linear, and curvilinear relationships.

7. What is the difference between the correlational method and the experimental method?

8. What is the difference between an independent variable and a dependent variable?

9. Distinguish between laboratory and field experiments.

10. What is meant by the problem of direction of cause and effect and the third-variable problem?

11. How do direct experimental control and randomization influence the possible effects of extraneous variables?

12. What are some reasons for using the correlational method to study relationships between variables?

13. What is meant by a "necessary and sufficient" cause?

ACTIVITY QUESTIONS

1. Males and females may differ in their approaches to helping others—for example, males may be more likely to help a person having car trouble, while females may be more likely to bring dinner to a sick friend. Develop two operational definitions for the concept of "helping behavior," one that emphasizes the "male style" and the other the "female style." How might the use of one or the other lead to different conclusions from experimental results regarding who helps more, males or females? What does this tell you about the importance of operational definitions?

2. You observe that classmates who get good grades tend to sit toward the front of the classroom, while those who receive poorer grades tend to sit toward the back. What are three possible cause-and-effect relationships for this correlational observation?

3. Consider the hypothesis that stress at work causes family conflict at home.
   a. What type of relationship is proposed (e.g., positive linear, negative linear)?
   b. Graph the proposed relationship.
   c. Identify the independent variable and the dependent variable in the statement of the hypothesis.

    d. How might you investigate the hypothesis using the experimental method?

    e. How might you investigate the hypothesis using the correlational method (recognizing the problems of determining cause and effect)?

    f. What factors might you consider in deciding whether to use the experimental or correlational method to study the relationship between work stress and family conflict?

4. Identify the independent and dependent variables in the following descriptions of experiments:

    a. Students watched a cartoon either alone or with others and then rated how funny they found the cartoon to be.

    b. A comprehension test was given to students after they had studied textbook material either in silence or with the television turned on.

    c. Some elementary school teachers were told that a child's parents were college graduates, and other teachers were told that the child's parents had not finished high school; they then rated the child's academic potential.

    d. Workers at a company were assigned to one of two conditions: One group completed a stress management training program, while another group of workers did not participate in the training; the number of sick days taken by these workers was examined for the two subsequent months.

CHAPTER 5

Descriptive Methods

Description is the first goal of scientific inquiry. Because behavior is so varied and occurs in so many settings, social scientists have developed many ways of achieving this goal. In this chapter, we will explore a variety of approaches to describing behavior. These include asking people to describe their behavior (self-report), directly observing behavior, and even examining existing records of behavior, such as census data or hospital records. Before describing some of these in detail, it will be helpful to understand the distinction between quantitative and qualitative methods of describing behavior.

QUANTITATIVE AND QUALITATIVE APPROACHES

Descriptive methods can be broadly classified as primarily quantitative or qualitative. To understand the distinction, imagine that you are interested in describing the ways that the lives of teenagers are affected by working. You might take a quantitative approach by developing a questionnaire for a sample population of teenagers to complete. You could ask about the number of hours they work, the type of work they do, their levels of stress, their school grades, and their use of drugs. After assigning numerical values to the responses, you could subject the data to a quantitative, statistical analysis. A quantitative description of the results would focus on such things as the percentage of teenagers who work and the way this percentage varies by age. Some of the results of such a survey are described later in this chapter.

Suppose, instead, that you took a qualitative approach to describing behavior. You might conduct a series of "focus groups" in which you gather together groups of 8–12 teenagers and engage them in a discussion about their perceptions and experiences with the world of work. You would allow the teenagers to tell you about the topic using their own words and cognitive frameworks. To record the focus group discussions, you might use a video- or audiotape recorder and later have a transcript prepared, or you might have observers take detailed notes during the discussions. A qualitative description of the findings would focus on the themes that emerge from the discussions and the manner in which the teenagers conceptualized the issues. Such description is qualitative because it is expressed in non-numerical terms using language and images.

Other methods, both qualitative and quantitative, could also be used to study teenage employment. Keep in mind the distinction between quantitative and qualitative approaches to describing behavior as you read about other specific descriptive methods discussed in this chapter. Both approaches are valuable and provide us with different ways of understanding.

NATURALISTIC OBSERVATION

Naturalistic observation is sometimes called "field work" or simply "field observation" (see Lofland & Lofland, 1995). In a **naturalistic observation** study, the researcher makes observations in a particular natural setting (the field) over an extended period of time, using a variety of techniques to collect information. The report includes these observations and the researcher's interpretations of the findings. This research approach has roots in anthropology and zoology (the study of human and animal behavior, respectively) and is currently widely used in the social sciences to study many phenomena in all types of social and organizational settings.

Gans' (1962) study of "urban villagers" living in Boston's West End is a good example of a naturalistic observation study. To examine the impact of living in what was considered a "slum" environment, Gans used a variety of techniques to watch people and listen to conversations in stores, bars, and other public settings. He attended meetings and public gatherings and made friends with local residents, who provided him with information. Gans concluded that, contrary to the beliefs of many city planners and urban renewal advocates, the West End was viewed by its inhabitants as a secure place. The effect of urban renewal (constructing new dwellings to replace the "slum") was to disrupt lives and break strong family and ethnic bonds that previously had existed in the neighborhood.

Naturalistic observation is undertaken when a researcher wants to describe and understand how people in a social or cultural setting live, work, and experience the setting. If you want to know about bars as a social setting, for example, you will need to visit one or more bars over an extended period of time, talk to people, observe interactions, and become accepted as a "regular" (cf. Cavan, 1966). If you want to know how people persuade or influence others, you can get a job as a car salesperson or take an encyclopedia sales training course (cf. Cialdini, 1988). If you are interested in how people become part of some social group (e.g., marijuana users, prostitutes, a particular religious cult), you can arrange to meet members of such groups to interview them about their experiences (cf. Becker, 1963, on marijuana users). Those who have studied what it is really like to be a patient in a mental hospital have had themselves admitted as patients (cf. Rosenhan, 1973). Of course, you might not want to do any of these things; however, if these questions interest you, the written reports of these researchers make for fascinating reading.

Description and interpretation of data

Naturalistic observation demands that researchers immerse themselves in the situation. The field researcher observes everything—the setting itself, the patterns of personal relationships, people's reactions to events, and so on. The goal is to provide a complete and accurate picture rather than to test hypotheses formed prior to the study. To achieve this goal, the researcher must keep detailed field notes; writing down or dictating on a regular basis (at least once each day) everything that has happened. Field researchers use a variety of techniques to gather information: observing people and events, interviewing key "informants" to provide inside information, talking to people about their lives, and examining documents produced in the setting, such as newspapers, newsletters, or memos. In addition to taking detailed field notes, researchers conducting naturalistic observation usually use audio- and video-tape recordings.

The researcher's first goal is to describe the setting, the events, and the persons observed. The second, equally important goal is to analyze what was observed. The researcher must interpret what occurred, essentially generating hypotheses that help explain the data and make them understandable. Such an analysis is done by building a coherent structure to describe the observations. The final report, while sensitive to the chronological order of events, is usually organized around the structure developed by the researcher. Specific examples of events that occurred during observation are used to support the researcher's interpretations.

A good naturalistic observation report will support the analysis by using multiple confirmations. For example, similar events may occur several times, similar information may be reported by two or more people, and several different events may occur that all support the same conclusion.

The data in naturalistic observation studies are primarily "qualitative" in nature; that is, they are the descriptions of the observations themselves rather than "quantitative" statistical summaries. Such qualitative descriptions are often "richer" and closer to the phenomenon being studied than are statistical representations. However, there is no reason that quantitative data cannot be gathered in a naturalistic observation study. If circumstances allow it, data can be gathered on income, family size, education levels, and other easily quantifiable variables. Such data can be reported and interpreted along with qualitative data gathered from interviews and direct observations.

Issues in naturalistic observation

Participation and concealment   Two related issues facing the researcher are whether to be a participant or nonparticipant in the social setting and whether to conceal his or her purposes from the other people in the setting. Do you become an active participant in the group, or do you observe from the outside? Do you conceal your purposes or even your presence, or do you openly let people know what you are doing?

A nonparticipant observer is an outsider who does not become an active part of the setting. In contrast, a participant observer assumes an active, insider role. Because participant observation allows the researcher to observe the setting from the inside, he or she may be able to experience events in the same way as natural participants. Friendships and other experiences of the participant observer may yield valuable data. A potential problem with participant observation, however, is that the observer may lose the objectivity necessary to conduct scientific observation. This may be particularly problematic when the researcher already belongs to the group being studied (e.g., a researcher who belongs to Parents Without Partners and who undertakes a study of that group). Remember that naturalistic observation requires accurate description and objective interpretation with no prior hypotheses. If a researcher has some prior reason to either criticize people in the setting or give a glowing report of a particular group, the observations will likely be biased and the conclusions will lack objectivity.

Should the researcher remain concealed or be open about the research purposes? Concealed observation may be preferable because the presence of the observer may influence and alter the behavior of those being observed. Imagine how a nonconcealed observer might alter the behavior of high school students in many situations at a school. Thus, concealed observation is less reactive than nonconcealed observation because people are not aware that their behaviors are being observed and recorded. Still, nonconcealed observation may be preferable from an ethical viewpoint. Consider the invasion of privacy when researchers hid under beds in dormitory rooms to discover what college students talk about (Henle & Hubbell, 1938)! Also, people often quickly become used to the observer and behave naturally in the observer's presence. Two well-known examples of nonconcealed observation are provided by television. In the PBS documentary series "An American Family" and in MTV's "Real World," people living together were filmed over an extended period of time. Many viewers of these series are surprised to see how quickly people forget about the cameras and spontaneously reveal many private aspects of their lives.

The decision as to whether to conceal one's purpose or presence depends on both ethical concerns and the nature of the particular group and setting being studied. Sometimes, a participant observer is nonconcealed to certain members of the group, who give the researcher permission to be part of the group as a concealed observer. Often, a concealed observer decides to say nothing directly about his or her purposes but will completely disclose the goals of the research if asked by anyone. Nonparticipant observers are also not concealed when they gain permission to "hang out" in a setting or use interview techniques to gather information (e.g., in Becker's study of marijuana users, some of the people who were interviewed first introduced Becker to their network of friends who were also marijuana users). In actuality, then, there are degrees of participation and concealment: A nonparticipant observer may not become a member of the group, for example, but may over time become accepted as a friend or simply part of the ongoing activities of the group. In sum, researchers who use naturalistic observation to study behavior must carefully determine what their role in the setting will be.

Defining the scope of the observation   A researcher employing naturalistic observation may want to study *everything* about a setting. However, this may not be possible, simply because a setting and the questions one might ask about it are so complex. Thus, researchers often must limit the scope of their observations to behaviors that are relevant to the central issues of the study. For example, we previously mentioned Cialdini's interest in social influence in settings such as car dealerships. In this case, Cialdini might focus only on sales techniques and ignore such things as management practices and relationships among salespersons.

Limits of naturalistic observation   Naturalistic observation obviously cannot be used to study all issues or phenomena. The approach is most useful when investigating complex social settings to both understand the settings and develop theories based on the observations. It is less useful for studying well-defined hypotheses under precisely specified conditions.

Field research is also very difficult to do (cf. Green & Wallaf, 1981). Unlike a typical laboratory experiment, field research data collection cannot always be scheduled at a convenient time and place. In fact, field research can be extremely time-consuming, often placing the researcher in an unfamiliar setting for extended periods. Also, in experimental research, the procedures are well defined and the same for each participant, and the data analysis is planned in advance. In naturalistic observation research, however, there is an ever-changing pattern of events, some important and some unimportant; the researcher must record them all and remain flexible in order to adjust to them as the research progresses. Finally, the process of analysis that follows the completion of the research is not simple. The researcher must repeatedly sort through the data, develop hypotheses to explain them, and make sure all the data are consistent with the hypotheses.

If some of the observations are not consistent, the researcher does more analysis. Judd, Smith, and Kidder (1991) emphasize the importance of **negative case analysis.** A negative case is an observation that does not fit the explanatory structure devised by the researcher. When a negative case is found, the researcher revises the hypothesis and reexamines all the data to make sure that they are consistent with the new hypothesis. The researcher may even collect additional data in order to examine more closely the circumstances that led to the negative case. Although naturalistic observation research is a difficult and challenging scientific procedure, it can yield invaluable knowledge when done well.

SYSTEMATIC OBSERVATION

Systematic observation refers to the careful observation of one or more specific behaviors in a particular setting. This research approach is much less global than naturalistic observation research. The researcher is interested in only a few very specific behaviors, the observations are quantifiable, and the researcher frequently has developed prior hypotheses about the behaviors.

For example, Bakeman and Brownlee (1980; also see Bakeman & Gottman, 1986) were interested in the social behavior of young children. Three-year-olds were videotaped in a room in a "free play" situation. Each child was taped for 100 minutes; observers viewed the videotapes and coded each child's behavior every 15 seconds, using the following coding system:

Unoccupied: Child is not doing anything in particular or is simply watching other children.

Solitary play: Child plays alone with toys but is not interested in or affected by the activities of other children.

Together: Child is with other children but is not occupied with any particular activity.

Parallel play: Child plays beside other children with similar toys but does not play with the others.

Group play: Child plays with other children, including sharing toys or participating in organized play activities as part of a group of children.

Bakeman and Brownlee were particularly interested in the sequence or order in which the different behaviors were engaged in by the children. They found, for example, that the children rarely went from being unoccupied to engaging in parallel play. However, they frequently went from parallel to group play, indicating that parallel play is a transition state in which children decide whether to go ahead and interact in a group situation.

Coding systems

Numerous behaviors can be studied using systematic observation. The researcher must decide which behaviors are of interest, choose a setting in which these behaviors can be observed, and most importantly, develop a **coding system,** such as the one described above, to measure the behaviors. Sometimes, the researcher develops the coding system to fit the needs of the particular study. Coding systems should be as simple as possible, allowing observers to easily categorize behaviors. This is especially important when observers are coding "live" behaviors rather than viewing videotapes that can be reviewed or even coded on a frame-by-frame basis. An example of a simple coding system comes from a study by Barton, Baltes, and Orzech (1980), in which nursing home residents and staff were observed. Only five categories were used: (1) resident independent behavior (e.g., doing something by oneself, such as grooming), (2) resident dependent behavior (asking for help), (3) staff independence-supporting behavior (praise or encouragement for independence), (4) staff dependency-supportive behavior (giving assistance or encouraging taking assistance), and (5) other, unrelated behaviors of both residents and staff. Their results illustrate one of the problems of care facilities: Staff perceive themselves as "care providers" and so most frequently engage in dependency-supportive behaviors. Does this lead to greater dependency by the residents and perhaps a loss of feelings of control? If so, the consequences may be serious: Recall the Rodin and Langer (1977) experiment discussed in Chapter 4, in which feelings of control led to greater happiness and general well-being among nursing home residents.

Sometimes, researchers can use coding systems that have been developed by others. For example, the Family Interaction Coding System (FICS; see Patterson & Moore, 1979) consists of 29 categories of interaction; these are grouped as aversive (hostility), prosocial (helping), and general activities. Most of the research using the FICS has centered on how children's aversive behaviors are learned and maintained in a family. Another coding system is SYMLOG, the System for the Multiple Level Observation of Groups (Bales & Cohen, 1979). SYMLOG provides a way of coding interactions of individuals in groups on three major dimensions: unfriendly-friendly, emotionally expressive–instrumentally controlled, and submissive-dominant. A major advantage of using a previously developed coding system is that a body of research already exists in which the system has proven useful, and training materials are usually available.

Methodological issues

Equipment   We should briefly mention several methodological issues in systematic observation. The first concerns equipment. You can directly observe behavior and code it at the same time—for example, observing and recording the behavior of children in a classroom or couples interacting on campus. However, it is becoming more common to use videotape equipment to make such observations. Video recorders have the advantage of providing a permanent record of the behavior observed that can later be coded. Your observations can be coded on a clipboard, and a stopwatch is sometimes useful for recording the duration of events. Alternatively, you can use a computer recording device that is not much larger than a calculator. Keys on the device are pressed to code the behaviors observed, as well as to keep track of their duration. These recorders add to the expense of the research, and initial training of observers may take longer. However, research that requires observing several types of behavior and recording duration of behavior is facilitated by using these computer devices. Also, data analysis may be easier because the data can be automatically transferred from the device to the computer on which the analyses will be performed.

Reactivity   A second issue is reactivity—the possibility that the presence of the observer will affect people's behaviors (see Chapter 4). As noted previously, reactivity can be reduced by concealed observation. The use of one-way mirrors, "candid camera" techniques, and hidden microphones all can conceal the presence of an observer. Alternatively, reactivity can be reduced by allowing enough time for people to become used to the presence of the observer and any recording equipment.

Reliability   Recall from Chapter 4 that reliability refers to the degree to which a measure is stable or consistent: A reliable measure is precise. The method used to determine reliability when doing systematic observation is called *inter-rater* or *inter-observer reliability*. This is an index of how closely two observers agree when coding the same observations. Usually, such reliability is expressed as a percentage of the time that two or more observers coded the same behavior in the same way. Very high levels of agreement are reported in virtually all published research using systematic observation (generally 80% agreement or higher). For some large-scale research programs in which many observers will be employed over a period of years, observers are first trained using videotapes, and their observations during training are checked for agreement with previous observers (cf. Bakeman & Gottman, 1986).

Sampling Finally, sampling of behaviors should be mentioned. For many research questions, samples of behavior taken over a long period will provide more accurate and useful data than single short observations. Consider a study on television viewing in homes (Anderson, Lorch, Field, Collins, & Nathan, 1986). The researchers wanted to know how members of families actually watch TV. They could have studied short periods of TV watching, perhaps during a single evening; however, such data could be distorted by short-term trends—time of day, a particular show, or the variations in family activities that influence TV viewing. A better method of addressing the question would be to observe TV viewing over a longer period. This is exactly what the researchers did. Video recorders and cameras were installed in the homes of 99 families; the equipment was set to record in a time-lapse mode whenever the TV was turned on. Using this method, almost 5,000 hours of TV viewing were recorded. Because coding this much data would be so time-consuming, to analyze the data, Anderson et al. sampled a segment of TV viewing every 55 minutes. Among other things, they found that no one is watching the TV 15% of the time and that TV viewing increases up to age 10 and then begins to decrease.

CASE STUDIES

A **case study** provides a description of an individual. This individual is usually a person, but it may also be a setting such as a business, school, or neighborhood. Sometimes, a naturalistic observation study is called a case study, and in fact the naturalistic observation and case study approaches frequently overlap. We have included case studies as a separate category in this chapter because case studies do not necessarily involve naturalistic observation. Instead, the case study may be a description of a patient by a clinical psychologist or a historical account of an event such as a model school that failed. A *psychobiography* is a type of case study in which a researcher applies psychological theory to explain the life of an individual—usually an important historical figure (cf. Elms, 1994; Runyan, 1981). Thus, case studies may use such techniques as library research and telephone interviews with persons familiar with the case but no direct observation (cf. Yin, 1994).

Depending on the purpose of the investigation, the case study may present the individual's history, symptoms, characteristic behaviors, reactions to situations, or responses to treatment. Typically, a case study is done when an individual possesses a particularly rare, unusual, or noteworthy condition.

85

One famous case study in clinical psychology involved "Sybil," a woman with a rare multiple personality disorder (Schreiber, 1973). Over the course of therapy, it was discovered that Sybil had experienced severe beatings and other traumas during childhood. One explanation for the disorder, then, was that Sybil unconsciously created other personalities who would suffer the pain instead of her. Another case study, reported by Luria (1968), involved a man with an amazing ability to recall information. The man, called "S.," could remember long lists and passages with ease, apparently using mental imagery for his memory abilities. Luria also described some of the drawbacks of S.'s ability. For example, he frequently had difficulty concentrating because mental images would spontaneously appear and interfere with his thinking. A final case study example concerns language development; it was provided by "Genie," a child who was kept isolated in her room, tied to a chair, and never spoken to until she was discovered at the age of 14 (Curtiss, 1977). Genie, of course, lacked any language skills. Her case provided psychologists and linguists with the opportunity to attempt to teach her language skills and discover which skills could be learned. Apparently, Genie was able to acquire some rudimentary language skills, such as forming childlike sentences, but she never developed full language abilities.

Case studies are valuable in informing us of conditions that are rare or unusual and thus not easily studied in any other way. Insights gained through the case study may also lead to the development of hypotheses that can be tested using other methods. However, like field research, case studies are very difficult to do, and they present unique challenges to the researcher in terms of providing explanations for the events that are described. For instance, Runyan (1981), in a discussion of psychobiography research, presents 13 potential explanations for why Vincent van Gogh cut off his ear. Runyan's analysis emphasized the need to critically examine each explanation in terms of its plausibility and the available evidence.

ARCHIVAL RESEARCH

Archival research involves using previously compiled information to answer research questions. The researcher doesn't actually collect the original data. Instead, he or she analyzes existing data such as statistics that are part of the public record (e.g., number of divorce petitions filed), reports of anthropologists, the content of letters to the editor, or information contained in computer databases. Judd, Smith, and Kidder (1991) distinguish between three types of archival research data: statistical records, survey archives, and written records.

Statistical records

Statistical records are collected by many public and private organizations. The U.S. Census Bureau maintains the most extensive set of statistical records available to researchers for analysis. There are also numerous less obvious ones such as public health statistics and test score records kept by testing organizations such as the Educational Testing Service.

Researchers Lillian Belmont and Francis Morolla used such statistical records when they examined the intelligence test scores of all 19-year-old men in the Netherlands. They discovered a very interesting pattern in the data: Intelligence was systematically related to both birth order and family size. Specifically, intelligence was higher in families with fewer children and also higher for early-born than later-born children. Later, Zajonc (1976) developed a mathematical model to explain the data, a model based on the amount of intellectual stimulation received by children of differing family size and birth order. Zajonc was also able to replicate the original findings by studying a database consisting of test scores obtained in the United States.

Various public records can also be used as sources of archival data. For example, Gwaltney-Gibbs (1986) used marriage license applications in one Oregon county in 1970 and 1980 to study changing patterns of premarital cohabitation. She found that only 13% of the couples used the same address on the application in 1970 but that 53% gave the same address in 1980. She was also able to relate cohabitation to other variables such as age and race. The findings were interpreted as support for the notion that premarital cohabitation has become a new step in patterns of courtship leading to marriage. Another example of the use of public records is research by Anderson and Anderson (1984) that demonstrated a relationship between temperature and violent crime statistics in two U.S. cities. Data on both variables are readily available from agencies that keep these statistics.

Survey archives

Survey archives consist of data from surveys that are stored on computers and available to researchers who wish to analyze them. Major polling organizations make many of their surveys available. Also, many universities are part of the Interuniversity Consortium for Political and Social Research (ICPSR), which makes survey archive data available. One very useful data set is the General Social Survey, a series of surveys funded by the National Science Foundation and intended as a resource for social scientists (Russell & Megaard, 1988). Each survey includes over 200 questions covering a range of topics such as attitudes, life satisfaction, health, religion, education, age, gender, and race. This and other survey archives may be available through the computer system on your campus. Survey archives are extremely important because most researchers do not have the financial resources to conduct surveys of representative national samples; the archives allow them to access such samples to test their ideas.

Written records

Written records consist of a variety of documents such as diaries and letters that have been preserved by historical societies; ethnographies of other cultures written by anthropologists; public documents such as speeches by politicians; and mass communications, including books, magazine articles, movies, and newspapers.

As an example of archival research using written records, Schoeneman and Rubanowitz (1985) studied Dear Abby and Ann Landers letters published in newspapers. They were interested in the causes people gave for problems they wrote about in their letters. Letters were coded according to whether the writers were discussing themselves or other people and whether the causes discussed in the letters were internal (caused by the person's own actions or personality) or external (caused by some situation external to the person). When people discussed themselves, the causes of the problems were primarily external, but when other people were described, more of the problems were seen as internally caused (also see Fischer, Schoeneman, & Rubanowitz, 1987).

Archival data may also be used in cross-cultural research that examines aspects of social structure that differ from society to society. A variable such as the presence versus absence of monogamous marital relationships cannot be studied in a single society. In North America, for example, monogamy is the norm and bigamy is illegal. By looking at a number of cultures, some monogamous and some not, we can increase our understanding of the reasons that one system or the other comes to be preferred. This method was adopted in a study by Rosenblatt and Cozby (1972) on the role of freedom of choice in mate selection. Some societies have considerable restrictions on whom one can marry; other societies give great freedom of choice to young people in deciding on a spouse. In the study, anthropologists' descriptions (called *ethnographies*) of a number of societies were used to rate the societies as either low or high in terms of freedom of choice of spouse. The ethnographies also provided information on a number of other variables. The results indicated that when there is freedom of choice of spouse, romantic love and sexual attraction are important bases for mate selection, but that greater antagonism also is present in the interactions among young males and females. The Rosenblatt and Cozby study used the Human Relations Area Files (HRAF), a resource available in many university libraries, to obtain information from the ethnographies. The HRAF consists of anthropologists' descriptions of many cultures, which have been organized according to categories such as courtship and marriage customs, child-rearing practices, and so on. Thus, it is relatively easy to find specific information from many societies by using the HRAF.

Content analysis of documents

Content analysis is the systematic analysis of existing documents such as the ones described in this section (see Holsti, 1969; Viney, 1983). Like systematic observation, content analysis requires researchers to devise coding systems that raters can use to quantify the information in the documents. Sometimes, the coding is quite simple and straightforward; for example, it is easy to code whether the addresses of the bride and groom on marriage license applications are the same or different. More often, the researcher must define categories in order to code the information. In the Rosenblatt and Cozby cross-cultural study, for example, raters had to read the ethnographic information and determine whether each culture was low or high on freedom of choice of spouse. Raters were trained to use the coding system, and inter-rater reliability coefficients were computed. Similar procedures would be used in studies examining archival documents such as speeches, magazine articles, television shows, and letters.

The use of archival data allows researchers to study interesting questions, some of which could not be studied in any other way. Archival data are a valuable supplement to more traditional data collection methods. There are at least two major problems with the use of archival data, however. First, the desired records may be difficult to obtain: They may be placed in long-forgotten storage places, or they may have been destroyed. Second, we can never be completely sure of the accuracy of information collected by someone else.

DESCRIBING PERSONALITY AND INDIVIDUAL DIFFERENCES

How do we study personality? A topic this complex requires both quantitative and qualitative approaches. A major area of psychology has been the development of quantitative measures of individual differences in psychological attributes such as intelligence, self-esteem, extraversion, and depression. For example, Costa and McCrae (1985) developed the NEO Personality Inventory (NEO-PI) to measure five major dimensions of personality: neuroticism, extraversion, openness to experience, agreeableness, and conscientiousness. Other tests focus on specific characteristics of a person, such as "sensation-seeking," "social anxiety," and "loving style." Still other measures focus on diagnosing psychological disorders, helping people decide on possible careers, and screening applicants for jobs.

One branch of personality research studies the way that personality characteristics are related to a person's behavior and interactions with others. For example, you might want to study how individuals who are categorized as introverted or extraverted recall material read under distracting versus quiet conditions. We will explore research designs that address such issues in Chapter 8.

It is usually wise to use existing personality measures rather than develop your own. Existing measures have reliability and validity data, and you can compare your findings with prior research that uses the measure. Sources of information about psychological tests that have been developed include the *Mental Measurements Yearbook* (Conoley & Kramer, 1989) and *Test Critiques* (Keyser & Sweetland, 1991). These reference books are published periodically and contain descriptions and evaluations of many psychological tests. *Psychological Abstracts* is, of course, another source of information about personality measures.

Although most attempts to understand personality in recent years have been quantitative, qualitative approaches to understanding personality are being increasingly used as an alternative to quantitative research. For example, researchers are focusing on narrative accounts of life histories to gain insights into the ways that personalities develop and are influenced by both common and unique, idiosyncratic life events (Baumeister & Newman, 1994; Josselson & Lieblich, 1993). These accounts may come from various sources such as interviews and autobiographical writings. They may be relatively unfocused accounts, or they may target particular parts of one's life such as personal relationships. Most importantly, such qualitative analyses may yield data that would be difficult to obtain with traditional personality measures, challenge traditional theories of personality, and lead to a more complete understanding of human behavior.

SURVEY RESEARCH

Surveys use self-report measurement techniques to question people about themselves—their attitudes, behaviors, and demographics (age, income, race, marital status, and so on). Surveys may employ careful sampling techniques to obtain an accurate description of an entire population; for example, the Gallup Poll conducts surveys to find out what people are thinking about issues such as abortion or nuclear power or to obtain data on preferences for political candidates. When scientific sampling techniques are used, the survey results can be interpreted as an accurate representation of the entire population. Such accuracy can be achieved by sampling an extremely small percentage of a very large population, such as an entire state or even the nation. Surveys on a much smaller scale are going on all the time. Students may be asked by their school to take part in a survey on student services. Employees of a large corporation might be asked for their opinions of current operations. Individuals might receive phone calls from marketing research firms asking about consumer preferences. Often, such surveys are used to help make important policy or marketing decisions.

Most people think of surveys as a way of taking a "snapshot" of current attitudes and behaviors. However, the survey method is also an important way for researchers to study relationships among variables and ways that attitudes and behaviors change over time. For example, Steinberg and Dornbusch (1991) examined the relationship between the number of hours that high school students work and variables such as grade point average, drug and alcohol use, and psychosomatic distress. The sample consisted of 3,989 students in grades 10–12 at nine high schools in California and Wisconsin. The researchers found that "long work hours during the school year are associated with lower investment and performance in school, greater psychological and somatic distress, drug and alcohol use, delinquency, and autonomy from parents" (Steinberg & Dornbusch, 1991, p. 304). Figure 5-1 shows a typical finding: There were frequently some positive aspects of working fewer

90

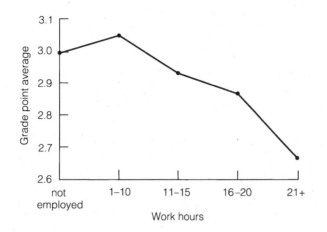

Figure 5-1
Relationship between hours of work and grade point average
Source: Steinberg, L., & Dornbusch, S. M. (1991). Negative correlates of part-time employment during adolescence: Replication and elaboration. *Developmental Psychology,* 27, 303–313. Copyright © 1991 by the American Psychological Association. Reprinted by permission.

than 10 hours per week (as opposed to not being employed); however, increasingly negative effects are associated with longer work hours.

We turn now to two major considerations in survey research: sampling techniques and constructing a survey instrument.

SAMPLING TECHNIQUES

Most research projects involve **sampling** participants from a population of interest. The **population** is composed of all of the individuals of interest to the researcher. One population of interest to a pollster, for instance, might be all the eligible voters in the United States. This implies that the pollster's population of interest does not include people under the age of 18, people serving prison terms, visitors from other countries, or anyone else not eligible to vote. With enough time and money, a pollster could conceivably contact everyone in the population who is eligible to vote. Fortunately, the pollster can avoid this massive undertaking by selecting a sample from the population of interest. With proper sampling, the pollster can use information obtained from the sample to determine key characteristics of the population as a whole. Sampling is therefore very important in the generalization of research results.

There are two basic types of sampling techniques: nonprobability sampling and probability sampling. In **nonprobability sampling,** we don't know the probability of any particular member of the population being chosen. In **probability sampling,** each member of the population has a specifiable probability of being chosen. Probability sampling is very important when you want to make precise statements about a population on the basis of the results of your survey. That is, probability sampling is necessary to accurately generalize results from a sample to the population from which that sample was drawn.

Nonprobability sampling

Nonprobability sampling techniques are quite arbitrary. A population may be defined, but little effort is expended to ensure that the sample accurately represents the population. However, among other things, nonprobability samples are cheap and convenient. Two types of nonprobability sampling are haphazard sampling and quota sampling.

Haphazard sampling   One form of nonprobability sampling is **haphazard sampling,** or "accidental" sampling. Haphazard sampling could be called a "take-them-where-you-find-them" method of obtaining participants (or *respondents*, the term that is typically used to describe individuals in survey research). For example, a television reporter might poll people who happen to walk past a particular street corner at a particular time of day and are willing to say a few words to the camera. The population of interest might be "people who live in this city," but the results of this poll could not really be generalized to this population. It would not be possible to specify the probability of a city resident being chosen as a participant in this poll. The probability would be high for some people (those who live or work near the street corner) and low for others. The haphazard sampling technique would exclude everyone who, for any reason, wasn't present at that location at that particular time. Thus, any generalization of the results to the entire city would probably be inaccurate.

Quota sampling   Another form of nonprobability sampling is **quota sampling.** A researcher who uses this technique chooses a sample that reflects the numerical composition of various subgroups in the population. For instance, suppose your city has the following composition: 60% white, 20% African American, 10% Latino, 8% Asian American, and 2% Native American. A quota sampling technique that uses nationality and ethnic subgroups would produce a sample that numerically reflects these percentages. Thus, a sample of 100 people from your city would have 60 whites, 20 African Americans, 10 Latinos, 8 Asian Americans, and 2 Native Americans. Similarly, subgroups might be based on age, gender, socioeconomic class, college majors, and so on. Although quota sampling is a bit more elegant than haphazard sampling, the problem remains that no restrictions are placed on how individuals in the various subgroups are chosen. The sample does reflect the numerical composition of the whole population of interest, but respondents within each subgroup are selected in a haphazard manner. Thus, quota sampling has the same problems of generalization as haphazard sampling.

Using haphazard sampling in basic research   Much of the research in psychology uses nonprobability sampling techniques to obtain participants for either surveys or experiments. The advantage of these techniques is that the investigator can obtain research participants without spending a great deal of money or time on selecting a specific sample group. It is, for example, common practice to select respondents from students in introductory psychology classes. Often, these students are required to participate in studies being conducted by faculty and other students; the introductory psychology students can then choose which experiments they wish to participate in. Even in studies that do not use college students, the sample is often selected based on convenience rather than the ability to generalize to a random sample.

If generalization is a potential problem, why do researchers use these techniques? The most important reason is that the research is being conducted to study relationships between variables rather than to accurately describe a population. Nonprobability samples are inexpensive and convenient, and so researchers prefer to spend their limited resources on conducting their experiments rather than on obtaining representative samples using probability sampling techniques. Also, it may be difficult to find a sample of the general population willing to come into the lab for an experiment. If a relationship between the variables being studied is found, one can ask whether the same relationship between variables would be observed with some other population. Usually, there isn't a compelling reason to believe or suspect that the relationship would not be found among other groups. When there is a reason to hypothesize that other groups (e.g., children, the elderly, or various ethnic groups) would behave differently, researchers typically conduct research to test their hypotheses. These issues are discussed further in Chapter 12.

Thus, generalization to a specific population is usually not the first priority in scientific studies designed to test ideas about relationships between variables. However, when the research goal is to accurately describe some particular aspect of a specific population, probability sampling techniques must be used. For example, research to determine how many people will vote for a particular political candidate or how many people use the parks in a city must use a truly representative sample. Let's examine three general types of probability sampling: simple random sampling, stratified random sampling, and cluster sampling.

Probability sampling

Simple random sampling   With **simple random sampling,** every member of the population has an equal probability of being selected for the sample. If the population has 1,000 members, each has one chance out of a thousand of being selected. Suppose you want to sample students who attend your school. A list of all students would be needed; from that list, students would be chosen at random to form the sample. Note that this procedure doesn't introduce any biases about who gets chosen. In contrast, a haphazard procedure in which you sampled from students walking by a certain location at 9 A.M. would involve all sorts of biases. For example, that procedure eliminates students who don't frequent this location, and it may also eliminate afternoon and evening students.

When conducting telephone interviews, researchers commonly have a computer randomly generate a list of telephone numbers with the dialing prefixes used in the city or area being studied. This will produce a random sample of the population because most people today have telephones. Some companies will even provide researchers with a list of telephone numbers for a survey in which the phone numbers of businesses and numbers that phone companies do not use have been removed.

Stratified random sampling   A somewhat more complicated procedure is **stratified random sampling.** This is analogous to quota sampling in that the population is divided into subgroups (or strata). Random sampling techniques are then used to select sample members from each stratum. Any number of dimensions could be used to divide the population, but the dimension (or dimensions) chosen should be relevant to the problem under study. For instance, a survey of sexual attitudes might stratify on the basis of age, gender, and amount of education, because these factors are related to sexual attitudes. Stratification on the basis of height or hair color would be ridiculous. Stratified random sampling has the advantage of a built-in assurance that the sample will accurately reflect the numerical composition of the various subgroups. This kind of accuracy is particularly important when some subgroups comprise very small percentages of the population. For instance, if African Americans comprise 5% of a city of 100,000 population, a simple random sample of 100 people might not include any African Americans. But a stratified random sample would include five African Americans chosen randomly from the population. In practice, when it is important to represent a small group within a population, researchers will "oversample" that group to ensure that a representative sample of the group is surveyed. Thus, if you need to compare attitudes of African Americans and whites on your campus, you might need to sample a large percentage of the African American students and only a small percentage of the white students in order to obtain a reasonable number of respondents from each group.

Cluster sampling   It might have occurred to you that obtaining a list of all members of a very large or unusual population (e.g., people who work in county health care agencies throughout the nation) might be difficult. In such situations, a technique called **cluster sampling** can be used. Rather than randomly sampling from a list of individuals, the researcher can identify "clusters" of individuals and then sample from these clusters. After the clusters have been sampled, all individuals in the cluster will be included in the sample. Most often, use of cluster analysis requires a series of samplings from larger to smaller clusters—a "multistage" approach. For example, a researcher interested in studying county health care agencies might first randomly determine a number of states to sample and then randomly sample counties from each state chosen. The researcher would then go to the health care agencies in each of these counties and study the people who work in them. The main advantage here is that the researcher does not have to sample from lists of individuals.

Critically evaluating survey samples

Response rate   The response rate in a survey is simply the percentage of people in the sample who actually completed the survey. Thus, if you mail 1,000 questionnaires to a random sample of adults in your community and 500 are completed and returned to you, the response rate is 50%. Response rate is important because it indicates how much bias there might be in the final sample of respondents. Nonrespondents may differ from respondents in any number of ways, including age, income, marital status, and education. The lower the response rate, the greater the likelihood that such biases may distort the findings and in turn limit the ability to generalize the findings to the population of interest.

In general, mail surveys have lower response rates than telephone surveys. With both methods, however, steps can be taken to maximize response rates. With mail surveys, an explanatory postcard or letter can be sent a week or so prior to mailing the survey. Follow-up reminders and even second mailings of the questionnaires are often effective in increasing response rates. With telephone surveys, respondents who aren't home can be called again, and people who can't be interviewed today can be scheduled for a call at a more convenient time.

Sampling frame   An important concept in survey research is the sampling frame: the actual set of people who might be included in the sample after the population is defined. If you define your population as "residents in my city," the actual sampling frame may be residents who can be contacted by telephone. This sampling frame excludes persons who do not have telephones or whose schedule prevents them from being at home when you are making calls. Also, if you are using the telephone directory to obtain numbers, you will exclude persons who have unlisted numbers. When evaluating the results of the survey, you need to consider how well the sampling frame matches the population of interest. In the study of high school students cited previously (Steinberg & Dornbusch, 1991), the population of interest was teenagers in the United States; however, the sample frame included only high school students in California and Wisconsin. Although this sample obviously excludes many potential respondents in other areas of the United States, it is superior to those used in previous studies of teenage employment. Again, it should be emphasized that research conducted to study relationships among variables is less concerned about generalization. In the Steinberg and Dornbusch study, for example, the researchers were not interested in accurately describing the number of hours that teenagers in the United States work; they were more interested in whether the number of hours that teenagers work is related to variables such as grade point average and alcohol use.

When research is intended to tell us precisely what a population is like (e.g., state or national opinion polls), careful sampling procedures must be used. This requires defining the population, sampling individuals from that population in some random fashion, and maximizing the response rate so no biases will be introduced into the sample. Thus, in order to learn what elderly people think about the social services available to them, a careful sample of the elderly population is needed. Obtaining the sample by going only to nursing homes would bias the results because these individuals are not representative of all elderly people in the population.

When evaluating survey data, it is important to examine how the responses were obtained and what population was investigated. Major polling organizations typically take great care to obtain representative samples of adults in our society. However, many other surveys, such as surveys on marital satisfaction or sexual practices that are published in a magazine, have limited generalizability because the results are based on people who read the particular magazine and are sufficiently motivated to complete and mail in the questionnaire. Likewise, when Dear Abby asks readers to write in to tell her whether they have ever "cheated" on their spouse, the results may be interesting but would not give a very accurate estimate of the true extent of extramarital activity in our society.

CONSTRUCTING SURVEYS

Questionnaires versus interviews

Survey research may use either questionnaires or interviews to ask people questions about themselves. With questionnaires, the questions are presented in written format and the respondents write their answers. Interviews involve a one-on-one verbal interaction between an interviewer and respondent, either face to face or over the phone. The questionnaire approach generally costs less than interviews, because questionnaires can be administered in groups or mailed to people. Further, they allow anonymity of the respondents. However, questionnaires require that the respondents be able to read and understand the questions. In addition, many people find it boring to sit by themselves reading questions and then writing down answers; thus, there may be a problem of motivation.

With interviews, there is a greater chance that the interviewer and respondent can establish a rapport, that the respondent will find it interesting to talk to the interviewer, and that all questions are understood. Telephone interviews are less expensive than face-to-face interviews, and new computerized telephone survey techniques lower the cost of telephone surveys by reducing labor and data analysis costs. With a computer-assisted telephone interview (CATI) system, the interviewer's questions are prompted on the computer screen, and the data are entered directly into the computer for analysis.

Constructing questions

A great deal of thought must be given to writing questions for a survey. This section describes some of the most important factors that a researcher must consider.

Defining the research questions When constructing questions for a survey, the first thing the researcher must do is explicitly determine the research questions: What is it that he or she wishes to know? The survey questions must be tied to the research questions. Too often, surveys get out of hand when researchers begin to ask any question that comes to mind about a topic without considering exactly what useful information will be gained by doing so.

Using closed- versus open-ended questions Questions may be either closed- or open-ended. With closed-ended questions, a limited number of response alternatives are given; with open-ended questions, respondents are free to answer in any way they like. Thus, you could ask a person, "Which of the following problems is the greatest one facing this city today?" (a closed-ended question) or simply, "What is the greatest problem facing this city today?" (an open-ended question). The closed-ended question would give the respondent a list to choose from (although an "other" category can be added to allow other possibilities). The open-ended question would permit the respondent to generate the answer.

Using closed-ended questions is a more structured approach. They are easier to code, and the response alternatives are the same for everyone. Open-ended questions require time to categorize and code the responses and are therefore more costly. Sometimes, a respondent's response cannot be categorized at all because the response doesn't make sense or the person couldn't think of an answer. Still, an open-ended question can yield valuable insights into what people are thinking. Open-ended questions are most useful when the researcher needs to know what people are thinking and how they view their world; closed-ended questions are more likely to be used when the dimensions of the variables are well defined. With closed-ended questions, there are a fixed number of response alternatives; these must make sense to people in the context of the question asked. Also, there must be a sufficient number of alternatives to allow people to express themselves—for example, 5- or 7-point scales ranging from "agree to disagree" or "positive to negative" may be preferable to simple "yes versus no" or "agree versus disagree" alternatives.

Wording questions Once the questions have been written, it is especially important to edit them and test them out on others. You should look for "double-barreled" questions that ask two things at once; a question such as

"Senior citizens should be given more money for recreation centers and food assistance programs" is difficult to answer because it taps two potentially very different attitudes. Researchers must also avoid questions that "lead" people to answer in a certain way or that might be misinterpreted. For example, the questions "Do you favor eliminating the wasteful excesses in the public school budget?" and "Do you favor reducing the public school budget?" will likely elicit different answers. It is a good idea to give the questions to a small group of people and have them "think aloud" while answering them. Ask these individuals to tell you how they interpret each question and how they respond to the response alternatives. This procedure can provide valuable insights that you can use when editing the questions (Chapter 7 discusses the importance of pilot studies).

Ordering questions   It is always a good idea to carefully consider the sequence in which you will ask your questions. In general, it is best to ask the most interesting and important questions first in order to capture the attention of your respondents. Roberson and Sundstrom (1990) obtained the highest return rates in an employee attitude survey when important questions were presented first and demographic questions (age, gender, and so on) were asked last.

Interviewer bias and response sets

Two major sources of bias can arise when questionnaires and interviews are used: interviewer bias and response sets. **Interviewer bias** refers to all of the biases that can arise from the fact that the interviewer is a unique human being interacting with another human. Thus, one potential problem is that the interviewer could subtly bias the respondent's answers by inadvertently showing approval or disapproval of certain answers. Or, if there are several interviewers, each could possess different characteristics (e.g., level of physical attractiveness, age, or race) that might influence the way respondents answer. Another problem is that interviewers may have expectations that could lead them to "see what they are looking for" in the respondents' answers. Such expectations could bias their interpretations of responses or lead them to probe further for an answer from certain respondents but not others—for example, when questioning whites but not people from other groups or when testing boys but not girls. Careful screening and training of interviewers helps to limit such biases.

A **response set** is a tendency to respond to all questions from a particular perspective rather than to provide answers that are directly related to the questions. Thus, response sets can affect the usefulness of data obtained from self-reports.

The most common response set is called social desirability, or "faking good." The social desirability response set leads the individual to answer in the most socially acceptable way—the way that "most people" are perceived to respond or the way that would reflect most favorably on the person. Social desirability can be a problem in many research areas, but it is probably most acute when the question concerns a sensitive topic such as violent or aggressive behavior, substance abuse, or sexual practices. It should not be assumed, however, that people consistently misrepresent themselves. Jourard (1969) suggested that people are most likely to lie when they don't trust the researcher. If the researcher openly and honestly communicates the purposes and uses of the research, promises to provide feedback about the results, and assures anonymity, then the participants can reasonably be expected to give honest responses.

Another response set is the tendency of some participants to consistently agree or disagree with questions ("yea-saying" or "nay-saying"). The solution to this is relatively straightforward: Ask several questions, and pose response alternatives in both positive and negative directions. For example, in a study of family communication patterns, the researcher might ask people how much they agree with the following statements: "The members of my family spend a lot of time together" and "My family members don't usually eat dinner together." Although someone might legitimately agree with both items, consistently agreeing or disagreeing with a set of related questions posed in both directions indicates that the individual is using a response set.

Sources of self-report measures

If you engage in survey research, you may need to design your own questionnaires or interviews. Good references for advice on constructing such measures are Judd, Smith, and Kidder (1991) and Converse and Presser (1986). You may often find it beneficial to use questions developed by others, particularly if these have proven useful in other studies and have been shown to have high reliability. A variety of measures of social, political, and occupational attitudes developed by others have been compiled by Robinson and his colleagues (Robinson, Athanasiou, & Head, 1969; Robinson, Rusk, & Head, 1968; Robinson, Shaver, & Wrightsman, 1991).

STUDYING VARIABLES ACROSS TIME AND AGE

Survey designs to study changes over time

Surveys most frequently study people at one point in time. On many occasions, however, researchers wish to make comparisons over time. For example, in the county in which I live, a local newspaper hires a firm to conduct an annual random survey of residents. Because the questions are the same each year, it is possible to track changes over time in such variables as satisfaction with the area, attitudes toward the school system, and perceived major problems facing the county. Similarly, a large number of new freshman students are surveyed each year at colleges throughout the United States to study changes in the composition, attitudes, and aspirations of this group (Astin, 1987). Often, researchers will test hypotheses concerning how behavior may change over time. For example, Sebald (1986) compared surveys of teenagers in 1963, 1976, and 1982. The survey questions focused on the persons teenagers seek advice from on a variety of issues. The primary finding was that seeking advice from peers rather than parents increased from 1963 to 1976 but that this peer orientation decreased from 1976 to 1982.

Another way to study changes over time is to conduct a **panel study** in which the same people are surveyed at two or more points in time. In a "two-wave" panel study, people are surveyed at two points in time; in a "three-wave" panel study, there are three surveys; and so on. Panel studies are particularly useful when the research question addresses the relationship between one variable at "time one" and another variable at some later "time two." For example, Hill, Rubin, and Peplau (1976) surveyed dating couples to study variables such as attitude similarity. The same people were surveyed later to determine whether they were still in the dating relationship and, if so, how satisfied they were. The results showed that attitude similarity, measured at time one, is a predictor of how long the dating relationship will last.

Studying changes across ages in developmental research

One research question of interest to developmental psychologists is how individuals change as a function of age. A researcher might test a theory concerning changes in ability to reason as children grow older, the age at which self-awareness develops in young children, or the global values people have as they move from adolescence through old age. In all cases, the major variable is age. Studying changes across age is conceptually similar to studying changes over time; some unique issues arise, however, in developmental research. Two general methods are used to study individuals of different ages: the longitudinal method and the cross-sectional method.

Longitudinal method In the **longitudinal method,** the same group of people is observed repeatedly as they grow older. Perhaps the most famous longitudinal study is the Terman Life Cycle Study that was begun by Stanford psychologist Lewis Terman in 1921. Terman studied 1,528 California schoolchildren who had intelligence test scores of at least 135. The participants, who called themselves the Termites, were initially measured on numerous aspects of their cognitive and social development in 1921 and 1922. Terman and his colleagues continued studying the Termites during their childhood and adolescence and throughout their adult lives (cf. Terman, 1925; Terman & Oden, 1947, 1959). The study has provided a rich description of the lives of highly intelligent individuals and disconfirmed many negative stereotypes of high intelligence—the Termites were very well adjusted both socially and emotionally, for example. The data have now been archived for use by other researchers. For example, Friedman et al. (1995) used the Terman data to study social and health practice factors associated with age of death.

Most longitudinal investigations do not take on the proportions of the Terman study in which individuals were studied over a lifetime. However, any study that attempts to compare the same individuals at different ages is using the longitudinal method. Thus, a researcher could study the same children at two-year intervals from the ages of 5 to 13 to examine changes in social and cognitive variables.

Cross-sectional method   In a study using the **cross-sectional method,** persons of different ages are studied at only one point in time. Suppose you are interested in examining how the ability to learn a computer application changes as people grow older. Using the cross-sectional method, you might study people who are currently 20, 30, 40, and 50 years of age. The participants in your study would be given the same computer learning task, and you would compare the groups on their performance.

Comparison of longitudinal and cross-sectional methods   The cross-sectional method is much more common than the longitudinal method, primarily because it is less expensive and immediately yields useful results. Note that with a longitudinal design it would take 30 years to study the same group of individuals from age 20 to 50, but with a cross-sectional design, comparisons of different age groups can be obtained relatively quickly.

There are, however, some disadvantages to cross-sectional designs. Most importantly, the researcher must infer that differences among age groups are due to the developmental variable of age. The developmental change is not observed directly among the same group of people, but rather is based on comparisons among different cohorts of individuals. You can think of a **cohort** as a group of people born at about the same time, exposed to the same events in a society, and influenced by the same demographic trends such as divorce rates and family size. If you think about the hairstyles of people you know who are in their 30s, 40s, 50s, and 60s, you will immediately recognize the importance of cohort effects! More crucially, differences among cohorts reflect different economic and political conditions, different cultural climates, different educational systems, and different child-rearing practices. In a cross-sectional study, a difference among groups of different ages may reflect developmental age changes; however, the differences may result from cohort effects (Schaie, 1986).

Returning to our hypothetical study on learning to use computers, suppose you found that age is associated with a decrease in ability such that the people in the 50-year-old group score lower on the learning measure than the 40-year-olds, and so on. Should you conclude that the ability to learn to use a computer application decreases with age? That may be an accurate conclusion; alternatively, the differences could be due to a cohort effect: The older people had less experience with computers while growing up. The key point here is that the cross-sectional method confounds age and cohort effects (see Chapter 6 for a discussion of confounding and internal validity). Finally, you should note that cohort effects are most likely to be a problem when the

101

researcher is examining age effects across a wide range of ages (e.g., college students through older adults).

The only way to conclusively study changes that occur as people grow older is to use a longitudinal design. Also, longitudinal research is the best way to study how scores on a variable at one age are related to another variable at a later age. For example, if a researcher wants to study how the home environment of children at age 5 is related to school achievement at age 13, a longitudinal study provides the best data. The alternative in this case would be to study 13-year-olds and ask them or their parents about the earlier home environment; this *retrospective* approach has its own problems when one considers the difficulty involved in remembering events in the distant past.

Thus, the longitudinal approach, despite being expensive and difficult, has definite advantages. There is one major problem, however: Over the course of a longitudinal study, people may move, die, or lose interest in the study. Researchers who conduct longitudinal studies become adept at convincing people to continue, often travel anywhere to collect more data, and compare test scores of people who drop out with those who stay to provide better analyses of their results. In sum, a researcher shouldn't embark on a longitudinal study without considerable resources and a great deal of patience and energy!

Cross-sequential method   A compromise between the longitudinal and cross-sectional methods is the **cross-sequential method.** The first phase of this procedure begins with the cross-sectional method; for example, you could study groups of 5-, 9-, and 13-year-olds. These individuals are then studied using the longitudinal method, with each individual tested at least one more time. This method takes fewer years to complete than a longitudinal study, and the researcher reaps immediate rewards because data on the different age groups are available even in the first year of the study.

This chapter has provided you with a great deal of information about important qualitative and quantitative descriptive methods that can be used to study a variety of questions about behavior. Researchers are continually designing intriguing new ways to describe behavior, often by combining the methods described in this chapter in creative ways. For example, Csikszentmihalyi, Rathunde, and Whalen (1993) studied teenagers identified as exceptionally talented; the researchers had the teenagers note their activities in a diary whenever a pager randomly beeped them during the day. This technique produces a vast amount of data that can be analyzed to understand the lives of these individuals.

We noted in Chapter 4 that both experimental and nonexperimental research are necessary to fully understand behavior. This chapter has focused on many descriptive methods that are crucial for nonexperimental research. In the next chapter, we begin a detailed analysis of the design of experiments.

STUDY TERMS

Archival research

Case study

Closed-ended
   questions

Cluster sampling

Coding system

Cohort

Content analysis

Cross-sectional
   method

Cross-sequential
   method

Haphazard sampling

Inter-rater reliability

Interviewer bias

Longitudinal method

Naturalistic
   observation

Negative case analysis

Nonprobability
   sampling

Open-ended questions

Participant
   observation

Population

Probability sampling

Psychobiography

Quota sampling

Reactivity

Response rate

Response sets

Sampling

Sampling frame

Simple random
   sampling

Stratified random
   sampling

Survey research

Systematic
   observation

REVIEW QUESTIONS

1. What is naturalistic observation? How does a researcher collect data when conducting naturalistic observation research?

2. Why are the data in naturalistic observation research primarily "qualitative"?

3. Distinguish between participant and nonparticipant observation and between concealed and nonconcealed observation.

4. What is systematic observation? Why are the data from systematic observation primarily "quantitative"?

5. What is a coding system? What are some important considerations when developing a coding system?

6. What is a case study? When are case studies used? What is a psychobiography?

7. What is archival research? What are the major sources of archival data?

8. What is content analysis?

9. What is a survey? Describe some research questions you might address with a survey.

10. Distinguish between probability and nonprobability sampling techniques. What are the implications of each?

11. Distinguish between haphazard and quota sampling.

12. Distinguish between simple random, stratified random, and cluster sampling.

103

13. Why don't researchers who want to test hypotheses about the relationships between variables worry about random sampling?

14. What are the advantages and disadvantages of using questionnaires versus interviews in a survey?

15. What are some factors to take into consideration when constructing questions for surveys?

16. Define interviewer bias.

17. Discuss types of response sets and possible solutions to the problems associated with response sets.

18. Distinguish between longitudinal, cross-sectional, and cross-sequential methods.

19. What is a cohort effect?

ACTIVITY QUESTIONS

1. Some questions are more readily answered using quantitative techniques, while others are best addressed through qualitative techniques. Some questions may be answered best through a combination of both approaches. Suppose you are interested in how a parent's alcoholism affects the life of an adolescent. Develop a research question best answered using quantitative techniques and another research question better suited to qualitative techniques. For example, a quantitative question might be, "Are adolescents with alcoholic parents more likely to have criminal records?" while a qualitative question could be, "What issues do alcoholic parents introduce in their adolescent's peer relationships?"

2. Devise a simple coding system to do a content analysis of print advertisements in popular magazines. Apply the system to an issue of a magazine and describe your findings.

3. In the Steinberg and Dornbusch (1991) study on teenage employment (see Figure 5-1), longer work hours were associated with lower grade point averages. Can you conclude that working longer hours causes lower grades? Why or why not? How might you expand the scope of this investigation through a panel study?

4. Dr. Cardenas studied political attitudes among groups of 20-, 40-, and 60-year-olds. Political attitudes were found to be most conservative in the age-60 group and least conservative in the age-20 group.

    a. What type of method was used in this study?

    b. Can you conclude that people become more politically conservative as they get older? Why or why not?

    c. Propose alternative ways of studying this topic.

6

Experimental Design: Purposes and Pitfalls

In the experimental method, all extraneous variables are controlled. Suppose you want to test the hypothesis that crowding impairs cognitive performance. To do this, you might put one group of people in a crowded room and another group in an uncrowded room. The participants in each of the groups would then complete the same cognitive tasks. Now suppose that the people in the crowded group do not perform as well on the cognitive tests as those in the uncrowded condition. Can the difference in test scores be attributed to the difference in crowding? Yes, *if* there is no other difference between the groups. But what if the crowded group was tested in a room with no windows but the uncrowded group was tested in a room that did have windows—for example, they were in two different rooms in a high school? In that case, it would be impossible to know whether the poor scores of the participants in the crowded group were due to the crowding or to the lack of windows.

In this chapter, we will discuss the fundamental procedures of experimental design. Recall from Chapter 4 that the experimental method has the advantage of allowing a relatively unambiguous interpretation of results. The researcher manipulates the independent variable to create groups that differ in the *levels* of the variable and then compares the groups in terms of their scores on the dependent variable. All other variables are kept constant, either through direct *experimental control* or through *randomization*. If the scores of the groups are different, the researcher can conclude that the independent variable caused the results, because the only difference between the groups is the manipulated variable.

CONFOUNDING AND INTERNAL VALIDITY

Although the task of designing an experiment is logically elegant and exquisitely simple, you should be aware of potential pitfalls. In the hypothetical crowding experiment just described, the variables of crowding and window presence are confounded. **Confounding** occurs when the researcher fails to control some extraneous variable. A variable other than the manipulated variable has been allowed to exert a differential effect in the two conditions. If the window variable had been held constant, the presence or absence of windows might have affected performance, but the effect of the windows would have been identical in both conditions. Thus, the presence of windows would not be a factor to consider when interpreting the difference between the crowded and uncrowded groups. When the variables of crowding and windows are confounded, the effect of the window variable is *different* in the crowded and the uncrowded conditions.

In short, both rooms in the crowding experiment should have had windows or both should have been windowless. Because one room had windows and one room did not, any difference in the dependent variable (test scores) cannot be attributed solely to the independent variable (crowding). An alternative explanation can be offered: The difference in test scores may have been caused, at least in part, by the window variable.

Good experimental design involves eliminating possible confounding that results in alternative explanations. A researcher can claim that the independent variable caused the results only when there are no competing explanations. When the results of an experiment can confidently be attributed to the effect of the independent variable, the experiment is said to have *internal validity* (see Chapter 4). To achieve internal validity, the researcher must design and conduct the experiment so that only the independent variable can be the cause of the results.

When you design an experiment or read about someone else's research, it is important to consider internal validity. Several different experimental designs that have been described by Campbell and Stanley (1966) nicely illustrate a number of threats to the internal validity of an experiment.

POORLY DESIGNED EXPERIMENTS

The missing control group

Suppose you want to investigate whether sitting close to a stranger will cause the stranger to move away. You might try sitting next to a number of strangers and measure the number of seconds that elapse before they leave. Your design would look like this:

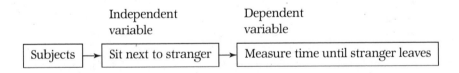

Now suppose that the average amount of time before the people leave is 9.6 seconds. Unfortunately, this finding is not interpretable. You don't know whether they would have stayed longer if you had not sat down or whether they would have stayed for 9.6 seconds anyway. It is even possible that they would have left sooner if you had not sat down—perhaps they liked you!

This design—called a "one-shot case study" by Campbell and Stanley (1966)—lacks a crucial element of an experiment: a control or comparison group. There must be some sort of comparison condition to enable you to interpret your results.[1]

---

1. The one-shot case study with its missing comparison group has serious deficiencies in the context of designing an experiment to precisely measure the effect of an independent variable on a dependent variable. As we noted in Chapter 5, case studies are valuable in other contexts.

The pitfalls of a one-group pretest-posttest design

One way to obtain a comparison would be to measure participants before the manipulation (a pretest) and again afterward (a posttest). An index of change from the pretest to the posttest could then be computed. Although this **one-group pretest-posttest design** sounds fine, there are some major problems with it.

To illustrate, suppose you wanted to test the hypothesis that a relaxation training program will result in a reduction in cigarette smoking. Using the one-group pretest-posttest design, you would select a group of people who smoke, administer a measure of smoking, have them go through relaxation training, and then re-administer the smoking measure. Your design would look like this:

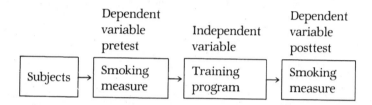

If you did find a reduction in smoking, you could not assume that the result was due to the relaxation training program. This design has failed to take into account several alternative explanations: history, maturation, testing, instrument decay, and statistical regression.

History   *History* refers to any event that occurs between the first and second measurements but is not part of the manipulation. Any such event is confounded with the manipulation. For example, suppose that a famous person dies of lung cancer during the time between the first and second measures. This event, and not the relaxation training, could be responsible for a reduction in smoking. Admittedly, the celebrity death example is dramatic and perhaps unlikely. However, **history effects** can be caused by virtually any confounding event that occurs at the same time as the experimental manipulation.

Maturation   People change over time. In a brief period, they become bored, fatigued, perhaps wiser, and certainly hungrier; over a longer period, children become more coordinated and analytical. Any changes that occur systematically over time are called **maturation effects.** Maturation could be a problem in the smoking reduction example if people generally become more concerned about health as they get older. Any such time-related factor might result in a change from the pretest to the posttest. If this happens, you might mistakenly attribute the change to the treatment rather than to maturation.

Testing   Testing becomes a problem if simply taking the pretest changes the participant's behavior. For example, the smoking measure might require people to keep a diary in which they note every cigarette smoked during the day. Simply keeping track of smoking might be sufficient to cause a reduction in the number of cigarettes a person smokes. Thus, with the **testing effect,** the reduction found on the posttest could be the result of taking the pretest rather than of the program itself. In other contexts, taking a pretest may sensitize people to the purpose of the experiment or make them more adept at a skill being tested. Again, the experiment would not have internal validity.

Instrument decay Sometimes, the basic characteristics of the measuring instrument change over time, particularly when human observers measure the behavior. Over time, an observer may gain skill, become fatigued, or change the standards on which observations are based. In our smoking example, participants might be highly motivated to record all cigarettes smoked during the pretest when the task is new and interesting, but by the time the posttest is given, they may be tired of the task and sometimes forget to record a cigarette. Such **instrument decay** would lead to an apparent reduction in cigarette smoking.

Statistical regression Sometimes called *regression toward the mean*, **statistical regression** is likely to occur whenever participants are selected because they score extremely high or low on some characteristic. When they are retested, their scores tend to change in the direction of the mean. Extremely high scores are likely to become lower, and extremely low scores are likely to become higher.

Statistical regression would be a problem in the smoking experiment if participants were selected because they were initially found to be extremely heavy smokers. By choosing people for the program who scored highest on the pretest, the researcher may have selected many participants who were, for whatever reason, smoking much more than usual at the particular time the measure was administered. The problem is actually rooted in the reliability of the measure. If there is measurement error in the score of a person who scores at the extreme, that score is likely to become less extreme when the measure is re-administered. The overall change from pretest to posttest of a group of very heavy smokers could be due to statistical regression, not the program.

Statistical regression occurs when we try to explain events in the "real world" as well. Sports columnists often refer to the hex that awaits an athlete who appears on the cover of *Sports Illustrated*. The performances of a number of athletes have dropped considerably after they were the subjects of *Sports Illustrated* cover stories. Although these cover stories might cause the lower performance (perhaps the notoriety results in nervousness and reduced concentration), statistical regression is also a likely explanation. An athlete is selected for the cover of the magazine because he or she is performing at an exceptionally high level; the principle of statistical regression states that very high performance is likely to deteriorate. We would know this for sure if

Sports Illustrated also did cover stories on athletes who were in a slump and this became a good omen for them!

All these problems can be eliminated by the use of an appropriate control group. A group that does not receive the experimental treatment provides an adequate control for the effects of history, statistical regression, and so on. For example, outside historical events would have the same effect on both the experimental and control groups. If the experimental group differs from the control group on the dependent measure administered after the manipulation, the difference between the two groups can be attributed to the effect of the experimental manipulation.

In forming a control group, the participants in the experimental condition and the control condition must be equivalent. If participants in the two groups differ *before* the manipulation, they will probably differ *after* the manipulation as well. The next design illustrates this problem.

The nonequivalent control group design

The **nonequivalent control group design** employs a separate control group, but the participants in the two conditions—the experimental group and the control group—are not equivalent. The differences become a confounding variable that provides an alternative explanation for the results. This problem, known as **selection differences,** usually occurs when participants who form the two groups in the experiment are chosen from existing natural groups. If the relaxation training program is studied with the nonequivalent control group design, the design will look like this:

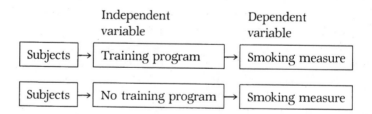

The participants in the first group are given the smoking frequency measure after completing the relaxation training. The people in the second group do not participate in any program. In this design, the researcher does not have any control over which participants are in each group. Suppose, for example, that the study is conducted in a division of a large company. All of the employees who smoke are identified and recruited to participate in the training program. The people who volunteer for the program are in the experimental group, and the people in the control group are simply the smokers who did not sign up for the training. The problem of selection differences arises because smokers who choose to participate may differ in some important way from those who do not. For instance, they may already be light smokers compared to the others and more confident that a program can help them. If so, any difference between the groups on the smoking measure, would reflect preexisting differences rather than the effect of the relaxation training.

It is important to note that the problem of selection differences arises in this design even when the researcher apparently has successfully manipulated the independent variable using two similar groups. For example, a researcher might have all smokers in the engineering division of a company participate in the relaxation training program while smokers who work in the marketing division serve as a control group. The problem here, of course, is that the smokers in the two divisions may have differed in smoking patterns *prior* to the relaxation program.

WELL-DESIGNED EXPERIMENTS

Now that you understand the way an experiment is designed and some problems to avoid, let's look at a well-designed experiment, a "true" experimental design. The simplest possible experimental design has two variables: the independent variable and the dependent variable. The independent variable has two levels: an experimental group and a control group. Researchers must make every effort to ensure that the only difference between the two groups is the manipulated variable. Remember, the experimental method involves control over extraneous variables, through either keeping such variables constant (experimental control) or using randomization to make sure that any extraneous variables will affect both groups equally. The simple experimental design can take one of two forms: a posttest-only design or a pretest-posttest design.

Posttest-only design

A researcher who uses the **posttest-only design** must (1) obtain two equivalent groups of participants, (2) introduce the independent variable, and (3) measure the effect of the independent variable on the dependent variable. The design looks like this:

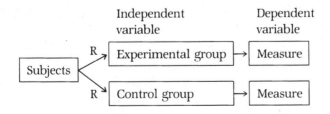

Thus, the first step is to choose the participants and assign them to two *equivalent* groups in order to eliminate the problem of selection differences. Groups can be made equivalent by randomly assigning participants to the two conditions or by having the same individuals participate in both conditions. The R in the diagram means that participants were randomly assigned to the two groups.

Next, the researcher must choose two levels of the independent variable, such as an experimental group that receives a treatment and a control group that does not. Thus, a researcher might study the effect of reward on motivation by offering a reward to one group of children before they play a game while offering no reward to children in the control group. Or a study testing the effect of a method of reducing smoking could compare one group that receives the treatment with a control group that does not. Another approach would be to use two different amounts of the independent variable—that is, to use more reward in one group than the other or to compare the effects of different amounts of relaxation training. Either of these approaches would provide a basis for comparison of the two groups.

Finally, the effect of the independent variable is measured. The same measurement procedure is used for both groups, so that comparison of the two groups is possible. Because the groups were equivalent to begin with, various factors—such as history or maturation—affect both groups equally. Thus, any difference between the groups on the dependent variable must be attributed to the effect of the independent variable. The result is an experimental design that has internal validity. In actuality, a statistical significance test would be used to assess the difference between the groups. However, we don't need to be concerned with statistics at this point. An experiment must be well designed, and confounding variables must be eliminated. If not, the results are useless, and statistics will be of no help at all.

Pretest-posttest design

The only difference between the posttest-only design and the *pretest-posttest design* is that in the latter a pretest is given before the experimental manipulation is introduced. This design makes it possible to ascertain that the groups were, in fact, equivalent at the beginning of the experiment. However, this precaution is usually not necessary if participants have been randomly assigned to the two groups. With a sufficiently large sample of participants, random assignment will produce groups that are virtually identical in all respects.

You are probably wondering how many participants are needed in each group to make sure that random assignment has made the groups equivalent. The larger the sample, the less likely the groups are to differ in any systematic way. Because of this, the statistical tests used to assess whether the independent variable did have an effect on the dependent variable are more likely to detect such an effect with larger sample sizes. There are formal procedures for determining the sample size needed to detect a statistically significant effect, but as a rule of thumb, you will probably need a minimum of 10–20 participants per condition. Further issues in determining the number of participants needed for an experiment are described in Chapter 11.

Advantages and disadvantages of the two designs

Each design has advantages and disadvantages that influence the decision whether to include or omit a pretest. The first decision factor concerns the equivalence of the groups in the experiment. Although randomization is likely to produce equivalent groups, it is possible that, with small sample sizes, the groups will not be equal. Thus, a pretest enables the researcher to assess whether the groups were in fact equivalent to begin with.

Sometimes, a pretest is necessary to select the participants in the experiment. A researcher might need to give a pretest to find the lowest or highest scorers on a smoking measure, a math anxiety test, or a prejudice measure. Once identified, the participants would be randomly assigned to the experimental and control groups. Also, the researcher who uses a pretest can measure the extent of change in each individual. If a smoking reduction program appears to be effective for some individuals but not others, attempts can be made to find out why.

A pretest is also necessary whenever the possibility exists that participants may drop out of the experiment, especially for a study that lasts over a long time period. The drop-out factor in experiments is called **mortality.** People may drop out for reasons unrelated to the experimental manipulation, such as illness; sometimes, however, mortality is related to the experimental manipulation. Even if the groups are equivalent to begin with, different mortality rates can make them nonequivalent. How might mortality affect a program designed to reduce smoking? The heaviest smokers in the experimental group might wind up leaving the program. Therefore, when the posttest is given, only the light smokers would remain, so that a comparison of the experimental and control groups would show less smoking in the experimental group even if the program had no effect. Use of a pretest enables you to assess the effects of mortality; you can look at the pretest scores of the dropouts and know whether mortality affected the final results.

Thus, pretests may offer some advantages in the experimental design. One disadvantage of a pretest, however, is that it may be time-consuming and awkward to administer in the context of the particular experimental procedures being used. Perhaps most importantly, a pretest can sensitize participants to what you are studying, enabling them to figure out your hypothesis. They may then react differently to the manipulation than they would have without the pretest. When a pretest affects the way participants react to the manipulation, it is difficult to generalize the results to people who have not received a pretest. That is, the independent variable may not have an effect in the real world, where pretests are rarely given. We will examine this issue more fully in Chapter 12.

**Table 6-1
Summary of
experimental
designs**

Design type	Problem(s)
1. One-shot case study	No comparison group
2. One-group pretest-posttest	History effect
	Maturation effect
	Testing effect
	Instrument decay
	Statistical regression
	Mortality
3. Nonequivalent control group	Selection differences
	Mortality
4. Posttest-only true experiment	None; possibly mortality
5. Pretest-posttest true experiment	None; possibly mortality but can assess with pretest information. Sensitizing subjects to the hypothesis is a potential problem.

If awareness of the pretest is a problem, the pretest can be disguised. One way to do this is by administering the pretest in a completely different situation with a different experimenter. Another approach is to embed the pretest in a set of irrelevant measures so that it is not obvious that the researcher is interested in a particular topic. Finally, the experiment can be structured to combine both the posttest-only and the pretest-posttest design. In this design, called a Solomon four-group design, half the participants receive only the posttest, and the other half receive both the pretest and the posttest. This design permits the direct assessment of the effect of the pretest; it will be discussed further in Chapter 12. Finally, concealed observation of behavior could be employed in a pretest, although ethical concerns would have to be addressed to do this. When reading about an experiment in which a pretest-posttest design was used, you should try to determine whether the pretest may have created a problem for interpreting the results.

The various designs described in this chapter are summarized in Table 6-1. You should familiarize yourself with the designs, the threats to internal validity, and the reasons that true experimental designs eliminate these threats.

ASSIGNING PARTICIPANTS TO EXPERIMENTAL CONDITIONS

Recall that there are two basic ways of assigning participants to experimental conditions. In one procedure, participants are randomly assigned to the various conditions so that each participates in only one group. This is called an **independent groups design.** In the other procedure, participants are in all conditions. In the simplest experiment, for example, each participant is assigned to both levels of the independent variable. This is called a **repeated measures design,** because each participant is measured after receiving each level of the independent variable. In the next two sections, we will examine each of these designs in detail.

INDEPENDENT GROUPS DESIGNS

In an independent groups design, different participants are assigned to each of the conditions in two ways: simple random assignment and matched random assignment.

Simple random assignment

The easiest method for assigning participants to different groups is **simple random assignment.** If there are two groups in the experiment, a possible randomization procedure would be to flip a coin to assign each individual to one or the other group. If there are more than two groups, the researcher would need to use a table of random numbers to assign participants. A table of random numbers and instructions for using it are shown in Appendix C. The table is made up of a series of the digits 0–99 that were arranged randomly by a computer. The researcher can use the arrangement of the numbers in the table to determine which group each participant will be assigned to. Random assignment will prevent any systematic biases, and the groups will be equivalent in terms of participant characteristics, such as social class, intelligence, age, and political attitudes.

Matched random assignment

A somewhat more complicated method of assigning participants to different groups is called **matched random assignment.** Matching procedures can be used when the researcher wants to ensure that the groups are equivalent on some subject characteristic. Typically, the matching variable will be a characteristic that is strongly related to the dependent variable; for example, in a learning experiment, participants might be matched on the basis of intelligence test scores. If intelligence is not related to the dependent measure, however, matching on the basis of intelligence would be a waste of time.

When matched random assignment procedures are used, the first step is to obtain a measure of the matching variable from each individual. The participants are then rank-ordered from highest to lowest on the basis of their scores on the matching variable. Now the researcher can form matched pairs that are approximately equal on the characteristic (the highest two participants form the first pair, the next two form the second pair, and so on). Finally, the members of each pair are randomly assigned to the conditions in the experiment.

Matched random assignment ensures that the groups are equivalent (on the matching variable) prior to introduction of the independent variable manipulation. This assurance could be particularly important with small

115

sample sizes, because random assignment procedures are more likely to produce equivalent groups as the sample size increases. Matched random assignment, then, is most likely to be used when only a few participants are available or when financial constraints limit the number of individuals in the experiment.

These advantages result in a greater ability to detect a statistically significant effect of the independent variable. This is because it is possible to account for individual differences in responses to the independent variable. Suppose you conduct an experiment in which the independent variable is "written versus audio presentation of material" and the dependent variable is "ability to recall the material." When you examine the results, you may find that the average ability to recall is different in the two groups. You will also find that, within each group, participants' recall scores vary; participants do not respond with the same score even though they were in the same experimental condition. With simple random assignment, we don't know why this variability exists; it is merely called "error" or unexplained variance in the scores. With matched random assignment to groups, however, we can account for much of the variability within each group. If intelligence is related to the ability to remember material, we can identify the extent to which individual differences in reactions to the independent variable are due to intelligence. The ability to explain the variability in scores on the dependent variable reduces the amount of "error," and when error or unexplained variability is reduced, we are more likely to find that the differences in the means are statistically significant.

These issues of variability and statistical significance are discussed further in Chapter 11 and Appendix B. The main point here is that matching on a variable makes it more likely that a statistically significant difference between groups will be found in an experiment. However, matching procedures can be costly and time-consuming because they require measuring participants on the matching variable prior to the experiment. Such efforts are worthwhile only when the matching variable is strongly related to the dependent measure and you know that the relationship exists prior to conducting your study. For these reasons, matching is less likely to be used than simple random assignment.

A compromise technique avoids the problems of matching while maintaining some of its statistical advantages. Rather than obtaining data on the subject variable (e.g., intelligence scores) in advance to establish matched pairs, the simple random assignment design is used, but time is allotted to collect data on the subject variable. Although these data are collected "after the fact," they can be used in the statistical analysis of the results. You may have seen research that reports the use of "analysis of covariance" or refers to a variable such as intelligence as a "covariate." Here, a technique called **analysis of covariance** statistically controls for the correlation between the subject variable and the dependent variable in the experiment. This procedure removes the error variance that results from the fact that variability in scores on the dependent variable is due in part to the effect of the subject variable. Analysis of covariance theory and procedures are beyond the scope of this book. After you have familiarized yourself with the simpler statistical methods described in Chapter 11 and Appendix B, however, you will be ready to use techniques such as these.

In both the simple and matched random assignment procedures, each individual participates in only one of the conditions in the experiment. An alternative procedure is to have the *same* individuals participate in all of the groups, in what is called a repeated measures experimental design.

REPEATED MEASURES DESIGNS

Consider an experiment to investigate the relationship between the meaningfulness of material and the learning of that material. In an independent groups design, one group of participants would be given highly meaningful material to learn and another group would receive less meaningful material. In a repeated measures design, the same participants would be used in both conditions. Thus, participants might first read low meaningful material and take a recall test to measure learning; the same participants would then read high meaningful material and take the recall test. You can see why this is called a repeated measures design; participants are repeatedly measured on the dependent variable after being in each condition of the experiment.

Advantages and disadvantages of repeated measures designs

The repeated measures design has several advantages. An obvious one is that fewer research participants are needed, because each individual participates in all conditions. When participants are scarce or when it is costly to run each individual in the experiment, a repeated measures design may be preferred. In much research on perception, for instance, extensive training of participants is necessary before the actual experiment can begin. Such research often involves only a few individuals who participate in all conditions of the experiment.

An additional advantage of repeated measures designs is that they are extremely sensitive to finding differences between groups. Because participants in the various groups are identical in every respect (they are the same people), error variability due to subject differences is minimized. As with the matched random assignment procedure described previously, the error variance or unexplained variability in the scores can be more readily identified, which results in a more sensitive statistical test. The principle is the same as with matching designs, but participants are not just matched on a single characteristic—they are identical on all characteristics. As a result, we are much more likely to detect an effect of the independent variable.

117

The major problem with a repeated measures design stems from the fact that the different conditions must be presented in a particular sequence. Suppose that there is greater recall in the high meaningful condition. Although this result could be caused by the manipulation of the meaningfulness variable, the result could also simply be an **order effect**—the order of presenting the treatments affects the dependent variable. Thus, greater recall in the high meaningfulness condition could be attributed to the fact that the high meaningful task came second in the order of presentation of the conditions. Performance on the second task might improve merely because of the practice gained on the first task.

There are several types of order effects. Order effects that are associated simply with the passage of time include practice effects and fatigue effects. A *practice effect* is an improvement in performance as a result of repeated practice with a task. A *fatigue effect* is a deterioration in performance as the research participant becomes tired, bored, or distracted. Time-related order effects are possible whenever there is a sequence of tasks to perform. For example, suppose you ask a child to play a videogame for half-hour periods under different conditions each time (e.g., different rewards for good performance or different amounts of distraction). The child playing the game for the first time might show a practice effect, with scores improving over time, but the child who is familiar with the game might show a fatigue effect, with scores deteriorating as boredom or weariness sets in.

Other types of order effects occur when the effect of the first treatment carries over to influence the response to the second treatment. For example, a *contrast effect* occurs when the response to the second condition in the experiment is altered because the two conditions are contrasted to one another. Suppose the independent variable is "severity of a crime." After reading about the less severe crime, the more severe one might seem much worse to participants than it normally would. In addition, reading about the severe crime might subsequently cause participants to view the less severe crime as much milder than they normally would.

There are two approaches to dealing with such problems. The first is to employ counterbalancing techniques. The second is to devise a procedure in which the interval between conditions is long enough to minimize the influence of the first condition on the second.

Counterbalancing

Complete counterbalancing   In a repeated measures design, it is very important to counterbalance the order of the conditions. With complete **counterbalancing,** all possible orders of presentation are included in the experiment. In the example of a study on learning high and low meaningful material, half of the participants would be randomly assigned to the low-high order, and the other half would be assigned to the high-low order. This design is illustrated as follows:

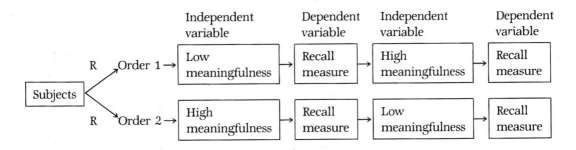

By counterbalancing the order of conditions, it is possible to determine the extent to which order is influencing the results. In the memory study example, you would know if the greater recall in the high meaningful condition is consistent for both orders; you would also know the extent to which a practice effect is responsible for the results.

Counterbalancing principles can be extended to experiments with three or more groups. With three groups, there would be 6 possible orders (3! = 3 × 2 × 1 = 6); with four groups, the number of possible orders increases to 24 (4! = 4 × 3 × 2 × 1 = 24); and so on. You would need a minimum of 24 participants to represent each order, and you would need 48 participants to have just two participants per order. Imagine the number of orders possible in an experiment by Shepard and Metzler (1971). In their basic experimental paradigm, each participant is shown a three-dimensional object along with the same figure rotated at one of 10 different angles ranging from 0 degrees to 180 degrees (see the sample objects in Figure 6-1). Each time, the participant presses a button when it is determined that the two figures are the same or different. The results show that reaction time becomes longer as the angle of rotation increases away from the original. In this experiment with 10 conditions, there are 3,628,800 possible orders! Fortunately, there are alternatives to complete counterbalancing that still allow researchers to draw valid conclusions about the effect of the independent variable.

Latin Squares   A technique to control for order effects without having all possible orders is to construct a **Latin Square**—a limited set of orders constructed to ensure that (1) each condition appears at each ordinal position and (2) each condition precedes and follows each condition one time. Using a

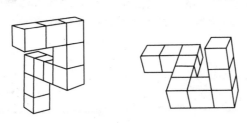

Figure 6-1
Three-dimensional figures

Source: Shepard, R. N., & Metzler, J. (1971). Mental rotation of three-dimensional objects. *Science, 171,* 701–703. Copyright © 1971 by the AAAS.

**Figure 6-2
A Latin Square
with four
conditions**

Note: The four
conditions were
randomly given the
letter designations. A =
60 degrees, B = 0
degrees, C = 180
degrees, and D = 120
degrees. Each row
represents a different
order of running the
conditions.

Order of conditions

	1	2	3	4
Row 1	A (60)	B (0)	D (120)	C (180)
Row 2	B (0)	C (180)	A (60)	D (120)
Row 3	C (180)	D (120)	B (0)	A (60)
Row 4	D (120)	A (60)	C (180)	B (0)

Latin Square to determine order controls for most order effects without having to include all possible orders. Suppose you replicated the Shepard and Metzler (1971) study using only 4 of the 10 rotations: 0, 60, 120, and 180 degrees. A Latin Square for these four conditions is shown in Figure 6-2. Each row in the square is one of the orders of the conditions (the conditions are labeled A, B, C, and D). The number of orders in a Latin Square is equal to the number of conditions; thus, if there are four conditions, there are four orders. When you conduct your study using the Latin Square to determine order, you need at least one participant per row. Usually, you will have two or more participants per row; the number of participants run in each order must be equal. The procedures for constructing Latin Squares with any number of conditions are provided in Appendix D.

Randomized blocks   In many areas of research that use repeated measures designs, the basic experimental procedure is repeated many times. For example, the 10 rotations in the Shepard and Metzler study might be repeated numerous times using different original figures. Each repetition of the basic experiment is called a *block of trials.* To control for order effects when there are many such blocks of trials, the order of presentation can be randomly determined each time.

We should note that, in an experiment in which individuals are tested over a series of trials, as in many learning studies, "trials" is a repeated measures variable. In this situation, counterbalancing is not an issue—in fact, the order effect of changes in performance over trials is of interest to the researcher.

Time interval between treatments

In addition to counterbalancing the order of treatments, researchers need to carefully determine the time interval between presentation of treatments and possible activities between them. Resting between treatments may counteract a fatigue effect; attending to an unrelated task between treatments may reduce the possibility of a contrast effect. If the treatment is the administration of a drug that takes time to wear off, the interval between treatments may have to be a day or more. Wilson, Ellinwood, Mathew, and Johnson (1994) examined the effects of three doses of marijuana on cognitive and motor task performance. Each participant was tested before and after smoking a marijuana cigarette. Because of the time necessary for the effects of the drug to wear off, the three conditions were run on separate days. A similar long time interval would be needed with procedures that produce emotional changes such as heightened anxiety or anger. You may have noted that introduction of an extended time interval may create a separate problem: Participants will have to commit to the experiment for a longer period of time. This can make it more difficult to recruit volunteers, and if the study extends over two or more days, some participants may not return.

Choosing between independent groups and repeated measures designs

Repeated measures designs have two major advantages over independent groups designs: (1) a reduction in the number of participants required to complete the experiment and (2) greater control over participant differences and thus greater ability to detect an effect of the independent variable. As noted previously, in certain areas of research, these advantages are very important. However, the disadvantages of repeated measures designs and the need to take precautions to deal with these are usually sufficient reasons for researchers to use independent groups designs.

A very different consideration in whether to use a repeated measures design concerns generalization to conditions in the "real world." Greenwald (1976) has pointed out that in actual everyday situations, we sometimes encounter independent variables in an independent groups fashion: We encounter only one condition without a contrasting comparison. However, some independent variables are most frequently encountered in a repeated measures fashion: Both conditions appear, and our responses occur in the context of exposure to both levels of the independent variable. Thus, for example, if you are interested in how characteristics of a defendant affect jurors, an independent groups design may be most appropriate because actual jurors focus on a single defendant in a trial. However, if you are interested in the effects of characteristics of a job applicant on employers, a repeated measures design would be reasonable because employers typically consider several applicants at once. Whether or not to use an independent groups or repeated measures design may be partially determined by these generalization issues.

Finally, any experimental procedure that produces a relatively permanent change in an individual cannot be used in a repeated measures design. Examples include a surgical procedure such as a brain lesion or a psychotherapy treatment.

121

You now have a fundamental understanding of the design of experiments. In the next chapter, we will consider issues that arise when you decide how to actually conduct an experiment.

STUDY TERMS

Confounding	Latin Square	Posttest-only design
Contrast effect	Matched random	Practice effect
Counterbalancing	assignment	Pretest-posttest design
Fatigue effect	Maturation effect	Randomized blocks
History effect	Nonequivalent control	Repeated measures
Independent groups	group design	design
design	One-group pretest-	Selection differences
Instrument decay	posttest design	Statistical regression
Internal validity	Order effect	Testing effect

REVIEW QUESTIONS

1. What is meant by confounding?
2. What is meant by the internal validity of an experiment?
3. Describe the threats to internal validity discussed in the text: history, maturation, testing, instrument decay, statistical regression, selection differences, and mortality.
4. Why does having a control group eliminate the problems associated with the one-group pretest-posttest design?
5. How do the two true experimental designs eliminate the problem of selection differences?
6. Distinguish between the posttest-only design and the pretest-posttest design. What are the advantages and disadvantages of each?
7. Distinguish between the simple random assignment and matched random assignment designs. When would a researcher decide to use the matched random assignment procedure? What would be the advantage of this design?
8. What is a repeated measures design? What are the advantages of using a repeated measures design? What are the disadvantages?
9. What are some of the ways of dealing with the problems of a repeated measures design?
10. The procedure used to obtain your sample (i.e., random and nonrandom sampling) is not the same as the procedure for assigning partici-

pants to conditions; distinguish between random sampling and random assignment.

ACTIVITY QUESTIONS

1. Dr. Smith learned that one sorority on campus had purchased several Macintosh computers and another sorority had purchased several IBM computers. Dr. Smith was interested in whether the type of computer affects the quality of students' papers and so went to each of the sorority houses to collect samples of papers. Two graduate students in the English department then rated the quality of the papers. Dr. Smith found that the quality of the papers was higher in one sorority than in the other. What are the independent and dependent variables in this study? Identify the type of design that Dr. Smith used. What variables are confounded with the independent variable? Design a true experiment that would address Dr. Smith's original question.

2. Gilovich (1991) described an incident that he read about during a visit to Israel. A large number of deaths had occurred during a short period of time in one region of the country. A group of rabbis attributed the deaths to a recent change in religious practice that allowed women to attend funerals. Women were immediately forbidden from attending funerals in that region, and the number of deaths subsequently decreased. How would you explain this phenomenon?

3. The captain of each precinct of a metropolitan police department selected two officers to participate in a program designed to reduce prejudice by increasing sensitivity to racial and ethnic group differences and community issues. The training program took place every Friday morning for three months. At the first and last meetings, the officers completed a measure of prejudice. To assess the effectiveness of the program, the average prejudice score at the first meeting was compared with the average score at the last meeting; it was found that the average score was in fact lower following the training program. What type of design is this? What specific problems arise if you try to conclude that the training program was responsible for the reduction in prejudice?

4. Design an experiment to test the hypothesis that single-gender math classes are beneficial to adolescent females. Operationally define both the independent and dependent variables. Your experiment should have two groups and use the matched random assignment procedure. Make a good case for your selection of the matching variable. In addition, defend your choice of either a posttest-only design or a pretest-posttest design.

5. Design a repeated measures experiment that investigates the effect of report presentation style on the grade received for the report. Use two levels of the independent variable: a "professional style" presentation (high-quality paper, laser printing, sophisticated font styles) and a "non-

professional style" (average-quality paper, dot-matrix printing, simple font style). Discuss the necessity for using counterbalancing. Create a table illustrating the experimental design.

6. Professor Foley conducted a cola taste test. Each participant in the experiment first tasted 2 ounces of Coca-Cola, then 2 ounces of Pepsi, and finally 2 ounces of RC Cola. A rating of the cola's flavor was made after each taste. What are the potential problems with this experimental design and the procedures used? Revise the design and procedures to address these problems. You may wish to consider several alternatives and think about the advantages and disadvantages of each.

7

Conducting Experiments

The previous chapters have laid the foundation for planning a research investigation. In this chapter, we will focus on some very practical aspects of conducting research. How do you select the research participants? What should you consider when deciding how to manipulate an independent variable? What should you worry about when you measure a variable? What do you do when the study is completed?

SELECTING RESEARCH PARTICIPANTS

The focus of your study may be children, college students, schizophrenics, rats, pigeons, rabbits, primates, or even cockroaches or flatworms; in all cases, the participants must somehow be selected. The method used to select participants has implications for generalizing the research results.

Recall from Chapter 5 that most research projects involve sampling research participants from a population of interest. The population is composed of all of the individuals of interest to the researcher. Samples may be drawn from the population using probability sampling or nonprobability sampling techniques. When it is important to accurately describe the population, you must use probability sampling. This is why probability sampling is so crucial when conducting scientific polls. Much research, however, is more interested in testing hypotheses about behavior. Here, the focus of the study is on examining the relationships between the variables being studied and testing predictions derived from theories of behavior. In such cases, the participants may be found in the most convenient way possible using a nonprobability haphazard or "accidental" sampling method. You may ask students in introductory psychology classes to participate, you may knock on doors in your dorm to find people to be tested, or you may choose a class in which to test children simply because you know the teacher. Nothing is wrong with such methods as long as you recognize that they affect the generalizability of your results. The issue of generalizing results is discussed in Chapter 12; despite the problems of generalizing results based on convenient haphazard samples, ample evidence supports the view that we *can* generalize findings to other populations and situations.

MANIPULATING THE INDEPENDENT VARIABLE

To manipulate an independent variable, you have to construct an operational definition of the variable (see Chapter 4). That is, you must turn a conceptual variable into a set of operations—specific instructions, events, and stimuli to be presented to the research participants. In addition, the independent and dependent variables must be introduced within the context of the total experimental setting. This has been called "setting the stage" (Aronson, Brewer, & Carlsmith, 1985).

126

Setting the stage

In setting the stage, you usually have to do two things: (1) provide the participants with the informed consent information needed for your study and (2) explain to participants why the experiment is being conducted. Sometimes, the rationale given is completely truthful, although only rarely will you want to tell participants the actual hypothesis. For example, you might say that you are conducting an experiment on memory when, in fact, you are studying a specific aspect of memory (your independent variable).

As noted in Chapter 3, participants sometimes are deceived about the actual purpose of the experiment. Deception is most common in social psychological research, because researchers in this area often find that people behave most naturally when they are unaware of the variable being manipulated. If participants know what you are studying, they may try to confirm the hypothesis or make themselves look good by behaving in the most socially acceptable way. As you plan the procedures for your study, remember as well that you will need to debrief the participants at the conclusion of the experiment.

There are no clear-cut rules for setting the stage, except that the experimental setting must seem plausible to the participants. Nor are there any clear-cut rules for translating conceptual variables into specific operations. Exactly how the variable is manipulated depends on the variable, as well as the cost, practicality, and ethics of the procedures being considered.

Types of manipulations

Straightforward manipulations   Researchers are usually able to manipulate a variable with relative simplicity by presenting written or verbal material to the participants. Such a straightforward manipulation is sometimes referred to as an *instructional manipulation* or a *judgment manipulation*.

How people use probabilities is a central element in decision theories. Tversky and Kahneman (1983), for example, had participants in one group estimate the probability that the following event would occur in the next year:

> A massive flood somewhere in North America, in which more than 1,000 people drown

Participants in the second group estimated the probability of a different event:

> An earthquake in California, causing a flood in which more than 1,000 people drown

The researchers were studying how people estimate the probability of joint occurrences (conjunctive events). Participants in the first group estimated a single event, a flood anywhere in North America, while participants in the second group estimated a joint occurrence, an earthquake *and* a flood. In theory, the probability of a single event is higher than that of a conjunctive event. The researchers found, however, that the probability estimates were higher in the conjunctive-event condition than in the single-event condition.

127

As another example, consider a study by Petty, Cacioppo, and Goldman (1981) on the effect of communicator credibility and personal involvement on attitude change. The participants were college seniors who read about the reasons that a comprehensive examination should be required for graduation from their university. To manipulate credibility, the arguments were said to be written by either a professor of education at Princeton University or a junior at a local high school. The researchers also manipulated personal involvement by telling the students that the examination was being considered for implementation either that same year (thus affecting the individuals participating in the study) or 10 years later. Although these manipulations involve deception, they are relatively straightforward because of the way they are presented. Participants in the low-involvement condition changed their attitudes more if the communicator was high in credibility, but the credibility of the communicator did not make a difference when the participants were highly involved. The Petty et al. study is an example of a factorial design in which more than one independent variable is manipulated. We will discuss factorial designs in detail in Chapter 8.

You will find that most manipulations of independent variables are straightforward. Researchers vary the difficulty of material to be learned, the level of motivation, the way questions are asked, characteristics of people to be judged, and a variety of other factors in a direct manner.

Staged manipulations   Other manipulations are less straightforward. Sometimes, it is necessary to stage events that occur during the experiment in order to manipulate the independent variable successfully. When this occurs, the manipulation is called a *staged* or *event manipulation*.

Staged manipulations are most frequently used for two reasons. First, the researcher may be trying to create some psychological state in the participants, such as frustration or a temporary lowering of self-esteem; second, a staged manipulation may be necessary to simulate some situation that occurs in the real world. For example, Fazio, Cooper, Dayson, and Johnson (1981) studied cognitive performance under conditions of multiple task demands. Participants in one condition spent 10 minutes proofreading a manuscript; participants in the other condition performed the same proofreading task but were interrupted by the experimenter from time to time and asked to go to another room to perform other tasks. These conditions simulate common real-world work environments.

Staged manipulations frequently employ a confederate—a person who poses as a participant but is actually part of the manipulation. Consider, for example, a typical study on aggression in which the confederate's role is to anger the participant. The confederate and the participant both report to the experiment and are told to wait in a room for the experiment to begin. During this waiting period, the confederate insults the participant in an "anger" condition but does not insult the participant in a "no-anger" condition. The experimenter then enters and informs the two individuals that learning is being studied and that one of them will be a teacher and the other will be a learner. The assignments to the roles of teacher and learner appear to be random but are actually rigged by the experimenter: The confederate is always the learner and the real participant is always the teacher. In the learning task, the participant is permitted to shock the confederate whenever an incorrect answer is given. The amount of shock that is chosen is the measure of aggression; the researcher compares the amount of shock given in the anger and no-anger conditions.

Staged manipulations demand a great deal of ingenuity and even some acting ability. They are used to involve the participants in an ongoing social situation, which the individuals perceive not as an experiment but as a real experience. Researchers assume that the result will be natural behavior that truly reflects the feelings and intentions of the participants. However, such procedures allow for a great deal of subtle interpersonal communication that is hard to put into words; this may make it difficult for other researchers to replicate the experiment. Also, a complex manipulation is difficult to interpret. If many things happened during the experiment, what *one* thing was responsible for the results? In general, it is easier to interpret results when the manipulation is relatively straightforward. However, the nature of the variable you are studying sometimes demands complicated procedures.

Strength of the manipulation

The simplest experimental design has two levels of the independent variable. In planning the experiment, the researcher has to choose these levels. A general principle to follow is to make the manipulation as strong as possible. A strong manipulation maximizes the differences between the two groups and increases the chances that the independent variable will have a statistically significant effect on the dependent variable.

To illustrate, suppose you hypothesize a positive linear relationship between attitude similarity and liking ("birds of a feather flock together"). In conducting the experiment, you could arrange for participants to encounter another person—a confederate. In one group, the confederate and the participant would share similar attitudes; in the other group, the confederate and the participant would be dissimilar. Similarity, then, is the independent variable, and liking is the dependent variable. Now you have to decide on the amount of similarity. Figure 7-1 shows the hypothesized relationship between attitude similarity and liking at 10 different levels of similarity. Level 1 represents the least amount of similarity, and level 10 the greatest. To achieve the strongest manipulation, the participants in one group would encounter a confederate of level-1 similarity, and those in the other group would encounter a confederate of level-10 similarity. This would result in a 9-point difference in mean liking. A weaker manipulation—using levels 4 and 7, for example—would result in a smaller mean difference.

A strong manipulation is particularly important in the early stages of research, when the researcher is most interested in demonstrating that a relationship does, in fact, exist. If the early experiments reveal a relationship

**Figure 7-1
Relationship
between attitude
similarity and
liking**

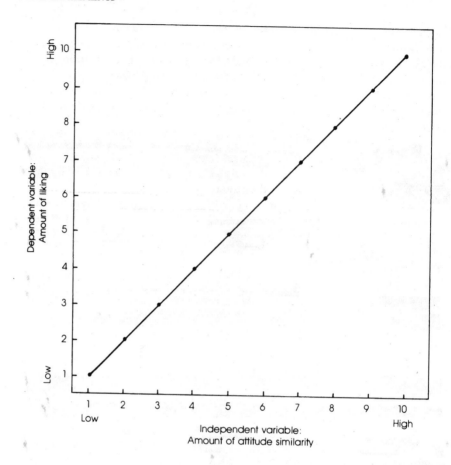

between the variables, subsequent research can systematically manipulate the other levels of the independent variable to provide a more detailed picture of the relationship.

The principle of using the strongest manipulation possible should be tempered by at least two considerations. First, the strongest possible manipulation may involve a situation that rarely, if ever, occurs in the real world. For example, an extremely strong crowding manipulation might involve placing so many people in a room that no one could move—a manipulation that might significantly affect a variety of behaviors. However, we wouldn't know if the results were similar to those occurring in more common, less crowded situations—such as many classrooms or offices.

A second consideration is ethics: A manipulation should be as strong as possible within the bounds of ethics. A strong manipulation of fear or anxiety, for example, might not be possible because of the potential physical and psychological harm.

Cost of the manipulation

Cost is another factor in the decision about how to manipulate the independent variable. Researchers who have limited monetary resources may not be able to afford expensive equipment, salaries for confederates, or payments to participants in long-term experiments. Also, a manipulation in which participants must be run individually requires more of the researcher's time than a manipulation that allows running many individuals in a single setting. In this respect, a manipulation that uses straightforward presentation of written or verbal material is less costly than a complex, staged, experimental manipulation. Some government and private agencies offer grants for research; because much research is costly, continued public support of these agencies is very important.

MEASURING THE DEPENDENT VARIABLE

In previous chapters, we have discussed various aspects of measuring variables. Reliability, validity, and reactivity of measures were described in Chapter 4, and descriptive methods such as systematic observation were presented in Chapter 5. Here, we focus on issues that are particularly relevant to experimental research.

Types of measures

The dependent variable in most experiments is one of three general types: self-report, behavioral, or physiological.

Self-report measures   Self-report measures simply ask people to describe their responses. Typically, the self-report is a paper-and-pencil measure in which the experimenter asks questions to which participants respond using a rating scale. For example, people rated the probability of events in the Tversky and Kahneman (1983) study described previously. Self-reports can be used to measure attitudes, liking for someone, judgments about someone's personality characteristics, intended behaviors, emotional states, attributions about why someone performed well or poorly on a task, confidence in one's judgments, and many other aspects of human thought and behavior.

As noted, self-report measures often have participants use a rating scale with two or more response alternatives from which to select. For example, you might ask someone to respond to the following 5-point scale:

Students at the university should be required to pass a comprehensive examination to graduate.

Strongly agree	Agree	Undecided	Disagree	Strongly disagree

Other rating scales do not label all the response alternatives, but only the end or anchor points. Thus, a participant could be asked to indicate liking for someone on the following scale, which has seven possible responses:

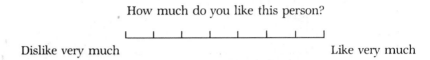

How much do you like this person?

Dislike very much   Like very much

Self-reports have many uses, and the exact method of obtaining a self-report measure will depend to a large degree on the topic being investigated. Perhaps the best way to gain an understanding of self-report scales is simply to look at a few; some examples of self-report scales are shown in Table 7-1.

Behavioral measures   Behavioral measures are direct observations of behaviors. As with self-reports, measurements of an almost endless number of behaviors are possible. Sometimes, the researcher may record whether or not a given behavior occurs—for example, whether or not an individual helps someone in distress, makes an error on a test, or chooses to engage in one activity rather than another. Often, the researcher must decide whether to record how often a behavior occurs in a given time period (the *rate*), how quickly a response occurs after a stimulus (the *reaction time*), or how long a behavior lasts (the *duration*). The decision of which aspect of behavior to measure depends on which is theoretically most relevant for the study of a particular problem or which measure logically follows from the independent variable manipulation.

Sometimes, the nature of the variable being studied requires either self-report or behavioral measurement. A measure of helping behavior is almost by definition a behavioral measure, while a measure of perception of the personality characteristics of someone will employ a self-report measure. For many variables, however, both self-reports and behavioral measures could be appropriate. Thus, liking or attraction could be measured on a rating scale or with a behavioral measure of the distance two people place between themselves or the amount of time they spend looking into each other's eyes. When both options are possible, a series of studies may be conducted to study the effects of an independent variable on both types of measures.

Physiological measures   Physiological measures are recordings of the physiological responses of the body. Many such responses are available; examples include the galvanic skin response (GSR), electromyogram (EMG), and electroencephalogram (EEG). The GSR is a measure of general emotional arousal and anxiety; it measures the electrical conductance of the skin, which changes when sweating occurs. The EMG measures muscle tension and is frequently used as a measure of tension or stress. The EEG is a measure of electrical activity of brain cells. It can be used to record general brain arousal as a

Table 7-1
Some self-report
scales

Example 1: A graphic rating scale. On a graphic rating scale, a check mark is made on a continuous line.

How would you rate the movie you just saw?

Very
unenjoyable

Very
enjoyable

_____✓_____

A ruler placed on this 100-mm line would show the score to be 84. Scores in the case could range from 0 to 100.

Example 2: A measure of interpersonal attraction. In a large number of studies, Byrne (1971) has used 7-point scales such as the following to measure liking for someone:

Personal feelings (check one)

_____ I feel that I would probably like this person very much.

_____ I feel that I would probably like this person.

_____ I feel that I would probably like this person to a slight degree.

_____ I feel that I would probably neither particularly like nor particularly dislike this person.

_____ I feel that I would probably dislike this person to a slight degree.

_____ I feel that I would probably dislike this person.

_____ I feel that I would probably dislike this person very much.

Example 3: A comparative rating scale. Sometimes it is useful to provide respondents with a frame of reference so that all ratings are made against some standard comparison. For example, a measure of student ratings of an instructor could ask the following question.

In comparison with other teachers at this university, how would you rate this instructor?

_____   _____   _____   _____   _____

Outstanding   Good   Average   Below
average   Poor

Example 4: Semantic differential scale. The semantic differential is a measure of the meaning of concepts that was developed by Osgood and his associates (Osgood, Suci, & Tannenbaum, 1957). Respondents rate any concept on a series of bipolar adjectives with 7-point scales. An example is the following rating of your local state senator, Ed Norton.

Ed Norton

Good	____:	____:	____:	____:	____:	____:	____: Bad
Foolish	____:	____:	____:	____:	____:	____:	____: Wise
Strong	____:	____:	____:	____:	____:	____:	____: Weak
Slow	____:	____:	____:	____:	____:	____:	____: Fast
Active	____:	____:	____:	____:	____:	____:	____: Passive

133

Table 7-1
(continued)

Research on the semantic differential shows that virtually anything may be measured using this technique. Respondents' ratings of specific things (e.g., marijuana, foreign cars), places (library, classroom), people (the president, one's mother), ideas (communism, abortion), or behaviors (going to church, riding a bus) can be measured. Research on the semantic differential has shown that ratings of concepts are along three basic dimensions: (1) *evaluation* (e.g., good-bad, wise-foolish, beautiful-ugly, kind-cruel), (2) *activity* (e.g., active-passive, slow-fast, excitable-calm), and (3) *potency* (e.g., weak-strong, large-small, hard-soft). Many researchers use evaluative adjectives only to measure attitude toward a concept (cf. Fishbein & Ajzen, 1975).

Example 5: A measure for children. Young children may not be able to comprehend many items and scales devised for adults. Nevertheless, they may be given self-report measures like this one:

Point to the face that shows how you feel about the toy.

---

response to different situations, activity in different parts of the brain as learning occurs, or brain activity during different stages of sleep.

The GSR, EMG, and EEG have long been used as physiological indicators of important psychological variables. Many other physiological measures are available, including temperature, heart rate, and blood or urine analysis. Often, such measures offer valuable alternatives to self-report and behavioral measures (also see Cacioppo & Tassinary, 1990).

Sensitivity of measures

The dependent variable should be sensitive enough to detect differences between groups. A measure of liking that asks, "Do you like this person?" with a simple "yes" or "no" response alternative is less sensitive than one that asks, "How much do you like this person?" on a 5- or 7-point scale. With the first measure, people may tend to be nice and say yes even if they have some negative feelings about the person. The second measure allows for a gradation of liking; such a scale would make it easier to detect differences in the amount of liking.

The issue of sensitivity is particularly important when measuring human performance. Memory can be measured using recall, recognition, or reaction time; cognitive task performance might be measured by examining speed or number of errors during a proofreading task; physical performance can be measured through various motor tasks. Such tasks vary in their difficulty. Sometimes, a task is so easy that everyone does well regardless of the conditions that are manipulated by the independent variable. This results in what is called a **ceiling effect**—the independent variable appears to have no effect on the dependent measure only because participants quickly reach the maximum performance level. The opposite problem occurs when a task is so difficult that hardly anyone can perform well; this is called a **floor effect.**

The need to consider sensitivity of measures is nicely illustrated in the Freedman, Klevansky, and Ehrlich (1971) study of crowding mentioned in Chapter 4. The study examined the effect of crowding on various measures of cognitive task performance and found that crowding did not impair performance. Thus, you could conclude that crowding has no effect on performance. However, it is also possible that the measures were either too easy or too difficult to detect an effect of crowding. In fact, subsequent research showed that the tasks may have been too easy; when participants were asked to perform more complex tasks, crowding did result in lower performance (Paulus, Annis, Seta, Schkade, & Matthews, 1976).

Multiple measures

It is often desirable to measure more than one dependent variable. One reason to use multiple measures stems from the fact that a variable can be measured in a variety of concrete ways (recall the discussion of operational definitions in Chapter 4). In a study on health-related behaviors, for example, researchers measured the number of workdays missed because of ill health, the number of doctor visits, and the use of aspirin and tranquilizers (Matteson & Ivancevich, 1983). Physiological measures might have been taken as well. If the independent variable has the same effect on several measures of the same dependent variable, our confidence in the results is increased. It is also useful to know if the same independent variable affects some measures but not others. For example, an independent variable designed to affect liking might have an effect on some measures of liking (e.g., desirability as a person to work with) but not others (e.g., desirability as a dating partner). Researchers also may be interested in studying the effects of an independent variable on several different behaviors. For example, an experiment on the effects of a new classroom management technique might examine academic performance, interaction rates among classmates, and teacher satisfaction.

Making multiple measurements in a single experiment is valuable when it is feasible to do so. However, it may be necessary to conduct a series of experiments to explore the effects of an independent variable on various behaviors.

Cost of measures

Another consideration is cost—some measures may be more costly than others. Paper-and-pencil self-report measures are generally inexpensive, but measures that require trained observers or various equipment can become quite costly. A researcher studying nonverbal behavior, for example, might

135

have to use a video camera to record each participant's behaviors in a situation. Two or more observers would then have to view the tapes to code behaviors such as eye contact, smiling, or self-touching (two observers are needed to ensure that the observations are reliable). Thus, there would be expenses for both equipment and personnel. Physiological recording devices are also expensive. Researchers need resources from the university or outside agencies to carry out such research.

Ethics

Ethical concerns are always important. Recall from Chapter 3 that participant anonymity must be protected in all research. Researchers must also be extremely careful about potential invasion of privacy.

ADDITIONAL CONTROLS

In the simplest case, the basic experimental design has two groups: (1) an experimental group that receives the manipulation and (2) a control group that does not. Use of a control group makes it possible to eliminate a variety of alternative explanations based on history, maturation, statistical regression, and so on. Sometimes, additional control procedures may be necessary to address other types of alternative explanations. Two general control issues concern expectancies on the part of both the participants and the experimenters.

Controlling for participant expectations

Demand characteristics   We noted previously that experimenters prefer not to inform participants about the specific hypotheses being studied or the exact purpose of the research. The reason for this lies in the problem of **demand characteristics** (Orne, 1962). A demand characteristic is any feature of an experiment that might inform participants of the purpose of the study. The concern is that when participants form expectations about the hypothesis of the study, they will then do whatever is necessary to confirm the hypothesis (assuming they are motivated to be cooperative). Orne conducted research to demonstrate that people are in fact cooperative. For example, he asked subjects to add numbers on a sheet of paper; when they had finished, they picked up a card from a large stack for further instructions. Each instruction card said to tear the sheet into 32 pieces and to go to the next page of numbers. The participants continued this ridiculous task for several hours with no protest or questioning! Although you can probably think of situations in which the individuals would try to be uncooperative, Orne's conception of the cooperative subject seems to be generally correct.

One way to control for demand characteristics is to use deception—to make participants think that the experiment is studying one thing when actually it is studying something else. The experimenter may devise elaborate cover stories to explain the purpose of the study and to disguise what is really being studied. The researcher may also attempt to disguise the dependent measure by using an unobtrusive measure or by placing the measure among a set of unrelated "filler-items" on a questionnaire. Another approach is simply to assess whether demand characteristics are a problem by asking participants about their perceptions of the purpose of the research. It may be that participants do not have an accurate view of the purpose of the study; or, if some individuals do guess the hypotheses of the study, their data may be analyzed separately.

Demand characteristics may be eliminated when people are not aware that an experiment is taking place or that their behavior is being observed. Thus, experiments conducted in field settings and observational research in which the observer is concealed or unobtrusive measures are used minimize the problem of demand characteristics.

Placebo groups   A special kind of participant expectation arises in research on the effects of drugs. Consider an experiment that is investigating whether a drug reduces depression in psychiatric patients. One group of people diagnosed as depressive receives the drug and the other group does not. Now suppose that the drug group shows an improvement. We don't know whether the improvement was caused by the properties of the drug or by the participants' expectations about the effect of the drug—what is called a *placebo effect*. In other words, merely administering a pill or an injection may be sufficient to cause an observed improvement in behavior. To control for this possibility, a **placebo group** can be added. An inert, harmless substance is given to members of the placebo group; they do not receive the drug given to members of the experimental group. If the improvement results from the active properties of the drug, the participants in the experimental group should show greater improvement than those in the placebo group. If the placebo group improves as much as the experimental group, the improvement is a placebo effect.

Sometimes, participants' expectations are the primary focus of an investigation. For example, Marlatt and Rohsenow (1980) conducted research to determine which behavioral effects of alcohol are due to alcohol itself as opposed to the psychological impact of believing one is drinking alcohol. The experimental design to examine these effects had four groups: (1) expect no alcohol—receive no alcohol, (2) expect no alcohol—receive alcohol, (3) expect alcohol—receive no alcohol, and (4) expect alcohol—receive alcohol. Their research suggests that the belief that one has consumed alcohol is a more important determinant of behavior than the alcohol itself. That is, people who believe they have consumed alcohol (groups 3 and 4) behaved very similarly, although those in group 3 were not actually given any alcohol.

Controlling for experimenter expectancies

Experimenters are usually aware of the purpose of the study and may thus develop expectations about how subjects should respond. These expectations can, in turn, bias the results. This general problem is called **experimenter bias** or **expectancy effects** (Rosenthal, 1966, 1967, 1969).

Expectancy effects may occur whenever the experimenter knows which condition subjects are in. There are two potential sources of experimenter bias. First, the experimenter might unintentionally treat participants differently in the various conditions of the study. For example, certain words might be emphasized when reading instructions to members of one group but not the other, or the experimenter might smile more when interacting with people in one of the conditions. The second source of bias can occur when experimenters record the behaviors of the participants; there may be subtle differences in the way the experimenter interprets and records the behaviors.

Research on expectancy effects   Expectancy effects have been studied in a variety of ways. Perhaps the earliest demonstration of the problem is the case of Clever Hans, a horse whose alleged brilliance was revealed by Pfungst (1911) to be an illusion. Robert Rosenthal describes Clever Hans:

> Hans, it will be remembered, was the clever horse who could solve problems of mathematics and musical harmony with equal skill and grace, simply by tapping out the answers with his hoof. A committee of eminent experts testified that Hans, whose owner made no profit from his horse's talents, was receiving no cues from his questioners. Of course, Pfungst later showed that this was not so, that tiny head and eye movements were Hans' signals to begin and to end his tapping. When Hans was asked a question, the questioner looked at Hans' hoof, quite naturally so, for that was the way for him to determine whether Hans' answer was correct. Then, it was discovered that when Hans approached the correct number of taps, the questioner would inadvertently move his head or eyes upward—just enough that Hans could discriminate the cue, but not enough that even trained animal observers or psychologists could see it.[1]

If a clever horse can respond to subtle cues, it is reasonable to suppose that clever humans can, too. In fact, research has shown that experimenter expectancies can be communicated to humans by both verbal and nonverbal means (Duncan, Rosenberg, & Finklestein, 1969; Jones & Cooper, 1971).

An example of more systematic research on expectancy effects is a study by Rosenthal (1966). In this experiment, graduate students trained rats that were described as coming from either "maze bright" or "maze dull" genetic strains. The animals actually came from the same strain and had been randomly assigned to the bright and dull categories; however, the "bright" rats *did* perform better than the "dull" rats. Subtle differences in the ways the students treated the rats or recorded their behavior must have caused this result. A generalization of this particular finding is called "teacher expectancy."

---

1. From Rosenthal, R. (1967). Covert communication in the psychological experiment. *Psychological Bulletin, 67,* 356–367. Copyright © 1967 by the American Psychological Association. Reprinted by permission.

Research has shown that telling a teacher that a pupil will bloom intellectually over the next year results in an increase in the pupil's IQ score (Rosenthal & Jacobson, 1968). In short, teachers' expectations can influence students' performance.

The problem of expectations influencing ratings of behavior is nicely illustrated in an experiment by Langer and Abelson (1974). Clinical psychologists were shown a videotape of an interview in which the person interviewed was described as either an applicant for a job or a patient; in reality, all saw the same tape. The psychologists later rated the person as more "disturbed" when they thought the person was a patient than when the person was described as a job applicant.

Solutions to the expectancy problem   Clearly, experimenter expectations can influence the outcomes of research investigations. How can this problem be solved? Fortunately, there are a number of ways of minimizing expectancy effects. First, experimenters should be well trained and should practice behaving consistently with all participants. The benefit of training was illustrated in the Langer and Abelson study with clinical psychologists. The bias of rating the "patient" as disturbed was much less among behavior-oriented than among traditional therapists. Presumably, the training of the behavior-oriented therapists led them to focus more on the actual behavior of the person, and so they were less influenced by the expectations stemming from the label of "patient."

Another solution is to run all conditions simultaneously so that the experimenter's behavior is the same for all participants. This solution is feasible only under certain circumstances, however, such as when the study can be carried out with the use of printed materials and the experimenter's instructions to participants are the same for everyone.

Expectancy effects are also minimized when the procedures are automated. As noted previously, it may be possible to manipulate independent variables and record responses using computers; with automated procedures, the experimenter's expectations are unlikely to influence the results.

A final solution is to use experimenters who are unaware of the hypothesis being investigated. In these cases, the person conducting the study or making observations is blind regarding what is being studied or which condition participants are in. This procedure originated in drug research using placebo groups. In a *single-blind* experiment, the participant is unaware of whether a placebo or the actual drug is being administered; in a *double-blind* experiment, neither the participant nor the experimenter knows whether the placebo or actual treatment is being given. To use a procedure in which the experimenter or observer is unaware of either the hypothesis or the group participants are in, you must hire other people to conduct the experiment and make observations.

Because researchers are aware of the problem of expectancy effects, solutions such as the ones just described are usually incorporated into the procedures of the study. If a study does have a potential problem of expectancy

139

effects, researchers are bound to notice and will attempt to replicate the experiment with procedures that control for them. A central tenet of the scientific method is that procedures are precisely defined so they can be replicated by others. This allows other researchers to build on previous research. It is also a self-correcting mechanism that ensures that methodological flaws will be discovered. The importance of replication will be discussed further in Chapter 12.

DEBUGGING THE STUDY

So far, we have discussed several of the factors that a researcher considers when planning a study. Actually conducting the study and analyzing the results is a time-consuming process. Before beginning the research, the investigator wants to be as sure as possible that everything will be done right. How can this be accomplished? There are a number of ways of eliminating the bugs from a study before it starts.

Research proposals

After putting considerable thought into planning the study, the researcher writes a research proposal. The proposal explains why the research is being done—what questions the research is designed to answer—and discusses what variables are being studied. The details of the procedures that will be used to test the idea are then given. A research proposal is very similar to the introduction and method sections of a journal article.

Such proposals must be included in applications for research grants; ethics review committees require some type of proposal as well (see Chapter 3 for more information on such committees). Preparing a proposal is a good idea in planning any research project. Simply putting your thoughts on paper helps to organize and systematize ideas. In addition, you can show the proposal to friends, colleagues, professors, and other interested parties who can provide useful feedback about the adequacy of your procedures. They may see problems that you didn't recognize, or they may offer ways of improving the study.

Pilot studies

When the researcher has finally decided on all the specific aspects of the procedure, it is possible to conduct a **pilot study** in which the researcher does a "trial run" with a small number of subjects. The pilot study will reveal whether participants understand the instructions, whether the total experimental setting seems plausible, whether any confusing questions are being asked, and so on.

Sometimes, participants in the pilot study are questioned in detail about the experience following the experiment. Another method is the "think-aloud"

140

protocol (described in Chapter 5), in which participants in the pilot study are instructed to verbalize their thoughts about everything that is happening during the study. Such procedures provide the researcher with an opportunity to make any necessary changes in the procedure before doing the entire study. Also, a pilot study allows the experimenters who are collecting the data to become comfortable with their roles and to standardize their procedures.

Manipulation checks

A **manipulation check** is an attempt to directly measure whether the independent variable manipulation has the intended effect on the participants. Manipulation checks provide evidence for the construct validity of the manipulation (construct validity was discussed in Chapter 4). If you are manipulating anxiety, for example, a manipulation check will tell you whether members of the high-anxiety group really were more anxious than those in the low-anxiety condition. The manipulation check might involve a self-report of anxiety, a behavioral measure (such as number of arm and hand movements), or a physiological measure. All manipulation checks, then, ask whether the independent variable manipulation was in fact a successful operationalization of the conceptual variable being studied. Consider an example of a manipulation of physical attractiveness as an independent variable. In a study, participants respond to someone who is supposed to be perceived as attractive or unattractive. The manipulation check in this case could determine whether participants do rate the highly attractive person as more physically attractive.

Manipulation checks are particularly useful in the pilot study to decide if the independent variable manipulation is in fact having the intended effect. They can also be used in the actual experiment to demonstrate the effectiveness of the manipulation. However, a manipulation check might not be included in the actual experiment if it would distract participants or reveal the purpose of the experiment.

A manipulation check has two advantages. First, if the check shows that your manipulation was not effective, you have saved the expense of running the actual experiment. You can turn your attention to changing the manipulation to make it more effective. For instance, if the manipulation check shows that neither the low- nor the high-anxiety group was very anxious, you could change your procedures to increase the anxiety in the high-anxiety condition.

Second, a manipulation check is advantageous if you get nonsignificant results—that is, if the results indicate that no relationship exists between the independent and dependent variables. A manipulation check can identify whether the nonsignificant results are due to a problem in manipulating the independent variable. If your manipulation is not successful, it is only reasonable that you will obtain nonsignificant results. If both groups are equally anxious after you manipulate anxiety, anxiety can't have any effect on the dependent measure. What if the check shows that the manipulation was successful, but you still get nonsignificant results? Then you know at least that the results were not due to a problem with the manipulation; the reason for not finding a relationship lies elsewhere. Perhaps you had a poor dependent measure, or perhaps there really is no relationship between the variables.

DEBRIEFING

After all the data are collected, a **debriefing** session usually is held. During debriefing, the researcher explains the purpose of the study and tells participants what kinds of results are expected; the practical implications of the results may also be discussed. In some cases, researchers may contact participants later in order to inform them of the actual results of the study. This is the educational purpose of debriefing.

If participants have been deceived in any way, debriefing is required for ethical reasons—the researcher needs to explain why the deception was necessary. If the research altered participants' physical or psychological state in some way—as in an experiment on the effects of stress—the researcher must make sure that the individuals have "calmed down" and are comfortable with having participated. The participants should leave the experiment without any ill feelings toward the field of psychology, and they may even leave with some new insight into their own behavior or personality.

Researchers may ask the participants to refrain from discussing the study with others. Such requests typically are made when more people will be participating and they might talk with one another in classes or residence halls. People who have already participated are aware of the general purposes and procedures, and it is important that these individuals not provide expectancies about the study to potential future participants.

The debriefing session also can provide an opportunity to learn more about what participants were thinking during the experiment. Researchers can ask participants what they believed to be the purpose of the experiment, how they interpreted the independent variable manipulation, and what they were thinking when they responded to the dependent measures. Such information can prove useful in interpreting the results and planning future studies.

USING COMPUTERS TO CONDUCT RESEARCH

It is becoming easier and more common for researchers to use computers as a tool for manipulating independent variables and measuring behaviors. An individual sitting at a computer screen can be presented with written material or graphical displays that replace traditional methods such as printed materials, tachistoscopes (devices that vary the length of presentation of a stimulus), and slides. Researchers can ask questions on a computer monitor instead of using the traditional paper-and-pencil method. Computers can also be used to record response times and control physiological recording devices and other equipment.

It has even become possible to conduct research over the Internet. People connected to the Internet from anywhere on the globe are potential participants in a research investigation. The existence of these global linkages raises many intriguing issues such as the integrity of the data and the nature of the sample.

ANALYZING AND INTERPRETING RESULTS

After the data have been collected, the next step is to analyze them. Statistical analyses of the data are carried out to allow the researcher to examine and interpret the pattern of results obtained in the study. The statistical analysis helps the researcher decide whether a relationship actually exists between the independent and dependent variables; the logic underlying the use of statistical tests is discussed in Chapters 10 and 11. It is not the purpose of this book to teach statistical methods; however, the calculations involved in several statistical tests are provided in Appendix B.

COMMUNICATING RESEARCH TO OTHERS

The final step is to write a report that details why you conducted the research, how you obtained the participants, what procedures you used, and what you found. A description of how to write such reports is included in Appendix A. After you have written the report, what do you do with it? How do you communicate the findings to others? Research findings are most often submitted as journal articles or as papers to be read at scientific meetings. In either case, the submitted paper is reviewed by two or more knowledgeable individuals, who decide whether the paper is acceptable for publication or presentation at the meeting.

Professional meetings

Meetings sponsored by professional associations are important opportunities for researchers to present their findings to other researchers and the public. National and regional professional associations such as the American Psychological Association (APA) and the American Psychological Society (APS) hold annual meetings at which psychologists and psychology students present their own research and learn about the latest research being done by their colleagues. Sometimes, verbal presentations are delivered to an audience. However, poster sessions are more common; here, researchers display a poster that summarizes the research and are available to discuss the research with others.

Journal articles

As we noted in Chapter 2, there are many journals in which research papers are published. Nevertheless, the number of journals is small compared to the number of reports written; thus, it isn't easy to publish research. When a researcher submits a paper to a journal, two or more reviewers read the paper and recommend acceptance (often with the stipulation that revisions be made) or rejection. As many as 75–90% of papers submitted to the more prestigious journals are rejected. Many rejected papers are submitted to other journals and eventually accepted for publication, but much research is never published. This isn't necessarily bad; it simply means that selection processes separate high-quality research from that of lesser quality.

Many of the decisions that must be made when planning an experiment were described in this chapter. The discussion focused on experiments that use the simplest experimental design with a single independent variable. In the next chapter, more complex experimental designs are described.

STUDY TERMS

Behavioral measure

Ceiling effect

Debriefing

Demand
  characteristics

Double-blind
  procedure

Expectancy effects
  (experimenter bias)

Floor effect

Manipulation check

Manipulation strength

Physiological measure

Pilot study

Placebo group

Self-report measure

Single-blind procedure

Staged manipulation

Straightforward
  manipulation

REVIEW QUESTIONS

1. Distinguish between staged and straightforward manipulations of an independent variable.
2. Distinguish between the general types of dependent variables.
3. What is meant by the sensitivity of a measure? What are ceiling and floor effects?
4. Discuss the ways that computers can be used in conducting an experiment.
5. What are demand characteristics? Describe ways to minimize demand characteristics.
6. What is the reason for a placebo group?
7. What are experimenter expectancy effects? What are some solutions to the experimenter bias problem?
8. What methods can be used to debug an experiment?
9. What is a pilot study?
10. What is a manipulation check? How does it help the researcher interpret the results of an experiment?

11. What does a researcher do with the findings after completing a research project?

ACTIVITY QUESTIONS

1. Dr. Mancini studied the relationship between age and reading comprehension, specifically predicting that older people will show lower comprehension than younger ones. Mancini was particularly interested in comprehension of material that is available in the general press. Groups of participants who were 20, 30, 40, and 50 years of age read a chapter from a book by physicist Stephen W. Hawking (1988) entitled *A Brief History of Time: From the Big Bang to Black Holes* (the book was on the best-seller list at the time). After reading the chapter, participants were given a comprehension measure. The results showed that there was no relationship between age and comprehension scores; all age groups had equally low comprehension scores. Why do you think no relationship was found? Identify at least two possible reasons.

2. Recall the experiment on facilitated communication by children with autism that was described in Chapter 2 (Montee, Miltenberger, & Wittrock, 1995). Interpret the findings of that study in terms of experimenter expectancy effects.

3. Your lab group has been assigned the task of designing an experiment to investigate the effect of time spent studying on a recall task. Thus far, your group has come up with the following plan: "Participants will be randomly assigned to two groups. Individuals in one group will study a list of 5 words for 5 minutes while those in the other group will study the same list for 7 minutes. Immediately after studying, the participants will read a list of 10 words and circle those that appeared on the original study list." Refine this experiment, giving specific reasons for any changes.

4. If you were investigating variables that affect helping behavior, would you be more likely to use a straightforward or staged manipulation? Why?

5. Design an experiment using a staged manipulation to test the hypothesis that when people are in a good mood, they are more likely to contribute to a charitable cause. Include a manipulation check in your design.

6. In a pilot study, Dr. Mori conducted a manipulation check and found no significant difference between the experimental conditions. Should she continue with the experiment? Explain your recommendations for Dr. Mori.

8

Complex Experimental Designs

Thus far we have focused primarily on the simplest experimental design in which one independent variable is manipulated with two levels and one dependent variable is measured. This simple design allows us to examine important aspects of research, such as internal validity and procedures for assigning participants to conditions. However, researchers often investigate problems that demand more complicated designs. These complex experimental designs are the subject of this chapter.

INCREASING THE NUMBER OF LEVELS
OF AN INDEPENDENT VARIABLE

In the simplest experimental design, there are only two levels of the independent variable. However, a researcher might want to design an experiment with more than two levels for several reasons. First, a design with only two levels of the independent variable cannot provide very much information about the exact form of the relationship between the independent and dependent variables. For example, Figure 8-1 shows the outcome of a hypothetical experiment on the relationship between motivation and performance on a motor task. The solid line describes the results when there are only two levels —no reward for good performance and $4.00 promised for high performance. Because there are only two levels, the relationship can only be described with a straight line. We don't know what the relationship would be if other amounts were included as levels of the independent variable. The broken line in Figure 8-1 shows the results when $1.00, $2.00, and $3.00 are

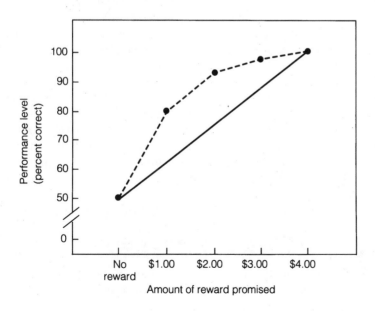

Figure 8-1
Results of a hypothetical experiment: Linear versus positive monotonic functions

147

**Figure 8-2
An inverted-U
curvilinear
relationship**

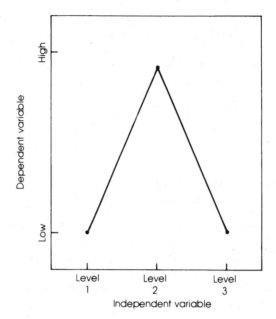

Note: At least three
levels of the
independent variable
are required to show
curvilinear
relationships.

also included. This result is a more accurate description of the relationship between amount of reward promised and performance. In the hypothetical experiment, the amount of reward is very effective in increasing performance up to a point, after which only modest increases in performance accompany increases in reward. Thus, the relationship is a monotonic positive relationship rather than a strictly linear relationship (see Chapter 4). An experiment with only two levels cannot yield such exact information.

Recall from Chapter 4 that variables are sometimes related in a curvilinear or nonmonotonic fashion—that is, the direction of relationship changes. Figure 8-2 shows an example of a curvilinear relationship; this particular form of curvilinear relationship is called an *inverted-U*. An experimental design with only two levels of the independent variable cannot detect curvilinear relationships between variables. If a curvilinear relationship is predicted, at least three levels must be used. As Figure 8-2 shows, if only levels 1 and 3 of the independent variable had been used, no relationship between the variables would have been detected. Many such curvilinear relationships exist in psychology. The relationship between fear arousal and attitude change is one example. Increasing the amount of fear aroused by a persuasive message increases attitude change up to a moderate level of fear; further increases in fear arousal actually reduce attitude change.

Finally, researchers frequently are interested in comparing more than two groups. For example, Punnett (1986) tested the hypothesis that setting specific and difficult goals improves performance more than does setting vague goals such as "do your best" or no specific goals at all. The participants were Caribbean women who work at home sewing children's clothes. One group was given the difficult goal of increasing production by 20%, another group was instructed to "do your best," and a third group served as a control. Results showed that the women in the difficult goal condition earned an average of $1.91 per day while the women in the "do your best" and control conditions earned $1.30 and $0.96 per day, respectively.

INCREASING THE NUMBER OF INDEPENDENT VARIABLES: FACTORIAL DESIGNS

Researchers often manipulate more than one independent variable in a single experiment. Typically, two or three independent variables are operating simultaneously. This type of experimental design is a closer approximation of real-world conditions, in which independent variables do not exist by themselves. Researchers recognize that in any given situation a number of variables are operating to affect behavior, so they design experiments with more than one independent variable.

Factorial designs are designs with more than one independent variable (or *factor*). In a factorial design, all levels of each independent variable are combined with all levels of the other independent variables. The simplest factorial design—known as a 2 × 2 (two-by-two) factorial design—has two independent variables, each having two levels.

An experiment by Smith and Ellsworth (1987) illustrates a 2 × 2 factorial design. Smith and Ellsworth studied the effects of asking misleading questions on the accuracy of eyewitness testimony. Participants in the experiment first viewed a videotape of a robbery and then were asked questions about what they saw. One independent variable was the type of question—misleading or unbiased. The second independent variable was the questioner's knowledge of the crime: The person asking the questions had either viewed the tape just once (a "naive" questioner) or had seen the tape a number of times (a "knowledgeable" questioner).

This 2 × 2 design results in four experimental conditions: (1) knowledgeable questioner—misleading questions, (2) knowledgeable questioner—unbiased questions, (3) naive questioner—misleading questions, and (4) naive questioner—unbiased questions. You may recall from Chapter 2 that Aronson's "blunder" experiment also studied two independent variables in a 2 × 2 design: There was a superior person who did or did not commit a blunder and an average person who did or did not commit a blunder (Aronson, 1984).

Note that a 2 × 2 design always has four groups. The general format for describing factorial designs is

$$\begin{bmatrix} \text{Number of levels} \\ \text{of first IV} \end{bmatrix} \times \begin{bmatrix} \text{Number of levels} \\ \text{of second IV} \end{bmatrix} \times \begin{bmatrix} \text{Number of levels} \\ \text{of third IV} \end{bmatrix}$$

Table 8-1
2 × 2 factorial
design: Results of
the eyewitness
testimony
experiment

Questioner type (independent variable B)	Type of question (independent variable A)		Overall means (main effect of B)
	Unbiased	Misleading	
Knowledgeable	13	41	27.0
Naive	13	18	15.5
Overall means (main effect of A)	13.0	29.5	

and so on. A design with two independent variables, one having two levels and the other having three levels, is a 2 × 3 factorial design; there are six conditions in the experiment. A 3 × 3 design has nine conditions.

Interpretation of factorial designs

Factorial designs yield two kinds of information. The first is information about the effect of each independent variable taken by itself: the **main effect** of an independent variable. In a design with two independent variables, there are two main effects—one for each independent variable. The second type of information is called an **interaction effect.** If there is an interaction between two independent variables, the effect of one independent variable depends on the particular level of the other variable. In other words, the effect that an independent variable has on the dependent variable depends on the level of the other independent variable. Interactions are a new source of information that cannot be obtained in a simple experimental design in which only one independent variable is manipulated.

To illustrate main effects and interactions, we can look at the results of the Smith and Ellsworth study on accuracy of eyewitness testimony. Table 8-1 illustrates a common method of presenting outcomes for the various groups in a factorial design. The number in each cell represents the mean percent of errors made in the four conditions.

Main effects   A main effect is the effect each variable has by itself. The main effect of independent variable A, type of question, is the overall effect of the variable on the dependent measure. Similarly, the main effect of independent variable B, type of questioner, is the effect of the different types of questions on accuracy of recall.

The main effect of each independent variable is the overall relationship between the independent variable and the dependent variable. For independent variable A, is there a relationship between type of question and recall errors? We can find out by looking at the overall means in the unbiased and misleading question conditions. These means are shown in the margins of the table. The overall percent of errors made by participants in the misleading questions condition is 29.5, while the error percent in the unbiased question condition is 13.0. These overall main effect means are obtained by averaging across all participants in each group, irrespective of the type of questioner (knowledgeable or naive). Note that the overall mean of 29.5 in the misleading question condition is the average of 41 in the knowledgeable—misleading group and 18 in the naive—misleading group (this calculation assumes equal numbers of participants in each group). You can see that, overall, more errors are made when the questions are misleading than when they are unbiased. Statistical tests would enable us to determine whether this is a significant main effect.

The main effect for independent variable B (questioner type) is the overall relationship between that independent variable, by itself, and the dependent variable. You can see in Table 8-1 that the overall score in the knowledgeable questioner condition is 27.0, while the overall score in the naive questioner group is 15.5. Thus, in general, more errors result when the questioner is knowledgeable.

Interaction effects   These main effects tell us that, overall, there are more errors when the questioner is knowledgeable and when the questions are misleading. There is also the possibility that an interaction exists; if so, the main effects of the independent variables must be qualified. This is because an interaction between independent variables indicates that the effect of one independent variable is different at different levels of the other independent variable. That is, an interaction tells us that the effect of one independent variable depends on the particular level of the other.

We can see an interaction in the results of the Smith and Ellsworth study. The effect of the type of question is different depending on whether the questioner is knowledgeable or naive. When the questioner is knowledgeable, misleading questions result in more errors (41% in the misleading question condition versus 13% in the unbiased condition). However, when the questioner is naive, the type of question has little effect (18% for misleading questions and 13% for unbiased questions). Thus, the relationship between type of question and recall errors is best understood by considering both independent variables: We must consider whether the questions are misleading *and* whether the questioner is knowledgeable or naive.

Interactions can be easily seen when the means for all conditions are presented in a graph. Figure 8-3 is a graph of the results of the eyewitness testimony experiment. Note that all four means have been graphed and that two lines describe the relationship between type of question and errors of recall. One line represents this relationship for the knowledgeable questioner, and the other line shows the relationship for the naive questioner. You can see the relationship that exists when the questioner is knowledgeable; when the questioner is naive, there is no relationship.

The concept of interaction is a relatively simple one that you probably use all the time. When we say "it depends," we are usually indicating that some sort of interaction is operating—it depends on some other variable. Suppose,

**Figure 8-3
Interaction
between type of
question and type
of questioner**

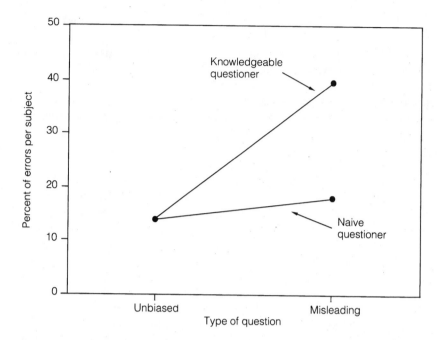

(Based on data from
Smith & Ellsworth,
1987)

for example, that a friend has asked you if you want to go to a movie.
Whether you go may reflect an interaction between two variables: (1) Is an
exam coming up? and (2) Who stars in the movie? If there is an exam coming
up, you won't go under any circumstance. If you do not have an exam to
worry about, your decision will depend on whether you like the person in the
movie. That is, you will go only if a favorite star is in the movie.

You might try graphing the movie example in the same way we graphed
the eyewitness testimony example in Figure 8-3. The dependent variable
(going to the movie) is always placed on the vertical axis. Independent variable A is placed on the horizontal axis. The results for the first level of independent variable B are then placed on the graph and a line is drawn to
connect the points. The same is then done for the second level of independent
variable B.

Graphing the results in this manner is a useful method of visualizing
interactions in a factorial design. In actual research, it is necessary to conduct
statistical analyses to determine whether either main effect is statistically significant and whether there is a significant interaction.

Outcomes of a 2 × 2 factorial design

A 2 × 2 factorial design has two independent variables, each with two levels.
When analyzing the results, there are several possibilities: (1) There may or
may not be a significant main effect for independent variable A, (2) there may

**Figure 8-4
Outcomes of a
factorial design
with two
independent
variables**

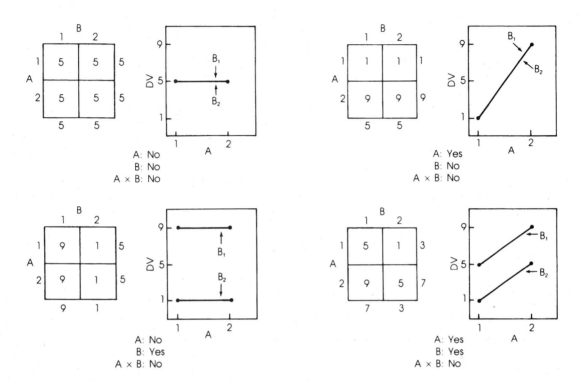

or may not be a significant main effect for independent variable B, and (3) there may or may not be a significant interaction between the independent variables.

Figure 8-4 illustrates the eight possible outcomes in a 2 × 2 factorial design. For each outcome, the means are given and then graphed. Note on each graph that the dependent variable is placed on the vertical axis and that independent variable A is placed on the horizontal axis. The two means for B_1 are plotted and a line is drawn to represent this level of B. Similarly, the B_2 means are plotted and a second line is drawn to represent this level. In the first two graphs, the lines representing B_1 and B_2 coincide, so only one line is seen.

The means that are given in the figure are idealized examples; such perfect outcomes rarely occur in actual research. Nevertheless, you should study the graphs to determine for yourself why, in each case, there is or isn't a main effect for A, a main effect for B, and an A × B interaction.

153

Figure 8-4
(continued)

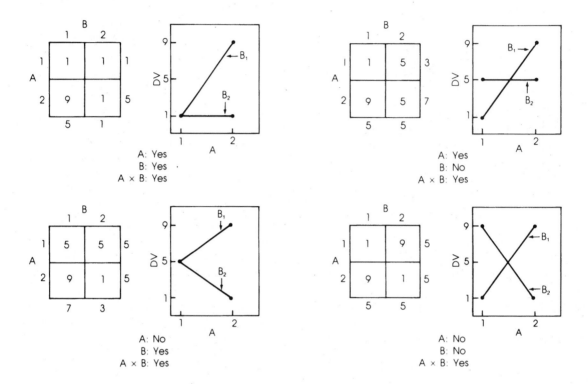

A: Yes
B: Yes
A × B: Yes

A: Yes
B: No
A × B: Yes

A: No
B: Yes
A × B: Yes

A: No
B: No
A × B: Yes

The first four graphs illustrate outcomes in which there is no A × B interaction effect, and the last four graphs depict outcomes in which there is an interaction. When there is a statistically significant interaction, you need to carefully examine the means to understand why the interaction occurred. In some cases, there is a strong relationship between the first independent variable and the dependent variable at one level of the second independent variable; however, there is no relationship or a weak relationship at the other level of the second independent variable. This pattern is evident in the Smith and Ellsworth (1987) data shown in Figure 8-3 and in the first two interactions shown in Figure 8-4. In other studies, the interaction may indicate that an independent variable has opposite effects on the dependent variable, depending on the level of the second independent variable. Look carefully at the last graph in Figure 8-4: There is a positive relationship between A and the dependent variable at B_1, and a negative relationship exists at B_2. An interesting feature of this last graph is that neither independent variable has an effect *by itself*. However, the interaction shows that A has strong (but opposite) effects, depending on the particular level of B. The interaction indicates that both independent variables must be considered if the relationships involved are to be understood. To make sure that you fully understand these graphs, you might test yourself. Cover the outcomes or draw a new set of graphs; see if you can say whether there are main effects or an interaction.

Factorial designs with manipulated and nonmanipulated variables: IV × SV designs

One common type of factorial design includes both experimental (manipulated) and correlational (nonmanipulated) variables. These designs—sometimes called **IV × SV designs** (i.e., independent variable by subject variable) —allow researchers to investigate how different types of individuals (i.e., subjects) respond to the same manipulated variable. The kinds of subject variables studied include gender, age, ethnic group, personality characteristics, and clinical diagnostic category.

The simplest IV × SV design includes one manipulated independent variable that has at least two levels and one subject variable with at least two levels. The two levels of the subject variable might be two different age groups, groups of low and high scorers on a personality measure, or groups of males and females. An example of this design is a study by Furnham, Gunter, and Peterson (1994). Do you ever try to study when there is a distraction such as a television program? Furnham et al. showed that the ability to study with such a distraction depends on whether you are more extraverted or introverted. The manipulated variable was distraction. College students read material in silence and within hearing range of a TV drama. Thus, a repeated measures design was used and the order of the conditions was counterbalanced. After they read the material, the students completed a reading comprehension measure. The subject variable was extraversion: Participants completed a measure of extraversion and then were classified as extraverts or introverts. The results are shown in Figure 8-5. There was a main effect of distraction: Overall, students had higher comprehension scores when they studied in silence. In addition, there was an interaction between extraversion and distraction. Without a distraction, the performance of extraverts and introverts was the same. However, extraverts performed better than introverts when the TV was on. If you are an extravert, be more understanding when your introverted friends want things quiet when studying!

Factorial designs with both manipulated independent variables and subject variables offer a very appealing method for investigating many interesting research questions. Such experiments recognize that full understanding of behavior requires knowledge of both situational variables and the personality and background characteristics of the individuals involved.

Assignment procedures and factorial designs

The considerations of assigning participants to conditions that were discussed in Chapter 6 can be generalized to factorial designs. There are two basic ways of assigning participants to conditions: (1) In an independent groups design,

155

Figure 8-5
Interaction in
IV × SV design

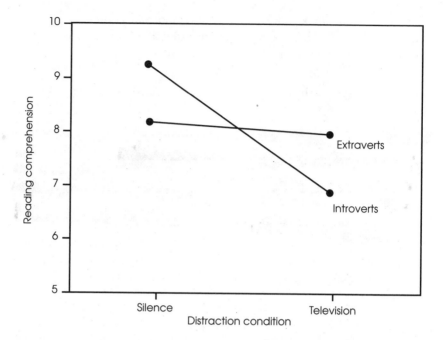

different participants are assigned to each of the conditions in the study; (2) in a repeated measures design, the same individuals participate in all conditions in the study. These two types of assignment procedures have implications for the number of participants necessary to complete the experiment. We can illustrate this fact by looking at a 2 × 2 factorial design. The design can be completely independent groups, completely repeated measures, or a **mixed factorial design**—that is, a combination of the two.

Independent groups   In a 2 × 2 factorial design, there are four conditions. If we want a completely independent groups design, a different group of participants will be assigned to each of the four conditions. The Smith and Ellsworth (1987) study on eyewitness testimony and the Petty, Cacioppo, and Goldman (1981) study on the effect of communicator credibility and personal involvement on attitude change that was described in Chapter 7 illustrate factorial designs with different individuals in each of the conditions. Suppose that you have planned a 2 × 2 design and want to have 10 participants in each condition; you will need a total of 40 *different* participants, as shown in the first table in Figure 8-6.

Repeated measures   In a completely repeated measures procedure, the same individuals will participate in *all* conditions. Suppose you have planned a study on the effects of marijuana similar to the one by Wilson, Ellinwood, Mathew, and Johnson (1994) that was described in Chapter 6: One factor is marijuana (marijuana treatment versus placebo control) and the other factor

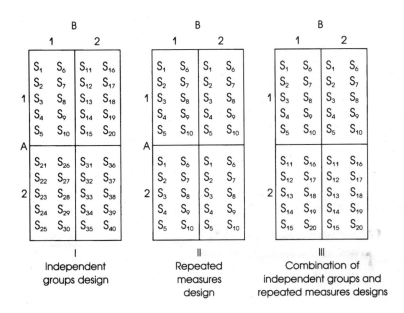

Figure 8-6
Number of
subjects required
to have 10 subjects
in each condition

is task difficulty (easy versus difficult). In a 2×2 completely repeated measures design, each individual would participate in all of the conditions by completing both easy and difficult tasks under both marijuana treatment conditions. If you wanted 10 participants in each condition, a total of 10 subjects would be needed, as illustrated in the second table in Figure 8-6. This design offers considerable savings in the number of participants required. In deciding whether to use a completely repeated measures assignment procedure, however, the researcher would have to consider the disadvantages of repeated measures designs.

Mixed factorial design using combined assignment   The Furnham, Gunter, and Peterson (1994) study on television distraction and extraversion illustrates the use of both independent groups and repeated measures procedures in a mixed factorial design. The subject variable, extraversion, is an independent groups variable. Distraction is a repeated measures variable; all participants studied with both distraction and silence. The third table in Figure 8-6 shows the number of subjects needed to have 10 per condition in a 2×2 mixed factorial design. In this table, independent variable A is an independent groups variable. Ten participants are assigned to level 1 of this independent variable, and another 10 participants are assigned to level 2. Independent variable B is a repeated measures variable, however. The 10 participants assigned to A_1 receive both levels of independent variable B. Similarly, the other 10 participants assigned to A_2 receive both levels of the B variable. Thus, a total of 20 participants is required.

Table 8-2
2 × 3 factorial
design

Task difficulty	Anxiety			Overall means (main effect)
	Low	Moderate	High	
Easy	4	7	10	7.0
Hard	7	4	1	4.0
Overall means (main effect)	5.5	5.5	5.5	

Age as a variable in factorial designs

As noted previously, age is frequently studied as a subject variable in experiments. The most common practice is to include age as an independent groups variable: Individuals from one age group are compared with those from a different age group. Researchers using this design typically are testing a theory that predicts an interaction between age and the manipulated independent variable. Age is included as a variable in such experiments because some psychological process is different in the age groups studied.

You may recognize this as the cross-sectional method described in Chapter 5. If the groups differ widely in age, cohort effects could be a factor to be considered when interpreting the results. It is possible to use the same individuals in both age groups in an IV × SV design; in this case, age is a repeated measures variable. However, this practice is rare for two reasons. Most importantly, researchers who employ this design usually are predicting the interaction on the basis of theoretical considerations that are independent of cohort effects. Further, using the longitudinal method is very difficult.

Further considerations in factorial designs

The 2 × 2 is the simplest factorial design. With this basic design, the researcher can arrange experiments that are more and more complex. One way to increase complexity is to increase the number of levels of one or more of the independent variables. A 2 × 3 design, for example, contains two independent variables: Independent variable A has two levels, and independent variable B has three levels. Thus, the 2 × 3 design has six conditions. Table 8-2 shows a 2 × 3 factorial design with the independent variables of task difficulty (easy, hard) and anxiety level (low, moderate, high).

The dependent variable is performance on the task. The numbers in each of the six cells of the design indicate the mean performance score of the group. The overall means in the margins show the main effects of each of the independent variables. The results in Table 8-2 indicate a main effect of task difficulty, because the *overall* performance score in the easy-task group is higher than the hard-task mean. However, there is no main effect of anxiety, because the mean performance score is the same in each of the three anxiety

	Class size		Table 8-3
	10	40	**2 × 2 × 2 factorial design**
Instruction method	*Male*		
Lecture			
Discussion			
	Female		
Lecture			
Discussion			

groups. Is there an interaction between task difficulty and anxiety? Note that increasing the amount of anxiety has the effect of increasing performance on the easy task but *decreasing* performance on the hard task. The effect of anxiety is different, depending on whether the task is easy or hard; thus, there is an interaction.

We can also increase the number of variables in the design. A 2 × 2 × 2 factorial design contains three variables, each with two levels. Thus, there are eight conditions in this design. In a 2 × 2 × 3 design, there are 12 conditions; in a 2 × 2 × 2 × 2 design, there are 16. The rule for constructing factorial designs remains the same throughout.

A 2 × 2 × 2 factorial design is constructed in Table 8-3. The independent variables are (1) instruction method (lecture, discussion), (2) class size (10, 40), and (3) student gender (male, female). Note that gender is a nonmanipulated variable while the other two variables are manipulated variables. The dependent variable is performance on a standard test.

Notice that the 2 × 2 × 2 design can be seen as two 2 × 2 designs, one for the males and another for the females. The design yields main effects for each of the three independent variables. For example, the overall mean for the lecture method is obtained by considering all participants who experience the lecture method, irrespective of class size or gender. Similarly, the discussion method mean is derived from all participants in this condition. The two means are then compared to see whether there is a significant main effect: Is one method superior to the other *overall?*

The design also allows us to look at interactions. In the 2 × 2 × 2 design, we can look at the interaction between (1) method and class size, (2) method and gender, and (3) class size and gender. We can also look at a three-way interaction that involves all three independent variables. Here, we want to determine whether the nature of the interaction between two of the variables differs depending on the particular level of the other variable. Three-way

159

interactions are rather complicated; fortunately, you won't encounter too many of these in your explorations of behavioral science research.

Sometimes students are tempted to include in a study as many independent variables as they can think of. A problem with this is that the design may become needlessly complex and require enormous numbers of participants. The design just discussed had 8 groups; a $2 \times 2 \times 2 \times 2$ design has 16 groups; adding yet another independent variable with two levels means 32 groups would be required. Also, when there are more than three or four independent variables, many of the particular conditions that are produced by the combination of so many variables do not make sense or could not occur under natural circumstances.

The designs described thus far all use the same logic for determining that the independent variable did in fact cause a change on the dependent variable measure. In the next chapter, we will consider alternative designs that use somewhat different procedures for examining the relationship between independent and dependent variables.

STUDY TERMS

Factorial design	IV × SV design	Mixed factorial design
Interaction effect	Main effect	

REVIEW QUESTIONS

1. Why would a researcher have more than two levels of the independent variable in an experiment?
2. What is a factorial design? Why would a researcher use a factorial design?
3. What are main effects in a factorial design? What is an interaction?
4. Describe an IV × SV factorial design.
5. Identify the number of conditions in a factorial design on the basis of knowing the number of independent variables and the number of levels of each independent variable.

ACTIVITY QUESTIONS

1. In a study by Chaiken and Pliner (1987), research participants read an "eating diary" of either a male or female stimulus person. The information in the diary indicated that the person ate either large meals or small meals. After reading this information, participants rated the person's femininity and masculinity.
   a. Identify the design of this experiment.
   b. How many conditions are in the experiment?

c. Identify the independent variable(s) and dependent variable(s).

d. Is there a subject variable in this experiment? If so, identify it. If not, can you suggest a subject variable that might be included?

2. Chaiken and Pliner reported the following mean femininity ratings (higher numbers indicate greater femininity): male—small meals (2.02), male—large meals (2.05), female—small meals (3.90), and female—large meals (2.82). Assume there are equal numbers of participants in each condition.

a. Are there any main effects?

b. Is there an interaction?

c. Graph the means.

d. Describe the results in a brief paragraph.

3. Using recent psychology journals, find an example of a 2 × 2 independent groups design. Identify each factor and the levels of each factor. Find another experiment that exemplifies a two-factor design using repeated measures for one or more variables; identify whether it is a completely repeated measures procedure or a mixed factorial design. Identify each factor and the levels of each factor. Was there an interaction effect? If so, describe the interaction.

4. Assume you want 15 participants in each condition of your experiment that uses a 3 × 3 factorial design. How many *different* participants do you need for (a) completely independent groups assignment, (b) completely repeated measures assignment, and (c) a mixed factorial design with both independent groups assignment and repeated measures variables?

9

Quasi-Experimental and Single-Subject Research Designs

In the classic experimental design described in Chapter 6, participants are randomly assigned to the independent variable conditions and a dependent variable is measured. The responses on the dependent measure by participants in the conditions are then compared to determine whether the independent variable had an effect. You will frequently encounter this experimental design when you explore research in the behavioral sciences. However, other research designs have been devised to address special research problems. This chapter focuses on quasi-experimental and single-subject research designs—research approaches that present interesting challenges to determining internal validity.

QUASI-EXPERIMENTAL DESIGNS

As we noted in Chapter 1, researchers frequently confront applied research questions and do evaluation research. Quasi-experimental designs emerged from the need to conduct applied research in settings in which the control features of true experimental designs cannot be achieved. **Quasi-experimental designs** attempt to approximate the control features of true experiments to infer that a given treatment did have its intended effect. Although quasi-experimental designs can be used to study many research problems, it is helpful to consider them in the context of program evaluation research.

Program evaluation

Program evaluation was briefly described in Chapter 1. This is research on programs that are proposed and implemented to achieve some positive effect on a group of individuals. Such programs may be implemented in schools, work settings, or even entire communities. In the schools, an example is the D.A.R.E. (Drug Abuse Resistance Education) program designed to reduce drug use.

The initial focus of evaluation research was "outcome evaluation": Did the program result in the positive outcome for which it was designed (e.g., reductions in drug abuse, higher grades, lower absenteeism, or lower recidivism)? However, as the field of program evaluation has progressed since Campbell's 1969 paper, evaluation research has become concerned with much more than outcome evaluation (Posavac & Carey, 1992; Rossi & Freeman, 1993).

There are four general types of evaluations, depicted in Figure 9-1 as the four phases of the evaluation process. The first is the evaluation of need. Needs assessment studies ask whether there are, in fact, problems that need to be addressed in a target population. For example, is there drug abuse by children and adolescents in the community? What services do the elderly lack? What is the pattern of high school drop-out rates among various ethnic

Figure 9-1
Four phases of
program
evaluation

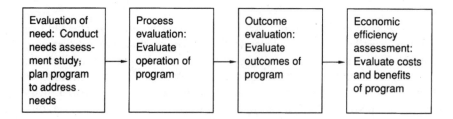

groups? Why do members drop out? Once a need has been established, programs can be planned to address the need.

The second type of program evaluation question is process evaluation or program monitoring. When the program is under way, the evaluation researcher monitors it to determine whether it is reaching the target population, whether it is attracting enough clients, and whether the staff is providing the planned services. In sum, the researcher wants assurance that the program is doing what it is supposed to do. This research is extremely important because we would not want to conclude that a program itself is ineffective if, in fact, it is the *implementation* of the program that is not working.

The third question concerns outcome evaluation: Are the intended outcomes of the program being realized? Is the goal—to reduce drug use, increase literacy, decrease the high school drop-out rate, or provide job skills —being achieved? To determine this, the evaluation researcher must devise a way of measuring the outcome and then study the impact of the program on the outcome measure.

The final program evaluation question addresses economic efficiency. Once it is shown that a program does have its intended effect, researchers must determine whether it is "worth it." The cost of the program must be weighed against its benefits. Also, the researchers must determine whether the resources used to implement the program might be put to some better use.

Evaluation research sometimes can be conducted using true experimental designs. However, this research often must be conducted in settings and under circumstances in which a true experimental design cannot be implemented. In such situations, an alternative to a true experimental design must be used. One alternative is a quasi-experimental design. Here we will look only at some of the more commonly used quasi-experimental designs. For more detailed discussions, see Campbell (1968, 1969), Cook and Campbell (1979), and Campbell and Stanley (1966).

Nonequivalent control group pretest-posttest design

The nonequivalent control group posttest-only design was described in Chapter 6. This design has an experimental group and a control group. However, the groups may not be equivalent because participants are not randomly assigned to conditions. Thus, any difference on the dependent measure posttest may be due to selection differences. The design can be greatly improved if a pretest is given. When this is done, we have a **nonequivalent control group pretest-posttest design,** one of the most useful quasi-experimental designs. It can be diagrammed as follows:

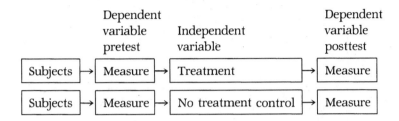

This is not a true experimental design because assignment to groups is not random; the two groups may not be equivalent. We have the advantage, however, of knowing the pretest scores. Thus, we can see whether the groups were the same on the pretest. Even if the groups are not equivalent, we can look at *changes* in scores from the pretest to the posttest. If the independent variable has an effect, the experimental group should show a greater change than the control group (see Kenny, 1979).

Joy, Kimball, and Zabrack (1986) used a nonequivalent control group pretest-posttest design to study the effect of television on children's aggressive behavior. A Canadian town that had not had television reception until 1974 was the focus of the study (this town was dubbed "Notel" by Joy et al.). Both before and after the introduction of television in Notel, the researchers measured children's physical and verbal aggression. At the same time, they measured aggression in two similar towns, one that received only a single Canadian station ("Unitel") and one that received both Canadian and U.S. networks ("Multitel"). Thus, it was possible to compare the change in aggression in Notel with that in the control communities of Unitel and Multitel. The results of the study showed that there was a greater increase in aggression in Notel than in either Unitel or Multitel.

Interrupted time series design

Campbell (1969) discusses at length the evaluation of one specific legal reform: the 1955 crackdown on speeding in Connecticut. Although seemingly an event in the distant past, the example is still a good illustration of an important methodological issue. The crackdown was instituted after a record high number of traffic fatalities occurred in 1955. The easiest way to evaluate this reform is to compare the number of traffic fatalities in 1955 (before the crackdown) with the number of fatalities in 1956 (after the crackdown). Indeed, there was a reduction in the number of traffic deaths, from 324 in 1955 to 284 in 1956. This single comparison is really a one-group pretest-posttest design with all of that design's problems of internal validity; there are many other reasons that traffic deaths might have declined.

**Figure 9-2
Connecticut traffic
fatalities:
1951–1959**

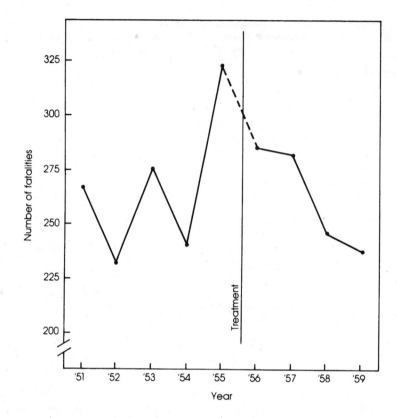

Source: Campbell, D. T.
(1969). Reforms as
experiments. *American
Psychologist, 24,*
409–429. Copyright
1969 by the American
Psychological
Association. Reprinted
by permission.

One alternative is to use an **interrupted time series design** that would examine the traffic fatality rates over an extended period of time, both before and after the reform was instituted. Figure 9-2 shows this information for the years 1951–1959. Campbell (1969) argues that the drop from 1955 to 1956 does not look particularly impressive, given the great fluctuations in previous years, but there is a steady downward trend in fatalities after the crackdown. Even here, however, Campbell sees a problem in interpretation. The drop could be due to statistical regression: Because 1955 was a record high year, the probability is that there would have been a drop anyway. Still, the data for the years extending before and after the crackdown allow for a less ambiguous interpretation than would be possible with only data for 1955 and 1956.

Control series design

One way to improve the interrupted time series design is to find some kind of control group—a **control series design.** In the Connecticut speed crackdown, this was possible because other states had not instituted the reform. Figure 9-3 shows the same data on traffic fatalities in Connecticut plus the fatality figures of four comparable states during the same years. The fact that

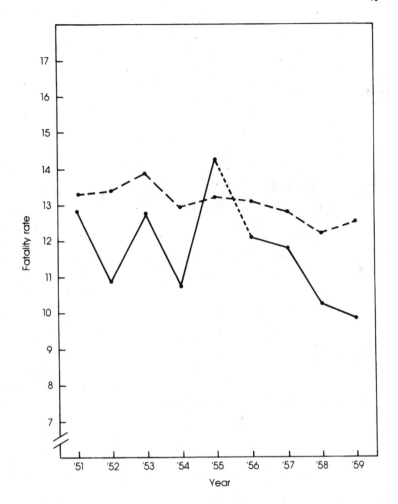

Figure 9-3
Control series
design comparing
Connecticut traffic
fatality rate (solid
line) with the
fatality rate of four
comparable states
(dashed line)

Source: Campbell, D. T. (1969). Reforms as experiments. *American Psychologist, 24,* 409–429. Copyright 1969 by the American Psychological Association. Reprinted by permission.

the fatality rates in the control states remained relatively constant while those in Connecticut consistently declined led Campbell to conclude that the crackdown did indeed have some effect.

You may be wondering about the evaluation of the D.A.R.E. program. Many researchers have, in fact, conducted outcome evaluation studies. For example, Becker, Agopian, and Yeh (1992) used a nonequivalent control group pretest-posttest design to examine drug use among 5th-graders in schools with a D.A.R.E. program in comparison to 5th-graders in schools that had not developed a D.A.R.E. program. The results of this study, along with others using different methods, have generally concluded that D.A.R.E. has very small effects on the participants (cf. Ennett, Tobler, Ringwalt, & Flewelling, 1994).

SINGLE-SUBJECT EXPERIMENTS

Single-subject experiments frequently take place within the context of research on reinforcement. This research tradition can be traced to the work of B. F. Skinner (1953) on reinforcement schedules, and it is often seen in applied and clinical settings when behavior modification techniques are used. However, the techniques and logic of **single-subject experiments** can be readily applied to other research areas as well.

Single-subject designs were developed from a need to determine whether an experimental manipulation had an effect on a single research participant. In a single-subject design, the subject's behavior is measured over time during a **baseline** control period. The manipulation is then introduced during a treatment period, and the subject's behavior continues to be observed. A change in the subject's behavior from baseline to treatment periods is evidence for the effectiveness of the manipulation. The problem, however, is that there could be many reasons for the change other than the experimental treatment. For example, some other event may have coincided with the introduction of the treatment. The single-subject designs described in the following sections address this problem.

Reversal designs

As noted, the basic issue in single-subject experiments is how to determine that the manipulation of the independent variable had an effect. One method is to demonstrate the reversibility of the manipulation. A simple **reversal design** takes the following form:

A (baseline period) ➔ B (treatment period) ➔ A (baseline period)

This design, called an ABA design, requires that behavior be observed during the baseline control (A) period and again during the treatment (B) period, and also during a second (A) baseline period after the experimental treatment has been removed. (Sometimes this is called a *withdrawal design*, in recognition of the fact that the treatment is removed or withdrawn.) For example, the effect of a reinforcement procedure on a child's academic performance could be assessed with an ABA design. The number of correct homework problems could be measured each day during the baseline. A reinforcement treatment procedure would then be introduced in which the child received stars for correct problems; the stars could be accumulated and exchanged for toys or candy. Later, this treatment would be discontinued during the second (A) baseline period. Hypothetical data from such an experiment are shown in Figure 9-4. The fact that behavior changed when the treatment was introduced and reversed when the treatment was withdrawn is evidence for its effectiveness.

The ABA design can be greatly improved by extending it to an ABAB design, in which the experimental treatment is introduced a second time, or even an ABABAB design that allows the effect of the treatment to be tested a

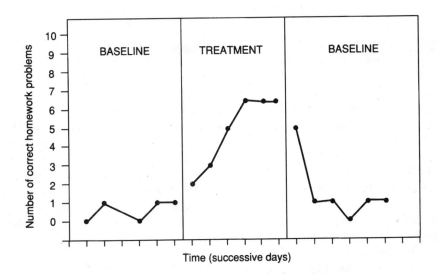

Figure 9-4
Hypothetical data from ABA reversal design

third time. This is done to address two problems with the ABA reversal design. First, a single reversal is not extremely powerful evidence for the effectiveness of the treatment. The observed reversal might have been due to a random fluctuation in the child's behavior. Or perhaps the treatment happened to coincide with some other event, such as the child's upcoming birthday, that caused the change (and the postbirthday reversal). These possibilities are much less likely if the treatment has been shown to have an effect two or more times; random or coincidental events are unlikely to be responsible for both reversals. The second problem is ethical. As Barlow and Hersen (1984) point out, it doesn't seem right to end the design with the withdrawal of a treatment that may be very beneficial for the participant. Using an ABAB design provides the opportunity to observe a second reversal when the treatment is introduced again. The sequence ends with the treatment rather than the withdrawal of the treatment.

A control group also may be used in a reversal design. For example, one group of researchers used reinforcement to increase ridership on a campus bus system (Everett, Hayward, & Meyers, 1974). Riders were counted on two different buses for 36 days. The experimental manipulation consisted of giving a token to each rider on one of the specially marked buses; the tokens could be exchanged for goods and services at local stores. No tokens were used on the control bus. An ABA design was used. The first 16 days were a baseline period, and during this phase, ridership on each bus was about 250 people per day. The experimental manipulation was introduced on days 17–24. During this period, ridership on the experimental bus was about 400 per day; there was no change in ridership on the control bus. The token system was discontinued on day 25, and ridership was monitored on both buses through day 36. Ridership on the experimental bus returned to baseline levels during this period and was no longer greater than ridership on the control bus.

Multiple baseline designs

It may have occurred to you that a reversal of some behaviors may be impossible or unethical. For example, it would be unethical to reverse treatment that reduces dangerous or illegal behaviors, such as indecent exposure or alcoholism, even if the possibility exists that a second introduction of the treatment might result in another change. Other treatments might produce a long-lasting change in behavior that is not reversible. In such cases, multiple measures over time can be made before and after the manipulation. If the manipulation is effective, a change in behavior will be immediately observed, and the change will continue to be reflected in further measures of the behavior. In a **multiple baseline design,** the effectiveness of the treatment is demonstrated when a behavior changes only after the manipulation is introduced. To demonstrate the effectiveness of the treatment, such a change must be observed under *multiple* circumstances to rule out the possibility that other events were responsible.

There are several variations of the multiple baseline design (Barlow & Hersen, 1984). In the multiple baseline *across subjects*, the behavior of several subjects is measured over time; for each subject, though, the manipulation is introduced at a different point in time. Figure 9-5 shows data from a hypothetical smoking reduction experiment with three subjects. Note that introduction of the manipulation was followed by a change in behavior for each subject. However, because this change occurred across individuals and the manipulation was introduced at a different time for each subject, we can rule out explanations based on chance, historical events, and so on.

In a multiple baseline *across behaviors*, several different behaviors of a single subject are measured over time. At different times, the same manipulation is applied to each of the behaviors. For example, a reward system could be instituted to increase the socializing, grooming, and reading behaviors of a psychiatric patient. The reward system would be applied to each of these behaviors at different times. Demonstrating that each behavior increased when the reward system was applied would be evidence for the effectiveness of the manipulation.

The third variation is the multiple baseline *across situations*, in which the same behavior is measured in different settings, such as at home and at work. Again, a manipulation is introduced at a different time in each setting, with the expectation that a change in the behavior in each situation will occur only after the manipulation.

Replications in single-subject designs

The procedures for use with a single subject can, of course, be replicated with other subjects, greatly enhancing the generalizability of the results. Usually, reports of research that employs single-subject experimental procedures do present the results from several subjects (and often in several settings). The tradition in single-subject research has been to present the results from each

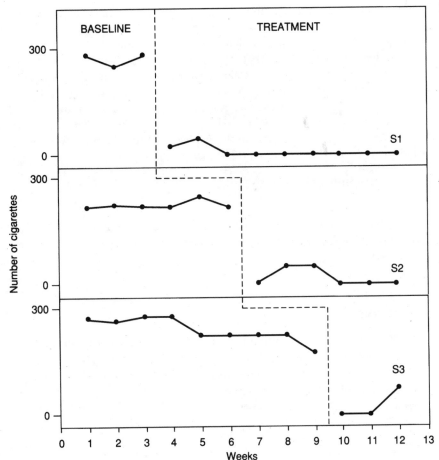

Figure 9-5 Hypothetical data from multiple baseline design across subjects

subject individually rather than grouping data and presenting overall means. Sidman (1960), a leading spokesperson for this tradition, has pointed out that grouping the data from a number of subjects by using group means can sometimes give a misleading picture of individual responses to the manipulation. For example, the manipulation may be effective in changing the behavior of some subjects but not others. This was true in a study of seat belt use (Barry & Geller, 1991). Different seat belt signal conditions were studied (e.g., a second signal that would come on if the subject did not buckle up after an initial signal). Among 13 subjects, 6 always used their seat belt irrespective of the condition, and 3 never used their seat belt. For the other 4 subjects, the signal conditions did have an effect. Because the emphasis of the study was on the individual subject, the pattern of results was quickly revealed.

Single-subject designs are useful for studying many research problems. They can be especially valuable for someone who is applying some change

171

technique in a natural environment—for example, a teacher who is trying a new technique in the classroom. In addition, complex statistical analyses are not required for single-subject designs. Despite this tradition of single-subject data presentation, however, the trend increasingly has been to study larger samples using the procedures of single-subject designs and presenting the average scores of groups during baseline and treatment periods (Barlow & Hersen, 1984). One reason for this is the relative lack of generalizability of single-subject research. A more important reason is that not all variables can be studied with the reversal and multiple baseline procedures used in single-subject experiments. Specifically, these procedures are useful only when the behavior is reversible or when one can expect a relatively dramatic shift in behavior after the manipulation.

We have now described most of the major approaches to designing research. In the next two chapters, methods of analyzing research data are considered.

STUDY TERMS

Baseline	Multiple baseline design	Quasi-experimental design
Control series design	Nonequivalent control group pretest-posttest design	Reversal design
Interrupted time series design		Single-subject experiment

REVIEW QUESTIONS

1. Describe what a program evaluation researcher's goals would be when addressing each of the four types of evaluation research questions.
2. Why might a researcher use a quasi-experimental design rather than a true experimental design?
3. Describe the nonequivalent control group pretest-posttest design. Why is this a quasi-experimental design rather than a true experiment?
4. Describe the interrupted time series and the control series designs. What are the strengths of the control series design as compared to the interrupted time series design?
5. What is a reversal design? Why is an ABAB design superior to an ABA design?
6. What is meant by *baseline* in a single-subject design?
7. What is a multiple baseline design? Why is it used? Distinguish between multiple baseline designs across subjects, across behaviors, and across situations.

ACTIVITY QUESTIONS

1. A student club is trying to decide whether to implement a peer tutoring program for students who are enrolled in the statistics class in your department. Club members who have completed the statistics class would offer to provide tutoring to students currently enrolled in the class. You decide to take the lessons of program evaluation seriously, and so you develop a strategy to conduct evaluation research.

   a. How would you measure whether there is a need for such a program?

   b. Briefly describe how you might implement a tutoring program. How would you monitor the program?

   c. Propose a quasi-experimental design to evaluate whether the program is effective.

   d. How might you determine the economic efficiency of such a program?

2. Many elementary schools have implemented a "sustained silent reading" period each day, during which students, faculty, and staff spend 15–20 minutes silently reading a book of their choice. Advocates of this policy claim that the activity encourages pleasure reading outside the required silent reading time. Design a nonequivalent control group pretest-posttest quasi-experiment to test this claim. Include a well-reasoned dependent measure as well.

3. For the preceding situation, discuss the advantages and disadvantages of using a quasi-experimental design in contrast to conducting a true experiment.

4. Your dog gets lonely while you are at work and consequently engages in destructive activities such as pulling down curtains or strewing wastebasket contents all over the floor. You decide that playing a radio while you are gone might help. How might you determine whether this "treatment" is effective?

5. Your best friend frequently suffers from severe headaches. You've noticed that your friend consumes a great deal of diet cola, and so you consider the hypothesis that the artificial sweetener in the cola is responsible for the headaches. Devise a way to test your hypothesis using a single-subject design. What do you expect to find if your hypothesis is correct? If you obtain the expected results, what do you conclude about the effect of the artificial sweetener on headaches?

10

Understanding Research Results: Description and Correlation

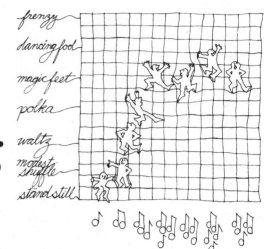

Statistics are used to help understand the data collected in research investigations. There are two reasons for using statistics. First, statistics are used to describe the data. Second, statistics are used to make inferences, on the basis of sample data, about a population. We examine descriptive statistics and correlation in this chapter; inferential statistics are discussed in Chapter 11. The focus is on the underlying logic and general procedures for statistical decision making. Specific calculations for a variety of statistics are provided in Appendix B.

SCALES OF MEASUREMENT

Before looking at any statistics, we need to consider the nature of the variables being studied. Whenever a variable is studied, there is an operational definition of the variable. The operational definition is the specific method used to manipulate or measure the variable (see Chapter 4). There must be at least two values or levels of the variable. The levels can be conceptualized as a scale that uses one of four kinds of measurement scales: nominal, ordinal, interval, and ratio. The scale that is used determines the types of statistics that are appropriate when the results of a study are analyzed. Also, the conclusions one draws about the meaning of a particular score on a variable depend on which type of scale was used for measuring the variable.

Nominal scales

Nominal scales have no numerical or quantitative properties. Instead, categories or groups simply differ from one another (sometimes nominal variables are called "categorical" variables). An obvious example is the variable of sex or gender. A person is classified as either male or female. Being male does not imply a greater amount of "sexness" than being female; the two levels are merely different. This is called a nominal scale because we simply assign names to different categories. Another example is the classification of undergraduates according to major. A psychology major would not be entitled to a higher number than a history major, for instance. Even if you were to assign numbers to the different categories, the numbers would be meaningless, except for identification.

In an experiment, the independent variable can also be a nominal or categorical variable. For example, in an experiment described in Chapter 8, Punnett (1986) motivated workers with either a specific, difficult goal or a vague goal to "do your best." The goal-setting variable is clearly nominal because the two groups used different goals that had no numerical properties.

Ordinal scales

Ordinal scales do involve quantitative distinctions. Ordinal scales allow us to rank order the levels of the variable being studied.

175

One example of an ordinal scale is provided by the movie rating system used in the television section of my local newspaper. Movies on TV are given one, two, three, or four checks, based on these descriptions:

✓✓✓✓ New or old, a classic

✓✓✓   First-rate

✓✓   Flawed; may have moments

✓   Desperation time

The rating system is not a nominal scale because the number of checks is meaningful in terms of a continuum of quality. However, the checks allow us only to rank order the movies. A four-check movie is better than a three-check movie; a three-check movie is better than a two-check movie; and so on. Although we have this quantitative information about the movies, we cannot say that the difference between a one-check and a two-check movie is always the same or that it is equal to the difference between a two-check and a three-check movie. No particular value is attached to the intervals between the numbers used in the rating scale.

Interval and ratio scales

In an **interval scale,** the difference between the numbers on the scale is meaningful. Specifically, the intervals between the numbers are equal in size. The difference between 1 and 2 on the scale, for example, is the same as the difference between 2 and 3. Interval scales generally have five or more quantitative levels.

A household thermometer (Fahrenheit or Celsius) measures temperature on an interval scale. The difference in temperature between 40° and 50° is equal to the difference between 70° and 80°. However, there is no absolute zero on the scale that would indicate the absence of temperature. The zero on any interval scale is only an arbitrary reference point. This means that we cannot form ratios of the numbers on interval scales. That is, we cannot say that one number on the scale represents twice as much (or three times as much, and so forth) temperature as another number. You cannot say, for example, that 60° is twice as warm as 30°.

An example of an interval scale in the behavioral sciences might be a personality measure of a trait such as extraversion. If the measurement is an interval scale, we cannot make a statement such as "the person who scored 20 is twice as extraverted as the person who scored 10" because there is no absolute zero point that indicates an absence of the trait being measured.

In the behavioral sciences, it is often difficult to know precisely whether an ordinal or an interval scale is being used. However, it is often useful to assume that the variable is being measured on an interval scale, because interval scales allow for more sophisticated statistical treatments than do ordinal scales. Of course, if the measure is a rank ordering (for example, a rank ordering of students in a class on the basis of popularity), an ordinal scale clearly is being used.

Ratio scales do have an absolute zero point that indicates the absence of the variable being measured. Examples include many physical measures, such as length, weight, or time. With a ratio scale, such statements as "a person who weighs 220 pounds weighs twice as much as a person who weighs 110 pounds" are possible.

Ratio scales are used in the behavioral sciences when variables that involve physical measures are being studied—particularly time measures such as reaction time, rate of responding, and duration of response. However, many variables in the behavioral sciences are less precise and so use nominal, ordinal, or interval scale measures. It should also be noted that the statistical tests for interval and ratio scales are the same.

ANALYZING THE RESULTS OF RESEARCH INVESTIGATIONS

Scales of measurement have important implications for the way that the results of research investigations are described and analyzed. Most research focuses on the study of relationships between variables. Depending upon the way that the variables were studied, there are three basic ways of describing the results: (1) comparing group percentages, (2) correlating scores of individuals on two variables, and (3) comparing group means.

Comparing group percentages

Suppose you want to know whether males and females differ in their interest in travel. In your study, you ask males and females whether they like or dislike to travel. To describe your results, you will need to calculate the percentage of females who like to travel and compare this with the percentage of males who like to travel. Suppose you tested 50 females and 50 males and found that 40 of the females and 30 of the males indicated that they like to travel. In describing your findings, you would report that 80% of the females like to travel in comparison to 60% of the males. Thus, a relationship between the gender and travel variables appears to exist. Note that we are focusing on percentages because the travel variable is nominal: Liking and disliking are simply two different categories. After describing your data, the next step would be to perform a statistical analysis to determine if there is a statistically significant difference. Statistical significance is discussed in Chapter 11; statistical analysis procedures are described in Appendix B.

Correlating individual scores

A second type of analysis is needed when you do not have distinct groups of subjects. Instead, individuals are measured on two variables, and each variable has a range of numerical values. Later in this chapter, we will consider an analysis of data on the relationship between location in a classroom and grades in the class: Do people who sit near the front receive higher grades?

177

**Table 10-1
Scores on
aggression
measure in a
hypothetical
experiment on
modeling and
aggression**

Model group	No-model group
3	1
4	2
5	2
5	3
5	3
5	3
6	4
6	4
6	4
7	5
$\Sigma X = 52$	$\Sigma X = 31$
$\bar{X} = 5.20$	$\bar{X} = 3.10$
$s^2 = 1.289$	$s^2 = 1.433$
$s = 1.135$	$s = 1.197$
$n = 10$	$n = 10$

Comparing group means

Much research is designed to compare the mean responses of two or more groups of subjects on a measured variable. For example, in an experiment designed to study the effect of exposure to an aggressive adult, children in one group might observe an adult "model" behaving aggressively while children in a control group do not. Each child then plays alone for 10 minutes in a room containing a number of toys while observers record the number of times the child behaves aggressively while playing.

In this case, you would be interested in comparing the mean number of aggressive acts by children in the two conditions to determine if the children who observed the model were more aggressive than the children in the control condition. Hypothetical data from such an experiment in which there were 10 children in each condition are shown in Table 10-1; the scores in the table represent the number of aggressive acts by each child. After completing an experiment, it is important to understand your results by carefully describing your data. We begin by constructing frequency distributions.

FREQUENCY DISTRIBUTIONS

When analyzing results, it is useful to start by constructing a frequency distribution of the data. A **frequency distribution** indicates the number of subjects who receive each possible score on a variable. Frequency distributions of exam scores are familiar to most college students—they tell how many students received a given score on an exam. Along with the number of individuals associated with each response, it is useful to examine the percentage associated with this number.

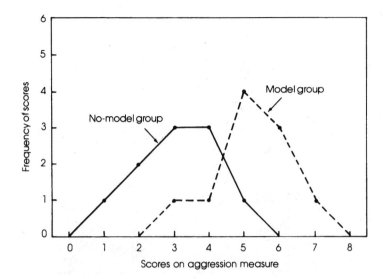

Figure 10-1 Frequency polygons illustrating the distributions of scores in Table 10-1

Note: Each frequency polygon is anchored at scores that were not obtained by anyone (0 and 6 in the no-model group; 2 and 8 in the model group).

Frequency polygons

Frequency distributions can be depicted in a graph such as Figure 10-1, which presents the data from the modeling aggression experiment. These two **frequency polygons**—one for each group—show how many people received each score on the aggression measure. The solid line represents the no-model group, and the dotted line stands for the model group.

Histograms

Histograms, or **bar graphs,** are an alternative method of presenting a frequency distribution. In a histogram, a bar is drawn for each score on the measure; the length of the bar depicts the number of persons who received that score. Figure 10-2 illustrates a histogram for the no-model group only.

What can you discover by examining frequency distributions? First, you can directly observe how your participants responded. You can see what scores are most frequent and you can look at the shape of the distribution of scores. You can tell if there are any "outliers"—scores that are unusual, unexpected, or very different from the scores of other participants. In an experiment, you can compare the distribution of scores in the groups. The information value of frequency distributions becomes greater as you increase the number of observations that you are trying to understand.

DESCRIPTIVE STATISTICS

In addition to examining the distribution of scores, you can calculate descriptive statistics. **Descriptive statistics** allow researchers to make precise statements about the data. Two statistics are needed to describe the data. A single

179

**Figure 10-2
Histogram
showing the
distribution of
scores in the no-
model group**

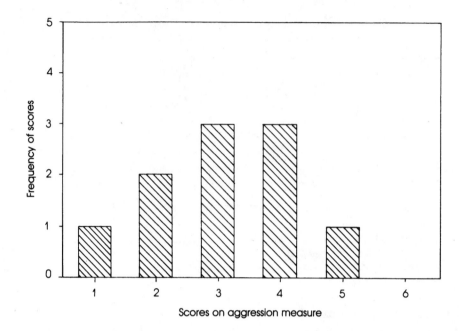

number can be used to describe the central tendency, or how subjects scored overall. Another number describes the variability, or how widely the distribution of scores is spread. These two numbers summarize the information contained in a frequency distribution.

Central tendency

A **central tendency** statistic tells us what the sample as a whole, or on the average, is like. There are three measures of central tendency—the mean, the median, and the mode. The **mean** of a set of scores is obtained by adding all the scores and dividing by the number of scores. It is symbolized as $\bar{X}$, and in scientific reports, it is abbreviated as M. The mean is an appropriate indicator of central tendency only when scores are measured on an interval or ratio scale, because the actual values of the numbers are used in calculating the statistic. In Table 10-1, the mean score for the no-model group is 3.10 and for the model group is 5.20. Note that the Greek letter Σ (sigma) in Table 10-1 is a statistical notation for summing a set of numbers. Thus, ΣX is shorthand for "sum of the values in a set of scores."

The **median** is the score that divides the group in half (with 50% scoring below and 50% scoring above the median). In scientific reports, the median is abbreviated as Mdn. The median is appropriate when scores are on an ordinal scale because it takes into account only the rank order of the scores. The median for the no-model group is 3 and for the model group is 5.

The **mode** is the most frequent score. The mode is the only measure of central tendency that is appropriate if a nominal scale was used. The mode does not use the actual values on the scale, but simply indicates the most frequently occurring value. There are two modal values for the no-model group —3 and 4 occur equally frequently. The mode for the model group is 5.

The median or mode can be a better indicator of central tendency than the mean if a few unusual scores bias the mean. For example, the median family income of a county or state is usually a better measure of central tendency than the mean family income. Because a relatively small number of individuals have extremely high incomes, using the mean would make it appear that the "average" person makes more money than is actually the case.

Variability

We can also determine how much **variability** exists in a set of scores. A measure of variability is a number that characterizes the amount of spread in a distribution of scores. One such measure is the **standard deviation,** symbolized as s, which indicates the average deviation of scores from the mean. In scientific reports, it is abbreviated as SD. The standard deviation is derived by first calculating the **variance,** symbolized as s^2 (the standard deviation is the square root of the variance). The standard deviation of a set of scores is small when most people have similar scores close to the mean. The standard deviation becomes larger as more people have scores that lie further from the mean value. For the model group, the standard deviation is 1.135, which tells us that most scores in that condition lie 1.135 units above and below the mean—that is, between 4.065 and 6.335. Thus, the mean and the standard deviation provide a great deal of information about the distribution. Note that, as with the mean, the calculation of the standard deviation uses the actual values of the scores; thus, the standard deviation is appropriate only for interval and ratio scale variables.

Another measure of variability is the *range,* which is simply the difference between the highest score and the lowest score. The range for both the model and no-model groups is 4.

GRAPHING RELATIONSHIPS

Graphing relationships between variables was discussed briefly in Chapter 4. A common way to graph relationships between variables is to use a line graph similar to the frequency polygons just discussed. Figure 10-3 illustrates the graphing of the means for the no-model and model groups. A point is placed representing the means in each group, and a line is drawn to connect the points. As an alternative to the line graph, a histogram could be prepared. A bar would be drawn for each group to the point that represents the mean of each group.

181

**Figure 10-3
Graph of the
results of the
modeling
experiment**

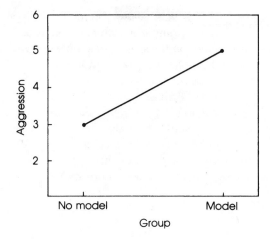

**Figure 10-4
Two ways to
graph the same
data**

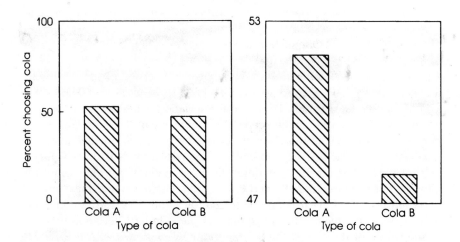

It is interesting to note a common trick that is sometimes used by scientists and all too commonly used by advertisers. The trick is to exaggerate the distance between points on the measurement scale to make the results appear more dramatic than they really are. Suppose, for example, that a cola company (cola A) conducts a taste test that shows that 52% of the participants prefer cola A and 48% prefer cola B. How should the cola company present these results? Figure 10-4 shows the most honest method, as well as one that is considerably more dramatic. It is always wise to look carefully at the numbers on the scales depicted in graphs.

CORRELATION COEFFICIENTS:
DESCRIBING THE STRENGTH OF RELATIONSHIPS

A **correlation coefficient** is a statistic that describes how strongly variables are related to one another. The values of a correlation coefficient can range

Subject identification number	Seating	Exam score	
01	2	95	**Table 10-2**
02	5	50	**Pairs of scores for**
03	1	85	**10 subjects on**
04	4	75	**seating pattern**
05	3	75	**and exam score**
06	5	60	**(fictitious data)**
07	2	80	
08	3	70	
09	1	90	
10	4	70	

from 0.00 to 1.00. A correlation of 0.00 indicates that there is no relationship at all. The nearer a correlation is to 1.00 (plus or minus), the stronger the relationship. Indeed, a 1.00 correlation is sometimes called a perfect relationship, because the two variables go together in a perfect fashion.

Data from studies examining similarities of intelligence test scores among siblings illustrate the connection between the magnitude of a correlation coefficient and the strength of a relationship. The relationship between scores of identical twins is very strong (correlation of .86), demonstrating a strong similarity of test scores in these pairs of individuals. The correlation for fraternal twins reared together is less strong, with a correlation of .60. The correlation among nontwin siblings raised together is .47, and the correlation among nontwin siblings reared apart is .24 (cf. Bouchard & McGue, 1981).

There are many different types of correlation coefficients. Each coefficient is calculated somewhat differently depending on the measurement scale that applies to the two variables. We will focus on the Pearson product-moment correlation coefficient, symbolized as r.

Pearson r correlation coefficient

The Pearson r correlation coefficient is appropriate when the values of both variables are on an interval or ratio scale. To calculate a correlation coefficient, we need to obtain pairs of observations from each subject. Thus, each individual has two scores, one on each of the variables. Table 10-2 shows fictitious data for 10 students who were measured on the variables of classroom seating pattern and exam grade. Students in the first row receive a seating score of 1, those in the second row receive a 2, and so on. Once we have made our observations, we can see if the two variables are related. Do the variables go together in a systematic fashion?

As with all correlation coefficients, the values of r can range from 0.00 to 1.00. However, the Pearson r yields additional information about the direction of the relationship. The values of r range from 0.00 to +1.00 in a positive direction and from 0.00 to –1.00 in a negative direction. The plus and minus

**Figure 10-5
Scatterplots of
perfect (±1.00)
relationships**

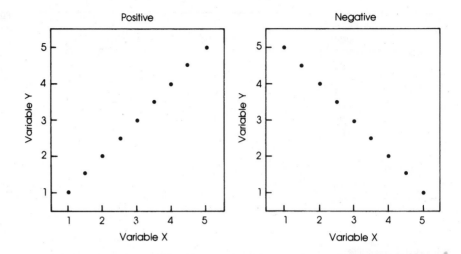

signs indicate whether there is a positive linear or negative linear relationship between the two variables. The absolute size of r is the coefficient that indicates the strength of the relationship: The nearer r is to 1.00 (plus or minus), the stronger the relationship (positive or negative).

The data in Table 10-2 can be visualized in a scatterplot in which each pair of scores is plotted as a single point in a diagram. Figure 10-5 shows scatterplots for a perfect positive relationship (+1.00) and for a perfect negative relationship (–1.00). You can easily see why these are perfect relationships: The scores on the two variables fall on a straight line that is on the diagonal of the diagram. Each person's score on one variable goes perfectly with his or her score on the other variable. If we know an individual's score on one of the variables, we can predict exactly what his or her score will be on the other variable. Such "perfect" relationships are rarely if ever observed in actuality.

The scatterplots in Figure 10-6 show patterns of correlation you are more likely to encounter in exploring research findings. The first diagram shows pairs of scores with a positive correlation of +.65; the second diagram shows a negative relationship, –.77. The data points in these two scatterplots reveal a general pattern of either a positive or negative relationship, but the relationships are not perfect. You can make a general prediction in the first diagram, for instance, that the higher the score on one variable, the higher the score on the second variable. However, if you know a person's score on the first variable, you can't *perfectly* predict what that person's score will be on the second variable. To confirm this, take a look at value 1 on variable X (the horizontal axis) in the positive scatterplot. Looking up, you will see that two individuals had a score of 1. One of these had a score of 1 on variable Y (the vertical axis), and the other had a score of 3. The data points do not fall on the perfect diagonal. Instead, there is a variation (scatter) from the perfect diagonal line.

The third diagram shows a scatterplot in which there is absolutely no correlation ($r = 0.00$). The points fall all over the diagram in a completely

184

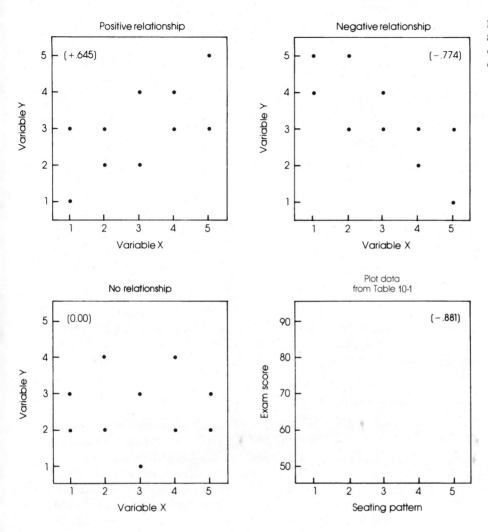

**Figure 10-6
Scatterplots
depicting patterns
of correlation**

random pattern. Thus, scores on variable X are not related to scores on variable Y.

The fourth diagram has been left blank so that you can plot the scores from the data in Table 10-2. The X (horizontal) axis has been labeled for the seating pattern variable, and the Y (vertical) axis for the exam score variable. To complete the scatterplot, you will need to plot the 10 pairs of scores. For each individual in the sample, find the score on the seating pattern variable; then go up until you reach that person's exam score. A point placed there will describe the score on both variables. There will be 10 points on the finished scatterplot.

The correlation coefficient calculated from these data shows a negative relationship between the variables ($r = -.88$). In other words, as the seating

185

Figure 10-7
Scatterplot of a curvilinear relationship (Pearson product-moment correlation coefficient = 0.00)

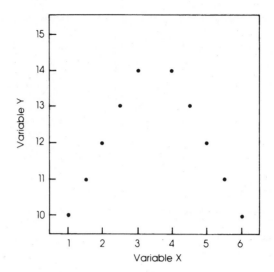

distance from the front of the class increases, the exam score decreases. Although these data are fictitious, they are consistent with actual research findings (Brooks & Rebata, 1991).

Important considerations

Restriction of range   It is important that the researcher sample from the full range of possible values of both variables. If the range of possible values is restricted, the magnitude of the correlation coefficient is reduced. For example, if the range of seating pattern scores is restricted to the first two rows, you will not get an accurate picture of the relationship between seating pattern and exam score. In fact, when only scores of students sitting in the first two rows are considered, the correlation between the two variables is exactly 0.00. The reason for needing a full range of values is the same as the reason for needing a strong manipulation when conducting an experiment (see Chapter 7). In both cases, it is easier to detect a relationship when low and high values of the variable are represented.

The problem of restriction of range occurs when the individuals in your sample are very similar or *homogenous*. If you are studying age as a variable, for instance, testing only 6- and 7-year-olds will reduce your chances of finding age effects. Likewise, trying to study the correlates of intelligence will be almost impossible if everyone in your sample is very similar in intelligence (e.g., the senior class of a prestigious private college).

Curvilinear relationship   The Pearson product-moment correlation coefficient (r) is designed to detect only linear relationships. If the relationship is curvilinear, as in the scatterplot shown in Figure 10-7, the correlation coeffi-

186

cient will not indicate the existence of a relationship. The Pearson *r* correlation coefficient calculated from these data is exactly 0.00, even though the two variables clearly are related.

When the relationship is curvilinear, another type of correlation coefficient must be used to determine the strength of the relationship. Because a relationship may be curvilinear, it is important to construct a scatterplot in addition to looking at the magnitude of the correlation coefficient. The scatterplot is valuable because it gives a visual indication of the shape of the relationship.

CORRELATION COEFFICIENTS AND THE CORRELATIONAL METHOD

There is a very confusing aspect of the term *correlation* as it has been used over many years by researchers in the behavioral sciences. We have reviewed the distinction between the experimental and correlational methods of studying relationships among variables. We have seen that a correlation coefficient functions as an index of the strength of relationships between variables. One might expect that researchers use correlation coefficients only in conjunction with the correlational method, because the term *correlation* is common to both. However, that is not correct. The term *correlational method* refers to a nonexperimental study, while *correlation coefficient* refers to an index of the strength of the relationship between two variables *irrespective of whether the experimental or correlational method was used.*

This confusion arises because historically the results of most studies using the correlational method have been analyzed using Pearson *r* correlation coefficients. However, researchers have become aware that correlation *coefficients* should always be used as an index of strength of relationships in both correlational and experimental research. The result is that more and more researchers are reporting correlation coefficients in both correlational and experimental research. The term *effect size* increasingly is being used to refer to all such correlation coefficients.

EFFECT SIZE

Effect size refers to the strength of association between variables. Use of this term eliminates some of the confusion over the terms *correlation* and *correlational method.* The Pearson *r* correlation coefficient is one indicator of effect size; it indicates the strength of the linear association between two variables. In an experiment with two or more treatment conditions, some other types of correlation coefficients can be calculated to indicate the magnitude of the effect of the independent variable on the dependent variable. For example, in our experiment on the effects of witnessing an aggressive model on children's aggressive behavior, we compared the means of two groups. In addition to knowing the means, it is valuable to know the effect size. An effect size correlation coefficient can be calculated for the modeling and aggression experiment. The effect size value is .68; the formula for calculating the effect size is described in Chapter 11. As with all correlation coefficients, the values of the effect size correlation can range from 0.00 to 1.00.

The advantage of reporting effect size is that it provides us with a scale of values that is consistent across all types of studies. The values range from 0.00 to 1.00, irrespective of the variables used, the particular research design selected, or the number of participants studied.

STATISTICAL SIGNIFICANCE

The emphasis in this chapter has been on *describing* the data obtained in a study. After describing the data, you will usually want to make a decision concerning the statistical significance of the results. Is the difference between the means of the model and no-model groups a statistically significant difference? This is largely a matter of inferring whether the results will hold up if the experiment is repeated several times, each time with a new sample of research participants. Inferential statistics are used to determine whether we can, in fact, make statements that the results reflect what would happen if we were to conduct the experiment over and over again with multiple samples. Statistical significance is discussed in Chapter 11. The remainder of this chapter focuses on additional topics of correlation.

REGRESSION EQUATIONS

Regression equations are calculations used to predict a person's score on one variable when that person's score on another variable is already known. They are essentially "prediction equations" that are based on known information about the relationship between the two variables. For example, after discovering that seating pattern and exam score are related, a regression equation may be calculated that predicts anyone's exam score based only on information about where the person sits in the class.

The general form of a regression equation is

$$Y = a + bX$$

where Y is the score we wish to predict, X is the known score, a is a constant, and b is a weighting adjustment factor that is multiplied by X (the weight is necessary because X and Y are measured on different scales). In our seating–exam score example, the following regression equation is calculated from the data:

$$Y = 99 + (-8)X$$

Thus, if we know a person's score on X (seating), we can insert that into the equation and predict what that person's score on Y (exam score) will be. If the person's X score is 2, we can predict that Y = 99 + (–16), or that the person's exam score will be 83. Through the use of regression equations such as these, colleges can use SAT scores to predict college grades.

When researchers are interested in predicting some future behavior (called the *criterion variable*) on the basis of a person's score on some other variable (called the *predictor variable*), it is first necessary to demonstrate that there is a reasonably high correlation between the criterion and predictor variables. The regression equation then provides the method for making predictions on the basis of the predictor variable score only.

MULTIPLE CORRELATION

Thus far we have focused on the correlation between two variables at a time. Researchers recognize that a number of different variables may be related to a given behavior. A technique called **multiple correlation** is used to combine a number of predictor variables to increase the accuracy of prediction of a given criterion variable.

A multiple correlation is the correlation between a combined set of predictor variables and a single criterion variable. Taking all of the predictor variables into account usually permits greater accuracy of prediction than if any single predictor is considered alone. For example, applicants to graduate school in psychology could be evaluated on a combined set of predictor variables using multiple correlation. The predictor variables might be (1) college grades, (2) scores on the Graduate Record Exam Aptitude Test, (3) scores on the Graduate Record Exam Psychology Test, and (4) favorability of letters of recommendation. No one of these factors is a perfect predictor of success in graduate school, but this combination of variables can yield a more accurate prediction. The multiple correlation is usually higher than the correlation between any one of the predictor variables and the criterion variable.

In actual practice, researchers would use an extension of the regression equation technique discussed previously. A multiple regression equation can be calculated that takes the following form:

$$Y = a + b_1 X_1 + b_2 X_2 + \ldots + b_n X_n$$

where Y is the criterion variable, X_1 to X_n are the predictor variables, a is a constant, and b_1 to b_n are weights that are multiplied by scores on the predictor variables. For example, a regression equation for graduate school admissions would be:

Predicted grade point average = $a + b_1$ (college grades)
$+ b_2$ (score on GRE Aptitude Test)
$+ b_3$ (score on GRE Psychology Exam)
$+ b_4$ (favorability of recommendation letters).

189

More and more researchers are using multiple correlation and regression analysis to study basic research topics. For example, Ajzen and Fishbein (1980) have developed a model that uses multiple correlation and regression to predict specific behavioral intentions (e.g., to attend church on Sunday, buy a certain product, or join an alcohol recovery program) on the basis of two predictor variables. These are (1) attitude toward the behavior and (2) perceived normative pressure to engage in the behavior. In one study, these researchers demonstrated that the multiple correlation between intention to buy a brand of beer and the combined predictors of attitude and norm was +.79. The regression equation was as follows:

$$Intention = .76(attitude) + .27(norm)$$

This equation is somewhat different from the ones described previously. In basic research, you are not interested in predicting an exact score (such as an exam score or GPA), and so the mathematical calculations can assume that all variables are measured on the same scale. When this is done, the weighting factor reflects the magnitude of the correlation between the criterion variable and each predictor variable. In the beer purchase example, the weight for the attitude predictor is higher than the weight for the norm predictor; this shows that, in this case, attitudes are more important as a predictor of intention than are norms. However, for other behaviors, it may be found that attitudes are less important than norms.

It is also possible to visualize the regression equation. In the beer purchase example, the relationships among variables could be diagrammed as follows:

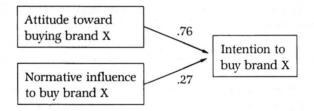

PARTIAL CORRELATION AND THE THIRD-VARIABLE PROBLEM

Researchers face the third-variable problem in correlational research when some uncontrolled third variable may be responsible for the relationship between the two variables of interest. The problem doesn't exist in experimental research, because all extraneous variables are controlled either by keeping the variables constant or by using randomization. A technique called **partial correlation** provides a way of statistically controlling third variables. A partial correlation is a correlation between the two variables of interest, with the influence of the third variable removed from, or "partialed out of," the original correlation.

Suppose a researcher finds that the correlation between residential crowding and performance on a test is –.50. The researcher suspects that a

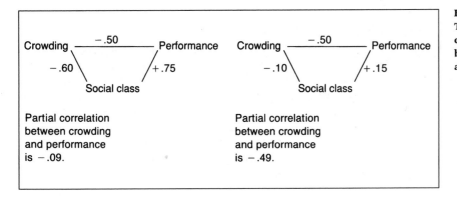

Figure 10-8
Two partial
correlations
between crowding
and performance

third variable may be operating. Social class, for example, could influence both crowding and performance. The use of partial correlations involves measuring subjects on the third variable in addition to the two primary variables. Thus, the researcher has to measure participants on all the variables: crowding, performance, and social class.

When a partial correlation between crowding and performance, with social class partialed out, is calculated, we can determine whether the original correlation is substantially reduced. Is our original correlation of –.50 lowered very much when the influence of social class is removed? Figure 10-8 shows two different partial correlations—in both, there is a –.50 correlation between crowding and performance. However, the first partial correlation drops to –.09 when social class is statistically controlled, and the second partial correlation remains high even when the influence of social class is removed. The outcome of the partial correlation depends on the magnitude of the correlations between the third variable and the two variables of primary interest.

STRUCTURAL MODELS

Recent advances in statistical theory and methods have resulted in techniques for testing **structural models** of relationships among variables using the correlational method. Although these methods are beyond the scope of this book, you should be aware that they exist (see James, Mulaik, & Brett, 1982; Coovert, Penner, & MacCallum, 1990; Tanaka, Panter, Winborne, & Huba, 1990). A structural model is an expected pattern of relationships among a set of variables. The proposed pattern is based on a theory of how the variables are causally related to one another. Thus, a popular term for conducting the statistical analysis is *causal modeling*. However, a more general term is *structural modeling*, because the techniques really allow researchers to test how well obtained data fit a theoretical "structure" among variables. (Also, the

**Figure 10-9
Example of a
causal or
structural model**

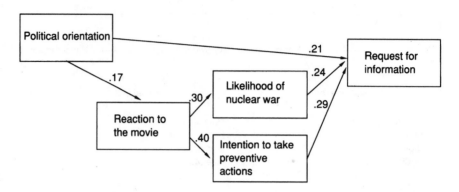

mathematical operations underlying the technique are based on structural equations.)

The diagram on attitudes and intentions shown previously is a very simple structural model. An example of a more complex model is shown in Figure 10-9. King (1985) developed the model from a study of reactions to viewing a television movie entitled *The Day After* (Oskamp, King, Burn, Konrad, Pollard, & White, 1985). The movie depicted the events that might follow a nuclear attack on the United States and was regarded as a film that contained an antinuclear message. The model shows the relationships among variables leading to a behavioral request to receive information from an antinuclear-war group. The variables in the model, in addition to the request for information, are political orientation (conservative–liberal), reaction to the movie (negative–positive), rated likelihood of nuclear war (low–high), and intention to take preventive actions concerning nuclear war (low–high).

Arrows leading from one variable to another depict obtained paths that relate the variables in the model. The coefficients are similar to the weights derived in the regression equations described previously. Focus your attention on the request for information variable. There are three arrows or paths to this variable: These are direct influences on the variable. The direct influences are political orientation, rated likelihood of nuclear war, and intention to take preventive actions. Reaction to the movie has an indirect effect on requests for information by directly influencing respondents' rated likelihood of nuclear attack and intentions to take preventive actions. Research that develops structural models such as this enables researchers to better understand complex networks of relationships among variables.

STUDY TERMS

Central tendency	Descriptive statistics	Frequency polygon
Correlation coefficient	Effect size	Histogram
Criterion variable	Frequency distribution	Interval scales

Mean	Partial correlation	Restriction of range
Median	Pearson r coefficient	Scatterplot
Mode	Predictor variable	Standard deviation
Multiple correlation	Range	Statistical significance
Nominal scales	Ratio scales	Structural model
Ordinal scales	Regression equations	Variability

REVIEW QUESTIONS

1. Distinguish between nominal, ordinal, interval, and ratio scales.
2. What is a frequency distribution?
3. Distinguish between a frequency polygon and a histogram, and construct one of each.
4. What is a measure of central tendency? Distinguish between the mean, median, and mode.
5. What is a measure of variability? Distinguish between the standard deviation and the range.
6. What is a correlation coefficient? What do the size and sign of the correlation coefficient tell us about the relationship between variables?
7. What is a scatterplot?
8. What happens when a scatterplot shows the relationship to be curvilinear?
9. What is the difference between a correlation coefficient/effect size and the correlational method?
10. What is a regression equation? How might an employer use a regression equation?
11. How does multiple correlation increase accuracy of prediction?
12. What is the purpose of partial correlation?
13. When a structural model is diagrammed, what information is conveyed by the arrows leading from one variable to another?

ACTIVITY QUESTIONS

1. Your favorite newspaper or news magazine is a rich source of descriptive statistics on a variety of topics. Examine the past week's newspapers and any news magazines in your home; describe at least five instances of actual data presented. These can include surveys, experiments, business data, and even sports information.
2. Hill (1990) studied the correlations between final exam score in an introductory sociology course and several other variables such as number of absences. The following Pearson r correlations with final exam score were obtained:

193

Overall college GPA	.72
Number of absences	–.51
Hours spent studying on weekdays	–.11 (not significant)
Hours spent studying on weekends	.31

Describe each correlation and draw graphs depicting the general shape of each relationship. Why might hours spent studying on weekends be correlated with grades but weekday studying not be?

3. Ask 20 students on campus how many units they are carrying this term, as well as how many hours per week they work in paid employment. Create a frequency distribution and find the mean for each data set. Construct a scatterplot showing the relationship between class load and hours per week employed. Does there appear to be a relationship between the variables? (Note: If there might be a restriction of range problem on your campus because few students work or most students take about the same number of units, ask different questions, such as the number of hours spent studying and watching television each week.)

4. Here are a number of references to variables. For each, identify whether a nominal, ordinal, interval, or ratio scale is being used:

   a. The temperatures in cities throughout the country that are listed in most newspapers.

   b. The birth weights of babies who were born at Wilshire General Hospital last week.

   c. The number of hours you spent studying each day during the past week.

   d. The amount of the tip left after each meal at a restaurant during a 3-hour period.

   e. The number of votes received by the Republican and Democratic candidates for Congress in your district in the 1996 election.

   f. The brand that is listed third in a consumer magazine's ranking of VCRs.

   g. Connecticut was voted the number one team in the poll of sportswriters, and Kansas was number two.

   h. Your friend's score on an intelligence test.

   i. The wall color in my office is yellow and the boss's office is white.

   j. The type of programming on each radio station in your city (e.g., KPSY plays jazz, KSOC is talk radio, etc.).

5. Prior to the start of the school year, Mrs. King reviewed the cumulative folders of the students in her 4th-grade class. She found that the standard deviation of the students' scores on the reading readiness test was exactly 0.00. What information does this provide her? How might that information prove useful?

CHAPTER

11

Understanding Research Results: Statistical Inference

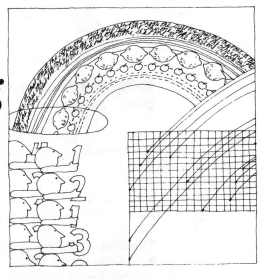

In the previous chapter, we examined ways of describing the results of a study. In addition to descriptive statistics, researchers are interested in inferential statistics. We need to infer whether the results that were obtained in a particular study would still occur if the study were repeated over and over again. In this chapter, we examine methods for doing so.

SAMPLES AND POPULATIONS

Inferential statistics are necessary because the results of a given study are based on data obtained from a single sample of research participants. Researchers rarely, if ever, study entire populations; the findings are based on sample data. In addition to describing the sample data, we want to make statements about populations. Would the results hold up if the experiment were conducted repeatedly, each time with a new sample?

In the hypothetical experiment described in Chapter 10 (see Table 10-1), mean aggression scores were obtained in model and no-model conditions. These means are different: Children who observe an aggressive model subsequently behave more aggressively than children who don't see the model. **Inferential statistics** are used to determine whether we can, in fact, make statements that the results reflect what would happen if we were to conduct the experiment again and again with multiple samples. In essence, we are asking whether we can infer that the difference in the sample means shown in Table 10-1 reflects a true difference in the population means.

You may be familiar with the basic issue here if you have paid attention to polling data reported in the media. The poll might tell you that 57% prefer the Republican candidate for an office while 43% favor the Democratic candidate. The report then says that these results are accurate to within 5 percentage points, with a 95% confidence level. This means that the researchers are very confident that, if they were able to study the entire population rather than a sample, the actual percentage who preferred the Republican candidate would be between 62 and 52% while the percentage preferring the Democrat would be between 48 and 38%. In this case, the researcher could predict with a great deal of certainty that the Republican candidate will win because there is no overlap in the projected population values.

Inferential statistics allow us to arrive at such conclusions on the basis of sample data. In our study with the model and no-model conditions, are we confident that the means are sufficiently different to infer that the difference would be obtained in an entire population?

INFERENTIAL STATISTICS

Much of the previous discussion of experimental design centered on the importance of making sure that the groups are equivalent in every way except the independent variable manipulation. Equivalency of groups is achieved by experimentally controlling all other variables or by randomization. The assumption is that if the groups are equivalent, any differences in the dependent variable must be due to the effect of the independent variable.

This assumption is usually valid. However, it is also true that the difference between any two groups will almost never be zero. In other words, there will be some difference in the sample means, even when all of the principles of experimental design are utilized. This happens because we are dealing with samples rather than populations. Random or chance error will be responsible for some difference in the means even if the independent variable had no effect on the dependent variable.

The point is that the difference in the sample means reflects any true difference in the population means (i.e., the effect of the independent variable) plus any random error. Inferential statistics allow researchers to make inferences about the true difference in the population on the basis of the sample data. Specifically, inferential statistics give the probability that the difference between means reflects random error rather than a real difference.

One way of thinking about inferential statistics is to use the concept of reliability that was introduced in Chapter 4. Recall that reliability refers to the stability or consistency of scores; a reliable measure will yield the same score over and over again. Inferential statistics allow researchers to assess whether the results of a study are reliable: Would the same results be obtained if the study were repeated again and again? You could, of course, repeat your study many times, each time with a new sample of research participants. However, this is not practical. Instead, inferential statistics are used to tell you the probability that your results would be obtained if you repeated the study on many occasions.

NULL AND RESEARCH HYPOTHESES

Statistical inference begins with a statement of the null hypothesis and a research (or alternative) hypothesis. The **null hypothesis** is simply that the population means are equal—the observed difference is due to random error. The **research hypothesis** is that the population means are, in fact, not equal. The null hypothesis states that the independent variable had no effect; the research hypothesis states that the independent variable did have an effect. In the aggression modeling experiment, the null and research hypotheses are:

H_0 (null hypothesis):   The population mean of the no-model group is equal to the population mean of the model group.

H_1 (research hypothesis):   The population mean of the no-model group is not equal to the population mean of the model group.

197

The logic of the null hypothesis is this: If we can determine that the null hypothesis is incorrect, then we accept the research hypothesis as correct. Acceptance of the research hypothesis means that the independent variable had an effect on the dependent variable.

The null hypothesis is used because it is a very precise statement—the population means are exactly equal. This permits us to know precisely the probability of the outcome of the study occurring if the null hypothesis is correct. Such precision isn't possible with the research hypothesis, so we infer that the research hypothesis is correct only by rejecting the null hypothesis. The null hypothesis is rejected when there is a very low probability that the obtained results could be due to random error. This is what is meant by **statistical significance:** A significant result is one that has a very low probability of occurring if the population means are actually equal. More simply, significance indicates that there is a low probability that the difference between the obtained sample means was due to random error. Significance, then, is a matter of probability.

PROBABILITY AND SAMPLING DISTRIBUTIONS

Probability is the likelihood of the occurrence of some event or outcome. We all use probabilities frequently in everyday life. For example, if you say that there is a high probability that you will get an A in this course, you mean that this outcome likely will occur. Your probability statement is based on specific information, such as your grades on examinations. The weather forecaster says there is a 10% chance of rain today; this means that the likelihood of rain is very low. A gambler gauges the probability that a particular horse will win a race on the basis of the past records of that horse.

Probability in statistical inference is used in much the same way. We want to specify the probability that an event (in this case, a difference between means in the sample) will occur if there is no difference in the population. The question is, What is the probability of obtaining this result if only random error is operating? If this probability is very low, we reject the possibility that only random or chance error is responsible for the obtained difference in means.

Probability: The case of ESP

The use of probability in statistical inference can be understood intuitively from a simple example. Suppose that a friend claims to have ESP (extrasensory perception) ability. You decide to test your friend with a set of five cards commonly used in ESP research; a different symbol is presented on each card. In the ESP test, you look at each card and think about the symbol, and your friend tells you which symbol you are thinking about. In your actual experiment, you have 10 trials; each of the five cards is presented two times in a random order. Your task is to know whether your friend's answers reflect random error (guessing) or whether they indicate that something more than random error is occurring. The null hypothesis in your study is that only random error is operating. The research hypothesis is that the number of correct answers shows more than just random or chance guessing. (Note, however, that accepting the research hypothesis could mean that your friend has ESP ability, but it could also mean that the cards were marked, that you had somehow cued your friend when thinking about the symbols, and so on.)

You can easily determine the number of correct answers to expect if the null hypothesis is correct. Just by guessing, one out of five answers (20%) should be correct. On 10 trials, two correct answers are expected under the null hypothesis. If, in the actual experiment, more (or less) than two correct answers are obtained, would you conclude that the obtained data reflect random error or something more than just random guessing?

Suppose that your friend gets three correct. Then you would probably conclude that only guessing is involved, because you would recognize that there is a high probability that there would be three correct answers *even though only two correct are expected under the null hypothesis*. You expect that exactly two answers in 10 trials would be correct in the long run, if you conducted this experiment with this subject over and over again. However, small deviations away from the expected two are highly likely in a sample of 10 trials.

Suppose, though, that your friend gets seven correct. You might conclude that the results indicate more than random error in this one sample of 10 observations. This conclusion would be based on your intuitive judgment that an outcome of 70% correct when only 20% is expected is very unlikely. At this point, you would decide to reject the null hypothesis and state that the result is significant. A significant result is one that is very unlikely if the null hypothesis is correct.

How unlikely does a result have to be before we decide it is significant? A decision rule is determined prior to collecting the data. The probability required for significance is called the *alpha level*. The most common alpha level probability used is .05. The outcome of the study is considered significant when there is a .05 or less probability of obtaining the results—that is, there are only 5 chances out of 100 that the results were due to random error in one sample from the population. If it is very unlikely that random error is responsible for the obtained results, the null hypothesis is rejected.

Sampling distributions

You may have been able to judge intuitively that obtaining seven correct on the 10 trials is very unlikely. Fortunately, we don't have to rely on intuition to determine the probabilities of different outcomes. Table 11-1 shows the probability of actually obtaining each of the possible outcomes in the ESP experiment with 10 trials and a null hypothesis expectation of 20% correct. An

Table 11-1
Exact probability of each possible outcome of the ESP experiment with 10 trials

Number of correct answers	Probability
10	.00000+
9	.00000+
8	.00007
7	.00079
6	.00551
5	.02642
4	.08808
3	.20133
2	.30199
1	.26844
0	.10737

outcome of two correct answers has the highest probability of occurrence. Also, as intuition would suggest, an outcome of three correct is highly probable, but an outcome of seven correct is highly unlikely.

The probabilities shown in Table 11-1 were derived from a probability distribution called the *binomial distribution;* all statistical significance decisions are based on probability distributions such as this one. Such distributions are called *sampling distributions.* The sampling distribution is based on the assumption that the null hypothesis is true; in the ESP example, the null hypothesis is that the person is only guessing and should therefore get 20% correct. Such a distribution assumes that if you were to conduct the study with the same number of observations over and over again, the most frequent finding would be 20%. However, because of the random error possible in each sample, there is a certain probability associated with other outcomes. Outcomes that are close to the expected null hypothesis value of 20% are very likely. However, outcomes further from the expected result are less and less likely if the null hypothesis is correct. When your obtained results are highly unlikely if you are, in fact, sampling from the distribution specified by the null hypothesis, you conclude that the null hypothesis is incorrect. Instead of concluding that your sample results reflect a random deviation from the long-run expectation of 20%, you decide that the null hypothesis is incorrect. That is, you conclude that you have not sampled from the sampling distribution specified by the null hypothesis. Instead, in the case of the ESP example, you decide that your data are from a different sampling distribution in which, if you were to test the person repeatedly, most of the outcomes would be near your obtained result of seven correct answers.

All statistical tests rely on sampling distributions to determine the probability that the results are consistent with the null hypothesis. When it is highly unlikely that the null hypothesis is correct (usually a .05 probability or less), the researcher decides to reject the null hypothesis and therefore to accept the research hypothesis.

Sample size

The ESP example also illustrates the importance of sample size—the total number of observations—on determinations of statistical significance. Suppose you had tested your friend on 100 trials instead of 10 and had observed 30 correct answers. Just as you had expected 2 correct answers in 10 trials, you would now expect 20 of 100 answers to be correct. However, 30 out of 100 has a much lower likelihood of occurrence than 3 out of 10. This is because, with more observations sampled, you are more likely to obtain an accurate estimate of the true population value. Thus, as the size of your sample increases, you are more confident that your outcome is actually different from the null hypothesis expectation.

EXAMPLE: THE *t* AND *F* TESTS

Different statistical tests allow us to use probability to decide whether to reject the null hypothesis. In this section, we will examine the *t*-test and the *F* test. The *t*-test is most commonly used to examine whether two groups are significantly different from each other. In the hypothetical experiment on the effect of a model on aggression, a *t*-test is appropriate because we are asking whether the mean of the no-model group differs from the mean of the model group. The *F* test is a more general statistical test that can be used to ask whether there is a difference among three or more groups or to evaluate the results of factorial designs (discussed in Chapter 8).

To use a statistical test, you must first specify the null hypothesis and the research hypothesis that you are evaluating. The null and research hypotheses for the modeling experiment were described previously. You must also specify the significance level that you will use to decide whether to reject the null hypothesis; this is the alpha level. As noted, researchers generally use a significance level of .05.

t-test

A value of *t* is calculated from the obtained data and evaluated in terms of the sampling distribution of *t* that is based on the null hypothesis. If the obtained *t* has a low probability of occurrence (.05 or less), then the null hypothesis is rejected. The *t* value is a ratio of two aspects of the data, the difference between the group means and the variability within groups. The ratio may be described as follows:

$$t = \frac{\text{group difference}}{\text{within-group variability}}$$

The group difference is simply the difference between your obtained means; under the null hypothesis, you expect this difference to be zero. The value of *t* increases as the difference between your obtained sample means increases. Note that the sampling distribution of t assumes that there is no difference in the population means; thus, the expected value of t under the null hypothesis is zero. The within-group variability is the amount of variability of scores about the mean. The denominator of the t formula is essentially an indicator of the amount of random error in your sample. Recall from Chapter 10 that s, the standard deviation, and s^2, the variance, are indicators of how much scores deviate from the group mean.

A concrete example of a calculation of a t-test should help clarify these concepts. The formula for the t-test for two groups with equal or nearly equal numbers of participants in each group is

$$t = \frac{\overline{X}_1 - \overline{X}_2}{\sqrt{\dfrac{s_1^2}{N_1} + \dfrac{s_2^2}{N_2}}}$$

The numerator of the formula is simply the difference between the means of the two groups. In the denominator, we first divide the variance (s^2) of each group by the number of subjects in the group and add these together. We then find the square root of the result. This yields an estimate of the overall amount of variability within the groups.

When this formula is applied to the data in Table 10-1, we find:

$$t = \frac{5.2 - 3.1}{\sqrt{\dfrac{1.289}{10} + \dfrac{1.433}{10}}}$$

$$= \frac{2.1}{\sqrt{.1289 + .1433}}$$

$$= 4.025$$

Thus, the t value calculated from the data is 4.025. Is this a significant result? A computer program analyzing the results would immediately tell you the probability of obtaining a t value of this size with a total sample size of 20. Without such a program, however, you can refer to a table of "critical values" of t, such as Table C-4 in Appendix C. We will discuss the use of the appendix tables in detail in Appendix B. Before going any further, you should know that the obtained result is significant. Using a significance level of .05, the critical value from the sampling distribution of t is 2.101. Any t value greater than or equal to 2.101 has a .05 or less probability of occurring under the assumptions of the null hypothesis. Because our obtained value is larger than the critical value, we can reject the null hypothesis and conclude that the difference in means obtained in the sample reflects a true difference in the population.

Degrees of freedom

You are probably wondering how the critical value was selected from the table. To use the table, you must first determine the **degrees of freedom** for the test. When comparing two means, the degrees of freedom are equal to $N_1 + N_2 - 2$, or the total number of subjects in the groups minus the number of groups. In our experiment, the degrees of freedom would be $10 + 10 - 2 = 18$. The degrees of freedom are the number of scores free to vary once the means are known. For example, if the mean of a group is 6.0 and there are five scores in the group, there are 4 degrees of freedom; once you have any four scores, the fifth score is known because the mean must remain 6.0.

One-tailed versus two-tailed tests

In the table, you must choose a critical *t* for the situation in which your research hypothesis either (1) specified a direction of difference between the groups (e.g., group 1 will be greater than group 2) or (2) did not specify a predicted direction of difference (e.g., group 1 will differ from group 2). Somewhat different critical values of *t* are used in the two situations: The first situation is called a one-tailed test, while the second situation is called a two-tailed test.

The issue can be visualized by looking at the sampling distribution of *t* values for 18 degrees of freedom, as shown in Figure 11-1. As you can see, a value of 0.00 is expected most frequently. Values greater than or less than zero are less likely to occur. The first distribution shows the logic of a two-tailed test. We used the value of 2.101 for the critical value of *t* with a .05 significance level because a direction of difference was not predicted. This critical value is the point beyond which 2.5% of the positive values and 2.5% of the negative values of *t* lie (hence, a total probability of .05 combined from the two "tails" of the sampling distribution). The second distribution illustrates a one-tailed test. If a directional difference had been predicted, the critical value would have been 1.734. This is the value beyond which 5% of the values lie in only one "tail" of the distribution. Whether to specify a one-tailed or two-tailed test will depend on whether you originally designed your study to test a directional hypothesis.

F test

The **analysis of variance,** or **F test,** is an extension of the *t*-test. The analysis of variance is a more general statistical procedure than the *t*-test. When a study has only one independent variable with two groups, *F* and *t* are virtually identical—the value of *F* equals t^2 in this situation. However, analysis of variance is also used when there are more than two levels of an independent variable and when a factorial design with two or more independent variables has been used. Thus, the *F* test is appropriate for the simplest experimental design, as well as for the more complex designs discussed in Chapter 8. The *t*-test was presented because the formula allows us to demonstrate easily the

203

**Figure 11-1
Sampling
distribution of *t*
with 18 degrees of
freedom**

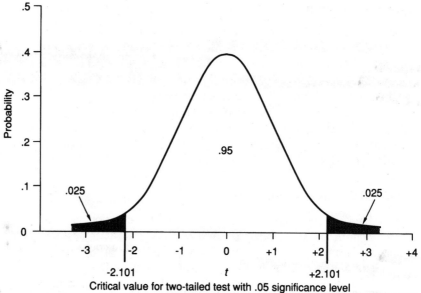

Critical value for two-tailed test with .05 significance level

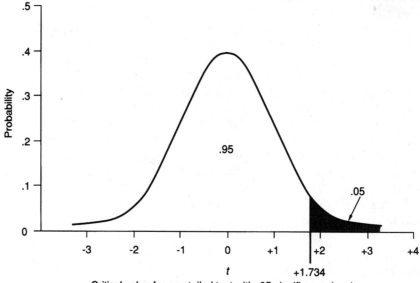

Critical value for one-tailed test with .05 significance level

relationship of the group difference and the within-group variability to the outcome of the statistical test. However, in practice, analysis of variance is the more common procedure. The calculations necessary to conduct an *F* test are provided in Appendix B.

The *F* statistic is a ratio of two types of variance: systematic variance and error variance (hence the term *analysis of variance*). **Systematic variance** is the deviation of the group means from the grand mean, or the mean score of all individuals in all groups. Systematic variance is small when the difference between group means is small and increases as the group mean differences increase. **Error variance** is the deviation of the individual scores in each group from their respective group means. Terms that you may see in research instead of systematic and error variance are *between-group variance* and *within-group variance*. Systematic variance is the variability of scores between groups, and error variance is the variability of scores within groups. The larger the *F* ratio, the more likely it is that the results are significant.

Calculating effect size

The concept of effect size was discussed in Chapter 10. In addition to knowing whether there was a statistically significant effect of the independent variable, it is useful to know the magnitude of the effect. Therefore, we want to calculate an estimate of effect size, a type of correlation coefficient that can range from 0.00 to 1.00. For a *t*-test, the calculation is

$$\text{Effect size } r = \sqrt{\frac{t^2}{t^2 + df}}$$

where df is the degrees of freedom. Thus, using the obtained value of *t*, 4.025, and 18 degrees of freedom, we find

$$\text{Effect size } r = \sqrt{\frac{(4.025)^2}{(4.025)^2 + 18}} = \sqrt{\frac{16.201}{34.201}} = .688$$

For additional information on effect size calculation, see Rosenthal (1991).

Statistical significance: An overview

The logic underlying the use of statistical tests rests on statistical theory. There are some general concepts, however, that should help you understand what you are doing when you conduct a statistical test. First, the goal of the test is to allow you to make a decision about whether your obtained results are reliable; you want to be confident that you would obtain similar results if you conducted the study over and over again. Second, the significance level (alpha level) you choose indicates how confident you wish to be when making the decision. A .05 significance level says that you are 95% sure of the reliability of your findings; however, there is a 5% chance that you could be wrong. There are few certainties in life! Third, you are most likely to obtain significant results when you have a large sample size, because larger sample sizes provide better estimates of true population values. Finally, you are most likely to obtain significant results when differences between groups are large and variability of scores within groups is small.

Figure 11-2
Decision matrix:
Type I and Type II
errors

	Population	
	Null hypothesis is true	Research hypothesis is true
Reject the null hypothesis	Type I error	Correct decision
Accept the null hypothesis	Correct decision	Type II error

Decision

In the remainder of the chapter, we will expand on these issues. We will examine the implications of making a decision about whether results are significant, the way to determine a significance level, and the way to interpret nonsignificant results. We will then provide some guidelines for selecting the appropriate statistical test in various research designs.

TYPE I AND TYPE II ERRORS

The decision to reject the null hypothesis is based on probabilities rather than certainties. That is, the decision is made without direct knowledge of the true state of affairs in the population. Thus, the decision might not be correct; errors may result from the use of inferential statistics.

A decision matrix is shown in Figure 11-2. Notice that there are two possible decisions: (1) Reject the null hypothesis or (2) accept the null hypothesis. There are also two possible truths about the population: (1) The null hypothesis is true or (2) the research hypothesis is true. In sum, as the decision matrix shows, there are two kinds of correct decisions and two kinds of errors.

Correct decisions

One correct decision occurs when we reject the null hypothesis and the research hypothesis is true in the population. Here, our decision is that the population means are not equal, and in fact, this is true in the population.

The other correct decision is to accept the null hypothesis, and the null hypothesis is true in the population: The population means are in fact equal.

Type I errors

A **Type 1 error** is made when we reject the null hypothesis but the null hypothesis is actually true. Our decision is that the population means are not equal when they actually are equal. Type I errors occur when, just by chance, we obtain a large value of t or F. For example, even though a t value of 4.025 is highly improbable if the population means are indeed equal (less than 5 chances out of 100), this *can* happen. When we do obtain such a large t value by chance, we *incorrectly* decide that the independent variable had an effect.

The probability of making a Type I error is determined by the choice of significance or alpha level. When the significance level for deciding whether to reject the null hypothesis is .05, the probability of a Type I error is .05. If the null hypothesis is rejected, there are 5 chances out of 100 that the decision is wrong. The probability of making a Type I error can be changed by either decreasing or increasing the significance level. If we use a lower significance level of .01, for example, there is less chance of making a Type I error. With a .01 significance level, the null hypothesis is rejected only when the probability of obtaining the results is .01 or less if the null hypothesis is correct.

Type II errors

A **Type II error** occurs when the null hypothesis is accepted although in the population the research hypothesis is true. The population means are not equal, but the results of the experiment do not lead to a decision to reject the null hypothesis.

The probability of making a Type II error is not directly specifiable, although the significance level is an important factor. If we set a very low significance level to decrease the chances of a Type I error, we increase the chances of a Type II error. In other words, if we make it very difficult to reject the null hypothesis, the probability of incorrectly accepting the null hypothesis increases.

The everyday context of Type I and Type II errors

The decision matrix used in statistical analyses can be applied to the kinds of decisions people frequently must make in everyday life. For example, consider the decision made by a juror in a criminal trial. As is the case with statistics, a decision must be made on the basis of evidence: Is the defendant innocent or guilty? However, the decision rests with individual jurors and does not necessarily reflect the true state of affairs: that the person really is innocent or guilty.

The juror's decision matrix is illustrated in Figure 11-3. To continue the parallel to the statistical decision, assume as the null hypothesis that the defendant is innocent (i.e., the dictum that a person is innocent until proven

Figure 11-3
Decision matrix
for a juror

True state

	Null is true (innocent)	Null is false (guilty)
Reject null (find guilty)	Type I error	Correct decision
Accept null (find innocent)	Correct decision	Type II error

Decision

guilty). Thus, rejection of the null hypothesis means deciding that the defendant is guilty, and acceptance of the null hypothesis means deciding that the defendant is innocent. The decision matrix also shows that the null hypothesis may actually be true or false. There are two kinds of correct decisions and two kinds of errors like those described in statistical decisions. A Type I error is finding the defendant guilty when the person really is innocent; a Type II error is finding the defendant innocent when the person actually is guilty. In our society, Type I errors by jurors generally are considered to be more serious than Type II errors. Thus, before finding someone guilty, the juror is asked to make sure that the person is guilty "beyond a reasonable doubt" or to consider that "it is better to have a hundred guilty persons go free than to find one innocent person guilty."

The decision that a doctor makes to operate or not operate on a patient provides another illustration of how a decision matrix works. The matrix is shown in Figure 11-4. Here, the null hypothesis is that no operation is necessary. The decision is whether to reject the null hypothesis and perform the operation or to accept the null hypothesis and not perform surgery. In reality, the surgeon is faced with two possibilities: Either the surgery is unnecessary (the null hypothesis is true) or the patient will die without the operation (a dramatic case of the null hypothesis being false). Which error is more serious in this case? Most doctors would believe that not operating on a patient who really needs the operation—making a Type II error—is more serious than making the Type I error of performing surgery on someone who does not really need it.

Figure 11-4
Decision matrix for a doctor

		True state	
		Null is true (no operation needed)	Null is false (operation is needed)
Decision	Reject null (operate on patient)	Type I error	Correct decision
	Accept null (don't operate)	Correct decision	Type II error

One final illustration of the use of a decision matrix involves the important decision to marry someone. If the null hypothesis is that the person is "wrong" for you, and the true state is that the person is either "wrong" or "right," you must decide whether to go ahead and marry the person. You might try to construct a decision matrix for this particular problem. Which error is more costly: a Type I error or a Type II error?

CHOOSING A SIGNIFICANCE LEVEL

Researchers traditionally have used either a .05 or a .01 significance level in the decision to reject the null hypothesis. If there is less than a .05 or a .01 probability that the results occurred because of random error, the results are said to be significant. However, there is nothing magical about a .05 or a .01 significance level. The significance level chosen merely specifies the probability of a Type I error if the null hypothesis is rejected. The significance level chosen by the researcher usually is dependent on the consequences of making a Type I versus a Type II error. As previously noted, for a juror, a Type I error is more serious than a Type II error; for a doctor, however, a Type II error may be more serious.

Researchers generally believe that the consequences of making a Type I error are more serious than those associated with a Type II error. If the null hypothesis is rejected, the researcher might publish the results in a journal, and the results might be reported by others in textbooks or in newspaper or magazine articles. Researchers don't want to mislead people or risk damaging their reputations by publishing results that aren't reliable and so cannot be replicated. Thus, they want to guard against the possibility of making a Type I error by using a very low significance level (.05 or .01). In contrast to the consequences of publishing false results, the consequences of a Type II error are not seen as being very serious.

Thus, researchers want to be very careful to avoid Type I errors when their results may be published. However, in certain circumstances, a Type I error is not serious. For example, if you were engaged in pilot or exploratory research, your results would be used primarily to decide whether your research ideas were worth pursuing. In this situation, it would be a mistake to overlook potentially important data by using a very conservative significance level. In exploratory research, a significance level of .25 may be more appropriate for deciding whether to do more research. Remember, the significance level chosen and the consequences of a Type I or a Type II error are determined by what the results will be used for.

INTERPRETING NONSIGNIFICANT RESULTS

Although "accepting the null hypothesis" is convenient terminology, it is important to recognize that researchers are not generally interested in accepting the null hypothesis. Research is designed to show that a relationship between variables does exist, not to demonstrate that variables are unrelated.

More importantly, a decision to accept the null hypothesis when a single study doesn't show significant results is problematic, because negative or nonsignificant results are difficult to interpret. First, it isn't possible to specify the probability that you could be wrong in the decision to accept the null hypothesis. Also, a single study might not show significant results even when a relationship between the variables in the population does exist. For example, a researcher might obtain nonsignificant results by providing incomprehensible instructions to the participants, by having a very weak manipulation of the independent variable, or by using a dependent measure that is unreliable and insensitive. When nonsignificant results are obtained, the researcher must re-examine all aspects of the procedures to try to discover if something went wrong.

Nonsignificant results can also be obtained by being very cautious in choosing the alpha level. If the researcher uses a significance level of .001 in deciding whether to reject the null hypothesis, there isn't much chance of a Type I error. However, a Type II error is possible, because the researcher has decreased the chances of wrongly rejecting the null hypothesis. In other words, a meaningful result is more likely to be overlooked when the significance level is very low.

A small sample size also might cause a researcher to wrongly accept the null hypothesis. A general principle is that the larger the sample size, the greater the likelihood of obtaining a significant result. This is because large sample sizes give more accurate estimates of the actual population than do small sample sizes. In any given study, the sample size may be too small to permit detection of a significant result.

This is not meant to imply that researchers should always use huge samples. A very large sample size (for example, 200 subjects in each group) might enable the researcher to find a significant difference between means. However, this difference, even though statistically significant, might have very little *practical* significance. For example, if an expensive new psychiatric treatment technique significantly reduces the average hospital stay from 60 days to 58 days, it might not be practical to use the technique despite the evidence for its effectiveness. In such cases, there can be a statistically significant effect, but the effect size will be very small.

The key point here is that *you should not accept the null hypothesis just because the results are nonsignificant*. Nonsignificant results do not necessarily indicate that the null hypothesis is correct. However, we can accept the null hypothesis and conclude that two variables are, in fact, not related. Frick (1995) describes several criteria that can be used in a decision to accept the null hypothesis. For example, we should look for well-designed studies with sensitive dependent measures and evidence from a manipulation check that the independent variable manipulation had its intended effect. In addition, the research should have a reasonably large sample to rule out the possibility that the sample was too small. Further, evidence that the variables are not related should come from multiple studies. Under such circumstances, you are justified in concluding that there is in fact no relationship.

THE IMPORTANCE OF REPLICATIONS

Throughout this discussion of statistical analysis, the focus has been on the results of a single research investigation. What were the means and standard deviations? Was the mean difference statistically significant? If the results are significant, you conclude that they would likely be obtained over and over again if we continued to sample from the population. We now have a framework for understanding the results of the study. Be aware, however, that scientists do not attach too much importance to the results of a single study. A rich understanding of any phenomenon comes from the results of numerous studies investigating the same variables. Instead of applying a statistical test to determine whether the results would hold up again and again, we can look at the results of studies that replicate previous investigations (see Cohen, 1994). The importance of replications is a central concept in Chapter 12.

SIGNIFICANCE OF A PEARSON *r* CORRELATION COEFFICIENT

Recall from Chapter 10 that the Pearson *r* correlation coefficient is used to describe the strength of the relationship between two variables when both variables have interval or ratio scale properties. However, there remains the issue of whether the correlation is statistically significant. The null hypothesis in this case is that the true population correlation is 0.00—the two variables are not related. What if you obtain a correlation of .27 (plus or minus)? A statistical significance test will allow you to decide whether to reject the null hypothesis and conclude that the true population correlation is, in fact, greater than 0.00. The technical way to do this is to perform a t-test that compares the obtained coefficient with the null hypothesis correlation of 0.00. The procedures for calculating a Pearson r and determining significance are provided in Appendix B.

COMPUTER ANALYSIS OF DATA

Although you can calculate statistics with a calculator using the formulas provided in this chapter and in Chapter 10 and Appendix B, most data analysis is carried out via computer programs. Sophisticated statistical analysis software packages make it easy to calculate statistics for any data set. Descriptive and inferential statistics are obtained quickly, the calculations are accurate, and information on statistical significance is provided in the output. Computers also facilitate graphic displays of data.

Some of the major statistical software programs are SPSS, SAS, Minitab, Systat, and BMDP; other programs may be used on your campus as well. Many people do most of their statistical analyses using a spreadsheet program such as Microsoft Excel. You will need to learn the specific details of the computer system used at your college or university. No one program is better than another; they all differ in the appearance of the output and the specific procedures needed to input data and have the program perform the test. However, the general procedures for doing analyses are quite similar in all of the statistics programs.

The first step in doing the analysis is to input the data. Suppose you want to input the data in Table 10-1, the modeling and aggression experiment. Data are entered into columns. It is easiest to think of data for computer analysis as a matrix with rows and columns. Data for each research participant are the rows of the matrix. The columns contain each participant's scores on one or more measures, and an additional column may be needed to indicate a code to identify which condition the individual was in (e.g., group 1 or group 2). A data matrix in SPSS for Windows is shown on the next page. The numbers in the "group" column indicate whether the individual is in group 1 (model) or group 2 (no model), and the numbers in the "aggscore" column are the aggression scores from Table 10-1.

Other programs may require somewhat different methods of data input. For example, in Excel, it is usually easiest to set up a separate column for each group, as shown on the next page.

The next step is to provide instructions for the statistical analysis. Again, each program uses somewhat different steps to perform the analysis; most require you to choose from various menu options. When the analysis is completed, you are provided with the output that shows the results of the statistical procedure you performed. You will need to learn how to interpret the output. Also on the next page is the output for a t-test using Excel.

	group	aggscore
1	1	3
2	1	4
3	1	5
4	1	5
5	1	5
6	2	1
7	2	2
8	2	2
9	2	3
10	2	3
11	1	5
12	1	6
13	2	3
14	2	4
15	2	4

Data matrix in SPSS for Windows

	A	B
1	Model	No Model
2	3	1
3	4	2
4	5	2
5	5	3
6	5	3
7	5	3
8	6	4
9	6	4
10	6	4
11	7	5
12		
13		

Excel method of data input

t-Test: Two-Sample Assuming Equal Variances

	Model	No Model
Mean	5.200	3.100
Variance	1.289	1.433
Observations	10.000	10.000
Pooled Variance	1.361	
Hypothesized Mean Difference	0.000	
df	18.000	
t Stat	4.025	
P(T<=t) one-tail	0.000	
t Critical one-tail	1.734	
P(T<=t) two-tail	0.001	
t Critical two-tail	2.101	

Output for a *t*-test using Excel

213

When you are first learning to use a statistical analysis program, it is a good idea to practice with some data from a statistics text to make sure that you get the same results. This will ensure that you know how to properly input the data and request the statistical analysis.

SELECTING THE APPROPRIATE SIGNIFICANCE TEST

Many statistical tests have been developed for different research designs. The appropriateness of a particular test of significance depends on the design used and the type of measurement scales employed for studying the variables. Recall from Chapter 10 that the values of variables have measurement scale properties. There are four such scales: (1) nominal, in which the values have no numerical properties; (2) ordinal, in which the values are only meaningful as a ranked order; (3) interval, in which the values are arranged along a continuum of equal intervals; and (4) ratio, in which there is a true zero point on the scale of values. This section will not provide guidelines for selecting a test in all situations; rather, only the appropriate tests for some of the more common designs will be presented.

One independent variable—two groups only

Nominal scale data   When individuals in two groups have been measured using a nominal scale, the appropriate test is a Chi-square test. Chi-square tests are used with all nominal data. Check a statistics book for the formula for your application.

Ordinal scale data   If an independent groups design was used, the Mann-Whitney U test is appropriate. This test is described in Appendix B. For a repeated measures or matched subjects design, Wilcoxon's T or the sign test is used. The procedures for these tests may be found in many statistics texts (see Siegel & Castellan, 1988).

Interval or ratio scale data   For independent groups designs, the t-test described in this chapter or a one-way analysis of variance is used. The analysis of variance calculations are given in Appendix B. With repeated measures or matched groups designs, a t-test with a slightly different calculation procedure or a repeated measures analysis of variance should be employed. The calculations for a repeated measures analysis of variance are shown in Appendix B.

One independent variable—three or more groups

Nominal scale data   A Chi-square test is used in this situation.

Ordinal scale data   The Kruskal-Wallace H test is appropriate for an independent groups design. For repeated measures designs, the Friedman T test is appropriate. Consult a statistics text for details on calculating these tests.

Interval or ratio scale data   A one-way analysis of variance is used here. The procedures to calculate this test for both independent groups and repeated measures designs are provided in Appendix B.

Two or more independent variables

Nominal scale data   Again, a Chi-square test is appropriate for nominal scale data. The formula for a Chi-square in which subjects are classified on two variables, both with nominal scale properties, is provided in Appendix B.

Ordinal scale data   No appropriate statistical test is available.

Interval or ratio scale data   A two-way analysis of variance is used for factorial designs with two independent variables. Analysis of variance can be extended to designs with any number of independent variables. It is appropriate for independent groups, repeated measures, or mixed designs with both independent groups and repeated measures variables.

You have now considered how to generate research ideas, conduct research to test your ideas, and evaluate the statistical significance of your results. In the final chapter, we will examine issues of generalizing research findings beyond the specific circumstances in which the research was conducted.

STUDY TERMS

Alpha level	Inferential statistics	Systematic variance
Analysis of variance (*F* test)	Null hypothesis	*t*-test
	Probability	Type I error
Chi-square test	Research hypothesis	Type II error
Degrees of freedom	Sampling distribution	Variance
Error variance	Statistical significance	

REVIEW QUESTIONS

1. Distinguish between the null hypothesis and the research hypothesis. When does the researcher decide to reject the null hypothesis?

2. What is meant by statistical significance?

3. What factors are most important in determining whether obtained results will be significant?

4. Distinguish between a Type I and a Type II error. Why is your significance level the probability of making a Type I error?

5. What factors are involved in choosing a significance level?

6. What is the difference between statistical significance and practical significance?

7. Discuss the reasons that a researcher might obtain nonsignificant results.

ACTIVITY QUESTIONS

1. In an experiment, one group of research participants is given 10 pages of material to proofread for errors. Another group proofreads the same material on a computer screen. The dependent variable is the number of errors detected in a 5-minute period. A .05 significance (alpha) level is used to evaluate the results.
   a. What statistical test would you use?
   b. What is the null hypothesis? The research hypothesis?
   c. What is the Type I error? The Type II error?
   d. What is the probability of making a Type I error?

2. When the preceding experiment was conducted by Professor Dre, the average number of errors detected in the print and computer conditions was 38.4 and 11.2, respectively; the difference was not statistically significant. When Professor Seuss conducted the experiment, the means of the two groups were 21.1 and 14.7, but the difference was statistically significant. Explain how this could happen.

3. Suppose that you work for the child social services agency in your county. Your job is to investigate instances of possible child neglect or abuse. After collecting your evidence, which may come from a variety of sources, you must decide whether to leave the child in the home or place the child in protective custody. Specify the null and research hypotheses in this situation. What constitutes a Type I and a Type II error? Is a Type I or Type II error the more serious error in this situation? Why?

4. A researcher investigated attitudes toward individuals in wheelchairs. The question was, Would people react differently if they perceived the person as being temporarily confined to the wheelchair as compared to a person who had a permanent disability? Participants were randomly assigned to two groups. Individuals in one group each worked on various tasks with a confederate in a wheelchair; members of the other group worked with the same confederate in a wheelchair, but this time the confederate wore a leg cast. After the session was over, participants filled out a questionnaire regarding their reactions to the study. One question asked, "Would you be willing to work with your test partner in the future on a class assignment?" with "yes" and "no" as the only response alternatives. What would be the appropriate significance test for this experiment? Can you offer a critique of the dependent variable? If you changed the dependent variable, would it affect your choice of significance tests? If so, how?

12

Generalizing Results

In this chapter, we will consider the problem of generalization of research findings. Can the results of a completed research project be generalized to other subject populations, to other age groups, or to other ways of manipulating or measuring the variables? Recall that internal validity refers to the adequacy of the procedures and design of the research; external validity is the extent to which the findings may be generalized. Internal validity is of primary importance; ideally, however, a study should have external validity as well.

GENERALIZING TO OTHER POPULATIONS OF RESEARCH PARTICIPANTS

Even though a researcher randomly assigns participants to experimental conditions, rarely are they randomly selected from the general population. As we noted in Chapters 5 and 7, the individuals who participate in psychological research are usually selected because they are available, and the most available population consists of college students—or more specifically, freshmen and sophomores enrolled in the introductory psychology course to satisfy a general education requirement. They may also be from a particular college or university, may be volunteers, or may be mostly males or mostly females.

College students

Smart (1966) found that college students were studied in over 70% of the articles published between 1962 and 1964 in the *Journal of Experimental Psychology* and the *Journal of Abnormal and Social Psychology*. Sears (1986) reported similar percentages in 1980 and 1985 in a variety of social psychology journals. The potential problem is that such studies use a highly restricted population. Sears points out that most of the students are freshmen and sophomores taking the introductory psychology class. They therefore tend to be very young and to possess the characteristics of late adolescence: a sense of self-identity that is still developing, social and political attitudes that are in a state of flux, a high need for peer approval, and unstable peer relationships. They also are intelligent, have high cognitive skills, and know how to win approval from authority (having done well enough in a school environment to get into college). Thus, what we know about "people in general" may actually be limited to a highly select and unusual group.

The problem of unrepresentative subjects is not confined to human research. A great deal of research with animals relies solely on the infamous white rat. Why? In part because, as Beach (1950) points out, "Rats are hardy, cheap, easy to rear, and well adapted to laboratory existence." Thus, like the younger students, they are easy to obtain on a college campus.

Volunteers

Researchers usually must ask people to volunteer to participate in the research. At many colleges, introductory psychology students are required either to volunteer for experiments or to complete an alternative project. If you are studying populations other than college students, you are even more dependent on volunteers—for example, asking people at a homeowner's association meeting to participate in a study of marital interaction. Research indicates that volunteers differ in various ways from nonvolunteers (Rosenthal & Rosnow, 1975). For instance, volunteers tend to be more highly educated, more in need of approval, and more social; they also tend to have a higher socioeconomic status.

Further, different kinds of people volunteer for different kinds of experiments. Again, in colleges, there may be a sign-up board with the titles of many studies listed. Different types of people may be drawn to the study titled "problem solving" than to the one titled "interaction in small groups." Available evidence indicates that the title does influence who signs up (cf. Hood & Back, 1971).

Gender, race, and ethnicity

Sometimes, researchers use either males or females (or a very disproportionate ratio of males to females) simply because this is convenient or the procedures seem better suited to either males or females. Given the possible differences between males and females, however, the results of such studies may not be generalizable (Denmark, Russo, Frieze, & Sechzer, 1988). Denmark et al. provide an example of studies on contraception practices that use only females because of stereotypical assumptions that only females are responsible for contraception. They also point out several other ways that gender bias may arise in psychological research, including confounding gender with age or job status and selecting response measures that are gender-stereotyped. Their paper offers several suggestions for avoiding such biases.

Denmark et al. (1988) also note that the issues they raise regarding gender apply to race and ethnicity as well. These variables are particularly interesting given the changes in the college student population. Until recently, the participants in most experiments conducted with college students in the United States were primarily White because this reflected the predominant population of college students. Today, however, there are likely to be large numbers of individuals with diverse backgrounds, and so it becomes increasingly important to include all groups when research is conducted.

Locale

Subjects in one locale may differ from subjects in another locale. For example, students at UCLA may differ from students at a nearby state university, who,

219

in turn, may differ from students at a community college. People in Iowa may differ from people in New York City. Thus, a finding obtained with the students in one type of educational setting or in one geographic region may not generalize to people in other settings or regions.

Generalization as a statistical interaction

The problem of generalization can be thought of as an interaction in a factorial design (see Chapter 8). An interaction occurs when a relationship between variables exists under one condition but not another or when the nature of the relationship is different in one condition than in another. Thus, if you question the generalizability of a study that used only males, you are suggesting that an interaction between gender and the treatment was manipulated. Suppose, for example, that a study examines the relationship between crowding and aggression among males and reports that crowding is associated with higher levels of aggression. You might then question whether the results are generalizable to females.

Figure 12-1 shows four potential outcomes of a hypothetical study on crowding and aggression that tested both males and females. In each graph, the relationship between crowding and aggression for males has been maintained. In Graph A, there is no interaction—the behavior of males and females is virtually identical. Thus, the results of the original all-male study could be generalized to females. In Graph B, there is also no interaction; the effect of crowding is identical for males and females. However, in this graph, males are more aggressive than females. Although such a difference is interesting, it is not a factor in generalization because the overall relationship between crowding and aggression is present for both males and females.

Graphs C and D do show interactions. In both, the original results with males cannot be generalized to females. In Graph C, there is no relationship between crowding and aggression for females. The answer to the generalization question, Is this true for females? is no! In Graph D, the interaction tells us that a positive relationship between crowding and aggression exists for males but that a negative relationship exists for females. As it turns out, Graph D describes the results of several studies (cf. Freedman, Levy, Buchanan, & Price, 1972).

Researchers can address generalization issues that stem from the use of different populations by including subject type as a variable in the study. By including variables such as gender, age, or ethnic group in the design of the study, the results may be analyzed to determine whether there are interaction effects like the ones illustrated in Figure 12-1.

In defense of college students and rats

It is easy to criticize research on the basis of subject characteristics, yet criticism by itself does not mean that the research necessarily is flawed. Al-

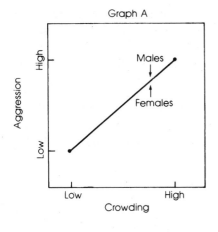

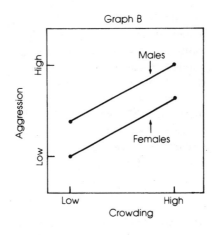

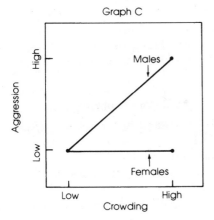

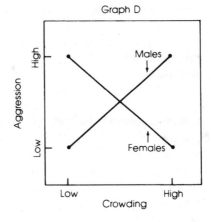

**Figure 12-1
Outcomes of a
hypothetical
experiment on
crowding and
aggression**

Note: The presence of
an interaction indicates
that the results for
males cannot be
generalized to females.

though we need to be concerned about the potential problems of generalizing from special populations such as college students (cf. Sears, 1986), we should also keep two things in mind when thinking about this issue. First, criticisms of the use of any particular type of subject, such as college students, in a study should be backed with good reasons that a relationship would not be found with other types of subjects. College students, after all, *are* human, and researchers should not be blamed for not worrying about generalization to a particular type of subject if there is no good reason to do so. Moreover, college students are increasingly diverse and representative of the society as a whole. Second, remember that replication of research studies provides a safeguard against limited generalizability. Studies are replicated at other colleges using different mixes of students, and many findings first established with college students are later applied to other populations, such as children, aging adults, and people in other countries. Also, while rats are, in fact, hardy and inexpensive, the value of studying rats has been demonstrated by research that applies findings to human problems. For example, research on reinforcement using rats and pigeons has been applied to modifying behavior, understanding personality, and studying choice behavior in humans.

You should also be aware that researchers have become more sensitive to such issues. There is a growing literature of research on the role of gender, ethnicity, race, and culture in determining behaviors and cognitions. This research is providing the data necessary to develop theories that include the influence of these variables.

GENERALIZING TO OTHER EXPERIMENTERS

The person who actually conducts the experiment is the source of another generalization problem. In most research, only one experimenter is used, and rarely is much attention paid to the personal characteristics of the experimenter (McGuigan, 1963). The main goal is to make sure that any influence the experimenter has on subjects is constant throughout the experiment. There is always the possibility, however, that the results are generalizable only to certain types of experimenters.

Some of the important characteristics of experimenters have been discussed by Kintz and his colleagues (1965). These include the experimenter's personality and gender and the amount of practice in the role of experimenter. A warm, friendly experimenter will almost certainly produce different results from those of a cold, unfriendly experimenter. Participants also may behave differently with male and female experimenters. It has even been shown that rabbits learn faster when trained by experienced experimenters (Brogden, 1962)! The influence of the experimenter may depend as well on the characteristics of the participants. For example, participants seem to perform better when tested by an experimenter of the opposite sex (Stevenson & Allen, 1964).

One solution to the problem of generalizing to other experimenters is to use two or more experimenters, preferably both male and female, to conduct the research. A fine example of the use of multiple experimenters is a study by Rubin (1975), who sent several male and female experimenters to the Boston airport to investigate self-disclosure. The experimenters revealed different kinds of information about themselves to both male and female travelers and recorded the passengers' return disclosures.

PRETESTS AND GENERALIZATION

Researchers are often faced with the decision of whether to give a pretest. Intuitively, pretesting seems to be a good idea. The researcher can be sure that the groups are equivalent on the pretest, and it is often more satisfying to see that individuals changed their scores than it is to look only at group means on a posttest. Pretesting, however, may limit the ability to generalize to populations that did not receive a pretest. In the real world, people are rarely pretested—attitudes are not measured prior to listening to a political speech or viewing an advertisement, for example (cf. Lana, 1969).

An important reason for using a pretest is that it enables the researcher to assess mortality effects when it is likely that some participants will withdraw from an experiment. If you give a pretest, you can determine whether the people who withdrew are different from those who completed the study. A Solomon four-group (Solomon, 1949) design can be used in situations in which a pretest is desirable but there is concern over the possible impact of taking the pretest. In the Solomon four-group design, half of the participants are given the pretest; the other half receive the posttest only. In other words, the same experiment is conducted with and without the pretest. Mortality effects can be assessed in the pretest conditions. Also, the researcher can examine whether there is an interaction between the independent variable and the pretest variable; that is, are posttest scores on the dependent variable different depending on whether the pretest was given? Sometimes, researchers find that it is not feasible to conduct the study with all four groups in a single experiment. In this case, the first study can include the pretest; the study can be replicated later without the pretest.

GENERALIZING FROM LABORATORY SETTINGS

Research conducted in a laboratory setting has the advantage of allowing the experimenter control over most extraneous variables. The question arises, however, whether the artificiality of the laboratory setting limits the ability to generalize what is observed in the laboratory to real-life settings. Field experiments, discussed in Chapter 4, represent one method of counteracting laboratory artificiality. In a field experiment, the researcher manipulates the independent variable in a natural setting—a factory, a school, or a street corner, for example.

Mundane and experimental realism

Aronson, Brewer, and Carlsmith (1985) point out that even field experiments can be contrived and artificial, having little real-world relevance. They propose a better distinction: mundane realism versus experimental realism. **Mundane realism** refers to whether the experiment bears similarity to events that occur in the real world. **Experimental realism** refers to whether the experiment has an impact on the participants, involves them, and makes them take the experiment seriously. Aronson et al. point out that experimental

223

and mundane realism are separate, independent dimensions. An experiment may have considerable mundane realism (and thus be very similar to real life) but be totally boring and uninvolving and thus lacking in experimental realism. Consider two examples:

Example 1: In a helping study, an experimenter drops some pencils outside a building on campus and waits to see whether anyone stops to help pick them up. The dependent variable is the helping by observers of the "accident." This study would possess considerable mundane realism but little experimental realism.

Example 2: In another helping experiment, participants are seated in individual cubicles that are interconnected via an intercom system. During the course of the study, the individual hears another (supposed) participant having an epileptic seizure and must decide whether to help the person (Darley & Latané, 1968). This study has relatively little mundane realism but a great deal of experimental realism.

Other experimental procedures, in both laboratory and field settings, may rate either high or low on both mundane and experimental realism. Experiments that are low on both mundane realism (bearing little similarity to real-world events or tasks) and experimental realism (failing to engage the participants' interest) are not likely to yield valuable results. The key point here, however, is that laboratory experiments are not automatically artificial; even when an experiment lacks mundane realism, it may be very realistic in terms of experimental realism.

Mutual benefits of lab and field research

Aronson et al. (1985) also point out that it is unwise to consider laboratory or field experiments in isolation. Conducting research in both laboratory and field settings provides the greatest opportunity for advancing our understanding of behavior. Recall the Langer and Rodin (1976) study on the effects of giving elderly nursing home residents greater control over decisions in their lives (see Chapter 4). This field experiment was part of a research tradition that includes laboratory studies of control over stressors using both animal and human subjects, the effects of stress in natural settings, and field experiments on the general effects of perceived control. Aronson et al. also point to research on the "jigsaw" technique to reduce conflict among different ethnic and racial groups in a school setting (Aronson, Stephan, Sikes, Blaney, & Snapp, 1978). In the "jigsaw" classroom, each student in a group learns a portion of a larger lesson. In order for all the students in the group to learn the lesson, they must work together cooperatively to teach one another the material. The effectiveness of the technique in reducing intergroup conflict has been demonstrated in both laboratory and field settings. These studies have also led to laboratory investigations of the exact processes that occur to produce the effect.

THE IMPORTANCE OF REPLICATIONS

Throughout this chapter, **replication** has been stressed as a way of overcoming any problems of generalization that occur in a single study. There are two types of replications to consider: exact replications and conceptual replications.

Exact replications

An **exact replication** is an attempt to replicate precisely the procedures of a study to see if the same results are obtained. A researcher who obtains an unexpected finding will frequently attempt a replication to make sure that the finding is reliable. If you are starting your own work on a problem, you may try to replicate a crucial study to make sure that you understand the procedures and can obtain the same results. Often, exact replications occur when a researcher builds on the findings of a prior study. For example, suppose you were intrigued by the Tversky and Kahneman (1983) study on the judgments of probabilities of single and joint events. In your research, you might replicate the procedures used in the original study while expanding on the original research. Specifically, you might study whether people who have had a course in statistics or probability respond differently to the problems, what happens when a third joint event is added, or whether it makes a difference if the events could actually happen to participants in the study. In all of these replication situations, confidence in the generalizability of the findings is increased because they were obtained with different subjects and often in a different locale with different experimenters.

Sometimes, a researcher will be unable to replicate a previous finding. A single failure to replicate doesn't reveal much, though; it is unrealistic to assume, on the basis of a single failure to replicate, that the previous research is invalid. Failures to replicate share the same problems as nonsignificant results, discussed in Chapter 11. A failure to replicate could mean that the original results are invalid, but it could also mean that the replication attempt was flawed. For example, if the replication is based on the procedure as reported in a journal article, it is possible that the article omitted an important aspect of the procedure. For this reason, it is usually a good idea to write the researcher to obtain detailed information on all of the materials that were used in the study.

A single failure to replicate is not adequate cause for discarding the original research finding. However, repeated failures to replicate do lead to reconsideration of the original findings. Eventually, we may conclude that the original results were a fluke—a Type I error was made. This is especially likely when unsuccessful attempts to replicate employ not only the original procedures but different procedures as well.

Conceptual replications

The use of different procedures to replicate a research finding is called a **conceptual replication.** Conceptual replications are even more important than exact replications in furthering our understanding of behavior.

In most research, the goal is to discover whether a relationship between conceptual variables exists. Thus, Tversky and Kahneman (1983) were interested in the effects of single versus conjoint events on probability judgments; the specific method of operationalizing the variable was to have subjects make judgments about the probability of a flood versus the probability of an earthquake *and* a flood. Or consider the Petty, Cacioppo, and Goldman (1981) study of the effect of issue involvement on attitude change. Here, involvement was manipulated by having subjects think either that a new graduation requirement would affect them or that it would only affect students who would graduate ten years later. The specific manipulations are operational definitions of the conceptual variables of interest. The same general point can be made about the operational definitions of dependent variables as well.

In a conceptual replication, the same independent variable is manipulated in a different way (and possibly the dependent variable is measured in a different way, too). Such conceptual replications are extremely important in the social sciences because the specific manipulations and measures are usually operational definitions of complex variables. A crucial generalization question is whether the relationship holds when other ways of manipulating or measuring the variables are studied. Do different types of single and conjoint probability problems lead to the same result? Does issue involvement result in the same conclusion when it is manipulated in different ways? When conceptual replications produce similar results, our confidence in the generalizability of relationships between variables is greatly increased.

This discussion should also alert you to an important way of thinking about research findings. The findings represent relationships between conceptual variables but are grounded in specific operations. You may read about the specific methods employed in a study conducted 20 years ago and question whether the study could be replicated today. Or the specific method may seem narrowly focused on one particular issue and setting—for example, issue involvement manipulated by having college seniors think that a proposal to institute a comprehensive examination as a graduation requirement might affect them. These concerns are not as serious when placed within the context of conceptual replications. Admittedly, a specific method from a study conducted at one time might not be effective today, given changes in

226

today's political and cultural climate. A conceptual replication of the manipulation, however, would demonstrate that the relationship between the conceptual theoretical variables is still present. Similarly, the narrow focus of a particular study is less problematic if the general finding is replicated with different procedures.

EVALUATING GENERALIZATIONS
VIA LITERATURE REVIEWS AND META-ANALYSIS

Researchers have traditionally drawn conclusions about the generalizability of research findings by conducting literature reviews. In a literature review, a reviewer reads a number of studies that address a particular topic and then writes a paper summarizing findings that are strongly supported by the research (e.g., obtained across numerous conceptual replications), findings that are less strongly supported (e.g., reported by only a few researchers), and findings that are puzzling because of contradictory results (e.g., results obtained in some studies but not others). Literature reviews provide valuable information because they organize many studies on a topic and point to areas in which there are well-established findings and others in which more research needs to be done.

The conclusions in a traditional literature review are based on the subjective impressions of the reviewer. There is nothing wrong with this practice; however, another technique for comparing a large number of studies in an area has emerged in recent years. This technique is termed **meta-analysis** (Rosenthal, 1991). You are likely to see references to meta-analysis studies as you become more familiar with research in psychology.

In a meta-analysis, the researcher combines the actual results of a number of studies. The analysis consists of a set of statistical procedures that employ effect sizes to compare a given finding across many different studies. Instead of relying on subjective judgments obtained in a traditional literature review, statistical conclusions can be drawn. The statistical procedures need not concern you. They involve examining several features of the results of studies, including the effect sizes and significance levels obtained. The important point here is that meta-analysis is a method for determining the reliability of a finding by examining the results from many different studies.

An example of a meta-analysis is a study by Smith and Glass (1977) on the effectiveness of psychotherapy techniques as reported in 375 studies. The researchers examined the reported effects of different modes of therapy (e.g., behavioral, psychodynamic, and client-centered therapies) across many different studies that used several different outcome measures (e.g., anxiety reduction, self-esteem). They then applied appropriate statistical techniques to combine and compare the different results. Their research allowed them to conclude that therapy does have a beneficial effect. In fact, they concluded that the "typical therapy client is better off than 75% of untreated controls." They were also able to make general statements that applied to different types of therapies. For example, some therapies, such as systematic desensitization, produce very large changes in behavior compared to others; however, overall there was no difference between the "behavioral" types of therapies and the "traditional" ones.

The information obtained from a meta-analysis such as the one conducted by Smith and Glass is very informative. In a traditional literature review, it would be very difficult to provide the type of general conclusion that was reached with the meta-analysis. Anyone would find it difficult to easily integrate the results of so many studies with different experimental designs, subject types, and measures. In fact, if you read all the studies and someone asked you the simple question "Does psychotherapy work?" you might proceed to spend a day telling the person about all the specific studies and the complexities you noted in reading the literature. This would be the result of information overload and the fact that it is difficult to integrate information from diverse sources.

An interesting study by Cooper and Rosenthal (1980) actually demonstrated that researchers are more likely to draw strong conclusions about a set of findings when using meta-analysis than when using traditional subjective judgments. In this study, the researchers read only seven articles on gender differences in task persistence; still, the researchers who used meta-analysis were more likely to conclude that females do show greater task persistence than do males. Beaman (1991) has also favorably compared meta-analysis with traditional reviews. It is interesting to note as well that meta-analyses are able to show that some findings are less robust than we previously thought them to be—for example, the physical attractiveness stereotype that "what is beautiful is good" (Eagly, Ashmore, Makhijani, & Longo, 1991).

GIVING PSYCHOLOGY AWAY

In a presidential address to the American Psychological Association, George Miller (1969) discussed "psychology as a means of promoting human welfare." He spoke of "giving psychology away." Miller was addressing the broadest issue of generalizability, taking what we know about human behavior and allowing it to be applied by many people in all areas of everyday life. Perhaps the strongest evidence for the generalizability of research findings is to view what has happened to psychology in the years since Miller urged us to give psychology away. The impact of psychological research can be seen in the fields of health care (programs to reduce stress and promote health-related behaviors), the environment (designing work spaces that promote worker satisfaction and productivity, providing energy companies with ways of encouraging conservation), law (providing data on the effects of 6- versus 12-person juries, showing how the testimony of eyewitnesses can be biased), and education (providing methods for encouraging academic performance or reducing conflict among different ethnic groups). These are only a few of the ways that basic research has been applied to help promote human welfare. Despite all the potential problems of generalizing research findings that were highlighted in this chapter, the evidence suggests that we can generalize our findings to many aspects of our lives.

STUDY TERMS

Conceptual replication	External validity	Mundane realism
Exact replication	Literature review	Solomon four-group
Experimental realism	Meta-analysis	design

REVIEW QUESTIONS

1. Why should a researcher be concerned about generalizing to other subject populations? What are some of the subject population generalization problems that a researcher might confront?

2. What is the source of the problem of generalizing to other experimenters? How can this problem be solved?

3. Why is pretesting a problem for generalization important? Describe how pretesting can affect generalization.

4. Distinguish between mundane and experimental realism.

5. Distinguish between an exact replication and a conceptual replication. What is the value of a conceptual replication?

6. What is a meta-analysis?

ACTIVITY QUESTIONS

1. It is now possible to collect data for experiments and surveys using the World Wide Web on the Internet. Anyone in the world who is connected to the Internet can access a researcher's computer and take part in the study. What issues of generalization might arise when interpreting the results of such studies?

2. Use *Psychological Abstracts* or *PsycLIT* to find abstracts of articles that included race, ethnicity, gender, or nationality as a variable in the study.

What conclusions do you draw about generalization to these populations?

3. Find a meta-analysis published in a journal; two good sources are the *Review of Educational Research* and *Psychological Bulletin*. What conclusions were drawn from the meta-analysis?

4. Obtain an article from a social psychology journal. After briefly summarizing the experimental procedure, discuss the experiment in terms of mundane realism and experimental realism.

APPENDIX

Writing Research Reports

INTRODUCTION

This appendix presents the information you will need to prepare a written report of your research for a course and for possible publication in a professional journal. We will consider the specific rules that should be followed in organizing and presenting research results. These rules are a great convenience for both the writer and the reader. They provide structure for the report and a uniform method of presentation, making it easier for the reader to understand and evaluate the report.

Specific rules vary from one discipline to another. A rule for presenting research results in psychology may not apply to the same situation in, for example, sociology research. Also, the rules may vary depending on whether you are preparing the report for a class, a thesis, or submission to a journal. Fortunately, the variation is usually minor, and the general rules of presentation are much the same across disciplines and situations.

The format presented here for writing research reports is drawn from the *Publication Manual of the American Psychological Association*, 4th ed. (1994). APA style is used in many journals in psychology, mental health, family relations, and education. If you are concerned about specific rules for a particular journal, consult a recent issue of that journal. You may purchase a copy of the *Publication Manual* through your college bookstore or directly from the American Psychological Association (APA Order Department, P.O. Box 2710, Hyattsville, MD 20784-0710; 1-800-374-2721). APA has also published a student workbook and training guide for the *Publication Manual* (Gelfand & Walker, 1990). Other useful sources for preparing papers are brief books by Rosnow and Rosnow (1995) and Sternberg (1993).

The fourth edition of the APA *Publication Manual* is a major revision and was guided by principles of "specificity and sensitivity." First, papers should be written at a level of specificity and detail that will allow others to replicate the research. Second, papers should be free of inappropriate language that might be interpreted as biased and insensitive. The manual also includes new manuscript preparation guidelines that take advantage of the features of word processing software. Throughout this appendix, examples that are intended to appear as you would type them in your papers appear in a `typewriter font`; this convention is also used in the APA *Publication Manual*.

WRITING STYLE

In any format for preparing your report, writing style is important. A poorly written report that is difficult to understand is of no value (and almost certainly will earn you a low grade!). Also, a good paper should be neatly typed and free of spelling and typographical errors.

Clarity

Clarity in writing is essential. Be precise and clear in presenting ideas. It is often a good idea to think about your intended audience. Usually, it is best to direct your paper to an audience that is unfamiliar with your general topic and the methods you used to study the topic. At the same time, you should usually assume that the reader has a general familiarity with statistics and hypothesis testing. Thus, you would want to eliminate jargon that most readers will not comprehend. Sometimes, a researcher will develop an abbreviated notation for referring to a specific variable or procedure; such abbreviations may be convenient when communicating with others who are directly involved in the research project, but they are confusing to the general reader. At the same time, statistical outcomes can usually be presented without defining terms such as *mean, standard deviation*, or *significance*. These are only general guidelines, however. Rosnow and Rosnow (1995) point out that when your intended audience is your instructor, you should pay close attention to what the instructor has to say about expectations for the paper!

The entire report should have a coherent structure. Ideas should be presented in an orderly, logical progression to facilitate understanding. Again, if you write your report for someone who is just being introduced to your ideas and research findings for the first time, you will be more likely to clearly communicate with the reader.

One method for producing a more organized report is to use an outline. Many writers plan a paper by putting their thoughts and ideas into outline form; in fact, computer word processing programs usually have features that facilitate outlining. The outline then serves as a writing guide. This method usually forces writers to develop a logical structure before writing the paper.

Other writers prefer to use a less structured approach for the first draft. They then try to outline what has been written. If the paper does not produce a coherent outline, the organization needs to be improved.

After completing your first draft, you would be wise to let it sit for a day or so and then reread it. Carefully proofread the paper, paying special attention to grammar and spelling. Some common grammatical considerations are described here, and you can also use a computer word processor to check for spelling and grammar. After you make changes and corrections, you may want to get feedback from others. Find one or more people who will read your report critically and suggest improvements. Be prepared, then, to write several drafts before you have a satisfactory finished product.

Acknowledging the work of others

It is extremely important to clearly distinguish your own words and ideas from those obtained from other sources. If you use a passage drawn from an article or book, make sure that the passage is presented as a direct quotation. There is nothing wrong with quoting another author as long as you acknowledge your source. Never present another person's idea as your own. This is plagiarism and is inexcusable.

Sometimes, writers are tempted to fill a paper with quotes from other sources or to quote another paper at great length (e.g., several paragraphs or more). This practice is usually distracting and counterproductive. Be direct and use your own descriptions and interpretations while at the same time acknowledging your sources. If you have any questions about how to properly include material from your source articles in your own paper, consult your instructor.

Active versus passive voice

Many writers rely too much on the passive voice in their reports, perhaps because they believe that the passive voice makes their writing seem more "scientific." Consider the following sentences:

It was found by Yee and Johnson (1996) that rats prefer . . .

Participants were administered the test after a 10-minute rest period.

Participants were read the instructions by the experimenter.

Now consider those same sentences written in a more active voice:

Yee and Johnson (1996) found that rats prefer . . .

Participants took the test after a 10-minute rest period.

I read the instructions to the participants.

The prose that seems stilted with the passive voice is much more direct and natural when phrased in the active voice. It is, of course, possible that the active voice can become distracting if used too much. "I" in particular can

233

become awkward if it begins too many sentences. A good practice is to vary sentence constructions.

Biased language

As noted previously, APA style is guided by the principles of specificity and sensitivity. Be sensitive to the possibility that your writing might convey a bias, however unintentional, regarding age, gender, sexual orientation, and race or ethnicity. As a general principle, you should be as specific as possible when referring to groups of people. For example, referring to the participants in your study as "Korean Americans and Vietnamese Americans" is more specific and accurate than "Asians." Also, be sensitive to the use of labels that might be offensive to members of certain groups. In practice, this means that you refer to people using the terms that these people prefer. Also, you should avoid implicit labels, such as "The lesbian sample, in contrast to the sample of normal women . . ." or "We tested groups of autistics and normals." The latter phrase could be written as "We tested people with autism and without autism."

The APA *Publication Manual* gives numerous examples of ways of being sensitive to gender, racial and ethnic identity, age, sexual orientation, and disabilities. The term *gender* refers to males and females as social groups. Thus, *gender* would be the proper term to use in a phrase such as "gender difference in average salary." The term *sex* refers to biological aspects of men and women—for example, "sex fantasies" or "sex differences in the size of certain brain structures." The use of gender pronouns can be problematical. For example, you should not use *he*, *his*, *man*, *man's*, and so on when both males and females are meant. Sentences can usually be rephrased or specific pronouns deleted to avoid linguistic biases. For example, "The worker is paid according to his productivity" can be changed to "The worker is paid according to productivity" or "Workers are paid according to their productivity." In the first case, the "his" was simply deleted; in the second case, the subject of the sentence was changed to plural. Do *not* try to avoid sexist language by simply substituting "s/he" whenever that might appear convenient.

There are certain rules when referring to racial and ethnic groups as well. These groups are capitalized and never hyphenated—for example, Black, White, African American, Latino, Asian, Asian American. The manual also reminds us that the terms that members of racial and ethnic groups use to describe themselves may change over time, and there may be a lack of consensus about a preferred term. Currently, for example, both Black and African American are generally acceptable. Depending on a number of factors, participants may prefer to be called Hispanic, Latino, Chicano, or Mexican American. You are urged to use the term most preferred by your participants.

The APA *Publication Manual* includes a great deal of information and numerous examples to encourage sensitivity in writing reports. The best advice is to review your papers for possible problems at least once prior to writing your final draft. If you have any questions about appropriate language, consult the manual and others whose opinions you respect.

Typing and word processing

You will eventually have to prepare a typed copy of your paper. In APA style, the paper should be *entirely double-spaced*. The margins for text should be *at least 1 inch* on all four sides of the page; in the example paper, the margins are set at 1¼ inches. Page headers should set approximately ½ inch from the top of the page. All pages must be numbered except for figure pages at the end of the paper. Words should never be hyphenated at the end of a line. Rather than break a word, let lines run a little short or a little long. Such details used to be called typing rules; in the era of word processing, they become rules for printing.

Many students use word processing computer programs to prepare their papers. With a computer, you can improve your writing and submit a high-quality paper far more easily. If you are not already using a word processor, you should consider purchasing your own computer system or at least investigate word processing facilities on your campus. When you use a word processor, your writing is no longer typed copy but simply characters on a computer screen. Correcting, revising, moving, and deleting text is no longer a chore; such changes are easily made on the computer screen using the word processing program. Writing several drafts of a paper is easy because you don't have to retype the paper each time you wish to make a change.

Many word processing programs also include writing tools such as a spell check, thesaurus, grammar analysis, and outliner (if not, separate writing tool programs can be used with the word processor). The spelling checker examines your paper for spelling errors and even suggests possible corrections for misspelled words; the thesaurus feature allows you to examine possible alternative words to express an idea. Grammar programs analyze the grammar and readability of your paper; such programs look for overlong sentences, obscure words, and simple grammatical mistakes. Finally, an outlining tool can facilitate the process of preparing an outline and help you better plan your actual paper.

Word processors also provide many advanced printing options such as full justification of text against the margins, different type styles and type sizes, italics and boldface, and other features that make the paper resemble an actual published report. Never use full justification of text; set justification to the left margin only. Use a font that is normal in size (10 or 12 characters per inch) and appearance (Courier, Times Roman, or Ariel), and use the same font throughout. When submitting papers for publication, you should not use boldface type and you should always underline any text that you would italicize in a published paper (pay attention to the use of underlining in the headings and references in the examples given later in the appendix). When you are preparing a paper for a class or a thesis, using the boldface and italics capability of a word processing program may be acceptable; your instructor will provide you with the definitive guidelines. Finally, you need to have only *one* space between a sentence-ending punctuation and the beginning of the following sentence. This practice can make the paper look more attractive when using a proportional font, and it saves a step when publishing the paper.

ORGANIZATION OF THE REPORT

A research report is organized into five major parts: abstract, introduction, method, results, and discussion. References must be listed using a particular format. The report may also include tables and figures used in presenting the research results. We will consider the parts of the paper in the order prescribed by APA style. You should refer to the sample paper at the end of Appendix A as you read the material that follows.

Title page

The first page of the paper is the title page. It is a separate page and is numbered as page 1. You should note in the sample paper that the title page does in fact list the title; however, there are other important items of information as well.

At the top of the title page is a page header. The page header includes a short title, consisting of the first two or three words of the title of your paper, and a page number. These should be typed so that the page number is flush to the right margin of the paper. If you are using a word processor, use the page header feature to create a header that will be printed approximately halfway between the text of the paper and the top of each page (in the sample paper, the header is set for ½ inch from the top). Do not try to manually type a page header at the top of every page of your paper; instead, use the page header function of your word processing program. The page header will appear on every page of your paper except the figures. The page header provides a heading for your readers; more importantly, if the pages get separated accidentally, it will be easy for the reader to put them together again in proper order.

The first line of the title page will be the running head for publication; it is typed flush against the left margin (note that all letters in the running head are capitalized). The running head is an abbreviated title and should be no more than 50 characters (letters, numbers, spaces) in length. If the paper is published in a journal, the running head is printed as a heading at the top of pages to help readers identify the article. Note that the running head is used for publication purposes and appears only once; the page header, in contrast, is used by readers of your paper and appears on every page. Do not confuse the running head and the page header. In the sample paper, the short title is "Smell of Success"—a brief description drawn from the first few words of the title of the paper. However, the running head is "EVALUATIONS OF JOB

236

APPLICANTS"—which is longer than the short title and more descriptive of the content of the paper.

The remainder of the title page consists of the title, author byline, and institutional affiliation. All are centered on the page.

The title should be fairly short (usually no more than 12–15 words) and should inform the reader of the nature of your research. A good way to do this is to include the names of your variables in the title. For example, the following titles are both short and informative:

Effect of Anxiety on Mathematical Problem Solving

Memory for Faces Among Elderly and Young Adults

Sometimes, a colon in the title will help to convey the nature of your research or even add a bit of "flair" to your title:

Cognitive Responses in Persuasion: Affective and Evaluative Determinants

Comparing the Tortoise and the Hare: Gender Differences and Experience in Dynamic Spatial Reasoning Tasks

Another method of titling a paper is to pose the question that the research addresses. For example:

Do Response Modality Effects Support Multiprocessor Models of Divided Attention?

Does Occupational Stereotyping Still Exist?

Abstract

The abstract is a brief summary of the research, 100–150 words in length (no more than 900 characters including spaces and punctuation marks). It should describe the research problem that was studied, the method used to study the problem (including information on the characteristics of the participants), the results, and the major conclusions.

The abstract should provide enough information so that the reader can decide whether to read the entire report, and it should make the report easier to comprehend when it is read. Although the abstract appears at the beginning of your report, you will probably want to wait until the body of the report is completed before you write the abstract.

The abstract is typed on a separate page and is numbered page 2. The word "Abstract" is centered at the top of the page. The abstract is always typed as a single paragraph in a "block" format with no paragraph indention.

Introduction

The introduction section begins on a new page (page 3), with the title of your report typed at the top of the page. Note that the author's name doesn't appear on this page; this allows a reviewer to read the paper while blind regarding the name of the author. This section introduces the reader to the

237

problem being investigated, reviews past research and theory relevant to the problem, presents the predicted outcomes of the research, and gives the method used for testing the predictions. After reading the introduction, the reader should know why you decided to do the research and how you decided to go about doing it.

Bem (1981) has suggested that, whenever possible, the introduction should begin with an opening statement of two or three sentences. The opening statement is intended to give the reader an appreciation of the broad context and significance of the topic being studied. This is worthwhile if it can be done: It helps readers, even those who are unfamiliar with the topic, to understand and appreciate why the topic was studied in the first place.

Following the opening statement, the introduction provides a description of past research and theory. This called the literature review. An exhaustive review of past research is not necessary (if there are major literature reviews of the topic, you would of course refer the reader to the reviews). Rather, you want to describe only the research and theoretical issues that are clearly related to your study. You should state explicitly how this previous work is logically connected to your research problem. This tells the reader why your research was conducted.

The final part of the introduction tells the reader exactly what hypothesis is being tested or what specific question is being addressed. Here, you state what variables you are studying, what results you expect, and why you expect these results.

Method

The method section begins immediately after you have completed the introduction (on the same page if space permits). This section provides the reader with detailed information about how your study was conducted. Ideally, there should be enough information in the method section to allow a reader to replicate your study.

The method section typically is divided into a number of subsections. The nature of the subsections is determined by the details of the research you are describing. The subsections should be organized to present the method as clearly as possible. Some of the most commonly used subsections include the overview, participants, apparatus, and procedures.

Overview   If the experimental design and procedures used in the research are complex, a brief overview of the method should be presented to help the reader understand the information that follows.

Participants   A subsection on the participants or respondents is always necessary. The number and nature of the participants should be described. Age, sex, ethnicity, and any other relevant characteristics should be described. State explicitly how participants were recruited and what incentives for participating might have been used. The number of individuals in each experimental condition also can be included here.

In animal research, it is common practice to report the species, strain number, and any other information that identifies the type of animal. The number of animals and their age and sex also are indicated. If information about care, feeding, or handling conditions in the laboratory is relevant, it should be described as well.

Apparatus   An apparatus subsection may be necessary if special equipment is used in the experiment. The brand name and model number of the equipment may be specified; some apparatus may be described in detail. This information would be included if it is needed to replicate the experiment.

Procedure   The procedure subsection tells the reader exactly how the study was conducted. One way to report this information is to describe, step by step, what occurred in the experiment.

The procedure subsection should tell the reader what instructions were read to the participants, how the independent variables were manipulated, and how the dependent variables were measured. The methods used to control extraneous variables also should be described. These would include randomization procedures, counterbalancing, and special means that were used to keep a variable constant across all conditions. Finally, the method of debriefing should be described. If your study used a nonexperimental method, you would still provide details on exactly how you conducted the study and what measurement techniques you used.

It is up to you to decide how much detail to include here. Use your own judgment to determine the importance of a specific aspect of the procedure and the amount of detail that is necessary for the reader to clearly understand what was done in the study. If any detail might be important in a replication of the study, it should be included.

Other subsections   Other subsections should be included if warranted by the nature of the experiment and needed for clear presentation of the method. For example, a subsection on "testing materials" might be necessary instead of an "apparatus" subsection.

Results

In the results section, you present the results as clearly as possible. Be sure to state the alpha (probability) level that you used in making decisions about statistical significance: this will usually be .05 or .01 and only requires a simple sentence such as "an alpha level of .05 was used for statistical analyses." It is best to refer to your predictions as stated in the introduction section of your paper. The order in which your results are presented should correspond to the order of your predictions. If a manipulation check measure was made, it should be presented before the major results are described.

The results should be stated in simple sentences. For example, the results of the modeling experiment described in Chapter 10 might be expressed as follows:

```
As predicted, the model group was significantly more aggressive
than the no-model group, t(18) = 4.025, p < .01. The mean
aggression score in the model group was 5.20, and the no-model
group mean was 3.10.
```

These two sentences inform the reader of the general pattern of the results, the obtained means, and the statistical significance of the results (note the placement of the results of the t-test, degrees of freedom, and significance level).

If the results are relatively straightforward, they can be presented entirely in sentence form. If the study involved a complex design, tables and figures may be needed to clarify presentation of the results.

Tables and figures   Tables are generally used to present large arrays of data. For example, a table might be useful in a design with several dependent measures; the means of the different groups for all dependent measures would be presented in the table. Tables are also convenient when a factorial design has been used. For example, in a $2 \times 2 \times 3$ factorial design, a table could be used to present all 12 means.

Figures should be included when a visual display of the results would help the reader understand the outcome of the study. Figures may be used to illustrate a significant interaction or show trends over time.

In APA style, tables and figures are not presented in the main body of the manuscript. Rather, they are placed at the end of the paper. Each table and figure appears on a separate page. A table or figure is noted in the text by referring to a table or figure number and describing the content of the table or figure. Never make a reference to the placement of the figure because the placement is determined by the typesetter.

When you are writing a research report for a purpose other than publication—for example, to fulfill a course or degree requirement—it may be more convenient to place each figure and table on a separate page within the main body of the paper. Because rules about the placement of tables and figures may vary, you should check on the proper format before writing your report.

Tables and figures are supplements to your written report of the results. They do not diminish your responsibility to clearly state the nature of the results in the text of your report. In fact, when tables or figures are used, you must also describe the important features of them.

Discussion of the results   It is usually *not* appropriate to discuss the implications of the results within the results section. However, the results and discussion section may be combined if the discussion is brief and greater clarity is achieved by doing so.

Discussion

The discussion section is the proper place to discuss the implications of the results. One way to organize the discussion is to begin by summarizing the original purpose and expectations of the study and then to state whether the results were consistent with your expectations. If the results do support your original ideas, you should discuss how your findings contribute to knowledge of the problem that you investigated. You will want to consider the relationship between your results and past research and theory. If you did not obtain the expected results, you will want to discuss possible explanations. The explanations would be quite different, of course, depending on whether the results were the opposite of what you expected or were nonsignificant.

It is often a good idea to include your own criticisms of the study. Try to anticipate what a reader might find wrong with your methodology. For example, if you used the correlational method, you might point out problems of cause and effect and possible extraneous variables that might be operating. Sometimes, there may be major or minor flaws that could be corrected in a subsequent study (if you had the time, money, etc.). You can describe such flaws and suggest corrections. If there are potential problems of generalizing your results, state the problems and give reasons that you think the results would or would not generalize.

The results will probably have implications for future research. If so, you should discuss the direction that research might take. It is also possible that the results have practical implications—for example, for rearing children or improving learning in the classroom. Discussion of these larger issues is usually placed at the end of the discussion section. Finally, you will probably want to include a brief concluding paragraph that provides "closure" to the entire paper.

References

The list of references begins on a new page. The references must contain complete citations for all sources mentioned in your report. Do not omit any sources from the list of references; also, do not include any sources that are not mentioned in your report. The exact procedures for citing sources within the body of your report and in your list of references are described in detail later in Appendix A.

Appendix

An appendix is rarely provided in manuscripts submitted for publication. The APA *Publication Manual* notes that an appendix might be appropriate when necessary material would be distracting in the main body of the report. Examples of appendices include a sample of a questionnaire or survey instrument, a complex mathematical proof, or a long list of words used as stimulus items. An appendix (or several appendices) are much more appropriate for a student research project or a thesis. The appendix might include the entire questionnaire that was used, a new test that was developed, or other materials employed in the study. Check with your instructor concerning the appropriateness of an appendix for your paper. If an appendix is provided, it begins on a new page with the word *Appendix* centered at the top.

Author note

An author note may be provided. The author note typically begins with a paragraph that gives the department affiliations of the authors (this is necessary only when a paper has multiple authors or when an author's current affiliation has changed since the study was completed). Another paragraph may give details about the background of the study (e.g., that it is based on the first author's master's thesis) and acknowledgments (e.g., grant support, colleagues who assisted with the study, and so on). A final paragraph begins with "Correspondence concerning this article should be addressed to . . ." followed by the mailing address of the person designated for that purpose. An author note will probably be unnecessary for class research reports.

Footnotes

Footnotes, if used, are not typed in the body of the text. Instead, all footnotes are typed on a separate page and placed at the end of the paper. Avoid using footnotes unless they are absolutely necessary. They tend to be distracting to readers, and the information usually can and should be integrated into the actual body of the paper.

Tables

Each table should be on a separate page. As noted previously, APA style requires placement of tables at the end of the paper, but for a class you may be asked to place your tables on separate pages within the body of the paper. A table is included in the sample paper at the end of Appendix A. In preparing your table, allow enough space so that the table does not appear cramped in a small portion of the page. Areas of the table are defined by typed horizontal lines (do not use vertical lines). Give some thought to the title so that it accurately and clearly describes the content of the table. You may wish to use an explanatory note in the table to show significance levels or the range of possible values on a variable. Before you make up your own tables, examine the tables in a recent issue of one of the journals published by the American Psychological Association (see Chapter 2).

Figures

There are two special APA style rules for the placement and preparation of figures: (1) Figures are placed after the tables, and (2) a separate page containing the figure captions is provided before the figures. However, either or both of these rules may not apply to student reports or theses. You may be asked to place each figure on a separate page at the appropriate point in the body of the text, and you may not need a figure caption page (this is only for the convenience of typesetting and printing the paper). Also, if you are following true APA style, there is no page number or short title on the figure pages (the figure number is written on the back of the figure in pencil).

If you are preparing your figure by hand, it is a good idea to buy graph paper with lines that do not photocopy (a photocopy of the graph is turned in with your final report. Lines are drawn using black ink and a ruler (alternatively, you can use press-on type and rules, available at a graphics supply store). In deciding on the size of the figure, a good rule is that the horizontal axis should be about 5 inches wide and the vertical axis should be about 3½ inches long. Both the vertical and the horizontal axis must be labeled. Dependent and criterion variables are placed on the vertical axis. Independent and predictor variables are placed on the horizontal axis (see Chapter 4).

Instead of preparing your graphs by hand, consider using computer graphics software. You may have access to such software in your word processing or spreadsheet program. Graphics software makes preparation of graphs easier and reduces the frustration that arises when you make mistakes. The figure in the sample paper was prepared using a popular spreadsheet program.

Remember that the purpose of a figure is to increase readers' comprehension of results by having a graphical display of data. If the graph is cluttered with information so that it confuses a reader, it is not serving its purpose. You will need to carefully plan your graphs to make sure that you are accurately and clearly informing the reader. If you become interested in the topic of how to display information in graphs and charts, two books by Tufte (1983, 1990) are recommended. Tufte explores a variety of ways of presenting data, factors that lead to clarity, and ways that graphs can deceive the reader.

Summary: Order of pages

To summarize, the organization of your paper is as follows:

1. Title page (page 1)
2. Abstract (page 2)
3. Pages of text (start on new page 3)
    a. Title at top of first page begins the introduction
    b. Method
    c. Results
    d. Discussion
4. References (start on new page)
5. Appendix (start on new page if included)
6. Author note (start on new page if included)

7. Footnotes (start on new page if included)

8. Tables, with table captions (each on separate page)

9. Figure caption(s) (all together on one separate page)

10. Figures (each on separate page)

You should now have a general idea of how to structure and write your report. The remainder of Appendix A will focus on some of the technical rules that may be useful as you prepare your own research report.

THE USE OF HEADINGS

Papers written in APA style use one to five levels of headings. Most commonly, you will use "level 2" and "level 4" headings, and you may need to use "level 5" headings as well. These are

(Level 2)   `Centered Heading`

(Level 4)   `Margin heading`

       `The text begins indented on a new line.`

(Level 5)   `Paragraph heading`. `The heading is indented and the`

    `text begins on the same line.`

Level 1 and level 3 headings will not be described because they are used in more complex papers in which multiple experiments are presented.

Level 2, or centered, headings are used to head major sections of the report: Abstract, Title (on page 3), Method, Results, Discussion, References, and so on. Level 2 headings are typed with initial capitals and lowercase letters (i.e., the first letter of each word is capitalized).

Level 4, or margin, headings are used to divide major sections into subsections. Level 4 headings are typed flush to the left margin. They are initial capped and underlined. For example, the Method section is divided into at least two subsections: Participants and Procedure. The correct format is

                       `Method`

`Participants`

   `The description of the participants begins on a new line.`

`Procedure`

   `The procedure is now described in detail.`

Level 5, or paragraph, headings are used to organize material within a subsection. For example, the Procedure subsection might be broken down into separate categories for describing instructions to participants, the independent variable manipulation, measurement of the dependent variable, and debriefing. Each of these would be introduced through the use of a paragraph heading.

Paragraph headings begin on a new line, indented five spaces. The first word begins with a capital letter; the remaining words are all typed in lower-case letters. The heading ends with a period. The entire heading including the period is underlined. All information that appears between a paragraph heading and the next heading (of any level) must be related to the paragraph heading.

CITING AND REFERENCING SOURCES

Citation style

Whenever you refer to information reported by other researchers, you *must* accurately identify the sources. APA journals use the author-date citation method: The author name(s) and year of publication are inserted at appropriate points. The citation style depends on whether the author name(s) are part of the narrative or are in parentheses.

One author   When the author's name is part of the narrative, include the publication date in parentheses immediately after the name:

```
Dion (1972) found that adults judged the misbehavior of

unattractive children to be more undesirable than the same

misbehavior of attractive children.
```

When the author's name is not part of the narrative, the name and date are cited in parentheses at the end of an introductory phrase or at the end of the sentence:

```
In one study (Dion, 1972), adults judged the misbehavior . . .

It has been reported that adults judge the misbehavior of

unattractive children to be highly undesirable (Dion, 1972).
```

Two authors   When the work has two authors, both names are included in each reference citation. The difference between narrative and parenthetical citations is in the use of the conjunction "and" and the ampersand "&." When the names are part of a sentence, use the word "and." When the complete citation is in parentheses, use the "&" symbol:

```
Parke and Sawin (1977) reported that fathers spend much more

time playing with their infants than in caregiving activities.

Fathers are more likely to spend time playing with their

infants than in caregiving (Parke & Sawin, 1977).
```

Three to five authors   When a report has three to five authors, all author names are cited the first time the reference occurs. Thereafter, cite the first author's surname followed by the abbreviation "et al." ("and others") along with the publication date. The abbreviation may be used in narrative and parenthetical citations:

First citation

Cunningham, Roberts, Barbee, Druen, and Wu (1995) reported that members of different cultural groups were highly similar in their ratings of facial attractiveness.

Research suggests that members of different cultural groups use similar criteria in judging facial attractiveness (Cunningham, Roberts, Barbee, Druen, & Wu, 1995).

Subsequent citations

Cunningham et al. (1995) also examined judgments of bodies made by Blacks and Whites.

The judgments made by members of different groups were highly correlated (Cunningham et al., 1995).

Another question about subsequent citations is whether to include the publication date each time an article is referenced. Within a paragraph, you do *not* need to include the year in subsequent citations as long as the study cannot be confused with other studies cited in your report.

First citation

In a recent study of reaction times, Smith and Jones (1995) found . . .

Subsequent citations within a paragraph

Smith and Jones also reported that . . .

When subsequent citations are in another paragraph or in another section of the report, the publication date should be included.

Six or more authors   Occasionally, you will reference a report with six or more authors. In this case, use the abbreviation "et al." after the first author's last name in *every* citation. Although you would not list all author names in the text, the citation in the references section of the report should include the names of all authors.

References with no author   When an article has no author (e.g., some newspaper or magazine articles), cite the first two or three words of the title in quotation marks, followed by the publication date:

Citation in reference list

```
Study finds free care used more. (1982, September 5). Los
Angeles Times, p. A14.
```

Citation in text

```
In an article on free care ("Study finds," 1982), data . . .
```

Multiple works within the same parentheses   A convenient way to cite several studies on the same topic or several studies with similar findings is to reference them as a series within the same parentheses. When two or more works are by the same author(s), report them in order of year of publication, using commas to separate dates:

```
Hasam and Grammick (1981, 1982) found . . .

Past research (Hasam & Grammick, 1981, 1982) indicates . . .
```

When two or more works by different authors are cited within the same parentheses, arrange them in alphabetical order and separate citations by semicolons:

```
Memory for large amounts of information can be improved by
visual imagery techniques (Bower & Clark, 1969; Jonides, Kahn,
& Rozin, 1975; Paivio, 1971).
```

Reference list style

The APA *Publication Manual* specifies different reference formats for journal articles, books, chapters in books, technical reports, convention presentations, dissertations, and videos, among many others. Only a few of these are presented here. When in doubt about how to construct a reference, consult the APA manual (especially pages 174–222). The general format for a reference list is:

1. The references are listed in alphabetical order by first author's last name. Do not categorize references by type (i.e., books, journal articles, and so on).
2. The first line of each reference is indented as if it were the first line of a paragraph. You might think of each reference as a different paragraph.
3. Elements of a reference (authors' names, article title, publication data) are separated by periods.

Notice the spacing in typing of author's names in the examples.

When the paper is typeset for publication in the journal, the citation will appear differently than it does in the manuscript. A reference in the manuscript might appear as follows:

```
Ortiz, G. (1994). Effectiveness of PC-based flight
simulation. International Journal of Aviation Psychology, 4,
285-291.
```

However, when published it would appear as follows:

Ortiz, G. (1994). Effectiveness of PC-based flight simulation. *International Journal of Aviation Psychology*, 4, 285–291.

Format for journal articles   Most journals are organized by volume and year of publication (e.g., Volume 62 of the *Journal of Clinical and Consulting Psychology* consists of journal issues published in 1994). A common confusion is whether to include the journal issue number in addition to the volume number. The rule is simple: If the issues in a volume are paginated consecutively throughout the volume, do *not* include the journal issue number. If each issue in a volume begins with page 1, the issue number should be included. Specific examples are shown below.

In the reference list, both the name of the journal and the volume number are underlined. Also, note that only the first letter of the first word in article titles is capitalized (unless the title has a colon; then the first word after the colon is also capitalized). Here are some examples of different types of references:

One author—no issue number

```
Pavio, A. (1975). Perceptual comparisons through the mind's
eye. Memory and Cognition, 3, 635-647.
```

Two authors—use of issue number

```
Greenwald-Robbins, J., & Greenwald, R. (1994). Environmental
attitudes conceptualized through developmental theory: A
qualitative analysis. Journal of Social Issues, 50(3), 29-47.
```

Format for books   When a book is cited, the title of the book is underlined. Only the first word of the title is capitalized; however, proper nouns and the first word after a colon are also capitalized. The city of publication and the publishing company follow the title. If the city is not well known, include the U.S. Postal Service two-letter abbreviation for the state (e.g., AZ, NY, MN, TX). For example:

One-author book

```
Norman, D. A. (1988). The design of everyday things. New
York: Doubleday.
```

One-author book—second or later edition

```
Lippa, R. A. (1994). Introduction to social psychology (2nd
ed.). Pacific Grove, CA: Brooks/Cole.
```

Edited book

>   Plomin, R., & McClearn, G. E. (Eds.). (1993). <u>Nature,</u>
> <u>nurture, and psychology</u>. Washington, DC: American Psychological
> Association.

Format for articles in edited books   For edited books, the reference begins with the names of the authors of the article, not the book's editor(s). The title of the article follows. The name(s) of the editor(s), the book title, the inclusive page numbers for the article, and the publication data for the book follow, in that order. Only the book title is underlined, and only the first letters of the article and book titles are capitalized. Here are some examples:

One editor

>   Brown, A. L., & Campione, J. C. (1994). Guided discovery in
> a community of learners. In K. McGilly (Ed.), <u>Classroom</u>
> <u>lessons: Integrating cognitive theory and classroom practice</u>
> (pp. 229-270). Cambridge, MA: MIT Press.

Two editors

>   Nguyen, N. A. (1992). Living between two cultures: Treating
> first-generation Asian Americans. In L. A. Vargas & J. D. Koss-
> Chioino (Eds.), <u>Working with culture: Psychotherapeutic</u>
> <u>interventions with ethnic minority children and adolescents</u>
> (pp. 204-222). San Francisco: Jossey-Bass.

Chapter from book in multivolume series

>   Kagan, J. (1992). Temperamental contributions to emotion and
> social behavior. In M. S. Clark (Ed.), <u>Review of Personality</u>
> <u>and Social Psychology: Vol. 14. Emotion and social behavior</u>
> (pp. 99-118). Newbury Park, CA: Sage.

Format for "popular articles"   The reference styles shown below should be used for articles from magazines and newspapers. As a general rule, popular press articles are used sparingly (e.g., when no scientific articles on a topic can be found or when you want to provide an example of an event that is related to your topic). For example:

Magazine—continuous pages

>   Begley, S. (1995, March 27). Gray matters. <u>Newsweek, 125,</u>
> 48-54.

Newspaper—no author

>   Study finds free care used more. (1982, September 5). <u>Los</u>
> <u>Angeles Times,</u> p. A14.

Newspaper—discontinuous pages

> Cole, K. C. (1995, May 1). Way the brain works may play role in bias, experts say. <u>Los Angeles Times,</u> pp. A1, A18.

Format for papers and poster sessions presented at conferences   Occasionally, you may need to cite an unpublished paper or poster session that was presented at a professional meeting. Here are two examples:

Paper

> Kee, D. W., McBride, D., Neale, P., & Segal, N. (1995, November). <u>Manual and cerebral laterality in hand-discordant monozygotic twins.</u> Paper presented at the annual meeting of the Psychonomics Society, Los Angeles, CA.

Poster session

> Collins, M. A., & Zebrowitz, L. A. (1994, July). <u>The contribution of appearance to occupational outcomes in civilian and military settings.</u> Poster session presented at the annual meeting of the American Psychological Society, Washington, DC.

ABBREVIATIONS

Abbreviations are not extensively used in APA-style papers. They can be distracting because the reader must constantly try to translate the abbreviation into its full meaning. However, APA style does allow for the use of abbreviations that are accepted as words in the dictionary (specifically, Webster's *New Collegiate Dictionary*). These include IQ, REM, ESP, and AIDS.

Certain well-known terms may be abbreviated when it would make reading easier, but the full meaning should be given when the term first appears in the paper. Examples of commonly used abbreviations are:

MMPI	Minnesota Multiphasic Personality Inventory
STM	short-term memory
CS	conditioned stimulus
RT	reaction time
CVC	consonant-vowel-consonant
ANOVA	analysis of variance

Statistical terms are sometimes used in their abbreviated or symbol form. These are always underlined in a manuscript. For example:

<u>M</u>	mean
<u>SD</u>	standard deviation
<u>Mdn</u>	median

df	degrees of freedom
n	number of individuals in a group or experimental condition
N	total number of participants or respondents
p	probability (significance) level
SS	sum of squares
MS	mean square
F	value of F in analysis of variance
r	Pearson correlation coefficient
R	multiple correlation coefficient

Finally, certain abbreviations of Latin terms are regularly used in papers. Some of these abbreviations and their meanings are:

cf.	compare
e.g.	for example
etc.	and so forth
i.e.	that is
viz.	namely
vs.	versus

SOME GRAMMATICAL CONSIDERATIONS

Transition words and phrases

One way to produce a clearly written research report is to pay attention to how you connect sentences within a paragraph and connect paragraphs within a section. The transitions between sentences and paragraphs should be smooth and consistent with the line of reasoning. Some commonly used transition words and phrases and their functions are described in this section.

Adverbs   Adverbs can be used as introductory words in sentences. However, you must use them to convey their implied meanings.

Adverb	Implied meaning
(Un)fortunately	It is (un)fortunate that . . .
Similarly	In a similar manner . . .
Certainly	It is certain that . . .
Clearly	It is clear that . . .

One adverb that is frequently misused as an introductory or transition word is *hopefully*. "Hopefully" means "in a hopeful manner," *not* "it is hoped that . . ."

Incorrect

Hopefully, this is not the case.

251

Correct

I *hope* this is not the case.

Words suggesting contrast   Some words and phrases suggest a contrast or contradiction between what was written immediately before and what is now being written:

Between sentences	*Within sentences*
By contrast,	whereas
On the other hand,	although
However,	but

The words in the left list refer to the previous sentence. The words in the right list connect phrases within a sentence; that is, they refer to another point in the same sentence.

Words suggesting a series of ideas   Words and phrases that suggest that information after the transition word is related or similar to information in the sentence are:

First	In addition	Last	Further
Second	Additionally	Finally	Moreover
Third	Then	Also	Another

Words suggesting implication   These words and phrases indicate that the information following the transition word is implied by or follows from the previous information:

Therefore	If . . . then
It follows that	Thus
In conclusion	Then

When you use transition words, be sure that they convey the meaning you intend. Sprinkling them around to begin sentences leads to confusion on the reader's part and thus defeats your purpose.

Troublesome words and phrases

"That" versus "which"   *That* and *which* are relative pronouns that introduce subordinate clauses and reflect the relationship of the subordinate clause to the main clause. *That* clauses are called restrictive clauses and are essential to the meaning of the sentence; *which* clauses are nonrestrictive and simply add more information. Note the different meanings of the same sentence using *that* and *which*:

The mice that performed well in the first trial were used in the second trial.

The mice, which performed well in the first trial, were used in the second trial.

The first sentence states that only mice that performed well in the first trial were used in the second. The second sentence states that all the mice were used in the second trial and they also happened to perform well in the first trial.

"While" versus "since"   *While* and *since* are subordinate conjunctions that also introduce subordinate clauses. To increase clarity in scientific writing, the APA manual suggests that *while* and *since* should be used only to refer to time. *While* is used to describe simultaneous events, and *since* is used to refer to a subsequent event:

```
The participants waited together while their personality tests
were scored.
```
```
Since the study by Dion (1972), many studies have been
published on this topic.
```

The APA manual suggests other conjunctions to use to link phrases that do not describe temporal events. *Although*, *whereas*, and *but* can be used in place of *while*, and *because* should be substituted for *since*:

Incorrect

While the study was well-designed, the report was poorly written.

Correct

Although the study was well-designed, the report was poorly written.

"Effect" versus "affect"   A common error in student reports is incorrect use of *effect* and *affect*. *Effect* is a noun that is used in scientific reports to mean "what is produced by a cause," as in "The movie had a strong effect on me." *Affect* can be a noun or a verb. As a noun, it means emotion, as in "The patient seemed depressed but she displayed very little affect." As a verb, it means "to have an influence on," as in "The listeners' responses were affected by the music they heard."

Incorrect

The independent variable *effected* their responses.

Correct

The independent variable *affected* their responses.

Incorrect

The independent variable had only a weak *affect* on the participants' behavior.

253

Correct

The independent variable had only a weak *effect* on the participants' behavior.

Singular and plural   The following words are often misused. The left list shows singular nouns requiring singular verb forms. The right list contains plural nouns that must be used with plural verbs.

Singular	*Plural*
datum	data
stimulus	stimuli
analysis	analyses
phenomenon	phenomena
medium	media
hypothesis	hypotheses
schema	schemata

Probably the most frequently misused word is *data*.

Incorrect

The data *was* coded for computer analysis.

Correct

The data *were* coded for computer analysis.

REPORTING NUMBERS AND STATISTICS

Virtually all research papers will report numbers: number of participants, number of groups, the values of statistics such as t, F, or r. Should you use numbers (e.g., 43) or should you use words (e.g., forty-three)? The general rule is to use words when expressing the numbers zero through nine but to use numbers for 10 and above. There are some important qualifications, however.

If you start a sentence with a number, you should use words even if the number is 10 or larger (e.g., "Eighty-five Introductory Psychology students participated in the study"). Starting a sentence with a number is often awkward, especially with large numbers. Therefore, you should usually try to revise the sentence to avoid the problem (e.g., "The participants were 85 students enrolled in Introductory Psychology classes").

When numbers both above and below 10 are being compared in the same sentence, use numerals for both (e.g., "Participants read either 8 or 16 paragraphs"). However, the following sentence contains an appropriate mix of numbers and words: "Participants read eight paragraphs and then answered

20 multiple-choice questions." The sentence is correct because paragraphs and questions are different entities and so are not being compared.

When reporting a percentage, always use numerals followed by a percent sign, except when beginning a sentence. This is true irrespective of whether the number is less than 10 (e.g., "Only 6% of the computer games appealed to females") or greater than 10 (e.g., "When using this technique, 85% of the participants improved their performance").

Always use numbers when describing money (e.g., "The top scorer received either $1 or $5"), ages (e.g., "5-year-olds"), points on a scale (e.g., "a 3 on a 5-point scale"), and statistics (e.g., "The mean score in the no-model group was 3.10"). An odd but sensible exception to the word-number rule occurs when two different types of numbers must appear together. An example is "Teachers identified the most aggressive fifteen 7-year-olds." This sentence avoids an awkward juxtaposition of two numbers.

Finally, you need to know about presenting statistical results within your paper. As noted previously, statistical terms are abbreviated and underlined (e.g., $\underline{M}$, $\underline{r}$, $\underline{t}$, $\underline{F}$). In addition, when reporting the results of a statistical significance test, provide the name of the test, the degrees of freedom, the value of the test statistic, and the probability level. Here are two examples of sentences that describe statistical results:

> As predicted, participants in the high-anxiety condition took longer to recognize the words ($\underline{M}$ = 2.63) than did the individuals in the low-anxiety condition ($\underline{M}$ = 1.42), $\underline{t}$(20) = 2.34, $\underline{p}$ <.05.
>
> Job satisfaction scores were significantly correlated with marital satisfaction, $\underline{r}$(50) = .38, $\underline{p}$ <.05.

If your printer cannot produce a particular symbol, you may draw it in with black ink. Pay attention to the way that statistics are described in the articles that you read. You will find that you can vary your descriptions of results to best fit your data and presentation, as well as vary your sentence constructions.

CONCLUSION

When you have completed your research report, you should feel proud of your effort. You have considered past research on a problem, conducted a research project, analyzed the results, and reported the findings. Such a research effort may result in publication or presentation at a convention. This is not the most important part of your research, however. What is most important is that you have acquired new knowledge and that your curiosity has been aroused, so that you will want to learn even more.

SAMPLE PAPER

The following is a typed manuscript of a paper that was published in a professional journal. This is intended to be a useful guide when you write and organize your own reports in APA style. The margin notes point out important elements of APA style. Read through the manuscript, paying particular attention to the general format, and make sure you understand the rules concerning page numbering, section headings, reference citation, and the format of tables and figures. Writing your first research report is always a difficult and challenging task. It will become easier as you read the research of others and practice by writing reports of your own.

The sample paper by Robert A. Baron was originally published in the *Journal of Applied Psychology* (1983, Vol. 68, pp. 709–713). Certain modifications were made to illustrate various elements of APA style. Dr. Baron graciously gave his permission to reprint the paper in this form. After noting the title of the article, you will be interested to know that Dr. Baron has invented a desktop air filtration and noise reduction unit designed to enhance the working environment. He has also continued to do research on the role of fragrances and work-related behavior (cf. Baron & Bronfen, 1994).

Smell of Success 1

Running head: EVALUATIONS OF JOB APPLICANTS

"Sweet Smell of Success"? The Impact of Pleasant
Artificial Scents on Evaluations of Job Applicants

Robert A. Baron

Purdue University

Each page has a header with a page identification and page number.

The running head is used by the typesetter as a short title at the top of each page of the printed article. It is 50 spaces maximum, and capitalized.

Title, author, and affiliation are centered on the page.

The title is usually no more than 15 words.

Double-space the entire paper.

Set margins to at least 1 inch.

Abstract begins on a
new page.

The word "Abstract"
is centered and not
underlined.

There is no
paragraph
indentation in the
abstract.

The abstract is
usually 100–150
words in length.

The word "gender"
is now used more
commonly than
"sex."

Abstract

Male and female participants interviewed male or female
applicants for an entry-level management position.
Applicants were actually confederates of the researcher who
wore or did not wear a measured amount of a popular perfume
or cologne. Following the interview, participants rated
each applicant on a number of job-related dimensions (e.g.,
to what extent is this individual qualified for the job?)
and personal characteristics (e.g., how friendly is this
person?). Results indicated that sex of participant and the
presence or absence of scent interacted in affecting
ratings of the applicants. Males assigned lower ratings to
these persons when they wore perfume or cologne than when
they did not; females showed the opposite pattern.
Moreover, this was true both for job-related and personal
characteristics. These and other results are interpreted as
reflecting greater difficulty on the part of males than
females in ignoring extraneous aspects of job applicants'
appearance or grooming.

Smell of Success 3

"Sweet Smell of Success"? The Impact of Pleasant
Artificial Scents on Evaluations of Job Applicants

Each year, manufacturers of clothing, cosmetics, and
other grooming aids spend huge sums in an effort to
convince consumers that use of their products will yield
important benefits. Interestingly, a large body of research
concerned with the impact of personal attractiveness
suggests that to some degree, these claims may be justified
(Berscheid & Walster, 1978). For example, individuals who
are attractive in personal appearance have an advantage
over those who are not in hiring decisions (Dipboye, Arvey,
& Terpstra, 1977). Similarly, attractive persons are often
perceived as possessing more positive traits (e.g., greater
potential for success) than unattractive ones (e.g., Cash,
Gillen, & Burns, 1977). Additional evidence suggests that
these advantages do not exist in all situations or under
all circumstances. In particular, females may experience
negative rather than positive effects as a result of
physical attractiveness (e.g., Heilman & Saruwatari, 1979).
Yet the benefits of attractiveness appear to be general
enough in scope to suggest that efforts to enhance one's
personal appearance are often worthwhile.

Typically, people try to enhance others through
appropriate dress, cosmetics, and various forms of personal
grooming. In addition, they often adopt another tactic--the
use of perfume or cologne. Advertisements for these
artificial scents indicate that they can enhance one's
attractiveness and so contribute to both personal happiness

Page 3 begins the main body of the paper, including method, results, and discussion.

Center the title and then begin the introduction section. Do not give the author's name.

Use the author's last name and date for reference citations.

Use the "&" symbol when authors' names are within parentheses. Use "and" when authors' names are part of the text.

Give all authors' names in the first citation. When there are three or more authors, use "et al." for subsequent citations.

and career success. The millions of dollars spent on such products each year suggest that many consumers accept the accuracy of these claims.

But are these claims actually valid? Do perfumes and colognes yield the uniformly beneficial outcomes so often predicted. Surprisingly, no empirical evidence on these questions exists. While the behavioral impact of naturally occurring scents has been extensively studied (e.g., pheromones; Leshner, 1978), little research has focused on the effects of artificial aromas (Levine & McBurney, 1981). More to the point, no investigation has sought to determine the impact of such scents in work-related settings. The present research was designed to attain preliminary evidence on such effects. Specifically, it sought to determine whether wearing pleasant artificial scents can affect the ratings assigned to job candidates during employment interviews.

Past research on related topics suggests that such effects might arise in two distinct ways. First, because perfume and cologne are pleasant, they may induce positive moods among interviewers. These reactions, in turn, may enhance liking for interviewees (Clore & Byrne, 1974). Second, the use of artificial scents may lead interviewers to make negative attributions about the traits of people who use them (see Harvey & Weary, 1981). For example, individuals who wear perfume or cologne to a job interview may be perceived as overly concerned with their appearance or as manipulative. To the extent such perceptions occur,

Smell of Success 5

evaluations of job candidates may be reduced.

In the absence of directly relevant data, no firm predictions were offered concerning which of these two potential effects might predominate. However, because the results of one study (Baron, 1981) suggested that persons wearing perfume or cologne may evoke negative reactions even in purely social settings, it was tentatively predicted that the impact of such scents on evaluations of job candidates might be primarily unfavorable.

Method

<u>Participants</u>

Forty-six undergraduates (19 males, 27 females) enrolled in introductory psychology at Purdue University participated in the study. Participants took part in the investigation in order to satisfy a course requirement.

<u>Design</u>

A 2 x 2 x 2 factorial design based on the presence or absence of perfume or cologne, sex of participants (interviewers), and sex of confederates (interviewees) was employed. Participants were randomly assigned to each cell of this design as they appeared for their appointments with one exception: Because of the lingering qualities of the two scents employed, it was necessary to conduct scent and no scent sessions on alternate days. One male and one female undergraduate served as confederates throughout the study.

<u>Procedure</u>

<u>The employment interview.</u> The study was described as

The "Method" section begins immediately after the introduction (no new page). The word "Method" is centered.

Subsection headings (e.g., <u>Participants</u>) are flush to the left margin, underlined, and stand alone on the line.

The "Design" subsection was included by the author. It is not mandatory. There is always a "Participants" subsection, however.

Paragraph headings were included; these further divide the subsection. Only the first word in a paragraph heading begins with a capital letter. The heading ends with a period, and the paragraph starts on the same line.

being concerned with the manner in which individuals form first impressions of others. Within this general context, the participant played the role of a personnel manager and interviewed the confederate, who played the role of job applicant. The job in question was described as an entry-level management position involving a wide range of activities (e.g., visits to various plants and customer sites, preparation of written reports). During the interview the participant (i.e., the interviewer) read a series of questions to the applicant (i.e., the confederate). The questions were typed on index cards and were quite straightforward. For example, one asked, "What are the major goals you are seeking in your career?" Another was, "How do you get along with other people?" The confederate's responses to each question were prepared in advance and thoroughly memorized. Thus, they were identical for all participants. These replies were designed to be simple and noncontroversial and were found, during pretesting, to be both reasonable and believable by participants.

Dependent measures. Following the final interview question, the participant was taken to a separate room where he or she rated the applicant on a number of different dimensions. Four of these were directly job related (personal suitability for the job, qualifications for this position, potential for future success, and an overall recommendation about hiring). Four other items related to personal characteristics of the applicant (intelligence, warmth, friendliness, and modesty). All ratings were made on 7-point scales.

Presence or absence of pleasant scent. In the scent-present condition, the confederates applied two small drops of the appropriate perfume or cologne behind their ears prior to the start of each day's sessions. In the scent-absent condition, they did not make use of these substances. In both conditions, the confederates refrained from employing any scented cosmetics of their own. The two scents used were Jontue for the female complices and Brut for the males. These products were chosen through pretesting in which 12 undergraduate judges (8 females, 4 males) rated 11 popular perfumes and colognes presented in identical plastic bottles. Judges rated the pleasantness of each scent and its attractiveness when used by a member of the opposite sex. Jontue and Brut received the highest mean ratings in this preliminary study. Further, they were rated above the neutral point on both dimensions by all participants.

Additional pretesting indicated that two small drops of these products placed behind the ear produced a noticeable but far-from-overpowering aroma. Because data were collected in sessions lasting from 2 to 3 hours, little fading of these scents occurred in most cases. On those few occasions when data collection occupied a longer interval, an additional single drop of scent was applied. The confederates dressed neatly in all cases, in a manner suitable for an informal job interview (they wore slacks

Smell of Success 8

and a blouse). They did not wear more formal clothing because it was felt that such behavior, unusual for a college campus, might arouse suspicion among participants.

Results

Ratings of the applicants on job-related dimensions

A .05 alpha level was used for all statistical tests. A multivariate analysis of variance (ANOVA) was performed on the data for the four job-related items. This analysis yielded an interaction between sex of participant and presence of scent. Subsequent univariate analyses performed for each item separately revealed that the interaction was significant for three of the four dependent measures: qualification for the job in question, $F(1, 37) = 4.23$, $p <$ .05, potential for future success, $F(1, 37) = 8.21$, $p <$ .025, and overall hiring recommendation, $F(1, 37) = 4.32$, $p < .05$. Inspection of the appropriate means indicated that this interaction took the same form in each case. The interaction is illustrated in Figure 1 which presents the means for the overall hiring recommendation. Males assigned lower ratings to the applicants when they wore scent than when they did not, while females assigned higher ratings to the applicants when they used scent than when they did not. Thus, it appeared that male interviewers reacted negatively to the presence of artificial scent whereas female interviewers reacted in the opposite fashion.

Ratings of the applicants on personal dimensions

A multivariate ANOVA was performed on the data for the four items relating to personal characteristics of the

---

The "Results" section does not begin on a new page; the heading is centered and not underlined.

The author used optional subsection headings to break the "Results" section into two parts. If you do this, the title of each heading would depend on your particular study and the variables you investigated. You may have as many subsections as necessary for your study.

All nouns, pronouns, verbs, adjectives, adverbs, and other major words in a subsection heading begin with capital letters.

applicant (intelligence, warmth, friendliness, modesty). This analysis yielded a significant effect for sex of participant, $F(4, 34) = 4.29$, $p < .025$, and an interaction between sex of participant and scent that approached significance, $F(4, 34) = 2.51$, $p < .08$. Univariate analyses on each item revealed that the effect of sex of participant was significant for two of the four dependent measures: warmth and friendliness, $F(1, 37) = 6.24$, $p < .025$, and $F(1, 37) = 8.80$, $p < .01$, respectively. Inspection of the appropriate means indicated that this effect reflected the fact that males assigned higher ratings to the applicants on both dimensions than did females. Also, the interaction was significant for ratings of intelligence, $F(1, 37) = 4.50$, and friendliness, $F(1, 37) = 4.54$, $p < .05$. The means are shown in Table 1. Males rated the applicants as lower in intelligence and friendliness when wearing perfume or cologne than when not using these substances. In contrast, females rated the applicants higher in intelligence and friendliness when wearing perfume or cologne than when not wearing such substances.

A third multivariate analysis was performed on the three items relating to the applicants' personal appearance (attractiveness, personal grooming, neatness of dress). This analysis yielded two effects that closely approached significance: a main effect for scent and a main effect for sex of participant. Follow-up univariate analyses on each measure revealed that males rated the applicants as better groomed than did females, $F(1, 37) = 4.19$, $p < .05$, and

When presenting data showing statistical significance, the name of the statistical test is underlined and followed by the degrees of freedom in parentheses. Note the spacing. If your typewriter does not have a necessary symbol, write the symbol in black ink.

Most statistical symbols are underlined (e.g., F, t, M, p, df).

Figures and tables, when used, must be mentioned in the text.

almost significantly better dressed than did females, $F(1,$ 37) = 3.86, p < .06. Similar analyses performed to examine the main effect of scent revealed that the applicants were viewed as better dressed when wearing scent than when not using this substance, $F(1, 37)$ = 5.67, p < .025.

Note the spelling of "questionnaire."

An additional item on the questionnaire asked participants to rate their liking for the applicants. An ANOVA on these data yielded a significant interaction between sex of participant and scent, $F(1, 37)$ = 4.28, p < .05. Consistent with findings reported earlier, this interaction reflected the fact that males reported liking the applicants less in the presence of a pleasant scent (M = 3.56) than in its absence (M = 5. 10). In contrast, females reported liking the applicants more in the presence of such scent (M = 5.21) than in its absence (M = 4.62).

Note that the word "data" is plural; thus, "the data show" (not "shows"). Similarly, "criteria" is plural.

Participants' ratings of their own performance as interviewers

Two final items on the questionnaire dealt with participants' perceptions of their own performance as interviewers. The first of these required them to rate their effectiveness in this role. An ANOVA on these data yielded an interaction between sex of participant and scent that approached significance, $F(1, 37)$ = 3.52, p < .07. This interaction reflected the fact that males rated themselves as poorer interviewers when the applicants wore scent (M = 3.70) than when they did not (M = 4.78). In contrast, females rated themselves as slightly more effective in the presence of scent (M = 4.29) than in its

Smell of Success 11

absence ($\underline{M}$ = 3.92).

The second item asked participants to rate the extent to which their evaluations of the applicants' qualifications were affected by the grooming and personal appearance of these persons. An ANOVA on these data yielded a main effect for sex of participant that approached significance, $\underline{F}$(1, 37) = 3.13, $\underline{p}$ < .10. This reflected the fact that males reported being affected to a greater degree by the applicants' personal appearance ($\underline{M}$ = 4.47) than did females ($\underline{M}$ = 3.88).

Discussion

A substantial body of research findings indicates that various aspects of personal appearance can exert powerful effects on hiring decisions (e.g., Cash et al., 1977; Dipboye et al., 1977). The present study extends this previous work by indicating that such effects can also be produced by one aspect of personal grooming not previously investigated: the use of perfume or cologne. Specifically, it was found that ratings assigned to job applicants were significantly affected by the use of such substances. Moreover, this was true both for job-related and personal characteristics. The pattern of such effects, however, was not consistent with preliminary theorizing.

Initially, it was proposed that pleasant artificial scents might either enhance ratings of job applicants through the induction of positive mood states (e.g., Clore & Byrne, 1974) or reduce such ratings through unfavorable shifts in social perception or attributions (see Harvey &

The "Discussion" section immediately follows the "Results" section. The word "Discussion" is centered and not underlined.

Smell of Success 12

Weary, 1981). Neither of these patterns emerged. Instead, males and females reacted in sharply contrasting ways to the presence of perfume or cologne. Females assigned higher ratings to the applicants when they used artificial scents than when they did not, whereas the opposite was true for males: they assigned lower ratings to these persons when they wore perfume or cologne than when they did not. Given that both males and females reacted positively to the two scents used during pretesting, it seems unlikely that these opposite reactions in the main study stemmed from contrasting moods or affective states. Instead, cognitive factors seem more likely to have played a role in generating the obtained results. One possible mechanism in this regard is suggested by findings obtained with other dependent measures. As may be recalled, males reported being influenced to a greater extent than females by various aspects of the applicants' appearance or grooming. Similarly, they rated themselves as less effective in the role of interviewer in the presence of perfume or cologne than in its absence. In contrast, females perceived themselves as slightly more effective in this role in the presence of artificial scents than in their absence. Together, these findings suggest that males were more strongly affected by scent and other extraneous aspects of the applicants' appearance or grooming than females, and were quite aware of this fact. To the extent this was true, it is not surprising that they reacted negatively to the presence of perfume or cologne. Briefly, males may have

realized that such scents would interfere with their
ability to serve as an effective interviewer. This, in
turn, caused them to experience annoyance or resentment
toward the applicants for making use of these substances,
and so to downrate them on several key dependent measures.
Females, in contrast, were less likely to experience such
reactions. Thus, they may have responded more directly to
the pleasant nature of the two scents employed. In short,
the obtained interaction between presence of scent and sex
of participants may have stemmed from differences in the
ability of males and females to "filter out" irrelevant
aspects of the applicants' grooming or appearance. Although
this interpretation is consistent with the present
findings, it is, of course, only tentative in nature. It
should be noted, though, that it agrees with evidence
suggesting that in many species, males react more strongly
to certain naturally occurring scents (e.g., pheromones)
than do females (see Leshner, 1978).

At this point, it seems important to comment briefly
on the overall significance of the present findings. Past
research has called attention to the fact that job
applicants' appearance and grooming can strongly affect the
interview process (Dipboye et al., 1977). The present
results extend this previous work by indicating that the
direction of such effects is not uniformly positive. On the
contrary, it appears that interviewers may sometimes react
negatively to efforts at self-enhancement by job
applicants. Further, such reactions appear to stem from

complex cognitive mechanisms as well as from current affective states. Full comprehension of these mechanisms may add appreciably to our understanding of the job interview process. Thus, they seem worthy of further, detailed study. Until they are fully clarified, however, the practical implications of the present findings for applicants seem clear: Use artificial scents and other grooming aids with caution, for the impact may sometimes be negative.

Before concluding, it should be noted that several steps were taken to enhance the generalizability of the present research. The description of the job in question was quite realistic, and the questions asked during the interview were similar to ones that might well be posed to actual job candidates. The perfume or cologne worn by confederates were popular national brands, and the amount used was carefully adjusted to reflect levels typically applied under ordinary life conditions. These precautions, and the fact that earlier studies employing simulated interviews have often yielded valuable results (e.g., Imada & Hakel, 1977), suggest that the present findings may possess considerable generality. However, it is fully realized that the precise extent to which they may be generalized can only be established through further research conducted in a variety of different settings.

Smell of Success 15

References

Baron, R. A. (1981). The role of olfaction in human social behavior: Effects of a pleasant scent on attraction and social perception. <u>Personality and Social Psychology Bulletin, 7,</u> 611-617.

Berscheid, E., & Walster, E. (1978). <u>Interpersonal attraction</u> (2nd ed.). Reading, MA: Addison-Wesley.

Cash, T. F., Gillen, B., & Burns, D. S. (1977). Sexism and beautyism in personnel consultant decision-making. <u>Journal of Applied Psychology, 62,</u> 301-311.

Clore, G. L., & Byrne, D. A. (1974). A reinforcement affect model of attraction. In T. L. Huston (Ed.), <u>Foundations of interpersonal attraction</u> (pp. 143-170). New York: Academic Press.

Dipboye, R. L., Arvey, R. D., & Terpstra, D. E. (1977). Sex and physical attractiveness of raters and applicants as determinants of resume evaluations. <u>Journal of Applied Psychology, 62,</u> 288-294.

Harvey, J. H., & Weary, G. (1981). <u>Perspectives on attributional processes.</u> Dubuque, IA: William C. Brown.

Heilman, M. S., & Saruwatari, L. R. (1979). When beauty is beastly: The effects of appearance and sex on evaluations of job applicants for managerial and nonmanagerial jobs. <u>Organizational Behavior and Human Performance, 23,</u> 360-372.

Imada, A. S., & Hakel, M. D. (1977). Influence of nonverbal communication and rater proximity on impressions and decisions in simulated employment interviews. <u>Journal</u>

References begin on a new page. Each reference is a separate paragraph.

These references contain journal articles (Baron), books (Berscheid & Walster), chapters in books (Clore & Byrne), and unpublished papers (Levine & McBurney).

Smell of Success 16

of Applied Psychology, 62, 295-300.

Leshner, A. I. (1978). An introduction to behavioral
endocrinology. New York: Oxford University Press.

Levine, J. M., & McBurney, D. H. (1981, August). The
role of olfaction in social perception and behavior. Paper
presented at the Third Ontario Symposium on Personality and
Social Psychology, Toronto.

Smell of Success 17

Author Note

Robert A. Baron, Department of Psychological Science (now at the Managerial Policy and Organization Department, Rensselaer Polytechnic Institute).

The author wishes to express his thanks to Mark Mannella, Patti Schacht, Keith Short, and Linda Thiemrodt for their able assistance in collection of the data, and to Robert W. Horton for expert statistical analyses. Thanks are also due to Howard Weiss for insightful comments on an earlier draft of this article.

Correspondence concerning this article should be addressed to Robert A. Baron, Managerial Policy and Organization Department, Rensselaer Polytechnic Institute, Troy, NY 12180-3590.

The author note is a good place to thank people who assisted with the research. You can also identify your course and instructor.

Smell of Success 18

Each table is typed on a new page. Use Arabic, not Roman, numerals to number your tables.

Note that only horizontal lines are used to separate sections of the table.

Table 1

Mean Ratings of the Applicants on Personal Dimensions

	Scent condition	
Sex of participant	No scent	Scent
Intelligence ratings		
Males	5.44	5.10
Females	4.08	5.64
Friendliness ratings		
Males	6.68	6.10
Females	5.30	5.85

Smell of Success 19

Figure Caption

<u>Figure 1.</u> Mean hiring recommendation as a function of sex of participant and presence of scent.

Begin the figure captions on a new page. All figure captions will go here.

Underline the figure number to begin each figure caption. Only the first word of the caption is capitalized.

The figure caption page may not be necessary for student reports. Instead, the caption would appear on the figure page.

Each figure must go on a separate page.

Pages on which figures are drawn are not numbered, nor is there a page identification. To identify the figure, write the figure number in pencil on the back of the page.

Include all necessary labels for interpreting the figure.

Draw figures carefully and make sure everything is accurate.

Note that, as in all graphs, the independent variable is placed on the horizontal axis, and the dependent variable is placed on the vertical axis.

Always draw figures in black ink.

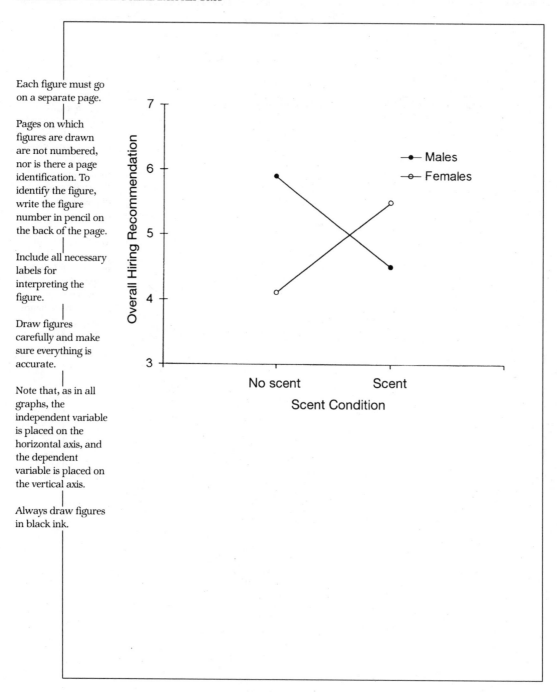

B

Statistical Tests

The purpose of this appendix is to provide the formulas and calculational procedures for analysis of data. All possible statistical tests are not included, but a variety of tests that should be appropriate for many of the research designs you might use are given.

We will examine both descriptive and inferential statistics. Before you study the statistics, however, you should review the properties of measurement scales described in Chapter 10. Remember that there are four types of measurement scales: nominal, ordinal, interval, and ratio. Nominal scales have no numerical properties, ordinal scales provide rank-order information only, and interval and ratio scales have equal intervals between the points on the scale. In addition, ratio scales have a true zero point. You will also recall from Chapter 11 that the appropriate statistical analysis is determined by the type of design and by the measurement scale that was used in the study. As we proceed, the discussion of the various statistical tests will draw to your attention the relevant measurement scale restrictions that apply.

The examples here use small and simple data sets so the calculations can be easily done by hand using a calculator. However, you will find that the calculations become tedious and that you are more likely to make errors when working with large data sets and when you have to perform many statistical analyses in your study. Computer programs to perform statistical analyses have been developed to make the process easier and reduce calculation errors.

Table B-1
Descriptive
statistics for a set
of scores

Score	Descriptive statistic
1	Mode = 5
2	
4	Median = 5
4	
5	$\overline{X} = \dfrac{\sum X}{N} = 4.5$
5	
5	
6	Range = 6
6	
7	

$$\sum X = \overline{45}$$

$$s^2 = \frac{\sum(X - \overline{X})^2}{N - 1} = \frac{\sum X^2 - N\overline{X}^2}{N - 1} = \frac{233 - 202.5}{9} = 3.388$$

$$\sum X^2 = 233$$

$$N = 10$$

$$s = \sqrt{s^2} = 1.84$$

DESCRIPTIVE STATISTICS

With a knowledge of the types of measurement scales, we can turn to a consideration of statistical techniques. We can start with two ways of describing a set of scores: central tendency and variability.

Measures of central tendency

A measure of central tendency gives a single number that describes how an entire group scores as a whole, or on the average. Three different central tendency measures are available: the mode, the median, and the mean.

The mode   The mode is the most frequently occurring score. Table B-1 shows a set of scores and the descriptive statistics that are discussed in this section. The most frequently occurring score in these data is 5: No calculations are necessary to find the mode. The mode can be used with any of the four types of measurement scales. However, it is the only measure of central tendency that can be used with nominal scale data. If you are measuring gender and find there are 100 females and 50 males, the mode is "female" because this is the most frequently occurring category on the nominal scale.

The median   The median is the score that divides the group in half: 50% of the scores are below the median and 50% are above the median. When the scores have been ordered from lowest to highest (as in Table B-1), the median is easily found. If there is an odd number of scores, you simply find the middle score. (For example, if there are 11 scores, the sixth score is the median, since there are 5 lower and 5 higher scores.) If there is an even number of scores, the median is the midpoint between the two middle scores. In the data in

Table B-1, there are 10 scores, so the fifth and sixth scores are the two middle scores. To find the median, we add the two middle scores and divide by 2. Thus, in Table B-1, the median is

$$\frac{5 + 5}{2} = 5$$

The median can be used with ordinal, interval, or ratio scale data. It is most likely to be used with ordinal data, however. This is because calculation of the median considers only the rank ordering of scores and not the actual size of the scores.

The mean   The mean does take into account the actual size of the scores. Thus, the mean is based on more information about the scores than either the mode or the median. However, it is appropriate only for interval or ratio scale data.

The mean is the sum of the scores in a group divided by the number of scores. The calculational formula for the mean can be expressed as

$$\bar{X} = \frac{\sum X}{N}$$

where $\bar{X}$ is the symbol for the mean. In this formula, X represents a score obtained by an individual, and the $\sum$ symbol indicates that scores are to be summed or added. The symbol $\sum X$ can be read as "sum of the Xs" and simply is an indication that the scores are to be added. Thus, $\sum X$ in the data from Table B-1 is

$$1 + 2 + 4 + 4 + 5 + 5 + 5 + 6 + 6 + 7 = 45$$

The N in the formula symbolizes the number of scores in the group. In our example, $N = 10$. Thus, we can now calculate the mean:

$$\bar{X} = \frac{\sum X}{N} = \frac{45}{10} = 4.5$$

Measures of variability

In addition to describing the central tendency of the set of scores, we want to describe how much the scores vary among themselves. How much spread is there in the set of scores?

The range   The range is the highest score minus the lowest score. In our example, the range is 6. The range is not a very useful statistic, however, because it is based on only two scores in the distribution. It doesn't take into account all of the information that is available in the entire set of scores.

The variance and standard deviation   The variance, and a related statistic called the standard deviation, uses all the scores to yield a measure of variability. The variance indicates the degree to which scores vary about the group mean. The formula for the variance (symbolized as s^2) is

$$s^2 = \frac{\Sigma(X - \bar{X})^2}{N - 1}$$

where $(X - \bar{X})^2$ is an individual score, X, minus the mean, $\bar{X}$, and then squared. Thus, $(X - \bar{X})^2$ is the squared deviation of each score from the mean. The Σ sign indicates that these squared deviation scores are to be summed. Finally, dividing by $N - 1$ gives the mean of the squared deviations. The variance, then, is the mean of the squared deviations from the group mean. (Squared deviations are used because simple deviations would add up to zero. $N - 1$ is used in most cases for statistical purposes because the scores represent a sample and not an entire population. As the sample size becomes larger, it makes little difference whether N or $N - 1$ is used.)

The data in Table B-1 can be used to illustrate calculation of the variance. $\Sigma (X - \bar{X})^2$ is equal to

$$(1 - 4.5)^2 + (2 - 4.5)^2 + (4 - 4.5)^2 + (4 - 4.5)^2 + (5 - 4.5)^2$$
$$+ (5 - 4.5)^2 + (5 - 4.5)^2 + (6 - 4.5)^2 + (6 - 4.5)^2 + (7 - 4.5)^2$$
$$= 30.50$$

The next step is to divide $\Sigma (X - \bar{X})^2$ by $N - 1$. The calculation for the variance, then, is

$$s^2 = \frac{\Sigma(X - \bar{X})^2}{N - 1} = \frac{30.50}{9} = 3.388$$

A simpler calculational formula for the variance is

$$s^2 = \frac{\Sigma X^2 - N\bar{X}^2}{N - 1}$$

where ΣX^2 is the sum of the squared individual scores, and $\bar{X}^2$ is the mean squared. You can confirm that the two formulas are identical by computing the variance using this simpler formula (remember that ΣX^2 tells you to square each score and then sum the squared scores). This simpler formula is much easier to work with when there are many scores, because each deviation doesn't have to be calculated.

The standard deviation is the square root of the variance. Because the variance uses squared scores, the variance doesn't describe the amount of variability in the same units of measurement as the original scale. The standard deviation (s) corrects this problem. Thus, the standard deviation is the average deviation of scores from the mean.

STATISTICAL SIGNIFICANCE TESTS

This section describes several statistical significance tests. All of these tests are used to determine the probability that the outcome of the research was due to the operation of random error. All use the logic of the null hypothesis discussed in Chapter 11. We will consider three significance tests in this section: the Chi-square test, the Mann–Whitney U test, and the analysis of variance or F test.

Chi-square (χ^2)

The Chi-square (Greek letter chi, squared) test is used when dealing with nominal scale data. It is used when the data consist of frequencies—the number of subjects who fall into each of several categories.

Chi-square can be used with either the experimental or correlational method. It is used in conjunction with the experimental method when the dependent variable is measured on a nominal scale. It is used with the correlational method when both variables are measured on nominal scales.

Example Suppose you want to know whether there is a relationship between gender and hand dominance. To do this, you sample 50 males and 50 females and ask whether they are right-handed, left-handed, or ambidextrous (use both hands with equal skill). Your data collection involves classifying each person as male or female and as right-handed, left-handed, or ambidextrous.

Fictitious data for such a study are presented in Table B-2. The frequencies labeled as "O" in each of the six cells in the table refer to the number of male and female subjects who fall into each of the three hand-dominance categories. The frequencies labeled "E" refer to frequencies that are expected if the null hypothesis is correct. It is important that each subject falls into only one of the cells when using Chi-square (that is, no subject can be counted as both male and female or both right- and left-handed).

The Chi-square test examines the extent to which the frequencies that are actually observed in the study differ from the frequencies that are expected if the null hypothesis is correct. The null hypothesis states that there is no relationship between sex and hand dominance: Males and females do not differ on this characteristic.

The formula for computing Chi-square is

$$\chi^2 = \sum \frac{(O - E)^2}{E}$$

where O is the *observed* frequency in each cell, E is the *expected* frequency in each cell, and the symbol Σ refers to summing over all cells. The steps in calculating the value of χ^2 are:

**Table B-2
Data for
hypothetical study
on hand
dominance:
Chi-square test**

| Sex of subject | Hand dominance | | | Row totals |
	Right	Left	Ambidextrous	
Male	$O_1 = 15$ $E_1 = 25$	$O_2 = 30$ $E_2 = 20$	$O_3 = 5$ $E_3 = 5$	50
Female	$O_4 = 35$ $E_4 = 25$	$O_5 = 10$ $E_5 = 20$	$O_6 = 5$ $E_6 = 5$	50
Column totals	50	40	10	$N = 100$

Computations:

Cell number	$\dfrac{(O - E)^2}{E}$
1	4.00
2	5.00
3	0.00
4	4.00
5	5.00
6	0.00
$\Sigma = \overline{18.00}$	

$$\chi^2 = \Sigma \frac{(O - E)^2}{E}$$
$$= 18.00$$

Step 1: Arrange the observed frequencies in a table such as Table B-2. Note that in addition to the observed frequencies in each cell, the table presents row totals, column totals, and the total number of observations (N).

Step 2: Calculate the expected frequencies for each of the cells in the table. The expected frequency formula is

$$E = \frac{\text{Row total} \times \text{Column total}}{N}$$

where the row total refers to the row total for the cell, and the column total refers to the column total for the cell. Thus, the expected frequency for cell 1 (male right-handedness) is

$$E_1 = \frac{50 \times 50}{100} = 25$$

The expected frequencies for each of the cells are shown in Table B-2 below the observed frequencies.

Step 3: Calculate the quantity $(O - E)^2/E$ for each cell. For cell 1, this quantity is

282

$$\frac{(15 - 25)^2}{25} = \frac{100}{25} = 4.00$$

Step 4: Find the value of χ^2 by summing the $(O - E)^2/E$ values found in step 3. The calculations for obtaining χ^2 for the example data are shown in Table B-2.

Significance of Chi-square   The significance of the obtained χ^2 value can be evaluated by consulting a table of critical values of χ^2. A table of critical χ^2 values is presented as Table C-2 in Appendix C. The critical χ^2 values indicate the value that the *obtained* χ^2 must equal or exceed to be significant at the .10 level, the .05 level, and the .01 level.

To be able to use the table of critical values of χ^2 as well as most other statistical tables, you must understand the concept of *degrees of freedom (df)*. The critical value of χ^2 for any given study depends on the degrees of freedom. Degrees of freedom refers to the number of scores that are free to vary. In the table of categories for a Chi-square test, the number of degrees of freedom is the number of cells in which the frequencies are free to vary once we know the row totals and column totals. The degrees of freedom for Chi-square is easily calculated:

$$df = (R - 1)(C - 1)$$

where R is the number of rows in the table and C is the number of columns. In our example in Table B-1, there are two rows and three columns, so there are 2 degrees of freedom. In a study with three rows and three columns, there are 4 degrees of freedom, and so on.

In order to use Table C-2, find the correct degrees of freedom and then determine the critical value of χ^2 necessary to reject the null hypothesis at the chosen significance level. With 2 degrees of freedom, the obtained χ^2 value must be *equal to* or *greater than* the critical value of 5.991 in order to be significant at the .05 level. There is only a .05 probability that a χ^2 of 5.991 would occur if only random error is operating. Because the obtained χ^2 from our example is 18.00, we can reject the null hypothesis that there is no relationship between sex and hand dominance. (The Chi-square was based on fictitious data, but it would be relatively easy for you to determine for yourself whether there is in fact a relationship.)

Concluding remarks   The Chi-square test is extremely useful and is used frequently in all of the behavioral sciences. The calculational formula described is generalizable to expanded studies in which there are more categories on either of the variables. One note of caution, however: When both variables have only two categories, so that there are only two rows and two columns, the formula for calculating Chi-square changes slightly. In such cases, the formula is

$$\chi^2 = \sum \frac{(\left|O - E\right|) - .5)^2}{E}$$

where $\left|O - E\right|$ is the absolute value of $O - E$, and .5 is a constant that is subtracted for each cell.

Analysis of variance (F test)

The analysis of variance, or F test, is used to determine whether there is a significant difference between groups that have been measured on either interval or ratio scales. The groups may have been formed using either the experimental or the correlational method; the important thing is that at least an interval scale measure was used. The analysis of variance may be used with either independent groups or repeated measures designs. Procedures for calculating F for both types of designs are presented.

Analysis of variance: One independent variable

To illustrate the use of the analysis of variance, let's consider a hypothetical experiment on physical distance and self-disclosure. You think that people will reveal more about themselves to an interviewer when they are sitting close to the interviewer than they will when sitting farther away. To test this idea, you conduct an experiment on interviewing. Subjects are told that interviewing techniques are being studied. Each subject is seated in a room; the interviewer comes into the room and sits at one of three distances from the subject: close (2 feet, or .61 meter), medium (4 feet, or 1.22 meters), or far (6 feet, or 1.83 meters). The distance chosen by the interviewer is the independent variable manipulation. Subjects are randomly assigned to the three distance conditions, and the interviewer's behavior is constant in all conditions. The interview consists of a number of questions, and the dependent variable is the number of personal, revealing statements made by the subject during the interview.

Fictitious data for such an experiment are shown in Table B-3. Note that this is an independent groups design with five subjects in each group. The calculations of the systematic variance and error variance involve computing the *sum of squares* for the different types of variance.

Sum of squares   Sum of squares stands for the *sum of squared deviations from the mean*. Computing an analysis of variance for the data in Table B-3 involves three sums of squares: (1) SS_{TOTAL}, the sum of squared deviations of each individual score from the grand mean; (2) SS_A, the sum of squared deviations of each of the group means from the grand mean; and (3) SS_{ERROR}, the sum of squared deviations of the individual scores from their respective group means. The "A" in SS_A is used to indicate that we are dealing with the systematic variance associated with independent variable A.

Table B-3
Data for
hypothetical
experiment on
distance and self-
disclosure:
Analysis of
variance

	Distance (A)	
Close (A1)	Medium (A2)	Far (A3)
33	21	20
24	25	13
31	19	15
29	27	10
34	26	14
$T_{A1} = 151$	$T_{A2} = 118$	$T_{A3} = 72$
$n_{A1} = 5$	$n_{A2} = 5$	$n_{A3} = 5$
$\overline{X}_{A1} = 30.20$	$\overline{X}_{A2} = 23.60$	$\overline{X}_{A3} = 14.40$
$\sum X_{A1}^2 = 4623$	$\sum X_{A2}^2 = 2832$	$\sum X_{A3}^2 = 1090$
$T_{A1}^2 = 22801$	$T_{A2}^2 = 13924$	$T_{A3}^2 = 5184$

$$SS_{TOTAL} = \sum X^2 - \frac{G^2}{N} = (4623 + 2832 + 1090) - \frac{(151 + 118 + 72)^2}{15}$$

$$= 8545 - 7752.07$$

$$= 792.93$$

$$SS_A = \sum \frac{T_a^2}{n_a} - \frac{G^2}{N} = \left[\frac{(151)^2}{5} + \frac{(118)^2}{5} + \frac{(72)^2}{5} \right] - 7752.07$$

$$= 8381.80 - 7752.07$$

$$= 629.73$$

$$SS_{ERROR} = \sum X^2 - \sum \frac{T_a^2}{n_a} = 8545 - 8381.80$$

$$= 163.20$$

The three sums of squares are deviations from a mean (recall that we calculated such deviations earlier when discussing the variance in a set of scores). We could calculate the deviations directly with the data in Table B-3, but such calculations are hard to work with, so we will use simplified formulas for computational purposes. The computational formulas are

$$SS_{TOTAL} = \sum X^2 - \frac{G^2}{N}$$

$$SS_A = \sum \frac{T_a^2}{n_a} - \frac{G^2}{N}$$

$$SS_{ERROR} = \sum X^2 - \sum \frac{T_a^2}{n_a}$$

You might note here that $SS_{TOTAL} = SS_A + SS_{ERROR}$. The actual computations are shown in Table B-3.

SS_{TOTAL}   The formula for SS_{TOTAL} is

$$\sum X^2 - \frac{G^2}{N}$$

$\sum X^2$ is the sum of the squared scores of all subjects in the experiment. Each of the scores is squared first and then added. Thus, for the data in Table B-3, $\sum X^2$ is $33^2 + 24^2 + 31^2$ and so on until all of the scores have been squared and added. If you are doing the calculations by hand or with a pocket calculator, it may be convenient to find the $\sum X^2$ for the scores in each group and then add these up for your final computation. This is what I did for the data in the table. The G in the formula stands for the grand total of all of the scores. This involves adding up the scores for all subjects. The grand total is then squared and divided by N, the total number of subjects in the experiment. When computing the sum of squares, you should always keep the calculations clearly labeled, because you can simplify later calculations by referring to these earlier ones. Once you have computed SS_{TOTAL}, SS_A can be calculated.

SS_A   The formula for SS_A is

$$\sum \frac{T_a^2}{n_a} - \frac{G^2}{N}$$

The T_a in this formula refers to the total of the scores in group a of independent variable A. (T_a is a shorthand notation for $\sum X$ in each group [recall the computation of $\sum X$ from our discussion of the mean]. The T_a symbol is used to avoid having to deal with too many $\sum$ signs in our calculational procedures.) The a is used to symbolize the particular group number; thus, T_a is a general symbol for T_1, T_2, and T_3. Looking at our data in Table B-3, $T_1 = 151$, $T_2 = 118$, and $T_3 = 72$. These are the sums of the scores in each of the groups. After T_a has been calculated, T_a^2 is found by squaring T_a. Now, T_a^2 is divided by n_a, the number of subjects in group a. Once the quantity T_a^2/n_a has been computed for each group, the quantities are summed as indicated by the $\sum$ symbol.

Notice that the second part of the formula, G^2/N, was calculated when SS_{TOTAL} was obtained. Because we already have this quantity, it needn't be calculated again when computing SS_A. After obtaining SS_A, we can now compute SS_{ERROR}.

SS_{ERROR}   The formula for SS_{ERROR} is

$$\sum X^2 - \sum \frac{T_a^2}{n_a}$$

Source of variance	Sum of squares	df	Mean square	F	Table B-4
					Analysis of variance summary table
A	SS_A	$a - 1$	SS_A/df_A	MS_A/MS_{ERROR}	
Error	SS_{ERROR}	$N - a$	SS_{ERROR}/df_{ERROR}		
Total	SS_{TOTAL}	$N - 1$			
A	629.73	2	314.87	23.15	
Error	162.20	12	13.60		
Total	792.93	14			

Both of these quantities were calculated above in obtaining SS_{TOTAL} and SS_A. To obtain SS_{ERROR}, we merely have to find these quantities and perform the proper subtraction.

As a check on the calculations, we can make sure that $SS_{TOTAL} = SS_A + SS_{ERROR}$.

The next step in the computation of the analysis of variance is to find the *mean square* for each of the sums of squares. We can then find the value of F. The necessary computations are shown in an analysis of variance summary table in Table B-4. Constructing a summary table is the easiest way to complete the computations.

Mean squares   After obtaining the sum of squares, it is necessary to compute the mean squares. Mean square stands for the *mean of the sum of the squared deviations from the mean* or, more simply, the mean of the sum of squares. The mean square (MS) is the sum of squares divided by the degrees of freedom. The degrees of freedom are determined by the number of scores in the sum of squares that are free to vary. The mean squares are the variances that are used in computing the value of F.

From Table B-4, you can see that the mean squares that concern us are the mean square for A (systematic variance) and the mean square for error (error variance). The formulas are

$$MS_A = SS_A /df_A$$

$$MS_{ERROR} = SS_{ERROR} /df_{ERROR}$$

where $df_A = a - 1$ (the number of groups minus one) and $df_{ERROR} = N - a$ (the total number of subjects minus the number of groups).

Obtaining the F value   The obtained F is found by dividing MS_A by MS_{ERROR}. If only random error is operating, the expected value of F is 1.0. The greater the F value, the lower the probability that the results of the experiment were due to chance error.

Significance of F   To determine the significance of the obtained F value, it is necessary to compare the obtained F to a critical value of F. Table C-4 in

Appendix C shows critical values of F for significance levels of .10, .05, and .01. To find the critical value of F, locate on the table the degrees of freedom for the numerator of the ratio (the systematic variance) and the degrees of freedom for the denominator of the F ratio (the error variance). The intersection of these two degrees of freedom on the table is the critical F value.

The appropriate degrees of freedom for our sample data are 2 and 12 (see Table B-4). The critical F value from Table C-4 is 3.89 for a .05 level of significance. For the results to be significant, the obtained F value must be equal to or greater than the critical value. Because the obtained value of F in Table B-4 (23.15) is greater than the critical value, we conclude that the results are significant and reject the null hypothesis that the means of the groups are equal in the population.

Concluding remarks   The analysis of variance for one independent variable with an independent groups design can be used when there are two or more groups in the experiment. The general formulas described are appropriate for all such designs. Also, the calculations are the same whether the experimental or the correlational method is used to form the groups. The formulas are also applicable to cases in which the number of subjects in each group is not equal (although you should have approximately equal numbers of subjects in the groups).

When the design of the experiment includes more than two levels of the independent variable (as in our example experiment, which had three groups), the obtained F value doesn't tell us whether any two specific groups are significantly different from one another. One way to examine the difference between two groups in such a study is to use the formula for SS_A to compute the sum of squares and the mean square for the two groups (the df in this case is $2 - 1$). When doing this, the previously calculated MS_{ERROR} should be used as the error variance term for computing F. More complicated procedures for evaluating the difference between two groups in such designs are available, but these are beyond the scope of this book.

Analysis of variance: Two independent variables

In this section, we will describe the computations for analysis of variance with a factorial design containing two independent variables. The formulas apply to an $A \times B$ factorial design with any number of levels of the independent variables. The formulas apply only to a completely independent groups design with different subjects in each group, and the number of subjects in each group must be equal. Once you understand this analysis, however, you should have little trouble understanding the analysis for more complicated designs with repeated measures or unequal numbers of subjects. With these limitations in mind, let's consider example data from a hypothetical experiment.

The experiment uses a 2×2 IV $\times$ SV factorial design. Variable A is the type of instruction used in a course, and variable B is the intelligence level of the students. The students are classified as of either "low" or "high" intelligence

	Intelligence (B)	
	Low (B1)	High (B2)

Table B-5
Data for
hypothetical
experiment on the
effect of type of
instruction and
intelligence level
on exam score:
Analysis of
variance

Traditional lecture (A1)

Low (B1)	High (B2)
75	90
70	95
69	89
72	85
68	91

$$T_{A1B1} = 354 \qquad T_{A1B2} = 450 \qquad T_{A1} = 804$$
$$\sum X^2_{A1B1} = 25094 \qquad \sum X^2_{A1B2} = 40552 \qquad n_{A1} = 10$$
$$n_{A1B1} = 5 \qquad n_{A1B2} = 5 \qquad \overline{X}_{A1} = 80.40$$
$$\overline{X}_{A1B1} = 70.80 \qquad \overline{X}_{A1B2} = 90.00$$

Individualized method (A2)

Low (B1)	High (B2)
85	87
87	94
83	93
90	89
89	92

$$T_{A2B1} = 434 \qquad T_{A2B2} = 455 \qquad T_{A2} = 889$$
$$\sum X^2_{A2B1} = 37704 \qquad \sum X^2_{A2B2} = 41439 \qquad n_{A2} = 10$$
$$n_{A2B1} = 5 \qquad n_{A2B2} = 5 \qquad \overline{X}_{A2} = 88.90$$
$$\overline{X}_{A2B1} = 86.80 \qquad \overline{X}_{A2B2} = 91.00$$

$$T_{B1} = 788 \qquad T_{B2} = 905$$
$$n_{B1} = 10 \qquad n_{B2} = 10$$
$$\overline{X}_{B1} = 78.80 \qquad \overline{X}_{B2} = 90.50$$

on the basis of intelligence test scores and are randomly assigned to one of two types of classes. One class uses the traditional lecture method; the other class uses an individualized learning approach with frequent testing over small amounts of material, proctors to help individual students, and a stipulation that students master each section of material before going on to the next section. The information presented to students in the two classes is identical. At the end of the course, all students take the same test, which covers all of the material presented in the course. The score on this examination is the dependent variable.

Table B-5 shows fictitious data for such an experiment, with five subjects in each condition. This design allows us to evaluate three effects—the main effect of A, the main effect of B, and the $A \times B$ interaction. The main effect of A is whether one type of instruction is superior to the other; the main effect of B is whether high-intelligence students score differently on the test than do low-intelligence students; the $A \times B$ interaction examines whether the effect of one independent variable is different depending on the particular level of the other variable.

**Table B-6
Computations for
analysis of
variance with two
independent
variables**

$$SS_{TOTAL} = \sum X^2 - \frac{G^2}{N}$$

$$= (25094 + 40552 + 37704 + 41439)$$

$$- \frac{(354 + 450 + 434 + 455)^2}{20}$$

$$= 144789 - 143312.45$$

$$= 1476.55$$

$$SS_A = \frac{\sum T_a^2}{n_a} - \frac{G^2}{N}$$

$$= \frac{(804)^2 + (889)^2}{10} - 143312.45$$

$$= 143673.70 - 143312.45$$

$$= 361.25$$

$$SS_B = \frac{\sum T_b^2}{n_b} - \frac{G^2}{N}$$

$$= \frac{(788)^2 + (905)^2}{10} - 143312.45$$

$$= 143996.90 - 143312.45$$

$$= 684.45$$

$$SS_{A \times B} = \frac{\sum T_{ab}^2}{n_{ab}} - \frac{G^2}{N} - SS_A - SS_B = \frac{(354)^2 + (450)^2 + (434)^2 + (455)^2}{5}$$

$$-143312.45 - 361.25 - 684.45$$

$$= 144639.40 - 143312.45 - 361.25 - 684.45$$

$$= 281.25$$

$$SS_{ERROR} = \sum X^2 - \frac{\sum T_{ab}^2}{n_{ab}}$$

$$= 144789 - 144639.40$$

$$= 149.60$$

The computation of the analysis of variance starts with calculation of the sum of squares for the following sources of variance in the data: SS_{TOTAL}, SS_A, SS_B, $SS_{A \times B}$, and SS_{ERROR}. The procedures for calculation are similar to the calculations performed for the analysis of variance with one independent variable. The numerical calculations for the example data are shown in Table B-6. We can now consider each of these calculations.

SS_{TOTAL}   The SS_{TOTAL} is computed in the same way as the previous analysis formula. The formula is

$$SS_{TOTAL} = \sum X^2 - \frac{G^2}{N}$$

where $\sum X^2$ is the sum of the squared scores of all subjects in the experiment, G is the grand total of all of the scores, and N is the total number of subjects.

It is usually easiest to calculate $\sum X^2$ and G in smaller steps by calculating subtotals separately for each group in the design. The subtotals are then added. This is the procedure followed in Tables B-5 and B-6.

SS_A   The formula for SS_A is

$$SS_A = \frac{\sum T_a^2}{n_a} - \frac{G^2}{N}$$

where $\sum T_a^2$ is the sum of the squared totals of the scores in each of the groups of independent variable A, and n_a is the number of subjects in each level of independent variable A. When calculating SS_A, we only consider the groups of independent variable A without considering the particular level of B. In other words, the totals for each group of the A variable are obtained by considering all subjects in that level of A, irrespective of which condition of B the subject may be in. The quantity of G^2/N was previously calculated for SS_{TOTAL}.

SS_B   The formula for SS_B is

$$SS_B = \frac{\sum T_b^2}{n_b} - \frac{G^2}{N}$$

SS_B is calculated in the same way as SS_A. The only difference is that we are calculating totals of the groups of independent variable B.

$SS_{A \times B}$ The formula for $SS_{A \times B}$ is

$$SS_{A \times B} = \frac{\sum T_{ab}^2}{n_{ab}} - \frac{G^2}{N} - SS_A - SS_B$$

The sum of squares for the $A \times B$ interaction is computed by first calculating the quantity $\sum T_{ab}^2$. This involves squaring the total of the scores in each of the ab conditions in the experiment. In our example experiment in Table B-5, there are four conditions; the interaction calculation considers *all* of the groups. Each of the group totals is squared, and then the sum of the squared totals is obtained. This sum is divided by n_{ab}, the number of subjects in each group. The other quantities in the formula for $SS_{A \times B}$ have already been calculated, so the computation of $SS_{A \times B}$ is relatively straightforward.

SS_{ERROR}   The quantities involved in the SS_{ERROR} formula have already been calculated. The formula is

$$SS_{ERROR} = \sum X^2 - \frac{\sum T_{ab}^2}{n_{ab}}$$

**Table B-7
Analysis of
variance summary
table: Two
independent
variables**

Source of variance	Sum of squares	df	Mean square	F
A	SS_A	$a-1$	SS_A/df_A	MS_A/MS_{ERROR}
B	SS_B	$B-1$	SS_B/df_B	MS_B/MS_{ERROR}
$A \times B$	$SS_{A \times B}$	$(a-1)(b-1)$	$SS_{A \times B}/df_{A \times B}$	$MS_{A \times B}/MS_{ERROR}$
Error	SS_{ERROR}	$N-ab$	SS_{ERROR}/df_{ERROR}	
Total	SS_{TOTAL}			
A	361.25	1	361.25	38.64
B	684.45	1	684.45	73.20
$A \times B$	281.25	1	281.25	30.08
Error	149.60	16	9.35	
Total	1476.55	19		

These quantities were calculated previously, so we merely have to perform the proper subtraction to complete the computation of SS_{ERROR}.

At this point, you may want to practice calculating the sums of squares using the data in Table B-5. As a check on the calculations, make sure that $SS_{TOTAL} = SS_A + SS_B + SS_{A \times B} + SS_{ERROR}$.

After obtaining the sums of squares, the next step is to find the mean square for each of the sources of variance. The easiest way to do this is to use an analysis of variance summary table like Table B-7.

Mean square   The mean square for each of the sources of variance is the sum of squares divided by the degrees of freedom. The formulas for the degrees of freedom and the mean square are shown in the top portion of Table B-7, and the computed values are shown in the bottom portion of the table.

Obtaining the F value   The F value for each of the three sources of systematic variance (main effects for A and B, and the interaction) is obtained by dividing the appropriate mean square by the MS_{ERROR}. We now have three obtained F values and can evaluate the significance of the main effects and the interaction.

Significance of F   To determine whether an obtained F is significant, we need to find the critical value of F from Table C-4 in Appendix C. For all of the Fs in the analysis of variance summary table, the degrees of freedom are 1 and 16. Let's assume that a .01 significance level for rejecting the null hypothesis was chosen. The critical F at .01 for 1 and 16 degrees of freedom is 8.53. If the obtained F is larger than 8.53, we can say that the results are significant at the .01 level. By referring to the obtained Fs in Table B-7, you can see that the main effects and the interaction are all significant. I'll leave it to you to interpret the main effect means and to graph the interaction. If you don't recall how to do this, you should review the material in Chapter 8.

Table B-8
Data for
hypothetical
experiment on
attractiveness
and judged
competence:
Repeated
measures analysis
of variance

| Subjects (or subject pairs) | Condition (A) | | T_s | T_s^2 |
	Unattractive candidate (A1)	Attractive candidate (A2)		
S#1	6	8	14	196
S#2	5	6	11	121
S#3	5	9	14	196
S#4	7	6	13	169
S#5	4	6	10	100
S#6	3	5	8	64
S#7	5	5	10	100
S#8	4	7	11	121

$$T_{A1} = 39 \qquad T_{A2} = 52 \qquad \sum T_s^2 = 1067$$
$$\sum X_{A1}^2 = 201 \qquad \sum X_{A2}^2 = 352$$
$$n_{A1} = 8 \qquad n_{A2} = 8$$
$$\overline{X}_{A1} = 4.88 \qquad \overline{X}_{A2} = 6.50$$

$$SS_{TOTAL} = \sum X^2 - \frac{G^2}{N} = (201 + 352) - \frac{(39 + 52)^2}{16}$$

$$= 553 - 517.56$$

$$= 35.44$$

$$SS_A = \frac{\sum T_a^2}{n_a} - \frac{G^2}{N} = \frac{(39)^2 + (52)^2}{8} - 517.56$$

$$= 528.13 - 517.56$$

$$= 10.57$$

$$SS_{SUBJECTS} = \frac{\sum T_s^2}{n_s} - \frac{G^2}{N} = \frac{1067}{2} - 517.56$$

$$= 533.50 - 517.56$$

$$= 15.94$$

$$SS_{ERROR} = SS_{TOTAL} - SS_A - SS_{SUBJECTS} = 35.44 - 10.57 - 15.94$$

$$= 8.93$$

Analysis of variance: Repeated measures and matched subjects

The analysis of variance computations considered thus far have been limited to independent groups designs. This section considers the computations for analysis of variance of a repeated measures or a matched random assignment design with one independent variable.

Fictitious data for a hypothetical experiment using a repeated measures design are presented in Table B-8. The experiment examines the effect of a job candidate's physical attractiveness on judgments of the candidate's competence. The independent variable is the candidate's physical attractiveness; the dependent variable is judged competence on a 10-point scale. Subjects in the experiment view two videotapes of different females performing a mechanical aptitude task that involved piecing together a number of parts. Both females do equally well, but one is physically attractive while the other is unattractive. The order of presentation of the two tapes is counterbalanced to control for order effects.

The main difference between the repeated measures analysis of variance and the independent groups analysis described earlier is that the effect of subject differences becomes a source of variance. There are four sources of variance in the repeated measures analysis of variance, and so four sums of squares are calculated:

$$SS_{TOTAL} = \sum X^2 - \frac{G^2}{N}$$

$$SS_A = \frac{\sum T_a^2}{n_a} - \frac{G^2}{N}$$

$$SS_{SUBJECTS} = \frac{\sum T_s^2}{n_s} - \frac{G^2}{N}$$

$$SS_{ERROR} = SS_{TOTAL} - SS_A - SS_{SUBJECTS}$$

The calculations for these sums of squares are shown in the lower portion of Table B-8. The quantities in the formula should be familiar to you by now. The only new quantity involves the calculation of $SS_{SUBJECTS}$. The term T_s^2 refers to the squared total score of each subject—that is, the squared total of the scores that each subject gives when measured in the different groups in the experiment. The quantity $\sum T_s^2$ refers to the sum of these squared totals for all subjects. The calculation of $SS_{SUBJECTS}$ is completed by dividing $\sum T_s^2$ by n_s and then subtracting by G^2/N. The term n_s refers to the number of scores that each subject gives. Because our hypothetical experiment has two groups, $n_s = 2$. The total for each subject is based on two scores.

An analysis of variance summary table is shown in Table B-9. The procedures for computing the mean squares and obtaining F are similar to our previous calculations. Note that the mean square and F for the subjects' source of variance are not computed. There is usually no reason to know or care whether subjects differ significantly from one another. The ability to calculate this source of variance does have the advantage of reducing the amount of error variance—in an independent groups design, subject differences are part of the error variance. Because there is only one score per subject in the independent groups design, it is impossible to estimate the influence of subject differences.

You can use the summary table and the table of critical F values to determine whether the difference between the two groups is significant. The procedures are identical to those discussed previously.

Source of variance	Sum of squares	df	Mean square	F
A	SS_A	$a-1$	SS_A/df_A	MS_A/MS_{ERROR}
Subjects	$SS_{SUBJECTS}$	$s-1$	—	
Error	SS_{ERROR}	$(a-1)(s-1)$	SS_{ERROR}/df_{ERROR}	
Total	SS_{TOTAL}	$N-1$		
A	10.57	1	10.57	8.26
Subjects	15.94	7	—	
Error	8.93	7	1.28	
Total	35.44	15		

Table B-9
Analysis of variance summary table: Repeated measures design

Analysis of variance: Conclusion

The analysis of variance is a very useful test that can be extended to any type of factorial design, including those that use both independent groups and repeated measures in the same design. The method of computing analysis of variance is much the same regardless of the complexity of the design. A section on analysis of variance as brief as this cannot hope to cover all of the many aspects of such a general statistical technique. You should now, however, have the background to compute an analysis of variance and to understand the more detailed discussions of analysis of variance in advanced statistics texts.

CORRELATION AND EFFECT SIZE

Finally, we will examine calculations for measures of correlation and effect size; these are indicators of the strength of association between variables. These are very important measures because they provide a common metric number that can be used in all types of studies. These numbers range from 0.00, indicating no relationship, to 1.00; correlations above .50 are considered to be indicative of very strong relationships. In much research, expect correlations between about .25 and .50. Correlations between about .10 and .25 are weaker, but correlations of this size can be statistically significant with large sample sizes; they can also be important for theoretical and even practical reasons.

Effect size for the Chi-square statistic

The Chi-square (χ^2) test was described previously. In addition to determining whether there is a significant relationship, you want an indicator of effect size to tell you the strength of association between the variables. This is obtained by calculating a phi coefficient, symbolized as ϕ. Phi is computed after obtaining the value of Chi-square. The formula is

295

$$\phi = \sqrt{\frac{\chi^2}{N}}$$

Thus, the value of ϕ for the sex and hand-dominance study analyzed previously (see Table B-2) is

$$\phi = \sqrt{\frac{18.00}{100}} = \sqrt{.18} = .42$$

Because the significance of the obtained Chi-square value has already been determined from Table C-2 in Appendix C, no further significance testing is necessary.

Effect size for the F statistic

After computing an analysis of variance and evaluating the significance of the F statistic, you need to examine effect size. Rosenthal (1991) provides the following formula for calculating the effect size r:

$$\text{Effect size } r = \sqrt{\frac{F}{F + df_{ERROR}}}$$

We can easily calculate the effect size for the value of F obtained in the experiment on interpersonal distance and disclosure (see Table B-4). The value of F was 23.15, and the degrees of freedom for the error term was 12. Effect size, then, is

$$\text{Effect size } r = \sqrt{\frac{23.15}{23.15 + 12}} = \sqrt{.6586} = .81$$

Pearson product-moment correlation coefficient

The Pearson product-moment correlation coefficient (r) is used to find the strength of the relationship between two variables that have been measured on interval scales.

Example   Suppose you want to know whether travel experiences are related to knowledge of geography. In your study, you give a 15-item quiz on North American geography, and you also ask how many states and Canadian provinces participants have visited. After obtaining the pairs of observations from each participant, a Pearson r can be computed to measure the strength of the relationship between travel experience and knowledge of geography.

Table B-10 presents fictitious data from such a study along with the calculations for r. The calculational formula for r is

Table B-10
Data for
hypothetical study
on travel and
knowledge of
geography:
Pearson r

Subject identification number	Travel score (X)	Knowledge score (Y)	XY
01	4	10	40
02	6	15	90
03	7	8	56
04	8	9	72
05	8	7	56
06	12	10	120
07	14	15	210
08	15	13	195
09	15	15	225
10	17	14	238

$$\sum X = 106 \qquad \sum Y = 116 \qquad \sum XY = 1302$$
$$\sum X^2 = 1308 \qquad \sum Y^2 = 1434$$
$$(\sum X)^2 = 11236 \qquad (\sum Y)^2 = 13456$$

Computation:
$$r = \frac{N\sum XY - \sum X \sum Y}{\sqrt{N\sum X^2 - (\sum X)^2}\,\sqrt{N\sum Y^2 - (\sum Y)^2}}$$

$$= \frac{10(1302) - (106)(116)}{\sqrt{10(1308) - 11236}\,\sqrt{10(1434) - 13456}}$$

$$= \frac{13020 - 12296}{\sqrt{13080 - 11236}\,\sqrt{14340 - 13456}}$$

$$= \frac{724}{\sqrt{1844}\,\sqrt{884}}$$

$$= \frac{724}{1276.61}$$

$$= .567$$

$$r = \frac{N\sum XY - \sum X \sum Y}{\sqrt{N\sum X^2 - (\sum X)^2}\,\sqrt{N\sum Y^2 - (\sum Y)^2}}$$

where X refers to a subject's score on variable X, and Y is a subject's score on variable Y. In Table B-10, the travel experience score is variable X, and the geography knowledge score is variable Y. In the formula, N is the number of paired observations (that is, the number of participants measured on both variables).

The calculation of r requires a number of arithmetic operations on the X and Y scores. $\sum X$ is simply the sum of the scores on variable X. $\sum X^2$ is the sum of the squared scores on X (each score is first squared and then the sum of the squared scores is obtained). The quantity $(\sum X)^2$ is the square of the sum of the scores: The total of the X scores $(\sum X)$ is first calculated and then this total is squared. It is important not to confuse the two quantities, $\sum X^2$ and $(\sum X)^2$. The same calculations are made, using the Y scores, to obtain $\sum Y$, $\sum Y^2$, and

$(\Sigma Y)^2$. To find ΣXY, each participant's X score is multiplied by the score on Y; these values are then summed for all subjects. When these calculations have been made, r is computed using the formula for r given above.

At this point, you may wish to examine carefully the calculations shown in Table B-10 to familiarize yourself with the procedures for computing r. You might then try calculating r from another set of data, such as the seating pattern and exam score study shown in Table 10-2.

Significance of r   To test the null hypothesis that the population correlation coefficient is in fact 0.00, we consult a table of critical values of r. Table C-5 in Appendix C shows critical values of r for .10, .05, and .01 levels of significance. To find the critical value, you first need to determine the degrees of freedom. The *df* for the significance test for r is $N - 2$. In our example study on travel and knowledge, the number of paired observations is 10, so the *df* = 8. For 8 degrees of freedom, the critical value of r at the .05 level of significance is .632 (plus or minus). The obtained r must be greater than the critical r to be significant. Because our obtained r (from Table B-10) of .567 is less than the critical value, we do not reject the null hypothesis.

Notice that we do not reject the null hypothesis in this case, even though the magnitude of r is fairly large. Recall the discussion of nonsignificant results from Chapter 10. It is possible that a significant correlation would be obtained if you used a larger sample size or more sensitive and reliable measures of the variables.

C

Statistical Tables

RANDOM NUMBER TABLE

The random number table can be used to select data when an arbitrary sequence of numbers is needed. To obtain a series of random numbers, enter the table at any arbitrary point and read in sequence either across or down.

To use the random number table, first order your subjects in some way. This could be by name or by assigning a number to each subject. Suppose that you have three groups and want 5 subjects per group, for a total of 15 subjects. On the next page is a list of 15 subjects ordered from first to fifteenth. Enter the random number table and assign a number to each subject (if there is a duplicate number, ignore it and use the next number in the sequence). In the example here, the table was entered in the upper left-hand corner and was read downward. Now assign the subjects to groups: The five subjects who receive the lowest random numbers are assigned to group 1, the next five subjects are assigned to group 2, and the five subjects with the highest numbers are assigned to group 3. These general procedures can be followed with any number of groups in an experiment.

To use the random number table for random sampling, first make a list of all members of your population. Enter the random number table and assign a number to each member of the population. Determine your desired sample size (N). Your sample, then, will be composed of the first N individuals. For example, if you want to take a random sample of 15 faculty members at your school, use the random number table to give each faculty member a number. The 15 faculty with the lowest numbers would be selected for the sample.

Subject order	Random number	Group assignment
1	10	1
2	37	2
3	08	1
4	09	1
5	12	1
6	66	2
7	31	2
8	85	3
9	63	2
10	73	2
11	98	3
12	11	1
13	83	3
14	88	3
15	99	3

Table C-1
Random number table

10 09 73 25 33	76 52 01 35 86	34 67 35 48 76	80 95 90 91 17	39 29 27 49 45
37 54 20 48 05	64 89 47 42 96	24 80 52 40 37	20 63 61 04 02	00 82 29 16 65
08 42 26 89 53	19 64 50 93 03	23 20 90 25 60	15 95 33 47 64	35 08 03 36 06
99 01 90 25 29	09 37 67 07 15	38 31 13 11 65	88 67 67 43 97	04 43 62 76 59
12 80 79 99 70	80 15 73 61 47	64 03 23 66 53	98 95 11 68 77	12 17 17 68 33
66 06 57 47 17	34 07 27 68 50	36 69 73 61 70	65 81 33 98 85	11 19 92 91 70
31 06 01 08 05	45 57 18 24 06	35 30 34 26 14	86 79 90 74 39	23 40 30 97 32
85 26 97 76 02	02 05 16 56 92	68 66 57 48 18	73 05 38 52 47	18 62 38 85 79
63 57 33 21 35	05 32 54 70 48	90 55 35 75 48	28 46 82 87 09	83 49 12 56 24
73 79 64 57 53	03 52 96 47 78	35 80 83 42 82	60 93 52 03 44	35 27 38 84 35
98 52 01 77 67	14 90 56 86 07	22 10 94 05 58	60 97 09 34 33	50 50 07 39 98
11 80 50 54 31	39 80 82 77 32	50 72 56 82 48	29 40 52 42 01	52 77 56 78 51
83 45 29 96 34	06 28 89 80 83	13 74 67 00 78	18 47 54 06 10	68 71 17 78 17
88 68 54 02 00	86 50 75 84 01	36 76 66 79 51	90 36 47 64 93	29 60 91 10 62
99 59 46 73 48	87 51 76 49 69	91 82 60 89 28	93 78 56 13 68	23 47 83 41 13
65 48 11 76 74	17 46 85 09 50	58 04 77 69 74	73 03 95 71 86	40 21 81 65 44
80 12 43 56 35	17 72 70 80 15	45 31 82 23 74	21 11 57 82 53	14 38 55 37 63
74 35 09 98 17	77 40 27 72 14	43 23 60 02 10	45 52 16 42 37	96 28 60 26 55
69 91 62 68 03	66 25 22 91 48	36 93 68 72 03	76 62 11 39 90	94 40 05 64 18
09 89 32 05 05	14 22 56 85 14	46 42 75 67 88	96 29 77 88 22	54 38 21 45 98
91 49 91 45 23	68 47 92 76 86	46 16 28 35 54	94 75 08 99 23	37 08 92 00 48
80 33 69 45 98	26 94 03 68 58	70 29 73 41 35	53 14 03 33 40	42 05 08 23 41
44 10 48 19 49	85 15 74 79 54	32 97 92 65 75	57 60 04 08 81	22 22 20 64 13
12 55 07 37 42	11 10 00 20 40	12 86 07 46 97	96 64 48 94 39	28 70 72 58 15
63 60 64 93 29	16 50 53 44 84	40 21 95 23 63	43 65 17 70 82	07 20 73 17 90

Table C-1
(continued)

61 19 69 04 45	26 45 74 77 74	51 92 43 37 29	65 39 45 95 93	42 58 26 05 27
15 47 44 52 66	95 27 07 99 53	59 36 78 38 48	82 39 61 01 18	33 21 15 94 66
94 55 72 83 73	67 89 75 43 87	54 62 24 44 31	91 19 04 23 92	92 92 74 59 73
42 48 11 62 13	97 34 40 87 21	16 86 84 87 67	03 07 11 20 59	25 70 14 66 70
23 52 37 83 17	73 20 88 98 37	68 93 59 14 16	26 25 22 96 63	05 52 28 25 62
04 49 35 24 94	75 24 63 38 24	43 86 25 10 25	61 96 27 93 35	65 33 71 24 72
00 54 99 76 54	64 05 18 81 39	96 11 96 38 96	54 89 28 23 91	23 28 72 95 29
35 96 31 53 07	26 89 80 93 54	33 35 13 54 62	77 97 45 00 24	90 10 33 93 33
59 80 80 83 91	45 42 72 68 42	83 60 94 97 00	13 02 12 48 92	78 56 52 01 06
46 05 88 32 36	01 39 00 22 86	77 28 14 40 77	93 91 08 36 47	70 61 74 29 41
32 17 90 05 97	87 37 92 52 41	05 56 70 70 07	86 74 31 71 57	85 39 41 18 38
69 23 46 14 06	20 11 74 52 04	15 95 66 00 00	18 74 39 24 23	97 11 89 63 38
19 56 54 14 30	01 75 87 53 79	40 41 92 15 85	66 67 43 68 06	84 96 28 52 07
45 15 51 49 38	19 47 60 72 46	43 66 79 45 43	59 04 79 00 33	20 82 66 95 41
94 86 43 19 94	36 18 81 08 51	34 88 88 15 53	01 54 03 54 56	05 01 45 11 76
09 18 82 00 97	32 82 53 95 27	04 22 08 63 04	83 38 98 73 74	64 27 85 80 44
90 04 58 54 97	51 98 15 06 54	94 93 88 19 97	91 87 07 61 50	68 47 68 46 59
73 18 95 02 07	47 67 72 62 69	62 29 06 44 64	27 12 46 70 18	41 36 18 27 60
75 76 87 64 90	20 97 18 17 49	90 42 91 22 72	95 37 50 58 71	93 82 34 31 78
54 01 64 40 56	66 28 13 10 03	00 68 22 73 98	20 71 45 32 95	07 70 61 78 13
08 35 86 99 10	78 54 24 27 85	13 66 15 88 73	04 61 89 75 53	31 22 30 84 20
28 30 60 32 64	81 33 31 05 91	40 51 00 78 93	32 60 46 04 75	94 11 90 18 40
53 84 08 62 33	81 59 41 36 28	51 21 59 02 90	28 46 66 87 93	77 76 22 07 91
91 75 75 37 41	61 61 36 22 69	50 26 39 02 12	55 78 17 65 14	83 48 34 70 55
89 41 59 26 94	00 39 75 83 91	12 60 71 76 46	48 94 27 23 06	94 54 13 74 08
77 51 30 38 20	86 83 42 99 01	68 41 48 27 74	51 90 81 39 80	72 89 35 55 07
19 50 23 71 74	69 97 92 02 88	55 21 02 97 73	74 28 77 52 51	65 34 46 74 15
21 81 85 93 13	93 27 88 17 57	05 68 67 31 56	07 08 28 50 46	31 85 33 84 52
51 47 46 64 99	68 10 72 38 21	94 04 99 13 45	42 83 60 91 91	08 00 74 54 49
99 55 96 83 31	62 53 52 41 70	69 77 71 28 30	74 81 97 81 42	43 86 07 28 34
33 71 34 80 07	93 58 47 28 69	51 92 66 47 21	58 30 32 98 22	93 17 49 39 72
85 27 48 68 93	11 30 32 92 70	28 83 43 41 37	73 51 59 04 00	71 14 84 36 43
84 13 38 96 40	44 03 55 21 66	73 85 27 00 91	61 22 26 05 61	62 32 71 84 23
56 73 21 62 34	17 39 59 61 31	10 12 39 16 22	85 49 65 75 60	81 60 41 88 80
65 13 85 66 06	87 64 88 52 61	34 31 36 58 61	45 87 52 10 69	85 64 44 72 77
38 00 10 21 78	81 71 91 17 11	71 60 29 29 37	74 21 96 40 49	65 58 44 96 98
37 40 29 63 97	01 30 47 75 86	56 27 11 00 65	47 32 46 26 05	40 03 03 74 38
97 12 54 03 48	87 08 33 14 17	21 81 53 92 50	75 23 76 20 47	15 50 12 95 78
21 82 64 11 34	47 14 33 40 72	64 63 88 59 02	49 13 90 64 41	03 85 65 45 52
73 13 54 27 42	95 71 90 90 35	85 79 47 42 96	08 78 98 81 56	64 69 11 92 02
07 63 87 79 29	03 06 11 80 72	96 20 74 41 56	23 82 19 95 38	04 71 36 69 94
60 52 88 34 41	07 95 41 98 14	59 17 52 06 95	05 53 35 21 39	61 21 20 64 55
83 59 63 56 55	06 95 89 29 83	05 12 80 97 19	77 43 35 37 83	92 30 15 04 98
10 85 06 27 46	99 59 91 05 07	13 49 90 63 19	53 07 57 18 39	06 41 01 93 62
39 82 09 89 52	43 62 26 31 47	64 42 18 08 14	43 80 00 93 51	31 02 47 31 67

Source: From tables of the Rand Corporation from *A Million Random Digits With 100,000 Normal Deviates* (New York: Free Press, 1955) by permission of the Rand Corporation.

Table C-2
Critical values of
Chi-square

Degrees of freedom	Probability level		
	.10	*.05*	*.01*
1	2.706	3.841	6.635
2	4.605	5.991	9.210
3	6.251	7.815	11.345
4	7.779	9.488	13.277
5	9.236	11.070	15.086
6	10.645	12.592	16.812
7	12.017	14.067	18.475
8	13.362	15.507	20.090
9	14.684	16.919	21.666
10	15.987	18.307	23.209
11	17.275	19.675	24.725
12	18.549	21.026	26.217
13	19.812	22.362	27.688
14	21.064	23.685	29.141
15	22.307	24.996	30.578
16	23.542	26.296	32.000
17	24.769	27.587	33.409
18	25.989	28.869	34.805
19	27.204	30.144	36.191
20	28.412	31.410	37.566

Source: Table adapted from Fisher and Yates. (1974). *Statistical Tables for Biological, Agricultural, and Medical Research*, 6th ed. London: Longman. Reprinted by permission.

Table C-3
Critical values of t

df	Significance level*			
	.05 .10	.025 .05	.01 .02	.005 .01
1	6.314	12.706	31.821	63.657
2	2.920	4.303	6.965	9.925
3	2.353	3.182	4.541	5.841
4	2.132	2.776	3.747	4.604
5	2.015	2.571	3.365	4.032
6	1.943	2.447	3.143	3.707
7	1.895	2.365	2.998	3.499
8	1.860	2.306	2.896	3.355
9	1.833	2.262	2.821	3.250
10	1.812	2.228	2.764	3.169
11	1.796	2.201	2.718	3.106
12	1.782	2.179	2.681	3.055
13	1.771	2.160	2.650	3.012
14	1.761	2.145	2.624	2.977
15	1.753	2.131	2.602	2.947
16	1.746	2.120	2.583	2.921
17	1.740	2.110	2.567	2.898
18	1.734	2.101	2.552	2.878
19	1.729	2.093	2.539	2.861
20	1.725	2.086	2.528	2.845
21	1.721	2.080	2.518	2.831
22	1.717	2.074	2.508	2.819
23	1.714	2.069	2.500	2.807
24	1.711	2.064	2.492	2.797
25	1.708	2.060	2.485	2.787
26	1.706	2.056	2.479	2.779
27	1.703	2.052	2.473	2.771
28	1.701	2.048	2.467	2.763
29	1.699	2.045	2.462	2.756
30	1.697	2.042	2.457	2.750
40	1.684	2.021	2.423	2.704
60	1.671	2.000	2.390	2.660
120	1.658	1.980	2.358	2.617
∞	1.645	1.960	2.326	2.576

*Use the top significance level when you have predicted a specific directional difference (a one-tailed test; e.g., group 1 will be greater than group 2). Use the bottom significance level when you have only predicted that group 1 will differ from group 2 without specifying the direction of the difference (a two-tailed test).

Table C-4
Critical values of F

df for denomi-nator (error)	α	df for numerator (systematic)											
		1	2	3	4	5	6	7	8	9	10	11	12
1	.10	39.9	49.5	53.6	55.8	57.2	58.2	58.9	59.4	59.9	60.2	60.5	60.7
	.05	161	200	216	225	230	234	237	239	241	242	243	244
2	.10	8.53	9.00	9.16	9.24	9.29	9.33	9.35	9.37	9.38	9.39	9.40	9.41
	.05	18.5	19.0	19.2	19.2	19.3	19.3	19.4	19.4	19.4	19.4	19.4	19.4
	.01	98.5	99.0	99.2	99.2	99.3	99.3	99.4	99.4	99.4	99.4	99.4	99.4
3	.10	5.54	5.46	5.39	5.34	5.31	5.28	5.27	5.25	5.24	5.23	5.22	5.22
	.05	10.1	9.55	9.28	9.12	9.01	8.94	8.89	8.85	8.81	8.79	8.76	8.74
	.01	34.1	30.8	29.5	28.7	28.2	27.9	27.7	27.5	27.3	27.2	27.1	27.1
4	.10	4.54	4.32	4.19	4.11	4.05	4.01	3.98	3.95	3.94	3.92	3.91	3.90
	.05	7.71	6.94	6.59	6.39	6.26	6.16	6.09	6.04	6.00	5.96	5.94	5.91
	.01	21.2	18.0	16.7	16.0	15.5	15.2	15.0	14.8	14.7	14.5	14.4	14.4
5	.10	4.06	3.78	3.62	3.52	3.45	3.40	3.37	3.34	3.32	3.30	3.28	3.27
	.05	6.61	5.79	5.41	5.19	5.05	4.95	4.88	4.82	4.77	4.74	4.71	4.68
	.01	16.3	13.3	12.1	11.4	11.0	10.7	10.5	10.3	10.2	10.1	9.96	9.89
6	.10	3.78	3.46	3.29	3.18	3.11	3.05	3.01	2.98	2.96	2.94	2.92	2.90
	.05	5.99	5.14	4.76	4.53	4.39	4.28	4.21	4.15	4.10	4.06	4.03	4.00
	.01	13.7	10.9	9.78	9.15	8.75	8.47	8.26	8.10	7.98	7.87	7.79	7.72
7	.10	3.59	3.26	3.07	2.96	2.88	2.83	2.78	2.75	2.72	2.70	2.68	2.67
	.05	5.59	4.74	4.35	4.12	3.97	3.87	3.79	3.73	3.68	3.64	3.60	3.57
	.01	12.2	9.55	8.45	7.85	7.46	7.19	6.99	6.84	6.72	6.62	6.54	6.47
8	.10	3.46	3.11	2.92	2.81	2.73	2.67	2.62	2.59	2.56	2.54	2.52	2.50
	.05	5.32	4.46	4.07	3.84	3.69	3.58	3.50	3.44	3.39	3.35	3.31	3.28
	.01	11.3	8.65	7.59	7.01	6.63	6.37	6.18	6.03	5.91	5.81	5.73	5.67
9	.10	3.36	3.01	2.81	2.69	2.61	2.55	2.51	2.47	2.44	2.42	2.40	2.38
	.05	5.12	4.26	3.86	3.63	3.48	3.37	3.29	3.23	3.18	3.14	3.10	3.07
	.01	10.6	8.02	6.99	6.42	6.06	5.80	5.61	5.47	5.35	5.26	5.18	5.11
10	.10	3.29	2.92	2.73	2.61	2.52	2.46	2.41	2.38	2.35	2.32	2.30	2.28
	.05	4.96	4.10	3.71	3.48	3.33	3.22	3.14	3.07	3.02	2.98	2.94	2.91
	.01	10.0	7.56	6.55	5.99	5.64	5.39	5.20	5.06	4.94	4.85	4.77	4.71
11	.10	3.23	2.86	2.66	2.54	2.45	2.39	2.34	2.30	2.27	2.25	2.23	2.21
	.05	4.84	3.98	3.59	3.36	3.20	3.09	3.01	2.95	2.90	2.85	2.82	2.79
	.01	9.65	7.21	6.22	5.67	5.32	5.07	4.89	4.74	4.63	4.54	4.46	4.40
12	.10	3.18	2.81	2.61	2.48	2.39	2.33	2.28	2.24	2.21	2.19	2.17	2.15
	.05	4.75	3.89	3.49	3.26	3.11	3.00	2.91	2.85	2.80	2.75	2.72	2.69
	.01	9.33	6.93	5.95	5.41	5.06	4.82	4.64	4.50	4.39	4.30	4.22	4.16

Table C-4
(continued)

df for de-nomi-nator (error)	α	\multicolumn{12}{c}{*df for numerator (systematic)*}
		1	2	3	4	5	6	7	8	9	10	11	12
13	.10	3.14	2.76	2.56	2.43	2.35	2.28	2.23	2.20	2.16	2.14	2.12	2.10
	.05	4.67	3.81	3.41	3.18	3.03	2.92	2.83	2.77	2.71	2.67	2.63	2.60
	.01	9.07	6.70	5.74	5.21	4.86	4.62	4.44	4.30	4.19	4.10	4.02	3.96
14	.10	3.10	2.73	2.52	2.39	2.31	2.24	2.19	2.15	2.12	2.10	2.08	2.05
	.05	4.60	3.74	3.34	3.11	2.96	2.85	2.76	2.70	2.65	2.60	2.57	2.53
	.01	8.86	6.51	5.56	5.04	4.69	4.46	4.28	4.14	4.03	3.94	3.86	3.80
15	.10	3.07	2.70	2.49	2.36	2.27	2.21	2.16	2.12	2.09	2.06	2.04	2.02
	.05	4.54	3.68	3.29	3.06	2.90	2.79	2.71	2.64	2.59	2.54	2.51	2.48
	.01	8.68	6.36	5.42	4.89	4.56	4.32	4.14	4.00	3.89	3.80	3.73	3.67
16	.10	3.05	2.67	2.46	2.33	2.24	2.18	2.13	2.09	2.06	2.03	2.01	1.99
	.05	4.49	3.63	3.24	3.01	2.85	2.74	2.66	2.59	2.54	2.49	2.46	2.42
	.01	8.53	6.23	5.29	4.77	4.44	4.20	4.03	3.89	3.78	3.69	3.62	3.55
17	.10	3.03	2.64	2.44	2.31	2.22	2.15	2.10	2.06	2.03	2.00	1.98	1.96
	.05	4.45	3.59	3.20	2.96	2.81	2.70	2.61	2.55	2.49	2.45	2.41	2.38
	.01	8.40	6.11	5.18	4.67	4.34	4.10	3.93	3.79	3.68	3.59	3.52	3.46
18	.10	3.01	2.62	2.42	2.29	2.20	2.13	2.08	2.04	2.00	1.98	1.96	1.93
	.05	4.41	3.55	3.16	2.93	2.77	2.66	2.58	2.51	2.46	2.41	2.37	2.34
	.01	8.29	6.01	5.09	4.58	4.25	4.01	3.84	3.71	3.60	3.51	3.43	3.37
19	.10	2.99	2.61	2.40	2.27	2.18	2.11	2.06	2.02	1.98	1.96	1.94	1.91
	.05	4.38	3.52	3.13	2.90	2.74	2.63	2.54	2.48	2.42	2.38	2.34	2.31
	.01	8.18	5.93	5.01	4.50	4.17	3.94	3.77	3.63	3.52	3.43	3.36	3.30
20	.10	2.97	2.59	2.38	2.25	2.16	2.09	2.04	2.00	1.96	1.94	1.92	1.89
	.05	4.35	3.49	3.10	2.87	2.71	2.60	2.51	2.45	2.39	2.35	2.31	2.28
	.01	8.10	5.85	4.94	4.43	4.10	3.87	3.70	3.56	3.46	3.37	3.29	3.23
22	.10	2.95	2.56	2.35	2.22	2.13	2.06	2.01	1.97	1.93	1.90	1.88	1.86
	.05	4.30	3.44	3.05	2.82	2.66	2.55	2.46	2.40	2.34	2.30	2.26	2.23
	.01	7.95	5.72	4.82	4.31	3.99	3.76	3.59	3.45	3.35	3.26	3.18	3.12
24	.10	2.93	2.54	2.33	2.19	2.10	2.04	1.98	1.94	1.91	1.88	1.85	1.83
	.05	4.26	3.40	3.01	2.78	2.62	2.51	2.42	2.36	2.30	2.25	2.21	2.18
	.01	7.82	5.61	4.72	4.22	3.90	3.67	3.50	3.36	3.26	3.17	3.09	3.03
26	.10	2.91	2.52	2.31	2.17	2.08	2.01	1.96	1.92	1.88	1.86	1.84	1.81
	.05	4.23	3.37	2.98	2.74	2.59	2.47	2.39	2.32	2.27	2.22	2.18	2.15
	.01	7.72	5.53	4.64	4.14	3.82	3.59	3.42	3.29	3.18	3.09	3.02	2.96
28	.10	2.89	2.50	2.29	2.16	2.06	2.00	1.94	1.90	1.87	1.84	1.81	1.79
	.05	4.20	3.34	2.95	2.71	2.56	2.45	2.36	2.29	2.24	2.19	2.15	2.12
	.01	7.64	5.45	4.57	4.07	3.75	3.53	3.36	3.23	3.12	3.03	2.96	2.90

Table C-4
(continued)

df for de-nomi-nator (error)	α	df for numerator (systematic)											
		1	2	3	4	5	6	7	8	9	10	11	12
30	.10	2.88	2.49	2.28	2.14	2.05	1.98	1.93	1.88	1.85	1.82	1.79	1.77
	.05	4.17	3.32	2.92	2.69	2.53	2.42	2.33	2.27	2.21	2.16	2.13	2.09
	.01	7.56	5.39	4.51	4.02	3.70	3.47	3.30	3.17	3.07	2.98	2.91	2.84
40	.10	2.84	2.44	2.23	2.09	2.00	1.93	1.87	1.83	1.79	1.76	1.73	1.71
	.05	4.08	3.23	2.84	2.61	2.45	2.34	2.25	2.18	2.12	2.08	2.04	2.00
	.01	7.31	5.18	4.31	3.83	3.51	3.29	3.12	2.99	2.89	2.80	2.73	2.66
60	.10	2.79	2.39	2.18	2.04	1.95	1.87	1.82	1.77	1.74	1.71	1.68	1.66
	.05	4.00	3.15	2.76	2.53	2.37	2.25	2.17	2.10	2.04	1.99	1.95	1.92
	.01	7.08	4.98	4.13	3.65	3.34	3.12	2.95	2.82	2.72	2.63	2.56	2.50
120	.10	2.75	2.35	2.13	1.99	1.90	1.82	1.77	1.72	1.68	1.65	1.62	1.60
	.05	3.92	3.07	2.68	2.45	2.29	2.17	2.09	2.02	1.96	1.91	1.87	1.83
	.01	6.85	4.79	3.95	3.48	3.17	2.96	2.79	2.66	2.56	2.47	2.40	2.34
200	.10	2.73	2.33	2.11	1.97	1.88	1.80	1.75	1.70	1.66	1.63	1.60	1.57
	.05	3.89	3.04	2.65	2.42	2.26	2.14	2.06	1.98	1.93	1.88	1.84	1.80
	.01	6.76	4.71	3.88	3.41	3.11	2.89	2.73	2.60	2.50	2.41	2.34	2.27
∞	.10	2.71	2.30	2.08	1.94	1.85	1.77	1.72	1.67	1.63	1.60	1.57	1.55
	.05	3.84	3.00	2.60	2.37	2.21	2.10	2.01	1.94	1.88	1.83	1.79	1.75
	.01	6.63	4.61	3.78	3.32	3.02	2.80	2.64	2.51	2.41	2.32	2.25	2.18

df	Level of significance for two-tailed test		
	.10	.05	01
1	.988	.997	.9999
2	.900	.950	.990
3	.805	.878	.959
4	.729	.811	.917
5	.669	.754	.874
6	.622	.707	.834
7	.582	.666	.798
8	.549	.632	.765
9	.521	.602	.735
10	.497	.576	.708
11	.476	.553	.684
12	.458	.532	.661
13	.441	.514	.641
14	.426	.497	.623
15	.412	.482	.606
16	.400	.468	.590
17	.389	.456	.575
18	.378	.444	.561
19	.369	.433	.549
20	.360	.423	.537
25	.323	.381	.487
30	.296	.349	.449
35	.275	.325	.418
40	.257	.304	.393
45	.243	.288	.372
50	.231	.273	.354
60	.211	.250	.325
70	.195	.232	.303
80	.183	.217	.283
90	.173	.205	.267
100	.164	.195	.254

Table C-5
Critical values of r (Pearson product-moment correlation coefficient)

The significance level is halved for a one-tailed test.

D

Constructing
a Latin Square

A Latin Square to determine the orders of any N number of conditions will have N arrangements of orders. Thus, if there are four conditions, there will be four orders in a 4×4 Latin Square; eight conditions will produce an 8×8 Latin Square. The method for constructing a Latin Square shown below will produce orders in which (1) each condition or group appears once at each order and (2) each condition precedes and follows each other condition one time.

Use the following procedures for generating a Latin Square when there is an even number of conditions:

1. Determine the number of conditions. Use letters of the alphabet to represent your N conditions: ABCD for four conditions, ABCDEF for six conditions, and so on.

2. Determine the order for the first row, using the following ordering:

$$A, B, L, C, L-1, D, L-2, E$$

and so on. L stands for the last or final treatment. Thus, if you have four conditions (ABCD), your order will be

$$A, B, D, C$$

With six conditions (ABCDEF), the order will be

$$A, B, F, C, E, D$$

because F is the final treatment (L), and E is the next to final treatment ($L-1$).

3. Determine the order for the second row, by increasing one letter at each position of the first row. The last letter cannot be increased, of course, so it reverts to the first letter. With six conditions, the order of the second row becomes

B, C, A, D, F, E

4. Continue this procedure for the third and subsequent rows. For the third row, increase one letter at each position of the second row:

C, D, B, E, A, F

The final 6 × 6 Latin Square will be

```
A  B  F  C  E  D
B  C  A  D  F  E
C  D  B  E  A  F
D  E  C  F  B  A
E  F  D  A  C  B
F  A  E  B  D  C
```

5. Randomly assign each of your conditions to one of the letters to determine which condition will be in the A position, the B position, and so on.

If you have an odd number of conditions, you must make two Latin Squares. For the first square, simply follow the procedures shown above. Now create a second square that reverses the first one; that is, in each row, the first condition becomes the last, the second condition is next to last, and so on. Join the two squares together to create the final Latin Square (actually a rectangle!). Thus, if there are five conditions, you will have 10 possible orders to run in your study.

Glossary

Alternate forms reliability
> A reliability coefficient determined by the correlation between scores on one form of a measure administered at one time with scores on an alternative version of the measure given at a later time.

Analysis of covariance
> A statistical technique to control for the correlation between a subject variable and a dependent variable in an experiment. This procedure removes the error variance that results from the fact that variability in scores on the dependent variable is due in part to the effect of the subject variable.

Analysis of variance
> *See* F test.

Archival research
> The use of existing sources of information for research. Sources include statistical records, survey archives, and written records.

Bar graph
> *See* Histogram.

Baseline
> In a single-subject design, the subject's behavior during a control period before introduction of the experimental manipulation.

Between-subjects design
> *See* Independent groups design.

Carry-over effect
> A problem that may occur in repeated measures designs if the effects of one treatment are still present when the next treatment is given.

Case study
> A descriptive account of the behavior, past history, and other relevant factors concerning a specific individual.

Ceiling effect
> Failure of a measure to detect a difference because it was too easy (*also see* Floor effect).

Central tendency
    A single number or value that describes the typical or central score among a set of scores.

Cluster sampling
    A method of sampling in which clusters of individuals are identified. Clusters are sampled, and then all individuals in each cluster are included in the sample.

Coding system
    A set of rules used to categorize observations.

Cohort
    A group of people born at about the same time and exposed to the same societal events; cohort effects are confounded with age in a cross-sectional study.

Conceptual replication
    Replication of research using different procedures for manipulating or measuring the variables.

Confederate
    A person posing as a subject in an experiment who is actually part of the experiment.

Confounding
    Failure to control for the effects of a third variable in an experimental design.

Construct validity
    The degree to which a measurement device accurately measures the theoretical construct it is designed to measure.

Content analysis
    Systematic analysis of the content of written records.

Control series design
    An extension of the interrupted time series quasi-experimental design in which there is a comparison or control group.

Convergent validity
    Assessment of the validity of a measure by demonstrating that the measure is related to other variables in predicted ways.

Correlation coefficient
    An index of how strongly two variables are related to each other in a group of subjects.

Correlational method
    A method of determining whether two variables are related by measurement or observation of the variables.

Counterbalancing
    A method of controlling for order effects in a repeated measures design by either including all orders of treatment presentation or randomly determining the order for each subject.

Criterion validity
    The degree to which a measurement device accurately predicts behavior on a criterion measure.

Criterion variable
    A behavior that a researcher wishes to predict using a predictor variable.

Cross-cultural research
    Research that studies the relationship between variables across different cultures.

311

Cross-sectional method
> A developmental research method in which persons of different ages are studied at only one point in time; conceptually similar to an independent groups design.

Cross-sequential method
> A combination of the cross-sectional and longitudinal methods to study developmental research questions in which separate cohorts are studied longitudinally.

Curvilinear relationship
> A relationship in which increases in the values of the first variable are accompanied by both increases and decreases in the values of the second variable.

Debriefing
> Explanation of the purposes of the research that is given to subjects following their participation in the research.

Degrees of freedom (df)
> A concept used in tests of statistical significance; the number of observations that are free to vary to produce a known outcome.

Demand characteristics
> Cues that inform the subject how he or she is expected to behave.

Dependent variable
> The variable that is the subject's response to, and dependent on, the level of the manipulated independent variable.

Descriptive statistics
> Statistical measures that describe the results of a study; descriptive statistics include measures of central tendency (e.g., mean), variability (e.g., standard deviation), and correlation (e.g., Pearson r).

Discriminant validity
> Assessment of the validity of a measure by demonstrating that the measure is *not* related to other variables that it theoretically should not be related to.

Effect size
> The extent to which two variables are associated. In experimental research, the magnitude of the impact of the independent variable on the dependent variable.

Electroencephalograph (EEG)
> An apparatus that measures the electrical activity of the brain.

Error variance
> Random variability in a set of scores that is not the result of the independent variable. Statistically, the variability of each score from its group mean.

Exact replication
> Replication of research using the same procedures for manipulating and measuring the variables that were used in the original research.

Experimental control
> In an experiment, keeping all extraneous variables constant so that only the independent variable can affect the dependent variable.

Experimental method
> A method of determining whether variables are related in which the researcher manipulates the independent variable and controls all other variables either by randomization or by direct experimental control.

Experimental realism
> The extent to which the independent variable manipulation has an impact on and involves subjects in an experiment.

Experimenter bias (expectancy effects)
> Any intentional or unintentional influence that the experimenter exerts on subjects to confirm the hypothesis under investigation.

External validity
> The degree to which the results of an experiment may be generalized.

F test (analysis of variance)
> A statistical significance test for determining whether two or more means are significantly different. *F* is the ratio of systematic variance to error variance.

Face validity
> The degree to which a measurement device appears to accurately measure a variable.

Factorial design
> A design in which all levels of each independent variable are combined with all levels of the other independent variables. A factorial design allows investigation of the separate main effects and interactions of two or more independent variables.

Field experiment
> An experiment that is conducted in a field rather than laboratory setting.

Filler items
> Items included in a questionnaire measure to help disguise the true purpose of the measure.

Floor effect
> Failure of a measure to detect a difference because it was too difficult (*also see* Ceiling effect).

Frequency distribution
> An arrangement of a set of scores from lowest to highest that indicates the number of times each score was obtained.

Frequency polygon
> A graphic display of a frequency distribution in which the frequency of each score is plotted on the vertical axis, with the plotted points connected by straight lines.

Functional design
> An experiment that contains many levels of the independent variable in order to determine the exact functional relationship between the independent and dependent variables.

Galvanic Skin Response (GSR)
> The electrical conductance of the skin, which changes when sweating occurs.

Haphazard sampling
> Selecting subjects in a haphazard manner, usually on the basis of availability, and not with regard to having a representative sample of the population; a type of nonprobability sampling.

Histogram
> Graphic display of the scores in a frequency distribution; vertical or horizontal bars represent the frequencies of each score.

History effect
> As a threat to the internal validity of an experiment, refers to any outside event that is not part of the manipulation that could be responsible for the results.

Hypothesis
> A statement that makes an assertion about what is true in a particular situation; often, a statement asserting that two or more variables are related to one another.

313

Independent groups design
> An experiment in which different subjects are assigned to each group. Also called between-subjects design.

Independent variable
> The variable that is manipulated to observe its effect on the dependent variable.

Inferential statistics
> Statistics designed to determine whether results based on sample data are generalizable to a population.

Informed consent
> In research ethics, the principle that participants in an experiment be informed in advance of all aspects of the research that might influence their decision to participate.

Institutional Review Board
> An ethics review committee established to review research proposals. The IRB is composed of scientists, nonscientists, and legal experts.

Instrument decay
> As a threat to internal validity, the possibility that a change in the characteristics of the measurement instrument is responsible for the results.

Interaction effect
> The differing effect of one independent variable on the dependent variable, depending on the particular level of another independent variable.

Internal validity
> The certainty with which results of an experiment can be attributed to the manipulation of the independent variable rather than to some other, confounding variable.

Interrupted time series design
> A design in which the effectiveness of a treatment is determined by examining a series of measurements made over an extended time period both before and after the treatment is introduced. The treatment is not introduced at a random point in time.

Interval scale
> A scale of measurement in which the intervals between numbers on the scale are all equal in size.

Interviewer bias
> Intentional or unintentional influence exerted by an interviewer in such a way that the actual or interpreted behavior of respondents is consistent with the interviewer's expectations.

Item-total reliability
> A reliability coefficient based on the average correlation between the score on each item of a measure with the total score.

IV × SV design
> A factorial design that includes both an experimental independent variable (IV) and a correlational subject variable (SV).

Latin Square
> A technique to control for order effects without having all possible orders.

Longitudinal method
> A developmental research method in which the same persons are observed repeatedly as they grow older; conceptually similar to a repeated measures design.

Main effect
> The direct effect of an independent variable on a dependent variable.

Manipulation check
> A measure used to determine whether the manipulation of the independent variable has had its intended effect on a subject.

Matched random assignment
> A method of assigning subjects to groups in which pairs of subjects are first matched on some characteristic and then individually assigned randomly to groups.

Maturation effect
> As a threat to internal validity, the possibility that any naturally occurring change within the individual is responsible for the results.

Mean
> A measure of central tendency, obtained by summing scores and then dividing the sum by the number of scores.

Measurement error
> The degree to which a measurement deviates from the true score value.

Median
> A measure of central tendency; the middle score in a distribution of scores that divides the distribution in half.

Meta-analysis
> A set of statistical procedures for combining the results of a number of studies in order to provide a general assessment of the relationship between variables.

Mixed factorial design
> A design that includes both independent groups (between-subjects) and repeated measures (within-subjects) variables.

Mode
> A measure of central tendency; the most frequent score in a distribution of scores.

Mortality
> The loss of subjects who decide to leave an experiment. Mortality is a threat to internal validity when the mortality rate is related to the nature of the experimental manipulation.

Multiple baseline design
> Observing behavior before and after a manipulation under multiple circumstances (across different individuals, different behaviors, or different settings).

Multiple correlation
> A correlation between one variable and a combined set of predictor variables.

Mundane realism
> The extent to which the independent variable manipulation is similar to events that occur in the real world.

Naturalistic observation
> Descriptive method in which observations are made in a natural social setting. Also called field observation.

Negative case analysis
> In field observation, an examination of observations that do not fit with the explanatory structure devised by the researcher.

Negative linear relationship
> A relationship in which increases in the values of the first variable are accompanied by decreases in the values of the second variable.

315

Nominal scale
> A scale of measurement with two or more categories that have no numerical (less than, greater than) properties.

Nonequivalent control group design
> A poor experimental design in which nonequivalent groups of subjects participate in the different experimental groups, and there is no pretest.

Nonequivalent control group pretest-posttest design
> A quasi-experimental design in which nonequivalent groups are used, but a pretest allows assessment of equivalency and pretest-posttest changes.

Nonprobability sampling
> Type of sampling procedure in which one cannot specify the probability that any member of the population will be included in the sample.

Nonsignificant results
> Results that are probably due to error factors and indicative of a decision to not reject the null hypothesis.

Null hypothesis
> The hypothesis, used for statistical purposes, that the variables under investigation are not related in the population, that any observed effect based on sample results is due to random error.

Odd-even reliability
> A reliability coefficient determined by the correlation between scores based on the odd-numbered items of a measure with scores on the even-numbered items.

One-group pretest-posttest design
> A poor experimental design in which the effect of an independent variable is inferred from the pretest-posttest difference in a single group.

Operational definition
> Definition of a concept that specifies the operation used to measure or manipulate the concept.

Order effect
> In a repeated measures design, the effect that the order of introducing treatment has on the dependent variable.

Ordinal scale
> A scale of measurement in which the measurement categories form a rank order along a continuum.

Panel study
> In survey research, questioning the same people at two or more points in time.

Partial correlation
> The correlation between two variables with the influence of a third variable statistically controlled for.

Pilot study
> A small-scale study conducted prior to conducting an actual experiment; designed to test and refine procedures.

Placebo group
> In drug research, a group given an inert substance to assess the psychological effect of receiving a treatment.

Population

The defined group of individuals from which a sample is drawn.

Positive linear relationship

A relationship in which increases in the values of the first variable are accompanied by increases in the values of the second variable.

Posttest-only design

A true experimental design in which the dependent variable (posttest) is measured only once, after manipulation of the independent variable.

Prediction

A statement that makes an assertion concerning what will occur in a particular research investigation.

Predictor variable

A measure that is used to predict behavior on another measure (a criterion variable).

Pretest-posttest design

A true experimental design in which the dependent variable is measured both before (pretest) and after (posttest) manipulation of the independent variable.

Probability

The likelihood that a given event (among a specific set of events) will occur.

Probability sampling

Type of sampling procedure in which one is able to specify the probability that any member of the population will be included in the sample.

Program evaluation

Research designed to evaluate programs (e.g., social reforms, innovations) that are designed to produce certain changes or outcomes in a target population.

Projective measure

A measure consisting of an ambiguous stimulus to which subjects respond and thus "project" elements of their personality, values, and so on.

Psychobiography

A type of case study in which the life of an individual is analyzed using psychological theory.

Quasi-experimental design

A type of design that approximates the control features of true experiments to infer that a given treatment did have its intended effect.

Quota sampling

A sampling procedure in which the sample is chosen to reflect the numerical composition of various subgroups in the population. A haphazard sampling technique is used to obtain the sample.

Random error

An unexplained and unsystematic variability from a true score.

Randomization

Controlling for the effects of extraneous variables by ensuring that the variables operate in a manner determined entirely by chance.

Ratio scale

A scale of measurement in which there is an absolute zero point, indicating an absence of the variable being measured. An implication is that ratios of numbers

317

on the scale can be formed (generally, these are physical measures such as weight or timed measures such as duration or reaction time).

Reactivity

A problem of measurement in which the measure changes the behavior being observed.

Regression equation

A mathematical equation that allows prediction of one behavior when the score on another variable is known.

Reliability

The degree to which a measure is consistent.

Repeated measures design

An experiment in which the same subjects are assigned to each group. Also called within-subjects design.

Replication

Repeating a research study to determine whether the results can be duplicated.

Research hypothesis

The hypothesis that the variables under investigation are related in the population, that the observed effect based on sample data is true in the population.

Response set

A pattern of individual response to questions on a self-report measure that is not related to the content of the questions.

Reversal design

A single-subject design in which the treatment is introduced after a baseline period and then withdrawn during a second baseline period. It may be extended by adding a second introduction of the treatment. Sometimes called a "withdrawal" design.

Role-playing

A procedure for studying behavior in which individuals are asked to indicate how they would respond to a given situation rather than being observed in action in the situation.

Sampling

The process of choosing members of a population to be included in a sample.

Selection differences

Differences in the type of subjects who make up each group in an experimental design; this situation occurs when subjects elect which group they are to be assigned to.

Sensitivity

The ability of a measure to detect differences between groups.

Sequential design

A combination of the cross-sectional and longitudinal design to study developmental research questions.

Significance level

The probability of rejecting the null hypothesis when it is true.

Significant result

An outcome of a study that has a low probability of occurrence if the null hypothesis is true; a result that leads to a decision to reject the null hypothesis.

Simple random assignment

    Assigning subjects to groups in a random manner such that assignment is determined entirely by chance.

Simple random sampling

    A sampling procedure in which each member of the population has an equal probability of being included in the sample.

Simulator group

    In hypnosis research, a group that is not actually hypnotized but whose members are instructed to act as if they were hypnotized.

Single-subject experiment

    An experiment in which the effect of the independent variable is assessed using data from a single subject.

Split-half reliability

    A reliability coefficient determined by the correlation between scores on the first half of the items on a measure with scores on the second half of a measure.

Standard deviation

    The average deviation of scores from the mean (the square root of the variance).

Statistical regression

    The tendency of extreme scores on a measure to become less extreme (regress toward the mean) when the measurement is made a second time.

Statistical significance

    Rejection of the null hypothesis when an outcome has a low probability of occurrence (usually .05 or less) if, in fact, the null hypothesis is correct.

Stratified random sampling

    A sampling procedure in which the population is divided into strata followed by random sampling from each stratum.

Stratum (*pl.* strata)

    Subdivision of a population based on specified characteristics of its members.

Structural model

    A model of an expected pattern of relationships among a set of variables. The proposed pattern is based on a theory of how the variables are causally related to one another.

Systematic observation

    Observations of one or more specific variables, usually made in a precisely defined setting.

Systematic variance

    Variability in a set of scores that is the result of the independent variable; statistically, the variability of each group mean from the grand mean of all subjects.

Testing effect

    A threat to internal validity in which taking a pretest changes behavior without any effect on the independent variable.

Test-retest reliability

    A reliability coefficient determined by the correlation between scores on a measure given at one time with scores on the same measure given at a later time.

Theory

    A set of explanatory statements about behavior that can be tested through empirical research.

True score

An individual's actual score on a variable being measured, as opposed to the score the individual obtained on the measure itself.

Type I error

An incorrect decision to reject the null hypothesis when it is true.

Type II error

An incorrect decision to accept the null hypothesis when it is false.

Unobtrusive measure

A measure of behavior that is made without the subject's awareness.

Validity

The extent to which a measurement instrument measures what it is intended to measure.

Variability

The amount of dispersion of scores about some central value.

Variable

A general class or category of objects, events, or situations within which specific instances are found to vary.

Variance

A measure of the variability of scores about a mean; the mean of the sum of squared deviations of scores from the group mean.

References

Aiello, J. R., Baum, A., & Gormley, F. P. (1981). Social determinants of residential crowding stress. *Personality and Social Psychology Bulletin*, 4, 643–649.

Ajzen, I., & Fishbein, M. (1980). *Understanding attitudes and predicting social behavior*. Englewood Cliffs, NJ: Prentice-Hall.

American Psychological Association. (1967). *Casebook on ethical standards of psychologists*. Washington, DC: Author.

American Psychological Association. (1973). Ethical principles in the conduct of research with human participants. *American Psychologist*, 28, 79–80.

American Psychological Association. (1981). *Ethical principles of psychologists*. Washington, DC: Author.

American Psychological Association. (1982). *Ethical principles in the conduct of research with human participants*. Washington, DC: Author.

American Psychological Association. (1986). Guidelines for ethical conduct in the care and use of animals. *Journal of the Experimental Analysis of Behavior*, 45, 127–132.

American Psychological Association. (1992). Ethical principles of psychologists and code of conduct. *American Psychologist*, 47, 1597–1611.

American Psychological Association. (1994). *Publication manual of the American Psychological Association* (4th ed.). Washington, DC: Author.

Anderson, C. A., & Anderson, D. C. (1984). Ambient temperature and violent crime: Test of the linear and curvilinear hypotheses. *Journal of Personality and Social Psychology*, 46, 91–97.

Anderson, D. R., Lorch, E. P., Field, D. E., Collins, P. A., & Nathan, J. G. (1986). TV viewing at home. *Child Development*, 57, 1024–1033.

Aristotle. (1954). Rhetoric. In *Aristotle, rhetoric, and poetics* (W. Rhys Roberts, Trans.). New York: Modern Library.

Aronson, E. (1984). *The social animal* (4th ed.). San Francisco: W. H. Freeman.

Aronson, E., Brewer, M., & Carlsmith, J. M. (1985). Experimentation in social psychology. In G. Lindzey & E. Aronson (Eds.), *Handbook of social psychology* (3rd ed.). New York: Random House.

Aronson, E., Stephan, C., Sikes, J., Blaney, N., & Snapp, M. (1978). *The jigsaw class-room*. Newbury Park, CA: Sage.

Astin, A. (1987). *The American freshman: Twenty year trends, 1966–1985*. Los Angeles: Higher Education Research Institute, Graduate School of Education, University of California.

Bakeman, R., & Brownlee, J. R. (1980). The strategic use of parallel play: A sequential analysis. *Child Development, 51*, 873–878.

Bakeman, R., & Gottman, J. M. (1986). *Observing interaction*. Cambridge: Cambridge University Press.

Bales, R. F., & Cohen, S. P. (1979). *SYMLOG: A system for the multiple level observation of groups*. New York: Free Press.

Barlow, D. H., & Hersen, M. (1984). *Single case experimental designs*. New York: Pergamon Press.

Baron, R. A., & Bronfen, M. I. (1994). A whiff of reality: Empirical evidence concerning the effects of pleasant fragrances on work-related behavior. *Journal of Applied Social Psychology, 24*, 1179–1203.

Barton, E. M., Baltes, M. M., & Orzech, M. J. (1980). Etiology of dependence in older nursing home residents during morning care; the role of staff behavior. *Journal of Personality and Social Psychology, 38*, 423–431.

Baum, A., Gachtel, R. J., & Schaeffer, M. A. (1983). Emotional, behavioral, and psychological effects of chronic stress at Three Mile Island. *Journal of Consulting and Clinical Psychology, 51*, 565–572.

Baumeister, R. F., & Newman, L. S. (1994). How stories make sense of personal experiences: Motives that shape autobiographical narratives. *Personality and Social Psychology Bulletin, 20*, 676–690.

Beach, F. A. (1950). The snark was a boojum. *American Psychologist, 5*, 115–124.

Beaman, A. (1991). An empirical comparison of meta-analytic and traditional reviews. *Personality and Social Psychology Bulletin, 17*, 252–257.

Becker, H. K., Agopian, M. W., & Yeh, S. (1992). Impact evaluation of Drug Abuse Resistance Education (D.A.R.E.). *Journal of Drug Education, 22*, 283–291.

Becker, H. S. (1963). *Outsiders: Studies in the sociology of deviance*. New York: Free Press.

Bem, D. J. (1981). Writing the research report. In L. H. Kidder (Ed.), *Research methods in social relations*. New York: Holt, Rinehart & Winston.

Berry, T. D., & Geller, E. S. (1991). A single-subject approach to evaluative vehicle safety belt reminders: Back to basics. *Journal of Applied Behavior Analysis, 24*, 13–22.

Berscheid, E., Baron, R. S., Dermer, M., & Libman, M. (1973). Anticipating informed consent: An empirical approach. *American Psychologist, 28*, 913–925.

Bouchard, T. J., Jr., & McGue, M. (1981). Familial studies of intelligence: A review. *Science, 212*, 1055–1059.

Brogden, W. J. (1962). The experimenter as a factor in animal conditioning. *Psychological Reports, 11*, 239–242.

Brooks, C. I., & Rebata, J. L. (1991). College classroom ecology: The relation of sex of student to classroom performance and seating preference. *Environment and Behavior, 23*, 305–313.

Byrne, D. (1971). *The attraction paradigm*. New York: Academic Press.

Byrne, D., Ervin, C. R., & Lamberth, J. (1970). Continuity between the experimental study of attraction and real-life computer dating. *Journal of Personality and Social Psychology, 16,* 157–165.

Byrne, G. (1988, October 7). Breuning pleads guilty. *Science, 242,* 27–28.

Cacioppo, J. T., & Petty, R. E. (Eds.). (1983). *Social psychophysiology: A sourcebook.* New York: Guilford Press.

Cacioppo, J. T., & Tassinary, L. G. (1990). Inferring psychological significance from physiological signals. *American Psychologist, 45,* 16–28.

Campbell, D. T. (1968). Quasi-experimental design. In D. L. Gillis (Ed.), *International encyclopedia of the social sciences* (Vol. 5). New York: Macmillan and Free Press.

Campbell, D. T. (1969). Reforms as experiments. *American Psychologist, 24,* 409–429.

Campbell, D. T., & Stanley, J. C. (1966). *Experimental and quasi-experimental designs for research.* Chicago: Rand McNally.

Cavan, S. (1966). *Liquor license: An ethnography of bar behavior.* Chicago: Aldine.

Chaiken, S., & Pliner, P. (1987). Women, but not men, are what they eat: The effect of meal size and gender on perceived femininity and masculinity. *Personality and Social Psychology Bulletin, 13,* 166–176.

Christensen, L. (1988). Deception in psychological research: When is its use justified? *Personality and Social Psychology Bulletin, 14,* 664–675.

Cialdini, R. B. (1988). *Influence: Science and practice* (2nd ed.). Glenview, IL: Scott, Foresman.

Cialdini, R. B., Borden, R., Walker, M. R., Freeman, S., Shuma, P., Braver, S. L., Ralls, M., Floyd, L., Reynolds, L., Crandall, R., & Jellison, J. M. (1974). Wearing the warm glow of success: A (football) field study. *Proceedings of the Division of Personality and Social Psychology, 1,* 13–15.

Clark, K. B., & Clark, M. P. (1947). Racial identification and preference in Negro children. In T. M. Newcomb & E. L. Hartley (Eds.), *Readings in social psychology.* New York: Holt, Rinehart & Winston.

Cohen, J. (1994). The earth is round (p < .05). *American Psychologist, 49,* 997–1003.

Coile, D. C., & Miller, N. E. (1984). How radical animal activists try to mislead humane people. *American Psychologist, 39,* 700–701.

Conoley, J. C., & Kramer, J. J. (1989). *Tenth mental measurements yearbook.* Lincoln: Buros Institute of Mental Measurements, University of Nebraska–Lincoln.

Converse, J. M., & Presser, S. (1986). *Survey questions: Handcrafting the standardized questionnaire.* Newbury Park, CA: Sage.

Cook, T. D., & Campbell, D. T. (1979). *Quasi-experimentation: Design and analysis issues for field settings.* Chicago: Rand McNally.

Cooper, H. M., & Rosenthal, R. (1980). Statistical versus traditional procedures for summarizing research findings. *Psychological Bulletin, 87,* 442–449.

Coovert, M. D., Penner, L. A., & MacCallum, R. (1990). Covariance structure modeling in personality and social psychological research: An introduction. In C. Hendrick & M. S. Clark (Eds.), *Review of personality and social psychology* (Vol. 11). Newbury Park, CA: Sage.

Costa, P. T., Jr., & McCrae, R. R. (1985). *The NEO personality inventory manual.* Odessa, FL: Psychological Assessment Resources.

Csikszentmihalyi, M., Rathunde, K. & Whalen, S. (1993). *Talented teenagers: The roots of success and failure.* New York: Cambridge University Press.

323

Curtiss, S. R. (1977). *Genie: A psycholinguistic study of a modern-day "wild child."* New York: Academic Press.

Darley, J. M., & Latané, B. (1968). Bystander intervention in emergencies: Diffusion of responsibility. *Journal of Personality and Social Psychology, 8,* 377–383.

Denmark, F., Russo, N. P., Frieze, I. H., & Sechzer, J. A. (1988). Guidelines for avoiding sexism in psychological research: A report of the Ad Hoc Committee on Nonsexist Research. *American Psychologist, 43,* 582–585.

Department of Health and Human Services. (1981, January 26). Final regulations amending basic HHS policy for the protection of human research subjects. *Federal Register, 46*(16), 8366–8392.

Dill, C. A., Gilden, E. R, Hill, P. C., & Hanslka, L. L. (1982). Federal human subjects regulations: A methodological artifact? *Personality and Social Psychology Bulletin, 8,* 417–425.

Duncan, S., Rosenberg, M. J., & Finklestein, J. (1969). The paralanguage of experimenter bias. *Sociometry, 32,* 207–219.

Eagly, A. H., Ashmore, R. D., Makhijani, M. G., & Longo, L. C. (1991). What is beautiful is good, but . . . : A meta-analytic review of research on the physical attractiveness stereotype. *Psychological Bulletin, 110,* 109–128.

Ellsworth, P. C., Carlsmith, J. M., & Henson, A. (1972). The stare as a stimulus to flight in human beings: A series of field experiments. *Journal of Personality and Social Psychology, 21,* 302–311.

Elms, A. C. (1994). *Uncovering lives: The uneasy alliance of biography and psychology.* New York: Oxford University Press.

Ennett, S. T., Tobler, N. S., Ringwalt, C. L., & Flewelling, R. L. (1994). How effective is drug abuse resistance education? A meta-analysis of Project D.A.R.E. outcome evaluations. *American Journal of Public Health, 84,* 1394–1401.

Epstein, Y. M., Suedfeld, P., & Silverstein, S. J. (1973). The experimental contract: Subjects' expectations of and reactions to some behaviors of experimenters. *American Psychologist, 28,* 212–221.

Everett, P. B., Hayward, S. C., & Meyers, A. W. (1974). The effects of a token reinforcement procedure on bus ridership. *Journal of Applied Behavior Analysis, 7,* 1–10.

Fazio, R. H., Cooper, M., Dayson, K., & Johnson, M. (1981). Control and the coronary-prone behavior pattern: Responses to multiple situational demands. *Personality and Social Psychology Bulletin, 7,* 97–102.

Fischer, K., Schoeneman, T. J., & Rubanowitz, D. E. (1987). Attributions in the advice columns: II. The dimensionality of actors' and observers' explanations of interpersonal problems. *Personality and Social Psychology Bulletin, 13,* 458–466.

Fishbein, M., & Ajzen, I. (1975). *Belief, attitude, intention, and behavior: An introduction to theory and research.* Reading, MA: Addison-Wesley.

Fiske, S. T., Bersoff, D. N., Borgida, E., Deaux, K., & Heilman, M. E. (1991). Social science research on trial: Use of sex stereotyping in Price Waterhouse v. Hopkins. *American Psychologist, 46,* 1049–1060.

Fiske, S. T., & Taylor, S. E. (1984). *Social cognition.* New York: Random House.

Flavell, J. H. (1985). *Cognitive development.* Englewood Cliffs, NJ: Prentice-Hall.

Freedman, J. L. (1969). Role-playing: Psychology by consensus. *Journal of Personality and Social Psychology, 13,* 107–114.

Freedman, J. L., Klevansky, S., & Ehrlich, P. R. (1971). The effect of crowding on human task performance. *Journal of Applied Social Psychology, 1*, 7–25.

Freedman, J. L., Levy, A. S., Buchanan, R. W., & Price, J. (1972). Crowding and human aggressiveness. *Journal of Experimental Social Psychology, 8*, 528–548.

Frick, R. W. (1995). Accepting the null hypothesis. *Memory and Cognition, 25*, 132–138.

Friedman, H. S., Tucker, J. S., Schwartz, J. E., Tomlinson-Keasy, C., Martin, L. R., Wingard, D. L., & Criqui, M. H. (1995). Psychosocial and behavioral predictors of longevity: The aging and death of the "Termites." *American Psychologist, 50*, 69–78.

Furnham, A., Gunter, B., & Peterson, E. (1994). Television distraction and the performance of introverts and extroverts. *Applied Cognitive Psychology, 8*, 705–711.

Gallup, G. G., & Suarez, S. D. (1985). Alternatives to the use of animals in psychological research. *American Psychologist, 40*, 1104–1111.

Gans, H. (1962). *Urban villagers.* New York: Free Press.

Gardner, G. T. (1978). Effects of federal human subjects regulations on data obtained in environmental stressor research. *Journal of Personality and Social Psychology, 34*, 774–781.

Gardner, L. E. (1988). A relatively painless method of introduction to the psychological literature search. In M. E. Ware & C. L. Brewer (Eds.), *Handbook for teaching statistics and research methods.* Hillsdale, NJ: Erlbaum.

Gelfand, H., & Walker, C. J. (1990). *Mastering APA style.* Washington, DC: American Psychological Association.

Geller, E. S., Russ, N. W., & Altomari, M. G. (1986). Naturalistic observations of beer drinking among college students. *Journal of Applied Behavior Analysis, 19*, 391–396.

Gergen, K. J. (1973). The codification of research ethics: Views of a Doubting Thomas. *American Psychology, 28*, 907–912.

Gilovich, T. (1991). *How we know what isn't so: The fallibility of human reason in everyday life.* New York: Free Press.

Green, B. F. (1992). Exposé or smear? The Burt affair. *Psychological Science, 3*, 328–331.

Green, J., & Wallaf, C. (1981). *Ethnography and language in educational settings.* New York: Ablex.

Greenwald, A. G. (1976). Within-subjects designs: To use or not to use? *Psychological Bulletin, 83*, 314–320.

Gross, A. E., & Fleming, I. (1982). Twenty years of deception in social psychology. *Personality and Social Psychology Bulletin, 8*, 402–408.

Gwaltney-Gibbs, P. A. (1986). The institutionalization of premarital cohabitation: Estimates from marriage license applications, 1970 and 1980. *Journal of Marriage and the Family, 48*, 423–434.

Hawking, S. W. (1988). *A brief history of time: From the big bang to black holes.* New York: Bantam Books.

Health and Human Services, Department of. (1981, January 26). Final regulations amending basic HHS policy for the protection of human research subjects. *Federal Register, 46*(16), 8366–8392.

Hearnshaw, L. S. (1979). *Cyril Burt, psychologist.* Ithaca, NY: Cornell University Press.

Henle, M., & Hubbell, M. B. (1938). "Egocentricity" in adult conversation. *Journal of Social Psychology, 9*, 227–234.

Hill, C. T., Rubin, Z., & Peplau, L. A. (1976). Breakups before marriage: The end of 103 affairs. *Journal of Social Issues, 32*, 147–168.

Hill, L. (1990). Effort and reward in college: A replication of some puzzling findings. In J. W. Neuliep (Ed.), *Handbook of replication in the behavioral and social sciences.* [Special issue] *Journal of Social Behavior and Personality, 5*(4), 151–161.

Holden, C. (1987). Animal regulations: So far, so good. *Science, 238*, 880–882.

Holsti, O. R. (1969). *Content analysis for the social sciences and humanities.* Reading, MA: Addison-Wesley.

Hood, T. C., & Back, K. W. (1971). Self-disclosure and the volunteer: A source of bias in laboratory experiments. *Journal of Personality and Social Psychology, 17*, 130–136.

Hostetler, A. J. (1987, May) Fraud inquiry revives doubt: Can science police itself? *APA Monitor*, pp. 1, 12.

Hovland, C., & Weiss, W. (1951). The influence of source credibility on communication effectiveness. *Public Opinion Quarterly, 15*, 635–650.

Humphreys, L. (1970). *Tearoom trade.* Chicago: Aldine.

James, L. R., Mulaik, S. A., & Brett, J. M. (1982). *Causal analysis: Assumptions, models, and data.* Newbury Park, CA: Sage.

Jones, R., & Cooper, J. (1971). Mediation of experimenter effects. *Journal of Personality and Social Psychology, 20*, 70–74.

Josselson, R., & Lieblich, A. (1993). *The narrative study of lives.* Newbury Park, CA: Sage.

Jourard, S. M. (1969). The effects of experimenters' self-disclosure on subjects' behavior. In C. Spielberger (Ed.), *Current topics in community and clinical psychology.* New York: Academic Press.

Joy, L. A., Kimball, M. M., & Zabrack, M. L. (1986). Television and children's aggressive behavior. In T. M. Williams (Ed.), *The impact of television: A natural experiment in three communities.* Orlando, FL: Academic Press.

Judd, C. M., Smith, E. R., & Kidder, L. H. (1991). *Research methods in social relations* (6th ed.). Ft. Worth: Holt, Rinehart & Winston.

Kamin, L. G. (1974). *The science and politics of IQ.* New York: Wiley.

Kelman, H. C. (1967). Human use of human subjects: The problem of deception in social psychological experiments. *Psychological Bulletin, 67*, 1–11.

Kenny, D. A. (1979). *Correlation and causality.* New York: Wiley.

Keyser, D. J., & Sweetland, R. C. (Eds.). (1991). *Test critiques.* Kansas City, MO: Test Corporation of America.

Kidder, L. H., & Judd, C. M. (1986). *Research methods in social relations* (5th ed.). New York: Holt, Rinehart & Winston.

King, J. C. (1985, August). *The impact of "The Day After" on anti-nuclear war behavior.* Paper presented at the annual meeting of the American Psychological Association, Los Angeles.

Kintz, N. L., Delprato, D. J., Mettee, D. R., Persons, C. E., & Schappe, R. H. (1965). The experimenter effect. *Psychological Bulletin, 63*, 223–232.

Koocher, G. P. (1977). Bathroom behavior and human dignity. *Journal of Personality and Social Psychology, 35*, 120–121.

Koop, C. E. (1987). Report of the Surgeon General's workshop on pornography and public health. *American Psychologist, 42,* 944–945.

Lana, R. E. (1969). Pretest sensitization. In R. Rosenthal & R. Rosnow (Eds.), *Artifact in behavioral research.* New York: Academic Press.

Langer, E. J., & Abelson, R. P. (1974). A patient by any other name . . . : Clinical group difference in labeling bias. *Journal of Consulting and Clinical Psychology, 42,* 4–9.

Langer, E. J., & Rodin, J. (1976). The effects of choice and enhanced personal responsibility for the aged: A field experiment in an institutional setting. *Journal of Personality and Social Psychology, 34,* 191–198.

Latané, B., & Darley, J. M. (1970). *The unresponsive bystander: Why doesn't he help?* New York: Appleton-Century-Crofts.

Leventhal, H. (1970). Findings and theory in the study of fear communications. In L. Berkowitz (Ed.), *Advances in experimental social psychology* (Vol. 5). New York: Academic Press.

Levin, J. R. (1983). Pictorial strategies for school learning: Practical illustrations. In M. Pressley & J. R. Levin (Eds.), *Cognitive strategy research: Educational applications* (pp. 213–238). New York: Springer-Verlag.

Levine, R. V. (1990). The pace of life. *American Scientist, 78,* 450–459.

Linz, D., Donnerstein, E., & Penrod, S. (1987). The findings and recommendations of the Attorney General's Commission on Pornography: Do the psychological "facts" fit the political fury? *American Psychologist, 42,* 946–953.

Lofland, J., & Lofland, L. H. (1995). *Analyzing social settings: A guide to qualitative observation and analysis* (3rd ed.). Belmont, CA: Wadsworth.

Loftus, E. (1979). *Eyewitness testimony.* Cambridge, MA: Harvard University Press.

Luria, A. R. (1968). *The mind of a mnemonist.* New York: Basic Books.

Markus, H., & Zajonc, R. B. (1985). The cognitive perspective in social psychology. In G. Lindzey & E. Aronson (Eds.), *The handbook of social psychology* (3rd ed.) (Vol. 1). New York: Random House.

Marlatt, G. A. (1983). The controlled-drinking controversy: A commentary. *American Psychologist, 38,* 1097–1110.

Marlatt, G. A., & Rohsenow, D. R. (1980). Cognitive processes in alcohol use: Expectancy and the balanced placebo design. In N. K. Mello (Ed.), *Advances in substance abuse* (Vol. 1). Greenwich, CT: JAI Press.

Matteson, M. T., & Ivancevich, J. M. (1983). Note on tension discharge rate as an employee health status predictor. *Academy of Management Journal, 26,* 540–545.

McGuigan, F. J. (1963). The experimenter: A neglected stimulus. *Psychological Bulletin, 60,* 421–428.

Middlemist, R. D., Knowles, E. S., & Matter, C. F. (1976). Personal space invasion in the lavatory: Suggestive evidence for arousal. *Journal of Personality and Social Psychology, 33,* 541–546.

Middlemist, R. D., Knowles, E. S., & Matter, C. F. (1977). What to do and what to report: A reply to Koocher. *Journal of Personality and Social Psychology, 35,* 122–124.

Milgram, S. (1963). Behavioral study of obedience. *Journal of Abnormal and Social Psychology, 67,* 371–378.

Milgram, S. (1964). Group pressure and action against a person. *Journal of Abnormal and Social Psychology, 69*, 137–143.

Milgram, S. (1965). Some conditions of obedience and disobedience to authority. *Human Relations, 18*, 57–76.

Milgram, S. (1970, June). The lost letter technique. *Psychology Today*, p. 30.

Miller, A. G. (1972). Role-playing: An alternative to deception? *American Psychologist, 27*, 623–636.

Miller, A. G. (1986). *The obedience experiments: A case study of controversy in social science.* New York: Praeger.

Miller, G. A. (1969). Psychology as a means of promoting human welfare. *American Psychologist, 24*, 1063–1075.

Miller, N. E. (1985). The value of behavioral research on animals. *American Psychologist, 40*, 423–440.

Montee, B. B., Miltenberger, R. G., & Wittrock, D. (1995). An experimental analysis of facilitated communication. *Journal of Applied Behavior Analysis, 28*, 189–200.

Nisbett, R. E., & Ross, L. (1980). *Human inference: Strategies and shortcomings of social judgment.* Englewood Cliffs, NJ: Prentice-Hall.

Nisbett, R. E., & Wilson, T. D. (1977). Telling more than we can know: Verbal reports on mental processes. *Psychological Review, 84*, 231–259.

Orne, M. T. (1962). On the social psychology of the psychological experiment: With particular reference to demand characteristics and their implications. *American Psychologist, 17*, 776–783.

Osgood, C. E., Suci, G. J. & Tannenbaum, P. H. (1957). *The measurement of meaning.* Urbana: University of Illinois Press.

Oskamp, S., King, J. C., Burn, S. M., Konrad, A. M., Pollard, J. A., & White, M. A. (1985). The media and nuclear war: Fallout from TV's "The Day After." In S. Oskamp (Ed.), *Applied social psychology annual* (Vol. 6). Newbury Park, CA: Sage.

Patterson, G. R, & Moore, D. (1979). Interactive patterns as units of behavior. In M. E. Lamb, S. J. Sumoi, & G. L. Stephenson (Eds.), *Social interaction analysis: Methodological issues* (pp. 77–96). Madison: University of Wisconsin Press.

Paulus, P. B., Annis, A. B., Seta, J. J., Schkade, J. K., & Matthews, R. W. (1976). Crowding does affect task performance. *Journal of Personality and Social Psychology, 34*, 248–253.

Pendery, M. L., Maltzman, I. M., & West, L. J. (1982). Controlled drinking by alcoholics? New findings and a reevaluation of a major affirmative study. *Science, 217*, 169–174.

Peterson, J. L., & Zill, N. (1986). Marital disruption, parent-child relationships, and behavior problems in children. *Journal of Marriage and the Family, 48*, 295–307.

Petty, R. E., & Cacioppo, J. T. (1986). *Communication and persuasion: Central and peripheral routes to attitude change.* New York: Springer-Verlag.

Petty, R. E., Cacioppo, J. T., & Goldman, R. (1981). Personal involvement as a determinant of argument-based persuasion. *Journal of Personality and Social Psychology, 41*, 847–855.

Pfungst, O. (1911). *Clever Hans (the horse of Mr. von Osten): A contribution to experimental, animal, and human psychology* (C. L. Rahn, Trans.). New York: Holt, Rinehart & Winston. (Republished 1965.)

Piaget, J. (1952). *The origins of intelligence in children.* New York: International Universities Press.

Piliavin, I. M., Rodin, J., & Piliavin, J. A. (1969). Good samaritanism: An underground phenomenon? *Journal of Personality and Social Psychology, 4,* 289–299.

Posavac, E. J., & Carey, R. G. (1992). *Program evaluation: Methods and case studies* (4th ed). Englewood Cliffs, NJ: Prentice-Hall.

Prinsky, L. E., & Rosenbaum, J. L. (1987). "Leer-ics" or lyrics: Teenage impressions of rock 'n' roll. *Youth and Society, 18,* 384–397.

Punnett, B. J. (1986). Goal setting: An extension of the research. *Journal of Applied Psychology, 71,* 171–172.

Reed, J. G., & Baxter, P. M. (Eds.). (1991). *Library use: A handbook for psychology* (2nd ed.). Washington, DC: American Psychological Association.

Richardson, B., Sorenson, J., & Soderstrom, E. J. (1987). Explaining the social and psychological impact of a nuclear power plant accident. *Journal of Applied Social Psychology, 17,* 507–518.

Ring, K. (1967). Experimental social psychology: Some sober questions about frivolous values. *Journal of Experimental Social Psychology, 3,* 113–123.

Ring, K., Wallston, K., & Corey, M. (1970). Mode of debriefing as a factor affecting subjective reaction to a Milgram-type obedience experiment: An ethical inquiry. *Representative Research in Social Psychology, 1,* 67–68.

Riordan, C. A., & Marlin, N. A. (1987). Some good news about some bad practices. *American Psychologist, 42,* 104–106.

Roberson, M. T., & Sundstrom, E. (1990). Questionnaire design, return rates, and response favorableness in an employee attitude questionnaire. *Journal of Applied Psychology, 75,* 354–357.

Robinson, J. P., Athanasiou, R., & Head, K. B. (1969). *Measures of occupational attitudes and occupational characteristics.* Ann Arbor, MI: Institute for Social Research.

Robinson, J. P., Rusk, J. G., & Head, K. B. (1968). *Measures of political attitudes.* Ann Arbor, MI: Institute for Social Research.

Robinson, J. P., Shaver, P. R., & Wrightsman, L. S. (1991). *Measures of personality and social psychological attitudes* (Vol. 1). San Diego, CA: Academic Press.

Rodin, J., & Langer, E. J. (1977). Long-term effects of a control-relevant intervention with the institutionalized aged. *Journal of Personality and Social Psychology, 35,* 897–902.

Rosenblatt, P. C., & Cozby, P. C. (1972). Courtship patterns associated with freedom of choice of spouse. *Journal of Marriage and the Family, 34,* 689–695.

Rosenblatt, P. C., de Mik, L., Anderson, R. M., & Johnson, P. A. (1985). *The family in business.* San Francisco: Jossey-Bass.

Rosenhan, D. (1973). On being sane in insane places. *Science, 179,* 250–258.

Rosenthal, R. (1965). The volunteer subject. *Human Relations, 18,* 389–406.

Rosenthal, R. (1966). *Experimenter effects in behavior research.* New York: Appleton-Century-Crofts.

Rosenthal, R. (1967). Covert communication in the psychological experiment. *Psychological Bulletin, 67,* 356–367.

Rosenthal, R. (1969). Interpersonal expectations: Effects of the experimenter's hypothesis. In R. Rosenthal & R. L. Rosnow (Eds.), *Artifacts in behavioral research.* New York: Academic Press.

Rosenthal, R. (1991). *Meta-analytic procedures for social research* (rev. ed.). Newbury Park, CA: Sage.

Rosenthal, R., & Jacobson, L. (1968). *Pygmalion in the classroom: Teacher expectation and pupils' intellectual development.* New York: Holt, Rinehart & Winston.

Rosenthal, R., & Rosnow, R. L. (1975). *The volunteer subject.* New York: Wiley.

Rosnow R. L., & Rosnow, M. (1995). *Writing papers in psychology* (3rd ed.). Belmont, CA: Wadsworth.

Rossi, P. H., & Freeman, H. E. (1993). *Evaluation: A systematic approach* (5th ed.). Newbury Park, CA: Sage.

Rubin, Z. (1970, December). Jokers wild in the lab. *Psychology Today*, pp. 18, 20, 22–24.

Rubin, Z. (1973). Designing honest experiments. *American Psychologist, 28,* 445–448.

Rubin, Z. (1975). Disclosing oneself to a stranger: Reciprocity and its limits. *Journal of Experimental Social Psychology, 11,* 233–260.

Rubin, Z. (1985). Deceiving ourselves about deception: Comment on Smith and Richardson's "Amelioration of deception and harm in psychological research." *Journal of Personality and Social Psychology, 48,* 252–253.

Rubin, Z., & Peplau, L. A. (1973). Belief in a just world and reactions to another's lot: A study of participants in the national draft lottery. *Journal of Social Issues, 29,* 73–93.

Runyan, W. K. (1981). Why did van Gogh cut off his ear? The problem of alternative explanations in psychobiography. *Journal of Personality and Social Psychology, 40,* 1070–1077.

Russell, C. H., & Megaard, I. (1988). *The general social survey, 1972–1986: The state of the American people.* New York: Springer-Verlag.

Schachter, S. (1959). *The psychology of affiliation.* Stanford, CA: Stanford University Press.

Schaie, K. W. (1986). Beyond calendar definitions of age, time, and cohort: The general developmental model revisited. *Developmental Review, 6,* 252–277.

Schoeneman, T. J., & Rubanowitz, D. E. (1985). Attributions in the advice columns: Actors and observers, causes and reasons. *Personality and Social Psychology Bulletin, 11,* 315–325.

Schreiber, F. R. (1973). *Sybil.* Chicago: Regnery.

Schwartz, S. (1986). *Classic studies in psychology.* Mountain View, CA: Mayfield.

Sears, D. O. (1986). College sophomores in the laboratory. Influences of a narrow data base on social psychology's view of human nature. *Journal of Personality and Social Psychology, 51,* 515–530.

Seaver, W. B. (1973). Effects of naturally induced teacher expectancy effects. *Journal of Personality and Social Psychology, 28,* 333–342.

Sebald, H. (1986). Adolescents' shifting orientation toward parents and peers: A curvilinear trend over recent decades. *Journal of Marriage and the Family, 48,* 5–13.

Shaw, M. E., & Wright, J. M. (1967). *Scales for the measurement of attitudes.* New York: McGraw-Hill.

Shepard, R. N., & Metzler, J. (1971). Mental rotation of three-dimensional objects. *Science, 171*, 701–703.

Sidman, M. (1960). *Tactics of scientific research.* New York: Basic Books.

Sieber, J. E. (1992). *Planning ethically responsible research: A guide for students and internal review boards.* Newbury Park, CA: Sage.

Sieber, J. E. (1995). Deception methods in psychology: Have they changed in 23 years? *Ethics and Behavior, 5*, 67–85.

Sieber, J. E., Iannuzzo, & Rodriguez (1995).

Siegel, S., & Castellan, N. J. (1988). *Nonparametric statistics for the behavioral sciences.* New York: McGraw-Hill.

Silverman, I. (1975). Nonreactive methods and the law. *American Psychologist, 30*, 764–769.

Skinner, B. F. (1953). *Science and human behavior.* New York: Macmillan.

Smart, R. (1966). Subject selection bias in psychological research. *Canadian Psychologist, 7*, 115–121.

Smith, C. P. (1983). Ethical issues: Research on deception, informed consent, and debriefing. In L. Wheeler & P. Shaver (Eds.), *Review of personality and social psychology* (Vol. 4). Newbury Park, CA: Sage.

Smith, M. L., & Glass, G. V. (1977). Meta-analysis of psychotherapy outcome studies. *American Psychologist, 32*, 752–760.

Smith, R. J., Lingle, J. H., & Brock, T. C. (1978). Reactions to death as a function of perceived similarity to the deceased. *Omega, 9*, 125–138.

Smith, S. M., & Shaffer, D. R. (1991). Celerity and cajolery: Rapid speech may promote or inhibit persuasion through its impact on message elaboration. *Personality and Social Psychology Bulletin, 17*, 663–669.

Smith, S. S., & Richardson, D. (1983). Amelioration of harm in psychological research: The important role of debriefing. *Journal of Personality and Social Psychology, 44*, 1075–1082.

Smith, S. S., & Richardson, D. (1985). On deceiving ourselves about deception: A reply to Rubin. *Journal of Personality and Social Psychology, 48*, 254–255.

Smith, V. L., & Ellsworth, P. C. (1987). The social psychology of eyewitness accuracy: Misleading questions and communicator expertise. *Journal of Applied Psychology, 72*, 294–300.

Sobell, M. B., & Sobell, L. C. (1973). Individualized behavior therapy for alcoholics. *Behavior Therapy, 4*, 49–72.

Solomon, R. L. (1949). An extension of control group design. *Psychological Bulletin, 46*, 137–150.

Steinberg, L., & Dornbusch, S. M. (1991). Negative correlates of part-time employment during adolescence: Replication and elaboration. *Developmental Psychology, 27*, 304–313.

Stephan, W. G. (1983). Intergroup relations. In D. Perlman & P. C. Cozby (Eds.), *Social psychology.* New York: Holt, Rinehart & Winston.

Sternberg, R. J. (1993). *The psychologist's companion: A guide to scientific writing for students and researchers.* Cambridge: Cambridge University Press.

Stevenson, H. W., & Allen, S. (1964). Adult performance as a function of sex of experimenter and sex of subject. *Journal of Abnormal and Social Psychology, 68*, 214–216.

331

Sullivan, D. S., & Deiker, T. E. (1973). Subject-experimenter perceptions of ethical issues in human research. *American Psychologist, 28,* 587–591.

Tanaka, J. S., Panter, A. T., Winborne, W. C., & Huba, G. J. (1990). Theory testing in personality and social psychology with structural equation models: A primer in 20 questions. In C. Hendrick & M. S. Clark (Eds.), *Review of personality and social psychology* (Vol. 11). Newbury Park, CA: Sage.

Terman, L. M. (1925). *Genetic studies of genius: Vol. 1. Mental and physical traits of a thousand gifted children.* Stanford, CA: Stanford University Press.

Terman, L. M., & Oden, M. H. (1947). *Genetic studies of genius: Vol. 4. The gifted child grows up: Twenty-five years' follow-up of a superior group.* Stanford, CA: Stanford University Press.

Terman, L. M., & Oden, M. H. (1959). *Genetic studies of genius: Vol. 5. The gifted group in med-life: Thirty-five years' follow-up of the superior child.* Stanford, CA: Stanford University Press.

Tufte, E. R. (1983). *The visual display of quantitative information.* Cheshire, CT: Graphics Press.

Tufte, E. R. (1990). *Envisioning information.* Cheshire, CT: Graphics Press.

Tversky, A., & Kahneman, D. (1983). Extensional vs. intuitive reasoning: The conjunction fallacy in probability judgment. *Psychological Review, 90,* 293–315.

Verdonik, F., & Sherrod, L. R. (1984). *An inventory of longitudinal research on childhood and adolescence.* New York: Social Science Research Council.

Viney, L. L. (1983). The assessment of psychological states through content analysis of verbal communications. *Psychological Bulletin, 94,* 542–563.

Vitz, P. C. (1966). Preference for different amounts of visual complexity. *Behavioral Science, 11,* 105–114.

Webb, E. J., Campbell, D. T., Schwartz, R. D., Sechrest, R., & Grove, J. B. (1981). *Nonreactive measures in the social sciences* (2nd ed.). Boston: Houghton Mifflin.

Wilson, D. W., & Donnerstein, E. (1976). Legal and ethical aspects of nonreactive social psychological research. *American Psychologist, 31,* 765–773.

Wilson, W. H., Ellinwood, E. H., Mathew, R. J., & Johnson, K. (1994). Effects of marijuana on performance of a computerized cognitive-neuromotor test battery. *Psychiatry Research, 51,* 115–125.

Winograd, E., & Soloway, R. M. (1986). On forgetting the location of things stored in special places. *Journal of Experimental Psychology: General, 115,* 366–372.

Yin, R. K. (1994). *Case study research: Design and methods.* Newbury Park, CA: Sage.

Zajonc, R. B. (1976). Family configuration and intelligence. *Science, 192,* 227–236.

Zimbardo, P. G. (1973). The psychological power and pathology of imprisonment. In E. Aronson & R. Helmreich (Eds.), *Social psychology.* New York: Van Nostrand.

Zuckerman, M. (1979). *Sensation seeking: Beyond the optimal level of arousal.* Hillsdale, NJ: Erlbaum.

Index